Lecture Notes in Computer Sci

T0230266

Commenced Publication in 1973
Founding and Former Series Editors:
Gerhard Goos, Juris Hartmanis, and Jan van Leeuwen

Matthias Hemmje   Claudia Niederee
Thomas Risse (Eds.)

From Integrated Publication and Information Systems to Virtual Information and Knowledge Environments

Essays Dedicated to Erich J. Neuhold
on the Occasion of His 65th Birthday

 Springer

Volume Editors

Matthias Hemmje
FernUniversität Hagen
Universitätsstr. 1, 58097 Hagen, Germany
E-mail: Matthias.Hemmje@fernuni-hagen.de

Claudia Niederee
Thomas Risse
Fraunhofer IPSI
Dolivostr. 15, 64293 Darmstadt
E-mail: {claudia.niederee,thomas.risse}@ipsi.fraunhofer.de

Library of Congress Control Number: 2004118429

CR Subject Classification (1998): H.3, H.4, H.2, H.5, I.2

ISSN 0302-9743
ISBN 3-540-24551-0 Springer Berlin Heidelberg New York

Springer is a part of Springer Science+Business Media

springeronline.com

© Springer-Verlag Berlin Heidelberg 2005
Printed in Germany

Typesetting: Camera-ready by author, data conversion by Markus Richter, Heidelberg
Printed on acid-free paper   SPIN: 11387336   06/3142   5 4 3 2 1 0

Preface

Matthias Hemmje

FernUniversität in Hagen, Department of Computer Science,
Universitätsstraße 1, D-58097 Hagen, Germany
Matthias.Hemmje@fernuni-hagen.de

This book is dedicated to Erich J. Neuhold, Director of Fraunhofer's Integrated Publication and Information Systems Institute (IPSI) and Professor of Computer Science at the Technical University of Darmstadt on the occasion of his 65th Birthday in January 2005.

Erich Neuhold's primary research and development interests are in heterogeneous multimedia database systems, in peer-to-peer- and Grid-based information environments, in Web-based distributed information technologies, in persistent information and knowledge repositories, and in content engineering. Within his interest in content engineering special emphasis is given to all technological aspects of the information and publishing process, i.e., the knowledge value chain that arises for the creation of digital products and services in Web application contexts. Besides his main areas of scientific work, Erich Neuhold also guides research and development in user interfaces including information visualization, computer-supported cooperative work, ambient intelligence, mobile and wireless technology, and security in Web application areas like e-learning, e-commerce, e-culture and e-government.

Building on its long-standing scientific expertise and reputation Erich Neuhold's Fraunhofer IPSI aimed at supporting information-, content- and knowledge-intensive applications by focusing on research and development towards the achievement of the following vision: the efficient and flexible implementation of technologies supporting the creation and effective utilization of virtual information and knowledge environments where such environments are Web-based distributed information systems that enable the corporate as well as the personal and cooperative acquisition, management, access, distribution and usage of information, content and explicitly encoded knowledge objects.

In accordance with the unifying vision and continuing research interest of Erich Neuhold and in correspondence with his scientific work, this book presents a selected number of invited papers by leading international researchers in the area, addressing a broad variety of related topics. It therefore reflects the breadth and the depth of Erich Neuhold's scientific work advocating the synergistically integrated approach towards supporting digital information and knowledge production on the one hand together with its corresponding access and usage support on the other hand.

As the introductions to the first, second, and fourth parts of this book are provided in the later opening sections by Tamer Özsu and Keith van Rijsbergen, I would now like to introduce the content of the other parts.

The third part is dedicated to issues related to Securing Dynamic Media Content Integration and Communication. In the first paper of this part, Ralf Steinmetz (who successfully headed the Fraunhofer IPSI together with Erich Neuhold for several years and is currently still his colleague as the Professor for Multimedia Communications at the Technical University of Darmstadt) and Oliver Heckmann, address the subject of video distribution with peer-to-peer file-sharing networks. They introduce one of the most successful peer-to-peer file-sharing applications – it was especially successful in Germany – and discuss traffic characteristics and user behavior in distributing video files based on the results of their experiments and measurements. In the next paper, Jana Dittmann, former division head at Erich Neuhold's Fraunhofer IPSI and now Professor for Multimedia and Security at the Otto-von-Guericke-University in Magdeburg, and Martin Steinebach, currently division head at IPSI, describe the design of a framework for media production environments, where mechanisms like encryption, digital signatures and digital watermarking help to enable a flexible yet secure handling and processing of the content. Finally, Andreas Meissner, also division head at IPSI, and Wolfgang Schönfeld propose a heterogeneous and flexible communication platform that complies with the reliability and coverage requirements of the Public Safety Organization.

The fifth part is titled Visualization – Key to External Cognition in Virtual Information Environments. In the first paper of this part Tiziana Catarci and her colleagues Enrico Bertini, Lucia Di Bello and Stephen Kimani of the University of Rome "La Sapienza" discuss how visualization has been and can be used to support interaction with the digital library environment. In the next paper, Gerald Jäschke, Piklu Gupta and I introduce an approach to design a declarative language for defining information visualization applications (IVML). Next to this, Ben Shneiderman and Jinwook Seo of the University of Maryland present a generalized knowledge integration framework to better understand the importance of an item or cluster by using multiple interactively coordinated visual displays and show examples of hierarchical clustering of gene expression data, coordinated with a parallel-coordinates view and with the gene annotation and gene ontology. The part is completed by Maria Francesca Costabile and Paolo Buono of the University of Bari presenting a visual strategy that exploits a graph-based technique and parallel coordinates to visualize the results of algorithms for mining association rules which helps data miners to get an overview of the rule set they are interacting with and enables them to deeper investigate inside a specific set of rules.

The sixth part takes us From Human Computer Interaction to Human Artefact Interaction. In the first paper of this part, Norbert Streitz, currently division head at Erich Neuhold's Fraunhofer IPSI, outlines his approach to designing environments that exploit the advantages of real objects and at the same time use the potential of computer-based support by moving from human-*computer* interaction to human-*artefact* interaction. In the next paper, Peter Tandler and Laura Dietz (also members of Fraunhofer IPSI) explain how to support ubiquitous computing by enabling an extended view on sharing which seamlessly integrates the view of "traditional" CSCW and additionally incorporates ubiquitous, heterogeneous and mobile devices used in a common context. In the following paper, Jörg Haake, formerly PhD student of Erich Neuhold and now a Professor of Computer Science at the FernUniversität in Hagen, and his wife Anja Haake (also a former PhD student of Erich Neuhold) together with Till Schümmer introduce a metaphor and user interface for managing access permissions in shared workspace systems. The part is then completed by the contribution of Jose Encarnação (a colleague of Erich Neuhold as a Professor of Computer Science at the Technical University of Darmstadt and as the Director of the Fraunhofer Institute for Computer Graphics (IGD) in Darmstadt) and his research collaborator Thomas Kirste; they introduce the new ICT paradigm of ambient intelligence, its concepts, system architectures, and enabling technologies.

Finally, the seventh part introduces Application Domains for Virtual Information and Knowledge Environments. In the first paper of this part, Thomas Kamps, a former PhD student of Erich Neuhold and currently a division head at the Fraunhofer IPSI, together with Richard Stenzel, Libo Chen and Lothar Rostek discusses an approach that shows how a mix of information extraction and classification methods can be used to automatically set up and update a network of business objects serving as a corporate memory index. In the next contribution, Hans-Jörg Bullinger, President of the Fraunhofer-Gesellschaft, Corporate Management and Research, and his research colleagues Alexander Slama, Oliver Schumacher, Joachim Warschat and Peter Ohlhausen of the Fraunhofer Institute for Industrial Engineering (IAO) in Stuttgart explain how ontologies can be applied to providing a model for the computer-supported representation of innovation projects and to enabling computer-aided identification of time-consuming constellations, and can therefore serve to provide a basis for achieving innovation-acceleration knowledge to ensure faster and better innovations. In the following paper, Claudia Niederée, Avaré Stewart and Claudio Muscogiuri (all of the Fraunhofer IPSI) and I discuss approaches for both creating context awareness as well as supporting specific working contexts by means of virtual information and knowledge environments. In the next paper, Patrick Baudisch, a former PhD student of Erich Neuhold and now a researcher at Microsoft Research, together with Lars Bruecker presents a recommendation system that provides users with personalized TV schedules. The final contribution of this part is by Junzhong Gu and presents an approach to integrating consumer electronics (e.g., TV sets, DVD players, HiFi sets, etc.), mobile multimedia devices, as well as traditional computing devices (PCs, laptops, printers, scanners, etc.) into a complete application solution.

I would like to continue by thanking a number of people who strongly supported the timely creation of this book.

First of all, I am grateful to all the authors who contributed efficiently in a very short period of time to provide their high-quality scientific content for this book in order to honor Erich Neuhold's 65th birthday.

Furthermore, I am grateful to Wolfgang Glatthaar, Chairman of Fraunhofer IPSI's Kuratorium (advisory board), for supporting this book with a statement honoring the occasion from Erich Neuhold's research institute's point of view.

Next, I am grateful to Tamer Öszu and Keith van Rijsbergen for supporting the book by providing introductions to selected parts of the book on the one hand, on the other hand for contributing laudations for Erich Neuhold on behalf of the scientific communities that Erich Neuhold has been operating in, collaborating with and serving during his outstanding academic career.

With respect to coping with the editorial work for this book, I am grateful to my co-editors Claudia Niederée and Thomas Risse who proved themselves as reliable collaborators in what turned out to be a more challenging and demanding endeavor than we originally expected, especially in already tough times of organizational demand and change.

Concerning assistance in the preparation of this book, I am grateful to Anja Rieber, a secretary of excellence at Fraunhofer IPSI, who provided invaluable office administration back-end support as well as a competent and reliable communication and coordination front end for the whole preparation process.

Giving credit to the organizational background support, I am grateful to Dieter Böcker, Deputy Director of the Fraunhofer IPSI, and Emil Wetzel, Head of Administration of Fraunhofer IPSI, for providing me with the opportunity to take over responsibility for this book on the one hand, and on the other hand for providing the formal approval and support to use IPSI's infrastructure to prepare it.

Finally, I am grateful to Alfred Hofmann of Springer's Lecture Notes in Computer Science and his whole team for providing excellent publication support.

The last paragraphs of my preface shall be addressed and dedicated to Erich Neuhold himself.

First, I would like to state at this point that it has been a pleasure for me to work on this book honoring Erich's life-time achievements on the occasion of his 65th birthday as it has been taking me back to many memories about our collaboration history since 1991.

Furthermore, I would like to congratulate and thank him especially with respect to the many career opportunities that his research and management work as well as his personal guidance have opened up and continuously provided for many of the contributors to this book, including myself.

All of us who share such a "direct collaboration experience" with Erich know that working with him is a VERY demanding activity in many dimensions. However, it still is and has always been rewarding on many levels, too! Therefore, I would not like to have missed it. This holds especially true because I experienced Erich not only as a researcher who always strives for excellence but also many times and especially in tough situations as a man with a high degree of professionalism, integrity, and – most important – dedication, loyalty, and reliability with respect to his responsibility for taking care of the personal welfare of his staff members and the further development of their professional future.

I would like to conclude by wishing Erich Neuhold and his family all the best for the years to come. Personally, I am looking forward to many more years of interesting and fruitful collaboration.

December 2004   Matthias Hemmje

Organizational Laudatio and Personal Note

Wolfgang Glatthaar

Chairman of the Board of Trustees of Fraunhofer IPSI

In spite of the rapid growth of knowledge and information and a variety of usage scenarios on the World Wide Web, the goal of delivering the "right answer" to a question universally available remains a goal which is yet to be attained. According to Erich Neuhold's research agenda, this "right answer" needs to be appropriate in its depth, context and timeliness, and should be available everywhere and adhere to social and legal conventions. This goal determines the basis for demanding and multi-faceted research topics. The application spectrum ranges from the repurposing of publishing products, and classroom-based and mobile distance learning, through to automatic content generation for mobile phones, handheld computers or navigation systems, and more. The Fraunhofer Integrated Publication and Information Systems Institute conducts research and applications development in these areas.

IPSI is a research institute that was founded in 1987 by the German National Research Center for Information Technology (GMD). Since its inception it has been under the direction of Prof. Dr. Erich J. Neuhold, who also leads the research and teaching group with the same focus in the Computer Science Department at the Technical University of Darmstadt. The close links with the university are reinforced through the teaching activities there of IPSI researchers. Over 100 people currently work in research at IPSI, of whom about 20% are from abroad.

Being responsible for continuing IPSI's success in the future, Erich Neuhold and his research and management team started a transition phase in the first years of the new millennium. Most importantly, on July 11, 2001 IPSI was one of the eight research institutes of the German National Research Center for Information Technology (GMD) that became members of the Fraunhofer-Gesellschaft. Through this merger the Fraunhofer-Gesellschaft now encompasses 17 institutes out of 58 with about 3000 scientists doing applied research in the area of computer science and information technology. According to Erich Neuhold's own statements, IPSI is still today in this transformation process, permanently assessing risks and challenges, and taking measures to adapt to the changed environment. Some of these consequences relate to the changes in the research paradigm – from basic research towards application-oriented and contract research – while others relate to rather mundane issues like building up the institute's own marketing and sales processes.

From Erich Neuhold's point of view, research at IPSI has never happened in an ivory tower. IPSI has always tried yout new ideas and solutions on real-world problems. Its prime mechanism for reaching out to the market and turning research results into products has been the foundation of spin-offs. Due to Erich Neuhold's vision and engagement, IPSI will continue to be an incubator of ideas in the years to come. Furthermore, many former employees of IPSI have started university careers in Germany and abroad. Building on these contacts, IPSI has constantly used this opportunity to integrate its alumni in cooperation projects.

Under the leadership of Erich Neuhold, Fraunhofer IPSI in Darmstadt has been successfully developing user-centered systems that flexibly, effectively and efficiently respond to end-user needs in the application areas of electronic publishing and dissemination of information, collaborative work, and learning at common locations or over distances. The systems are formed using novel concepts of information enhancement and of information and knowledge management. Furthermore, IPSI investigates and develops high-quality software solutions for computer-supported collaborative work, electronic publishing and lifelong learning in real and virtual environments. IPSI's research areas to a high degree reflect Erich Neuhold's personal research interests, and therefore include digital libraries and information systems, publication tools with underlying database layers, distributed editing environments for collaborative maintenance of large collections of data, media and document management, and the more loosely related fields of knowledge management and cooperative learning systems, and security and services for mobile communication.

Values can only be preserved through change – so said Richard Löwenthal, the Anglo-German publicist and political scientist, in the twentieth century. Since its incorporation into the Fraunhofer Corporation in summer 2001, IPSI has been engaged in putting this insight into practice. During rigorous portfolio discussions and restructuring measures – in the course of which many favorite subjects and group approaches had to be sacrificed to a focus on areas of expertise more relevant to industry – this policy was amended. In this process, departments were analyzed down to group level, and in some cases were reconstituted – all with the thoroughgoing cooperation of many staff members, who, at the same time, had to carry on their usual work involving research, EU and BMBF (German Federal Ministry of Education and Research) projects, teaching, and industrial business. While this was proceeding, a new "Marketing & Sales" Department was formed. As a consequence, many new marketing instruments were introduced, followed by more rigid instruments for financial and sales control. However, all these achievements do not mean that the change process is now complete. As the Fraunhofer Institute operates in the area of research, it will never, and must never, become like a sort of screw factory, where everyone can sell everything – it is only natural that the concept of change has to be omnipresent at all times, by definition.

Besides managing IPSI during its GMD times as well as during the initial phases of its transformation into a Fraunhofer Institute, Erich Neuhold has always provided flexibility on the management level as well as on the administrative and operational staff level, supporting not only technologically but also aesthetically motivated and driven endeavors. Besides regularly hosting art exhibitions in the institute's building, for example during open house phases, he supported and initiated a set of artistically driven activities for the IPSI. Besides more or less hybrid IT R&D projects serving both worlds, like the Virtual Gallery projects resulting in cyber:gallery – a system for exhibiting and selling art on the Internet that enables the perception of art sales exhibitions in a VR-technology-driven Web-based application solution – there has also been room for supporting, for example, real and virtual theatre projects.

One such project originated at the beginning of 1999 when the Richard Wagner Forum in Graz offered the opportunity to submit projects for the staging of Richard Wagner's Parsifal. One option of the competition was to submit a cyberstaged version of Parsifal with an emphasis on the use of new technologies within the presentation. Supported by Erich Neuhold and IPSI, such a contribution from the IPSI staff member Christoph Rodatz was successful in the contest. During the project, traditional theatre architecture linked the audience with the stage through an audiovisual window. The stage was separated from the auditorium using a closed iron curtain. Thus the audience was able to move in a free way between the auditorium and the stage, and therefore the audience was in effect operating as a "hiker" between the two perception dimensions. Furthermore, the auditorium was transformed into an acoustic space of experience. Here Parsifal could be heard in a concerto form as a live transmission from the stage, except that, apart from the conductor, the performers, the orchestra and the choir were not present. Similarly, the stage area was transformed into a stage museum space, where the singers and musicians performed. The conductor's signal for the singers' entry was communicated via video. Each individual sound was sent via microphones to a sound panel. From there the entire "virtual soundscape" was transmitted to the auditorium. This approach meant that during the entire staging the orchestra and the choir could operate while still being in their rehearsal rooms, each equipped with microphones and at the same time quasi-"exhibited" in 10 vitrines that were located on the borders of the revolving stage. Via video screens and headphones the actors and singers were connected with the conductor and the entire soundscape experience system. Within so-called picture spaces there were 10 separate exhibition areas that could be entered via the revolving space. Furthermore, Parsifal was the topic of associated installations that enabled a more open access to Wagner's opera. With respect to the orchestra pit, the installation hosted video screens that displayed the movement of the live performance produced by each group of musical instruments transmitted from the orchestra and choir rehearsal rooms. The positioning of the video screens followed the specific pattern of the orchestra's natural position. Even though the chronology of the entire opera was not changed, an individual member of the audience could experience the entire staging in a fragmented and individualized manner if he or she decided to become a "hiker" during the performance. Using this approach, the audience could physically participate in the opera, and this had a tremendous impact on the dramatic degrees of freedom available within the director's interpretation of the Parsifal plot, bearing in mind that Wagner conceived of a "Gesamtkunstwerk". The cyberstaging of Parsifal demonstrated the influence of new technologies on society's perception, and the transformation that could be brought about in the theatre and in the arts in general.

The first time I met Erich Neuhold was in 1972. Since then it has been a very exciting walk together, not always easy but in the end certainly fruitful. So, looking at IPSI's history and the current situation I think it is fair to say that Erich Neuhold, now retiring, can be proud of what he and his team hand over to his successor. I hope that Erich Neuhold can observe, now from a distance, "his IPSI" – continuously changing and growing in success. I wish he and his family a healthy and fascinating future.

December 2004   Wolfgang Glatthaar

First Introduction, Laudatio, and Personal Note

M. Tamer Özsu

University of Waterloo, School of Computer Science,
Waterloo, Ontario, Canada N2L 3G1
tozsu@db.uwaterloo.ca

I was honored and very pleased to be asked to write an introduction to this volume dedicated to Erich J. Neuhold. I don't quite recall when I first met Erich, which, in itself, is an indication that it was a long time ago. We had overlapping research interests – distributed data management, multimedia systems, heterogeneous databases – so it was natural that we would have a professional relationship. Erich, as the Director of the Fraunhofer Institute (when I first met him this was the German National Research Center for Information Technology, GMD) for Integrated Publication and Information Systems (IPSI) in Darmstadt, Germany, and as the Professor of Computer Science, Publication and Information Systems, at the Technical University of Darmstadt, has created very strong research groups that are conducting state-of-the-art research on a number of fronts. Particularly during the 1990s, IPSI was a place that I visited frequently, including a sabbatical leave in 1998. I have often referred to it as my European base of operations. Erich successfully managed the various technical and organizational transitions that IPSI went through over the years, the last one being the major transition from GMD to Fraunhofer. He, along with his colleagues at IPSI, deserves significant credit for building a world-class research organization.

Erich Neuhold's research over his career has been wide ranging and has covered a variety of topics. His past and present research interests that overlap with mine involve heterogeneous multimedia database systems, distributed systems (mainly peer-to-peer and Grid-based environments), and Web-based distributed information technologies. This volume contains a number of parts that focus on these topics.

The first part in this book is dedicated to issues related to Advanced Technologies for Adaptive Information Management Systems and contains a number of contributions by Erich Neuhold's former PhD students. Thomas Risse, who is currently a division head at Fraunhofer IPSI, reports his latest research in "An Overview on Automatic Capacity Planning". The issue that is addressed is finding a configuration of a distributed system that satisfies performance goals. This is a well-known complex search problem that involves many design parameters, such as hardware selection, job distribution and process configuration. Thomas describes the new approaches that he has been following to address this problem. In the second contribution, "Overview on Decentralized Establishment of Multi-lateral Collaborations", Andreas Wombacher describes service-oriented architectures that facilitate loosely coupled collaborations, which are established in a decentralized way. One challenge for such collaborations is to guarantee consistency, that is, fulfilment of all constraints of individual services and deadlock-freeness. The paper introduces a decentralized approach to consistency checking, which utilizes only bilateral views of the collaboration. "Dynamic Maintenance of an Integrated Schema" by Regina Motz considers the importance of schema integration methodologies as well as the growing use of cooperative engineering and the relevance of dynamic maintenance of an integrated schema in a federated database. A key characteristic of a federation is the autonomy of its component databases: their instances and schemas may evolve independently, requiring dynamic maintenance of an integrated schema. Regina's work presents a methodology to propagate structural and semantic modifications that occur in the local schemas of a federated database to the integrated schema. In the final paper of Part 1, entitled "Efficient Evaluation of Nearest-Neighbor Queries in Content-Addressable Networks", Klemens Böhm, a former PhD student of Erich Neuhold and currently a Professor of Computer Science at the University of Karlsruhe, and Erik Buchmann discuss top-k query processing within peer-to-peer (P2P) systems organized as content-addressable networks (CAN). CANs manage huge sets of (key, value)-pairs and cope with very high workloads while following the P2P paradigm in order to build scalable, distributed data structures on top of the Internet. As outlined in this paper, CANs are designed to drive Internet-scale applications like distributed search engines, multimedia retrieval systems and more. In such scenarios, the introduced top-k query model is very applicable, as the user specifies an objective and the engine responds with a set of the most likely query results.

The second part in this volume is dedicated to issues related to Semantic Web Drivers for Advanced Information Management. In the first contribution, Rudi Studer, a former PhD student of Erich Neuhold and now a Professor of Computer Science at the University of Karlsruhe, and his co-authors Jens Hartmann, Nenad Stojanovic and Lars Schmidt-Thieme focus on Semantic Web mining in a paper entitled "Ontology-Based Query Refinement for Semantic Portals". Semantic Web mining combines two fast-developing research areas: the Semantic Web and Web mining. On the one hand the authors suggest that this connection can be exploited to improve Web mining methods, using new formal semantics that utilize Web mining results, while on the other hand they build the Semantic Web. The authors also present the SemIPort project, in which methods and tools for semantic information portals are currently developed. In the paper that follows, Matthias Hemmje, another former PhD student of Erich Neuhold and now a Professor of Computer Science at the Distance University of Hagen, and Erich Neuhold's former PhD student Zhanzi Qiu discuss the issues in preparing legacy Web sites for querying in searches in their paper "Towards Supporting Annotation for Existing Web Pages Enabling Hyperstructure-Based Searching". They discuss how existing Web pages can be tagged with additional structural and semantic information that can be represented with new Web standards and can be applied in advanced hyperstructure-based Web search methods. This paper is followed by Tom Baker's fine contribution, entitled "Maintaining Dublin Core as a Semantic Web Vocabulary", where he describes the Dublin Core Metadata Initiative (DCMI) to maintain a vocabulary of several dozen metadata terms, most notably the 15-element Dublin Core. These metadata terms, along with historical versions of the terms, are identified with URIs, documented on Web pages and in formal schemas, indexed in registries, and cited in application profiles. Tom has been collaborating with researchers at Fraunhofer IPSI in various projects related to such metadata issues.

In addition to his research contributions, it is important to note Erich's technical contributions more broadly. His original appointment as Director of the then GMD

IPSI (now Fraunhofer IPSI) dates back to 1986. At the same time, he was appointed as the Professor of Computer Science, Chair for Publication and Information Systems, at the Technical University of Darmstadt. Prior to that, he served in various academic positions. He was a Professor of Computer Science, Chair of Applied Informatics and Systems Analysis, at the Technical University of Vienna between 1984 and 1986, and a Professor of Computer Science, Chair of Application Software, at the University of Stuttgart from 1972 to 1983. His research focus was always on information systems and databases, but with wide-ranging approaches. During his academic career, he has been the principal supervisor of 38 PhD students and over 250 master's students.

Erich has held a number of industrial research and development positions as well. While heading the Information Management Laboratory and later the Systems Software Laboratory of Hewlett-Packard Research Laboratories, Palo Alto (1983–1984), Erich took part in and managed research work and development efforts on distributed operating systems, based both on UNIX and new advanced operating system concepts. Communication systems and (distributed) databases were extended to handle multimedia, generalized data types (objects) that were expected to arise in the future office and engineering environments and also in knowledge-based systems. Knowledge-based techniques were investigated in relation to all these areas to determine their possible future impact and to start advanced activities for their incorporation.

During his early times as a research scientist at IBM Corporation (1963–1972) in the US as well as at the IBM laboratory in Vienna, Erich's research work, amongst other aspects, was concerned with synchronization strategies for data manipulation in database systems. Especially during his time at IBM Program Products and Advanced Technology in New York he actively participated in research, design and implementation of integrated databases, database management and information retrieval systems. He contributed to the design and implementation of a family of computational and query languages oriented toward non-professional users.

Finally, let me comment on his service to the scientific community. Erich deserves special thanks with respect to serving as chair/co-chair, organizer/co-organizer, member of program committees, and general supporter in different functions for numerous conferences and other international scientific events in the field. In particular, it is important to note his chairmanship of the International Federation for Information Processing (IFIP) Working Group (WG) 2.6, "Data Bases", and WG 2.2, "Formal Description of Programming Concepts", his Vice-Chairmanship of the IFIP Technical Committee "Information Systems" (TC-8), his membership of the board of the Very Large Data Base (VLDB) Endowment, and his co-presidency of the International Foundation on Cooperative Information Systems (IFCIS). He has also been on the boards of various other committees. Erich has been very active in organizing a large number of conferences – too many to list individually. He serves as the Editor-in-Chief of the Journal on Digital Libraries, and he is on the editorial boards of many other journals.

Clearly, a very productive professional life is about to have a phase shift. I do not for a moment expect Erich to take a rest; in fact, I expect to see him and hear him at technical events and meetings for many years to come.

December 2004   M. Tamer Özsu

Second Introduction, Laudatio, and Personal Note

Keith van Rijsbergen

University of Glasgow, Department of Computing Science,
17 Lilybank Gardens, Glasgow, G12 8RZ, UK
keith@dcs.gla.ac.uk

Following Tamer Öszus's introduction to the first two parts of this book it is my pleasure to introduce the fourth part of this book. As in the other cases, it reflects Erich Neuhold's research interests, this time in the research areas that are close to my own areas of research: digital libraries and, of course, information retrieval.

The fourth part, aiming to move "From Digital Libraries to Intelligent Knowledge Environments", starts out with a reflection by Edward Fox, Marcos André Gonçalves and Rao Shen on the role of digital libraries in making this move. He illustrates how suitable knowledge environments can be more easily prepared when designed and built on the basis of a variety of digital library metamodels (including those for education, computing and archaeology) thereby resulting in more usable and useful digital library applications. This discussion is followed by some notes by Rudi Schmiede on scientific work and the usage of digital scientific information – its structures, discrepancies, tendencies and strategies. His article discusses changes in scientific work (academic and applied) associated with the new potential benefits accruing from the use of digital library technology, but also the increased coercive powers arising from such use. The background of his interesting observations is discussed in the context of a scientific sphere, in terms of the contents, the quantity and the quality of supply in scientific IT systems, taking into account the user side in their communities of practice, and the technological and organizational basis of scientific information.

Ulrich Thiel and his colleagues at the Fraunhofer IPSI introduce the concept of "Queries in Context" supporting access to digitized historic documents in a so-called Collaboratory, where appropriate indexing and retrieval mechanisms are developed to give users adequate access to material to support their collaborative work. The part continues with Richard Furuta's contribution about the separation of concerns in hypertext where articulation points are expected to increase flexibility. Richard has explored a family of models in which hypertext is modelled by an automaton structure rather than a graph structure. He discusses further distinctions, other than the structure/presentation, that his work provides to interactive documents leading to so-called "articulation points" to support investigations into novel and flexible implementations of hypertext/hypermedia. The fifth paper is a contribution by Karl Aberer, a former division head of Erich Neuhold's Fraunhofer IPSI, now a Professor of Computer Science at EPFL in Geneva, together with Jie Wu. In their paper "Towards a Common Framework for Peer-to-Peer Web Retrieval", they first review existing studies about the algorithmic feasibility of realizing peer-to-peer Web search using text- and link-based retrieval methods. From their perspective realizing peer-to-peer Web retrieval also requires a common framework that enables interoperability of peers using different peer-to-peer search methods. Therefore they introduce a common framework consisting of an architecture for peer-to-peer information retrieval and a logical framework for distributed ranking computation.

Carol Peters of CNR in Pisa contributed a paper on the comparative evaluation of cross-language information retrieval systems. DELOS, the Network of Excellence on Digital Libraries, has supported the launch of a Cross-language Evaluation Forum (CLEF), with the objective of promoting cross-language information retrieval system development, providing the research community with an infrastructure for testing and evaluating systems operating in multilingual contexts and a common platform for the comparison of methodologies and results. In her paper, Carol outlines the various activities initiated by CLEF over the years in order to meet the emerging needs of the application communities, and traces the impact of these activities on advances in system development.

The final two contributions of this chapter are about providing more intelligent functions within information environments by the application of machine learning techniques. First, in "Personalization for the Web: Learning User Preferences from Text", Giovanni Semeraro of the University of Bari and his colleagues Marco Degemmis and Pasquale Lops deal with the application of supervised machine learning methods for user profiling and content-based information filtering. The paper presents a new method, based on the classical Rocchio algorithm for text categorization, which is able to discover user preferences from the analysis of textual data. Secondly, Thomas Hofmann and Justin Basilico apply collaborative machine learning by proposing a collaborative machine learning framework for exploiting interuser similarities. More specifically, they present a kernel-based learning architecture that generalizes the well-known Support Vector Machine learning approach by enriching content descriptors with interuser correlations.

Besides introducing the fourth part, it is also my pleasure to pay tribute to Erich Neuhold for enthusiastically supporting the publication of several scientific journal series in a variety of responsible functions. He is the former Editor-in-Chief and now, Co-editor-in-Chief of the Journal on Digital Libraries, and a member of the Editorial Advisory Board for ACM Transactions on Database Systems; Information Systems, Pergamon Press; Journal of Information Processing, Japan; IEEE Computing Futures, USA; and Computers & Graphics, Pergamon Press. Finally, he is a member of the Editorial Board for Decision Support Systems – The International Journal, North Holland; Fifth Generation Computer Systems, North Holland; The International Journal of Systems Integration, Springer; Data & Knowledge Engineering, Elsevier Science; Multimedia Tools and Applications – An International Journal, Springer; J.UCS – The Journal of Universal Computer Science, Springer; as well as for the International Journal on Digital Libraries, Springer,

With respect to supporting conferences and other events of the scientific communities in the field of information retrieval, information systems, information science, and digital libraries, over and above those that Tamer has already mentioned in his laudation from the database research communities point of view, Erich has served the ACM SIGIR International Conference on Research and Development in Information Retrieval, the Internationales Symposium für Informationswissenschaft, Digital Libraries (DL), the Forum on Research and Technology Advances in Digital Libraries

(ADL), Advances in Information Systems (ADVIS), the European Conference on Digital Libraries (ECDL), the Joint Conference on Digital Libraries (JCDL), the International Workshop on Digital Libraries (DLib2001), the DELOS Workshop of the International Conference on Digital Libraries (ICDL), as well as Document Image Analysis for Libraries (DIAL).

My own interaction with Erich started in the early 1990s. We began working together on an ESPRIT project IDOMENEUS (1992–1995). My lasting memory of Erich is when he took over as chair of the network and saved the day. It once again illustrated the American dictum: "When the going gets tough, the tough get going". The network ran to completion and delivered results of which all of us were rightfully proud. Soon after the beginning of that network I was appointed to the position of Beirat of the German National Research Center for Information Technology (GMD) (1993–1996); one of my tasks was to chair a review of the Institute for Integrated Publication and Information Systems in Darmstadt (IPSI), of which Erich had been director since 1986. It is no secret that if the review had gone badly the consequences could have been dire. Erich, in customary fashion, marshalled the troops and oversaw a response to the external review that was exemplary. Once again his courage and stamina saw to it that IPSI continued to flourish.

There is no doubt in my mind that Erich will continue to fight for academic excellence. We all owe him a great debt for the extent of his contributions to our field. Personally, I learnt from him that one can, with one's friends, overcome bureaucratic obstacles by simply keeping one's eye on the main goal: success in research. I speak for all when I wish him success in his new ventures.

December 2004   Keith van Rijsbergen

Table of Contents

Advanced Technologies for Adaptive Information Management Systems

An Overview on Automatic Capacity Planning
Thomas Risse (Fraunhofer IPSI) 1

Overview on Decentralized Establishment of Multi-lateral
Collaborations
Andreas Wombacher (University of Twente) 11

Dynamic Maintenance of an Integrated Schema
Regina Motz (University of Montevideo) 21

Efficient Evaluation of Nearest-Neighbor Queries in Content-
Addressable Networks
*Erik Buchmann (University of Magdeburg) and Klemens Böhm
(University of Karlsruhe)* 31

Semantic Web Drivers for Advanced Information Management

Ontology-Based Query Refinement for Semantic Portals
*Jens Hartmann, Nenad Stojanovic, Rudi Studer, and
Lars Schmidt-Thieme (University of Karlsruhe)* 41

Towards Supporting Annotation for Existing Web Pages Enabling
Hyperstructure-Based Searching
Zhanzi Qiu and Matthias Hemmje (FernUniversität Hagen) 51

Maintaining Dublin Core as a Semantic Web Vocabulary
Thomas Baker (Fraunhofer-Gesellschaft) 61

Securing Dynamic Media Content Integration and Communication

A Peer-to-Peer Content Distribution Network
*Oliver Heckmann, Nicolas Liebau, Vasilios Darlagiannis, Axel Bock,
Andreas Mauthe, and Ralf Steinmetz (TU Darmstadt)* 69

Secure Production of Digital Media
*Martin Steinebach (Fraunhofer IPSI) and Jana Dittmann
(University of Magdeburg)* 79

Data Communication Between the German NBC Reconnaissance
Vehicle and Its Control Center Unit
Andreas Meissner and Wolfgang Schönfeld (Fraunhofer IPSI) 87

From Digital Libraries to Intelligent Knowledge Environments

The Role of Digital Libraries in Moving Towards Knowledge
Environments
Edward A. Fox, Marcos André Gonçalves, and Rao Shen
(Virginia Tech) 96

Scientific Work and the Usage of Digital Scientific Information –
Some Notes on Structures, Discrepancies, Tendencies, and Strategies
Rudi Schmiede (TU Darmstadt) 107

Queries in Context: Access to Digitized Historic Documents in a
Collaboratory for the Humanities
Ulrich Thiel, Holger Brocks, Andrea Dirsch-Weigand, André Everts,
Ingo Frommholz, and Adelheit Stein (Fraunhofer IPSI) 117

Separation of Concerns in Hypertext: Articulation Points That
Increase Flexibility
Richard Furuta (Texas A&M University) 128

Towards a Common Framework for Peer-to-Peer Web Retrieval
Karl Aberer and Jie Wu (EPFL) 138

Comparative Evaluation of Cross-language Information Retrieval
Systems
Carol Peters (ISTI-CNR) 152

Personalization for the Web: Learning User Preferences from Text
Giovanni Semeraro, Pasquale Lops, and Marco Degemmis
(University of Bari) 162

Collaborative Machine Learning
Thomas Hofmann (Fraunhofer IPSI) and Justin Basilico
(Brown University) 173

Visualization – Key to External Cognition in Virtual Information Environments

Visualization in Digital Libraries
Enrico Bertini, Tiziana Catarci, Lucia Di Bello, and Stephen
Kimani (University of Rome) 183

Modelling Interactive, Three-Dimensional Information Visualizations
    *Gerald Jaeschke (Fraunhofer IPSI), Piklu Gupta (TU Darmstadt),
    and Matthias Hemmje (FernUniversität Hagen)* 197

A Knowledge Integration Framework for Information Visualization
    Jinwook Seo and Ben Shneiderman (University of Maryland) 207

Visualizing Association Rules in a Framework for Visual Data Mining
    Paolo Buono and Maria Francesca Costabile (University of Bari) ... 221

From Human Computer Interaction to Human Artifact Interaction

From Human-*Computer* Interaction to Human-*Artefact* Interaction:
Interaction Design for Smart Environments
    Norbert A. Streitz (Fraunhofer IPSI) 232

Cooperation in Ubiquitous Computing: An Extended View on
Sharing
    Peter Tandler and Laura Dietz (Fraunhofer IPSI) 241

A Metaphor and User Interface for Managing Access Permissions in
Shared Workspace Systems
    *Till Schümmer, Jörg Haake, and Anja Haake
    (FernUniversität Hagen)* 251

Ambient Intelligence: Towards Smart Appliance Ensembles
    José L. Encarnação and Thomas Kirste (Fraunhofer IGD) 261

Application Domains for Virtual Information and Knowledge Environments

Enterprise Information Integration – A Semantic Approach
    *Thomas Kamps, Richard Stenzel, Libo Chen, and Lothar Rostek
    (Fraunhofer IPSI)* 271

Ontology-Based Project Management for Acceleration of Innovation
Projects
    *Hans-Jörg Bullinger (Fraunhofer-Gesellschaft), Joachim Warschat,
    Oliver Schumacher, Alexander Slama, and Peter Ohlhausen
    (Fraunhofer IAO)* 280

Understanding and Tailoring Your Scientific Information
Environment: A Context-Oriented View on E-Science Support
    *Claudia Niederée, Avaré Stewart, Claudio Muscogiuri
    (Fraunhofer IPSI), Matthias Hemmje (FernUniversität Hagen),
    and Thomas Risse (Fraunhofer IPSI)* 289

TV Scout: Lowering the Entry Barrier to Personalized TV Program
Recommendation
Patrick Baudisch (Xerox PARC) and Lars Brueckner
(TU Darmstadt) 299

Intelligent Home-Enjoying Computing Anywhere
Junzhong Gu (ECNU-MMIT) 310

Author Index 321

An Overview on Automatic Capacity Planning

Thomas Risse

Fraunhofer IPSI
Integrated Publication and Information Systems Institute
Dolivostrasse 15, 64293 Darmstadt, Germany
thomas.risse@ipsi.fraunhofer.de

Abstract. The performance requirement for the transformation of messages within electronic business processes is our motivation to investigate in automatic capacity planning methods. Performance typically means the throughput and response time of a system. Finding a configuration of a distributed system satisfying performance goals is a complex search problem that involves many design parameters, like hardware selection, job distribution and process configuration. Performance models are a powerful tool to analyse potential system configurations, however, their evaluation is expensive, such that only a limited number of possible configurations can be evaluated. In this paper we give an overview of our automatic system design method and discuss the arising problems to achieve the performance during the runtime of the systems. Furthermore we make a discussion on the impact of our strategy on the current trends in distributed systems.

1 Introduction

Our motivation to investigate in automatic capacity planning methods arises from the electronic data interchange. Electronic data interchange is an important aspect in the implementation of business processes and often requires the conversion of EDI messages (e.g. between EDIFACT and an in-house format). One key criterion in the design of such a converter systems, but also for most other systems, is performance. Performance typically means the throughput and response time of a system. The effects of poor performing systems ranges from unsatisfied users to high penalties for companies due to missed processing deadlines. Due to the continuously increasing hardware performance, companies often solve performance problems by replacing their hardware with faster machines. One consequence can be that a performance increase can be achieved, as e.g. the processors itself are faster, but the overall performance increase is less then expected. The reason for this is that the combination of hardware and software often does not match. A typical example for this is that a multi-processor machine is used to execute an application, which is not fully parallelizable. In this case serialized parts of the processing workflow can become the bottleneck of the system. Fontenot [1] called this a *software bottleneck*. A software bottleneck means that parts of the executed software are fully utilized, while most of the

M. Hemmje et al. (Eds.): E.J. Neuhold Festschrift, LNCS 3379, pp. 1–10, 2005.

other system components (hard- and software) are idle. Hence, the system is saturated but not fully utilized. To simply increase the number of processors is in this case an economically bad decision, as the system performance cannot benefit from the larger number of processors, as the software would not support more processors. For system designers it would be helpful to have a systematic method, which supports them in the design of new and in the extension of existing systems.

In this paper we give an overview of our automatic performance oriented system design method and discuss the arising problems to achieve the performance during the runtime of the systems. Furthermore we make a discussion on the impact of our strategy on the current trends in distributed systems.

The paper is organized as follows. In the next Section we motivate our work with a typical B2B scenario from the financial area. Afterwards we give an introduction on capacity planning and related activities. Our proposed automatic method to achieve performance goals is given in Section 4. The impact on decentralized systems is discussed afterwards in Section 5. Finally, conclusions are given in Section 6.

2   A Motivating Application

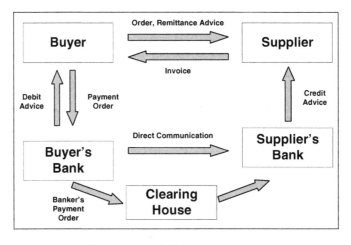

Fig. 1. Typical E-Business process

We motivate the need of a systematic configuration method by a typical procurement example application from the B2B world, which is depicted in Figure 1. It shows the information flow between a buyer and a supplier of goods and the communication with their banks. The instantiation of such a workflow requires the usage of several communication standards, e.g. the order handling is based on ebXML while the payments are done via EDIFACT, S.W.I.F.T. or DTA. Furthermore each party is using internally additional proprietary communication standards.

Let us now focus on the message processing on the bank side. In the banking sector often large EDI messages containing financial transaction information, e.g. collected payments or salary payments, need to be converted from a standard inbound format to formats of the in-house systems while keeping strict deadlines. The transformation of messages requires a sequence of different steps that are applied to each message. An example is shown in Figure 2.

Fig. 2. Sequential processing of messages

The 'Input Pre-Processor' regularly checks for the arrival of new messages. Afterwards it analyzes the messages regarding the syntax format (e.g. ebXML), message structure and size. The information about message structure and size is used for the distribution of messages among the available hosts performing the conversion. The 'Converter' task transforms the message to an intermediate format, which is finally converted to the target format by the 'Packer' task.

The processing goals regarding the performance (aka performance goals) are derived from a requirement analysis. Hence, we obtain information on the expected message volumes, the message size distribution and the requirements on response time and throughput. Qualitative requirements are scalability, availability, and constraints on the type of available hardware.

2.1   System Architecture

To satisfy requirements on availability, reliability, scalability and high throughput, a parallel and distributed architecture is used. The system can be built from different host types, allowing the use of existing hardware and the incremental extension of the system with new hardware. The generic architecture of the system is shown in Figure 3. The global scheduler distributes incoming messages to the individual hosts. The distribution strategy it uses will be based on the configuration determined by our system design method. The local scheduler controls the execution of tasks and the distribution of the tasks to the processors on the different hosts. The local scheduler is tightly coupled with the operating system. A more detailed description of this architecture and the processing steps can be found in [2].

The problem to solve is now the selection and combination of appropriate hardware. Furthermore the configuration of the software, which means to determine the optimal number of software process instances executed in parallel for each processing step. The process to identify such a configuration is called *Capacity planning*.

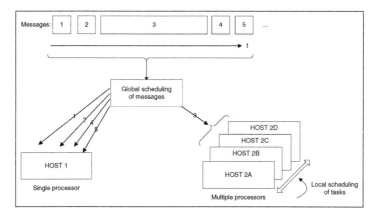

Fig. 3. System architecture

3   Capacity Planning

The process of *Capacity planning* is defined by Menascé et al. [3] as the prediction "when future load levels will *saturate* the system and determining the most cost-effective way of delaying system saturation as much as possible".

Capacity planning is used when hardware and software has to be selected and configured according to certain performance characteristics. Performance characteristics are throughput and response time of a system. Limited processing capacities together with increasing processing demands, large volumes of EDI messages, leads to systems saturation. Saturated systems have rapidly increasing response times, which lead to dissatisfaction of the users. Such architectural decisions are done very early in the design process of a system. Hence, it would be helpful for system designers to be able to assess the effects of design decisions on the system performance as early as possible.

Capacity planning requires a lot of knowledge about the software. Hence all major companies like IBM, Microsoft, etc. are providing tools and guidelines to configure their software systems manually. A more general methodology has been developed by Daniel Menascé. In a series of books he developed planning methods for client-server systems [4], for web servers [5] and web services [3].

Menascés' general methodology for capacity planning is depicted in Figure 4. The initial phase is a learning phase to understand the hardware, software, connectivities, etc. of the environment. Afterwards the systems' workload has to be precisely described. Typically the workload model is based on a clustered real workload. The workload model will be verified with the real workload and adapted accordingly until the differences are acceptable. Workload forecasting is the process of predicting future workloads, which is typically done by looking on the workload history. The same three steps have to be performed for the performance model.

In parallel to the workload and performance models, a cost model has to be developed to determine how costs vary with system size and architecture.

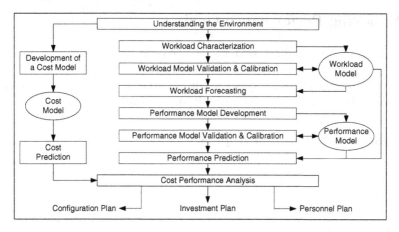

Fig. 4. A methodology for capacity planning [3]

The result of this process is a cost performance analysis, which is used to assess various scenarios of hardware and software configuration. This will results in a configuration plan, which specifies necessary hardware, configuration of software, architectural changes, etc.

Menascé formulated the cost performance analysis quite vague. He says that the performance model can be used to assess various configurations and scenarios, but he didn't describe a systematic way for testing different configurations or finding suitable hard- and software configurations.

An example for a systematic system configuration approach is described by Alvarez et al. [6]. He proposed the MINERVA system, whose goal was the rapid design of a storage system that meets certain workload requirements and has near-minimum cost. They combine fast analytical workload models, based on Markov chains, for the storage device with a heuristic search technique. The search mechanism is using a branch-and-bound strategy to find all suitable solutions.

El-Sayed et al. [7] proposed an automated method to optimize the response time of a pre-configured system. The optimization is performed by adapting the task priorities, the task allocations to processors and the splitting of tasks.

A methodology for the configuration of Java J2EE application servers for improved performance has been proposed by Raghavachari et al. [8]. The overall idea is to learn about application characteristics, interaction of configuration values, etc. during the random exploration of the configuration space. Unfortunately, no exact description of the learning process is available.

Up to our knowledge no further automatic process exists to support system designers in the cost performance analysis. Hence our approach published in [9] is the first automatic configuration approach, which integrates hardware and software configuration.

4   Achieving Performance Goals

The problem of achieving the performance goals is divided into two parts: system design and system runtime. We will first give an overview on our system configuration approach. Afterwards we discuss restrictions of this method and the way how they can be compensated during runtime.

4.1   System Configuration Approach

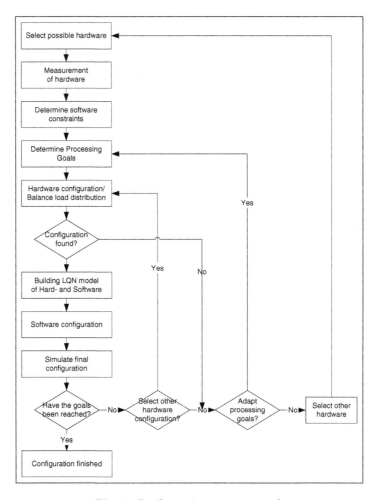

Fig. 5. Configuration process graph

In Figure 5 we provide an overview of the system configuration process. In a first step the available hardware is determined from the business constraints. For the available hardware, hardware measurements are performed for obtaining basic performance data that can be fed into the subsequent steps of the configuration process. Furthermore software constraints, e.g. the maximum number of process instances for a processing step, are determined. These constraints are used in the software configuration step to avoid the selection of unrealizable software configurations. Once the hardware and software properties are determined the processing goals in terms of throughput and response time for the different kinds of tasks are specified. The first main step in our method is hardware configuration. A system configuration selecting from the available hardware is determined, which has the capacity to achieve the processing goals. This step is based on approximate, analytical performance models that abstract from the properties of specific software configurations. They can be evaluated without using simulations.

Based on the selected hardware configuration a performance model based on Layered Queueing Networks (LQN) [10,11] is constructed, that considers also the software's process structure. Using simulations of the performance model and modifying the model by a greedy search method an optimized process configuration is identified, satisfying the processing goals achievable by the selected hardware configuration. A final simulation of the complete system is then performed in order to verify that the processing goals have been reached. This verification may fail when no software configuration can be found that satisfies the performance predicted in the hardware configuration step.

In such a case, a new iteration of the hardware configuration step is started. Other hardware configurations may be identified since hardware configuration is performed in a non-deterministic manner taking into account business requirements, such as available hardware and hardware cost. If no suitable hardware configuration can be found it is possible to adapt the processing goals. If this also does not result in a suitable configuration, as a last resort, alternative hardware needs to be considered. In general adaptations of processing goals and available hardware can be expected to occur rather rarely, since, on the one hand, the processing goals and hardware selection are mostly business-driven requirements and, on the other hand, the system designers have at least a very rough understanding of the necessary hardware performance required to satisfy the processing goals. To find within those constraints a solution with an optimal use of resources is where we provide support through our configuration method.

4.2   Runtime Optimization

The result of our configuration method is a combination of hosts and software process instances, which guarantees in average the performance goals. But our method requires to abstract from the reality, e.g. the models assume fixed arrival rates of jobs, which deviate in reality. Hence the real system handle all types of deviations in a flexible way. In the following we discuss the possibilities and limitations to handle runtime deviations.

During the system design phase we have to abstract from the reality in order to build the performance and workload models. For the workload model we are clustering the jobs by processing time, job size and arrival rates and calculate average values for each cluster. The deviations within the clusters are known but not respected in the performance model as we are only using the average values as fixed input values for our models. Furthermore, as we are using a stochastic performance model, we are only able to give probabilities for the execution of a specific task. Different arrival orders of jobs, which lead to different execution orders of tasks, are not respected by the performance model.

But both aspects, deviations of the average values and the arrival order of the jobs, have an impact on the runtime performance of the system. In contrast to the workload model the real workload has deviations of processing times, which has to be compensated during runtime. Another aspect is the arrival order of the jobs. It makes a big difference for the response time of an individual jobs if it has to be processed during peak arrivals of large jobs or during average arrival rates of jobs. In the first case all jobs will have much higher response times as they have to wait with a high probability for the termination of a large job. In the other case the response times are smaller as the probabilities for long waiting times is much lower. But if the performance is observed over a long time, then in average the performance goals are reached. Within short observation time ranges there might be deviations.

However, distributed systems are using schedulers to optimize the distribution of jobs among hosts with certain optimization goals. The scheduler has to decide just-in-time where and when a job will be executed. The optimization goal is to achieve the performance goal with any mixture of jobs if possible. The scheduler decisions are based on partial knowledge as future arrivals are not known. Such schedulers are also known as online schedulers.

Within a distributed system the online scheduling algorithm has to be selected according to the system environment and processing goals. Overall, several online scheduling algorithms exist. A good overview can be found in [12]. The selection of the right scheduling strategy is crucial. Most of the online scheduling algorithms are focused on the distribution of jobs among identical hosts. List scheduling is a very easy and popular algorithm, but Graham [13] showed that the quality depends on the number of machines and that the scheduler is in average $1.5 - 2$ times worse then the optimal solution. Albers [14] proposed a randomized algorithm, which has a better performance and is independent from the number of machines. In [15] we developed and evaluated a scheduler, based on Bin Stretching approach [16], for our motivating application from Section 2. Our evaluation in [9] showed that the combination of systematic system design and the optimal job distribution is able to achieve the performance goals. Our comparison with different algorithms also verified that the selection of the right distribution method is crucial.

To summarize, the results of the system design process will give a configuration, which guarantees that the performance goals are reached in average. Local deviations are possible and can be reduced by a scheduling component within the system. But one should have in mind that a complete compensation is not always possible. As the selection of the scheduling algorithm is crucial, this has to be done for every system and application separately.

5   Relevance for Distributed Systems

The problem of system sizing is not limited to system designers. The problem arises everywhere, where a limited number of resources have to be used to solve a specific problem. With the broader acceptance of GRID computing the problem of identifying suitable sets of resources from a pool of available resources arises every day. Foster defines in [17] the GRID as "coordinated resource sharing and problem solving in dynamic, multi-institutional virtual organizations". Hence in the GRID, organizations can provide resources, which are consumed by other institutions. Organizations, which collaborate in such a way, are forming a temporary virtual organization. Available resources are registered at some resource broker and can be discovered by other organizations. Currently the resource brokers work in a rather simple way. The users are only able to specify which type of resources they need (e.g. SUN Sparc Processor, 64 bit, 2 GHz). So the user has to guess, based on his experiences, which type of system would be the right one. This manual method works as long as the required systems are available and no processing guarantees or time constraints are given. If these prerequisites do not hold, a more sophisticated and flexible resource broker is desirable. Such a resource broker can take into account the processing goals and more detailed properties of the software. With the help of our system design method the resource broker could do the system design on the fly. The benefit for the user is that he does not need to care about the available systems. The benefit for the GRID infrastructure and user community is that only necessary resources are used.

6   Conclusion

In this paper we gave an overview on capacity planning and especially on the automatic configuration of distributed systems according to given performance requirements. Capacity planning methods provides already cost effective ways to delay system saturations. With our automatic configuration method this can be done more efficiently during the system design phase. Our analysis showed that processing time deviation during runtime can be handled by a good job distribution strategy, but that the performance goals can only be reached in average. During peak times the performance goals might not be reached. Furthermore, we motivated our approach with a typical B2B application, but showed also that an extension of the method is useful in the upcoming Grid computing. Other possible research directions lead to self-configuring systems. Hence, systems would be able to optimize themselves during runtime.

References

1. Fontenot, M.L.: Software congestion, mobile servers, and the hyperbolic model. IEEE Transactions on Software Engineering **SE-15, 8** (1989) 947–962
2. Risse, T., Wombacher, A., Aberer, K.: Efficient processing of voluminous edi documents. In: Proceedings of ECIS 2000, Vienna, Austria, Vienna University of Economics and Business Administration (2000)
3. Menascé, D.A., Almeida, V.A.F.: Capacity Planning for Web Services: Metrics, Models, and Methods. P T R Prentice-Hall, Englewood Cliffs, NJ 07632, USA (2002)
4. Menascé, D., Almeida, V., Dowdy, L.: Capacity Planning and Performance Modeling: From Mainframes to Client-Server Systems. Prentice-Hall (1994)
5. Menascé, D.A., Almeida, V.A.F.: Capacity Planning for Web Performance: metrics, models, and methods. Prentice-Hall, Englewood Cliffs, NJ 07632, USA (1998)
6. Alvarez, G.A., Borowsky, E., Go, S., Romer, T.H., Becker-Szendy, R., Golding, R., Merchant, A., Spasojevic, M., Veitch, A., Wilkes, J.: Minerva: An automated resource provisioning tool for large-scale storage systems. ACM Transactions on Computer Systems **19** (2001) 483–518
7. El-Sayed, H., Cameron, D., Woodside, M.: Automation support for software performance engineering. In: Proceedings of the 2001 ACM SIGMETRICS international conference on Measurement and modeling of computer systems, New York, ACM Press (2001) 301–311
8. Raghavachari, M., Reimer, D., Johnson, R.D.: The deployer's problem: configuring application servers for performance and reliability. In: Proceedings of the 25th international conference on Software engineering, IEEE Computer Society (2003) 484–489
9. Risse, T., Aberer, K., Wombacher, A., Surridge, M., Taylor, S.: Configuration of distributed message converter systems. Performance Evaluation **58** (2004) 43–80
10. Woodside, C.M., Neilson, J.E., Petriu, D.C., Majumdar, S.: The stochastic rendezvous network model for performance of synchronous client-server-like distributed software. IEEE Transactions on Computers **44** (1995) 20–34
11. Franks, G., Majumdar, S., Neilson, J., Petriu, D., Rolia, J., Woodside, C.: Performance analysis of distributed server systems. In: Proceedings of the 6th International Conference on Software Quality. (1996) 15–26
12. Sgall, J.: Online scheduling – a survey. Lecture Notes in Computer Science **1442** (1997) 196–231
13. Graham, R.: Bounds for certain multiprocessor anomalies. Bell System Technical Journal **45** (1966) 1563–1581
14. Albers, S.: On randomized online scheduling. In: Proceedings of the 34th annual ACM symposium on Theory of computing, New York, ACM Press (2002) 134–143
15. Risse, T., Wombacher, A., Surridge, M., Taylor, S., Aberer, K.: Online scheduling in distributed message converter systems. In: Proceedings of 13th Parallel and Distributed Computing and Systems (PDCS 2001), IASTED (2001)
16. Azar, Y., Regev, O.: On-line bin-stretching. Theoretical Computer Science **268** (2001) 17–41
17. Foster, I., Kesselman, C., Tuecke, S.: The anatomy of the Grid: Enabling scalable virtual organization. The International Journal of High Performance Computing Applications **15** (2001) 200–222

Overview on Decentralized Establishment of Multi-lateral Collaborations

Andreas Wombacher

Department of Computer Science, University of Twente, The Netherlands
a.wombacher@ewi.utwente.nl

Abstract. Service oriented architectures facilitate loosely coupled collaborations, which are established in a decentralized way. One challenge for such collaborations is to guarantee consistency, that is, fulfillment of all constraints of individual services and deadlock-freeness. This paper presents an overview on a decentralized approach to consistency checking, which utilizes only bilateral views of the collaboration.

1 Introduction

A multi-lateral collaboration is the act of several parties working jointly [1]. Several forms of collaboration exist covering almost all areas of people's life like for example at work, where people are employed by a company being involved in producing a good. Within this example, the employees have the same goal of producing a good. However, there exist collaborations where each party has its own goal that can only be achieved by interacting with other people, like for example, people going shopping at a market or companies having joint ventures.

These two generic types of collaborations exist also in Information Technology. The execution of such a collaboration usually involves several parties, each providing different tasks, that is, a "logical unit of work that is carried out as a single whole by one" party [2]. A collaboration can be characterized by a set of tasks that have to be performed and the causal and temporal dependencies between the different tasks. A model describing the coordination of tasks, that is, managing dependencies between these tasks [3], dependencies between activities" within a collaboration is known as a workflow.

Workflows have been studied for several years. Initially, workflows have been carried out completely by humans manipulating physical objects [4]. Later, with the introduction of Information Technology, processes are partially or totally be automated by information systems, which are controlling the execution of tasks and the performance of the tasks themselves. However, the main goal of workflow management systems is not the complete automation of workflows but the separation of control logic and logic contained in the tasks, where a task is either performed by a information system or by a human. Based on this separation reuse of tasks in different workflows is supported [5]. Electronic data interchange (EDI) performed over the Internet and the extendable markup language (XML) standard family are key factors for the emergence of Web-based workflows. Due

M. Hemmje et al. (Eds.): E.J. Neuhold Festschrift, LNCS 3379, pp. 11–20, 2005.

to this improved and simplified communication and coordination mechanisms, inter-organizational cooperations and virtual organization structures are evolving, where the interaction and work performed by several parties forming a multi-lateral collaboration have to be coordinated and controlled. Establishing such a multi-lateral collaboration is a major challenge, while the effort increases with the number of parties that have to agree on

- the connectivity, that is, the supported communication protocols (like for example FTP, HTTP, SMTP,...) as well as the communication languages, which are message formats in case of electronic data interchange (EDI).
- the tasks to be used within the collaboration, that is, the combination of tasks taken from different parties forming a successful collaboration.
- the coordination of the selected tasks, that is, the order in which the different tasks have to be executed guaranteeing a successful collaboration.

To achieve connectivity the transformation of protocols and messages might be required. An automated transformation of messages requires an "understanding" of the meaning of a message's content, which is expressed in terms of an ontology and is addressed by the Semantic Web community. The second and third aspect, that is, deriving the set of used tasks and the coordination of those tasks represents an establishment of a commonly agreed workflow specification. The approach sketched in this paper focus on these workflow aspects required to establish a multi-lateral collaboration.

2 Centralized Establishment of Multi-lateral Collaborations

Nowadays, multi-lateral collaborations are usually set up by a group of people representing the different parties involved in the collaboration. In particular, these people meet, discuss the different options, and finally decide on the definition of a multi-lateral collaboration: which communication protocols and messages are going to be used, and what are the workflow options that have to be supported by a collaboration.[1] The agreement on the multi-lateral collaboration derived by this group specifies a multi-lateral collaboration from a global point of view. Based on this specification a multi-lateral collaboration can be checked for consistency, that is deadlock-freeness: the specification of a multi-lateral collaboration has to ensure that all potential execution sequences of the collaboration guarantee a successful termination of the collaboration, that is, there exist no execution sequence resulting in a non-final state where no further interaction with any party is possible.

The global view specification of a multi-lateral collaboration can be used to derive a specification of the collaboration from a local point of view, that is, the

---

[1] As a basis for this discussion the different parties try to ensure that the integration effort needed to adapt the local infrastructure and processes to the multi-lateral collaboration is minimized.

view of an individual party. Approaches exist, which allow to derive the local point of view from the global one ensuring that the interaction of the local views implements the global view of a multi-lateral collaboration [6]. Further, it can be guaranteed that the interaction of the local views is consistent if the global specification of a multi-lateral collaboration has been consistent.

The approach described above starting with a global specification of a multi-lateral collaboration, deriving the local views of it, and finally implementing the local views at each party guaranteeing the properties of the global view is also known as top-down approach of a collaboration establishment. This way of collaboration establishment is quite expensive, because people have to come to an agreement and the implementation of the local views of a collaboration afterwards requires a considerable implementation effort. Further, changes of the collaboration require to go through the whole process again making changes also very expensive. As a consequence, the top-down approach of collaboration establishment works fine for well established and quite static multi-lateral collaborations. However, current development in IT technology supports more flexible structures like for example Service Oriented Architectures (SOA), which are used to realize loosely coupled systems inherently providing a high potential of establishing collaborations between parties in a quite flexible and dynamic way.

3   Web Services

A Service Oriented Architecture (SOA) is defined as "a set of components which can be invoked, and whose interface descriptions can be published and discovered" [7]. Where a component is a "software object interacting with other components, encapsulating certain functionality or a set of functionalities" [8] and maintaining an internal state [9]. Thus, a SOA consists of components accessible as services, where each service provides a certain functionality, an internal state, and an interface to publish the provided functionality to potential service requesters. Opposed to component based architectures, where components are combined during the development phase, in SOAs services are combined after the deployment of services, that is, at run-time [10]. This change can be characterized as a step from supply-driven collaborations to demand-driven ones [11].

A concrete technology implementing the SOA are Web Services. In particular, the W3C Web Service Architecture Working Group defines a Web Service as "a software system designed to support interoperable machine-to-machine interaction over a network. It has an interface described in a machine-processable format (specifically WSDL). Other systems interact with the Web service in a manner prescribed by its description using SOAP-messages, typically conveyed using HTTP with an XML serialization in conjunction with other Web-related standards." [7]

From the definition of SOA the following properties can be derived: i) the services are distributed, since each service can be provided by a different party, and ii) the services are autonomous, because state changes within a service are independent of other service's states. As a consequence, a stateless service representing a certain functionality is comparable to a single task within a workflow, while a stateful service represents a set of tasks and its inherent dependencies represent a local workflow. The interaction of several services results in a multi-lateral collaboration being constructed from a set of pre-existing local workflows provided by services, resulting in a global workflow. This approach is further called bottom-up approach opposed to the top-down approach introduced in Section 2.

4   Decentralized Establishment of Multi-lateral Collaborations

Bottom-up establishment of multi-lateral collaborations should always result in a consistent collaboration, that is, a consistent global workflow. As a consequence, the bottom-up approach has to guarantee that the resulting global workflow is consistent. Because the global workflow is never instantiated, the decision on the consistency of the global workflow has to be made by local decisions of the involved parties. Consistency of a multi-lateral collaboration can be decided locally by a single party in case of a hierarchical structure of services, where a single service requester centrally coordinates the services, which interact only with the service requester and are provided by the remaining parties of the multi-lateral collaboration. Due to the limitation of services to interact with the service requester only, a single party exists knowing all complete local workflows, which is able to derive the global workflow of the multi-lateral collaboration and to decide on the global workflow's consistency [12].

Opposed to this very specific case, in all other cases no party knows the global workflow, thus, the decision on consistency of the global workflow has to be made in a decentralized way based on partial knowledge of the global workflow. From decentralized systems it is known that this kind of decision can not be made directly from local decisions based on a bilateral comparison [13].

This paper addresses this issue and provides an overview on an approach to decide consistency of a multi-lateral collaboration in a decentralized way, that is, without instantiating the corresponding global workflow. The decision can be made in a decentralized way by deriving some additional consistency properties.

5   Workflow and Communciation Models

Before discussing the concrete approach, a sufficient workflow modeling approach has to be selected providing means to represent bilateral consistency as well as a centralized version of multi-lateral consistency as a starting point. Multi-lateral collaborations may rely on different communication infrastructure, which can be generally classified as synchronous, that is, a message sent by a party must be received by anotehr party immediately, and asynchronous, that is, a message sent by a party has to be received by another party later on, but latest before completion of the local workflow. While there exist several approaches for the asynchronous communication model, the synchronous communication model has not been addressed so far. In case of asynchronous communication Workflow Nets [2] have been used besides other approaches like for example [14,15]. For the synchronous case, an extension of Finite State Automata [16] called annotated Finite State Automata (aFSA) [17] has been proposed. In particular, standard Finite State Automata are extended by a notion of mandatory and optional transitions, that is, all messages sent by a party that must be supported by a recipient party are called mandatory messages, while messages received by a party are called optional messages, because they are not necessarily sent by another party.

Evaluation of Workflow Net properties are defined on the derived occurrence graph, which has the same expressiveness as aFSA. Thus, a mapping from Workflow Nets to aFSA can be defined, while it can be shown that the definitions of multi-lateral consistency consider the equivalent set of collaborations to be consistent. As a consequence, further discussion of decentralized consistency checking can be focused on the notion of aFSA.

6   Decentralized Consistency Checking

As discussed in detail in [18], the trivial approach of basing a decentralized multi-later consistency decision on bilateral consistency turned out to be incorrect, because of information loss introduced by having only a partial view on the multi-lateral collaboration. Especially, information loss has been observed on message parameter constraints, that is, parameter values are considered which have been excluded by other parts of the global workflow already, and occurrence graph constraints, that is, message sequences are considered although the execution of a message contained in this message sequence has been excluded already by another part of the global workflow.

Due to the loss of information, decentralized consistency checking requires to make use of transitivity properties on parameter and occurrence graph constraints. Thus, deciding consistency of a multi-lateral collaboration in a decentralized way proceeds in three steps:

1. Resolving Cycles:
   Local workflow models of parties are made acyclic by representing cycles as iterations of at most N steps.
2. Propagation:
   Parameter and occurrence graph constraints on already performed transitions are made available to all parties involved in the multi-lateral collaboration. This comprises:
   (a) Propagation of parameter constraints within local workflows, as well as between bilateral interactions until a fixed point has been reached.
   (b) Propagation of occurrence graph constraints within local workflows, as well as between bilateral interactions until a fixed point has been reached.

3. Decentralized Consistency Checking:
   Each party checks consistency of its bilateral interactions and local work-flow. If they are all consistent, then the party considers the multi-lateral collaboration to be consistent until any other party falsifies this decision by considering the multi-lateral collaboration to be inconsistent.

4. Consensus Making
   A protocol is required to decentrally check whether all parties consider their bilateral interactions and local workflows as consistent, and to inform all parties about the final consensus. This kind of problem is known in distributed systems as consensus making problem [13].

A decentralized decision requires to make use of transitivity properties of parameter and occurrence graph constraints, which requires the underlying work-flow model to support parameter constraint transitivity. Since cyclic graph structures are not transitive used workflow models have to be acyclic. As a consequence, cycles have to be resolved in step 1. In particular, cycles are resolved by explicitly representing all potential execution sequences of the cycle with at most N steps of a cycle within a single execution sequence of the local workflow.

Step 2 is required because bilateral workflows hide all parameter and occurrence graph constraints that is not immediately seen by the two involved parties. The goal of parameter constraint propagation is to make sure that all parameter constraints can be met, even though they may not immediately be visible in a bilateral workflow. The parameters of transitions are assumed to be immutable, that is, after they have been set initially they can not be changed. As a consequence, a parameter constraint holds for all transitions following the transition at which it has been specified. On these grounds parameter constraints can be propagated to all following transitions within a workflow as well as to the workflow of the partner. The goal of propagating occurrence graph constraints is to discard all those transitions, which cause a deadlock in a bilateral workflow but can never be executed due to constraints imposed by the invisible part of the global workflow.

Step 3 is the consistency checking itself, that is, making a local decision on local consistency of a local party. This step is performed by every party independently and the consensus making protocol is applied next.

Finally, step 4 aims to make an agreement between a set of parties having reached a fixed point with regard to parameter and occurrence graph constraint propagation, and forming a multi-lateral collaboration. Since no party knows all parties involved in the collaboration none can act as a coordinator of the collaboration. In particular, the following tasks must be performed:

- collect the local consistency decision of each party,
- check whether all parties consider the collaboration to be consistent, and finally
- inform all parties being involved on the final decision.

This generic consensus making problem is addressed by the distributed systems and algorithms community (see for example [13]). However, due to the fact that a fixed point on constraint propagation of constraints is required anyway, the aim is to define multi-lateral consistency as a kind of propagation to overcome the consensus making problem. The underlying idea is to reflect mandatory and optional messages as structural aspects of a workflow model effecting the occurrence graph, thus, being propagated via the corresponding propagation mechanism as discussed above. However, the modification of the occurrence graph with respect to mandatory and optional messages has to be performed via an explicit operation. As a consequence, a fixed point can be reached, where either non or all local workflows of the collaboration are consistent.

7   Evaluation

The evaluation of the sketched approach based on a synchronous communication model in the Web Services domain is two-fold: First, the applicability and expressiveness of the introduced annotated Finite State Automata (aFSA) as a workflow model is evaluated. In particular, a mapping of the Business Process Execution Language for Web Services (BPEL) [19] to aFSA is specified and realized. A detailed description of this mapping is contained in [20]. However, there exist some BPEL language constructs, which are not mapped to the aFSA workflow model, because they are irrelevant for consistency checking or can be added later on to the mapping by an additional processing step potentially increasing the complexity of the aFSA model significantly. Thus, the mapping works fine, which has been further evaluated by representing all potential workflows derived from the Internet Open Trading Protocol (IOTP) [21] specification in terms of aFSA. It turned out that all potential workflows covered by IOTP can be modeled as aFSAs.

Second, the process of establishing consistent multi-lateral collaborations has to be based on the propagation of constraints and consensus making as sketched above. To be able to set up these multi-lateral collaborations, a service discovery is required to find potential trading partners, which considers only thos service providers, which do have a consistent bilateral workflow with the own local workflow. In particular, this requires an implementation of a bilateral matchmaking based on the mapping from BPEL to aFSA as mentioned aboved. Such a service discovery based on the aFSA workflow model has been implemented and described in [22], where the supported queries are described as an extension of classical UDDI, the architecture is introduced, and a performance measurement based on the constructed IOTP data set is provided. The implementation is based on the assumption that receiving a message is always unconstraint, that is, the receiving party has to be able to handle all potential parameter values. As a consequence, the implementation does not consider the handling of parameters, hence, parameter constraint propagation can be neglected. Based on the derived service providers a multi-lateral collaboration can be established in a decentralized way requiring a unique collaboration identification to handle concurrent involvement of parties in several collaborations. In particular, a protocol is required to derive multi-lateral collaborations from bilateral collaborations in a decentralized way.

Thus, based on these two evaluation steps the sufficient expressiveness of aFSA to represent real world workflows is illustrated.

8   Summary and Outlook

The paper provides a high level description of an approach to establish consistent multi-lateral collaborations in a decentralized way. At various points references to further readings are provided. In particular, the aim of this paper is to sketch the basic ideas, which are the requirement of constraint propagation resulting in a fixed point allowing local consistency checking, and the consensus making on the multi-lateral consistency based on propagated structural workflow properties.

As an outlook, additional application scenarios are briefly sketched like for example ebXML, GRID, or Peer-to-Peer (P2P) environments, which all have in common a necessity of forming multi-lateral collaborations.

The electronic business XML initiative (ebXML) [23] specification provides a framework supporting XML based exchange of business data [11]. In particular, the Collaboration Partner Profiles (CPP) and the Collaboration Partner Agreements (CPA) are part of this framework, which are reflecting the description of a party and the subset of this description to be used within a concrete collaboration. Although, Patil and Newcomer [24] consider ebXML as a top-down collaboration establishment approach, this is not enforced by the framework since no centralized coordinator of a collaboration has to be specified and the assignment of potential trading partners supports late binding similar to the service discovery phase in Web Service.

Another technology is the GRID infrastructure. Foster defines in [25] the GRID as "coordinated resource sharing and problem solving in dynamic, multi-institutional virtual organizations". In particular, different organizations provide resources and request capacities for solving problems. However, the different parties are independent of each other although they agreed to participate in the GRID, which is right now a quite static relationship with high availability of the different participants. Due to this structure, there is no need for a more flexible handling of relationships. But, the GRID community started to think about more flexible relationships, where the availability of different parties is lower and more flexible and short to mid-term relationships have to be established and managed as for example addressed by the Diligent project [26].

A further example of a potential technology are Peer-to-Peer (P2P) systems. One definition of P2P considered suitable for this discussion is provided by the Intel P2P working group: "P2P is the sharing of computer resources and services by direct exchange between systems" [27]. In P2P environments every party (peer in P2P terminology) are considered to be independent. This means that a peer offers services or resources to a community, but at the same time, it can consume services/resources from others in the community. An important property of P2P systems is the lack of a central administration, the flexibility of the set of peers forming the community, and the decentralized organization of the community. As illustrated by Risse et.al. [28] P2P systems are on the move from well known file sharing to large scale decentralized and reliable systems relying on decentrally coordinated and established multi-lateral collaborations.

References

1. WordNet. (http://wordnet.princeton.edu)
2. Aalst, W., Hee, K.: Workflow Management - Models, Methods, and Systems. MIT Press (2002)
3. Malone, T.W., Crowston, K.: The interdisciplinary study of coordination. ACM Computing Surveys (CSUR) **26** (1994) 87–119
4. Georgakopoulos, D., Hornick, M., Sheth, A.: An Overview of Workflow Management: From Process Modelling to Workflow Automation Infrastructure. Distributed and Parallel Databases **3** (1995) 119–153
5. Mohan, C.: Workflow management in the internet age. In Litwin, W., Morzy, T., Vossen, G., eds.: Proceedings of the Second East European Symposium on Advances in Databases and Information Systems (ADBIS), Springer LNCS 1475 (1998) 26–34
6. Aalst, W.: Interorganizational workflows: An approach based on message sequence charts and petri nets. Systems Analysis - Modelling - Simulation **34** (1999) 335–367
7. Haas, H., Brown, A.: Web services gloassary. http://www.w3.org/TR/2004/NOTE-ws-gloss-20040211/ (2004)
8. Forum, C., Keahey, K.: CCA terms and definitions. http://www.cca-forum.org/glossary.shtml (2004)
9. Fielding, R.T.: Architectural Styles and the Design of Network-based Software Architectures. PhD thesis, University of Calivornia, Irvine (2000)
10. Kaye, D.: Loosely Coupled - The Missing Pieces of Web Services. RDS Press (2003)
11. Bussler, C.: B2B Integration - Concepts and Architecture. Springer (2003)
12. Wombacher, A., Mahleko, B., Risse, T.: Classification of ad hoc multi-lateral collaborations based on workflow models. In: Proceedings of Symposium on Applied Computing (ACM-SAC). (2003) 1185–1190
13. Lynch, N.A.: Distributed Algorithms. Morgan Kaufmann (1996)
14. Fu, X.: Formal Specification and Verification of Asynchronously Communicating Web Services. PhD thesis, University of California Santa Barbara (2004)
15. Kindler, E., Martens, A., Reisig, W.: Inter-operability of workflow applications: Local criteria for global soundness. In: Business Process Management, Models, Techniques, and Empirical Studies, Springer-Verlag (2000) 235–253
16. Hopcroft, J.E., Motwani, R., Ullman, J.D.: Introduction to Automata Theory, Languages, and Computation. Addison Wesley (2001)
17. Wombacher, A., Fankhauser, P., Mahleko, B., Neuhold, E.: Matchmaking for business processes based on choreographies. In: Proceedings of International Conference on e-Technology, e-Commerce and e-Service (EEE), IEEE Computer Society (2004) 28–31
18. Wombacher, A., Aberer, K.: Requirements for workflow modeling in P2P-workflows derived from collaboration establishment. In: Proceedings of International Workshop on Business Process Integration and Management (BPIM). (2004) 1036–1041

19. Andrews, T., Curbera, F., Dholakia, H., Goland, Y., Klein, J., Leymann, F., Liu, K., Roller, D., Smith, D., Thatte, S., Trickovic, I., Weerawarana, S.: Business process execution language for web services, version 1.1 (2003)

20. Wombacher, A., Fankhauser, P., Neuhold, E.: Transforming BPEL into annotated deterministic finite state automata enabling process annotated service discovery. In: Proceedings of International Conference on Web Services (ICWS). (2004) 316–323

21. Burdett, D.: Internet open trading protocol - IOTP - version 1.0. http://www.ietf.org/rfc/rfc2801.txt (2000)

22. Wombacher, A., Mahleko, B., Neuhold, E.: IPSI-PF: A business process match-making engine. In: Proceedings of Conference on Electronic Commerce (CEC). (2004) 137–145

23. ebXML: ebXML home page. (http://www.ebxml.org/)

24. Patil, S., Newcomer, E.: ebxml and web services. IEEE Internet Computing **7** (2003) 74–82

25. Foster, I., Kesselman, C., Tuecke, S.: The anatomy of the Grid: Enabling scalable virtual organization. The International Journal of High Performance Computing Applications **15** (2001) 200–222

26. diligent consortium: A digital library infrastructure on grid enabled technology. http://diligentproject.org/ (2004)

27. Milojičić, D., Kalogeraki, V., Lukose, R., Nagaraja, K., Pruyne, J., Richard, B., Rollins, S., Xu, Z.: Peer-to-peer computing. Technical report (2002)

28. Risse, T., Knezevic, P., Wombacher:, A.: P2P evolution: From file-sharing to de-centralized workflows. it-Information Technology (2004) 193–199

Dynamic Maintenance of an Integrated Schema

Regina Motz

Instituto de Computación
Universidad de la República
Montevideo - Uruguay
rmotz@fing.edu.uy

Abstract. This work presents a schema evolution methodology able to propagate structural and semantic modifications occurring in the local schemas of a federated database to the integrated schema. Our approach is to regard this problem from a schema integration point of view. Our theoretical framework is based on a declarative schema integration methodology, which reduces schema integration to the resolution of a set of equivalence correspondences between arbitrarily complex local subschemas.

1 Introduction

Considering the importance of schema integration methodologies in data warehousing, e-commerce as well as the growing use of cooperative engineering, the relevance of schema evolution of an integrated schema in a federated database becomes very important and necessary. Such an evolution may be due to: (a) changes in the structure of the component schemas, or (b) changes in the semantics of correspondences between the component databases. The former case is referred to as *structural modifications*, while the latter as *semantic modifications*.

A key characteristic of a federation is the autonomy of their component databases: their instances and schemas may evolve, but independently. This fact naturally leads to the introduction of the concept of *dynamic maintenance* of an integrated schema defined as the process of propagating changes of the component databases to the integrated one in an efficient, consistent and user-independent way. This means to avoid as much as possible re-integration steps during the propagation process.

In this paper, we present a methodology which reduces propagation to a form of *incremental schema integration*. In contrast with traditional integration methodologies, which always require as input the whole set of correspondences between the local schemas and a complete re-integration every time a component modification occurs, the one we present permits to provide new correspondences in an incremental manner and re-integrate only on the affected portions of the integrated schema.

Our approach is based on a declarative schema integration methodology, called SIM [6], which accomplishes schema integration by resolving a set of equivalence correspondences between arbitrary component subschemas. A relevant aspect of our work is the semi–automatic derivation of new states for the already acquired set of mappings from the local schemas to the integrated one after the occurrence of local schema changes. This is achieved by the development of a framework for the evolution of an integrated

M. Hemmje et al. (Eds.): E.J. Neuhold Festschrift, LNCS 3379, pp. 21–30, 2005.

schema based on a mechanism that incorporates *incrementality* in the integration process. Another contribution of our work is that we show how it is possible to propagate *purely structural changes, capacity augmenting changes* as well as *capacity reducing changes* in a uniform manner.

Motivated by the fact that some local schema changes may be considered as cases of more elaborated "semantic correspondences" between subschemas, we regard the propagation of local semantic modifications as a form of *incremental semantic* schema integration. For this purpose we extend SIM to deal with an enriched set of semantic correspondences, namely inclusion, overlapping and grouping, as well as equivalence correspondences between one class and multiple classes. From the set of semantic correspondences between the local schemas, our methodology automatically induces structural transformations that make it possible to regard the given correspondences as equivalences. On this basis, the propagation of local semantic modifications reduces to a process which identifies the original schema correspondences affected by the schema change and reintegrates the affected portions of the integrated schema.

The paper is organized as follows. Section 2 describes the schema integration methodology our work is based on. In Section 3 we make an account of local semantic and structural modifications and show, by means of examples, the problems that component schema changes may cause on the integrated schema. In Section 4 we describe our approach to the dynamic maintenance of an integrated schema. Section 5 summarizes related work. Finally, in Section 6 we draw some conclusions and present directions for further work.

2   The Schema Integration Methodology: SIM

SIM [6] is a declarative schema integration methodology that works on schema graphs. A *schema graph* $G = (V, E, S, K)$ is a directed graph that captures the inheritance hierarchies and relationships of a schema. The vertices of a schema graph are of two kinds, $V = C \cup T_I$, where C is a finite set of classes and T_I is a set of immutable types. $E = E_R \cup E_A$ is a set of labelled edges. E_R corresponds to a set of relationship edges between classes. We will denote relationship edges by $p \xrightarrow{a} q$, where $p, q \in C$ and $a \equiv (\alpha, \beta)$, for $\alpha, \beta \in L_E$ (a set of edge labels). $E_A \subseteq C \times L_E \times V$ is a set of attribute edges. $S \subseteq C \times C$ is a finite set of specialization edges, which will be denoted by $p \implies q$, meaning that p is a specialization of q. We will write $p{=}q$ to denote an arbitrary edge. Finally, $K = K_R \cup K_A$ is a function which associates cardinality constraints to relationship and attribute edges. Not every schema graph specifies a valid schema. A schema graph G is said to be a *proper schema* when it satisfies the following restrictions:

1. *Uniqueness in the context of a class.* The occurrence of a relationship/attribute edge in the context of a class is unique.
2. *Acyclicity of subtyping.* Class specializations are acyclic.
3. *Monotonicity of Inheritance.* Specialization is preserved along equal attributes / relationships.

SIM reduces schema integration to the resolution of a set of equivalence vertex/path correspondences between subschemas of the local databases. From such a set of correspondences, SIM semi-automatically derives mappings, called *schema augmentations*, from each local schema to the integrated one, in such a way that corresponding data among local databases is mapped to the same structure in the integrated database. The generated schema augmentations enhance the schemas with classes and paths, such that the resulting integrated schema is a non-redundant proper schema graph.

Formally, this means that it is the least upper bound $(G_1 \sqcup_{\mathcal{A}} G_2)$ of the local schemas G_1 and G_2 under an augmentation ordering $\sqsubseteq_{\mathcal{A}}$. Two proper schema graphs $G = (V, E, S, K)$ and $G' = (V', E', S', K')$ are in an augmentation ordering, denoted by $G \sqsubseteq_{\mathcal{A}} G'$, iff $V \subseteq V'$, $S \subseteq S'$ and there exists a mapping, denoted by $\mathcal{A} : G \to G'$ and called an *augmentation*, which maps each vertex/edge of G to a proper subschema of G', satisfying the following conditions:

1. The mapping of the empty graph is the empty graph.
2. Each class $p \in V$ is mapped to a subschema of G' which contains at least p.
3. The augmentation of two distinct classes in G do not contain a common class in G'.
4. Each specialization $p \Longrightarrow q$ in G is mapped to a specialization path $p \overset{*}{\Longrightarrow} q$ in G'.
5. Each relationship $p \overset{a}{\longleftrightarrow} q$ in G is mapped to a path in G' with begin and end given by p and q, respectively, and of this form: $p \overset{*}{\Longrightarrow} p' \overset{r_1}{\longleftrightarrow} A_1 \overset{r_2}{\longleftrightarrow} \ldots \overset{r_n}{\longleftrightarrow} A_n \overset{r_{n+1}}{\longleftrightarrow} q' \overset{*}{\Longleftarrow} q, n \geq 0$.

   If, in addition, the relationship occurs in the path of G' as $p' \overset{a}{\longleftrightarrow} q'$, then $p \overset{*}{\Longrightarrow} p'$ and $q \overset{*}{\Longrightarrow} q'$, and $K(p \overset{a}{\longleftrightarrow} q) \leq K'(p' \overset{a}{\longleftrightarrow} q')$.
6. Each attribute edge $p \overset{a}{\to} q$ in G is mapped to a path in G' of the form: $p \overset{*}{\Longrightarrow} p' \overset{r_1}{\longleftrightarrow} A_1 \overset{r_2}{\longleftrightarrow} \ldots \overset{r_n}{\longleftrightarrow} A_n \overset{a}{\to} q$, with $n \geq 0$, such that the path $p \overset{*}{\Longrightarrow} p' \overset{r_1}{\longleftrightarrow} A_1 \overset{r_2}{\longleftrightarrow} \ldots \overset{r_n}{\longleftrightarrow} A_n$ is included in the mapping of p.

An important aspect of SIM is that mappings are injective functions. The methodology recognizes inconsistent correspondences for which there is no augmentation possible, and identifies ambiguous correspondences, for which there exists no unique integrated schema. For consistent correspondences, the methodology generates appropriate augmentations and an integrated schema automatically. An important aspect is that all path correspondences that overlap in some subpath are grouped as a pair of trees and resolved together recursively. A complete description of SIM can be found in [6].

3   Component Modifications

The aim of this section is to illustrate the impact that component schema changes may produce on an already integrated schema. We consider two types of schema changes: semantic and structural modifications.

3.1   Semantic Modifications

A common criterion to identify the differences between two databases is to compare their intentions [7,12,8]. The *intention* of a schema graph G is defined as the set of all its possible valid instances. Semantic modifications on a schema may then be identified by inspecting the relationship that holds between its intentions before and after the change. On this basis, we can identify the following kinds of semantic modifications: *inclusion* (increment in the set of possible valid instances), *exclusion* (reduction in the set of valid instances), *overlapping* (some instances are maintained, others dismissed and new ones included) and *disjoint* (the new set of valid instances does not intersect with the old one). These local semantic modifications require the specification of new semantic correspondences between the local schemas. The enriched set of semantic correspondences contains equivalence ($\equiv$), inclusion ($\subset$), overlapping ($\odot$) and grouping ($\gg$). An important feature is that all kind of semantic correspondences can be expressed as a structural schema modification plus a set of equivalence correspondences. Based on this feature our approach is to treat semantic modifications as structural modifications.

Let us see this with an example. Consider the schemas of two travel agencies, Travel Makes Fun (TMF) and Easy Travel (ET). In both travel agencies, excursions need to be reserved in advance and this is represented by a class $Reservation$ in each schema. Suppose that, initially, there is a constraint in both schemas which states that reservations can only be carried out with advance the payment of an amount. After some time the Easy Travel agency changes its policy allowing reservations without any payment. This modification in the semantics of $Reservation_{ET}$ induces the following new semantic correspondence: $Reservation_{ET} \subset Reservation_{TMF}$. By applying a structural transformation this inclusion correspondence can be treated as follows:

- *Structural modification*: A class $PartiallyPaid_{ET}$, modeling those reservations that are made after paying some amount, is added as subclass of $Reservation_{ET}$. This means that $Reservation_{ET}$ permits doing reservations without initial payment. The definition of $Reservation_{ET}$ as a generalization of $PartiallyPaid_{ET}$ models the inclusion relationship between the extensions of $Reservation_{TMF}$ and $Reservation_{ET}$.
- *New equivalence correspondence*: With the definition of $PartiallyPaid_{ET}$, an equivalence correspondence between $Reservation_{TMF}$ and $PartiallyPaid_{ET}$ now holds.

This example shows the necessity of addressing the resolution of structural modifications for the propagation of local semantic modifications.

3.2   Structural Modifications

These are modifications to the structure of local schemas. They are more complex than semantic modifications because they can not only affect the instances of a class or relationship, but rather the whole schema. Therefore, as a consequence of a local structural modification a set of correspondences between local schemas can also be affected. The problem is that there are some cases in which it is not possible to automatically obtain an evolved integrated schema from the old one due to the occurrence of ambiguity or inconsistency in the new set of correspondences.

Modifications that lead to ambiguity: Consider the previous two travel agencies. In both schemas, excursions, represented by a class *Excursion*, follow predefined itineraries.

Each itinerary consists of a set of tours and a set of stops. While Easy Travel models itineraries as objects, in Travel Makes Fun they are given by the values of the attributes *tours* and *stops* that belong to the class *Excursion*. For simplicity reasons, we assume that elements with equal names in both schemas correspond with each other. Therefore, the following correspondences hold initially:

$$Excursion \xrightarrow{stops} string \equiv Excursion \leftrightarrow Itinerary \xrightarrow{stops} string$$
$$Excursion \xrightarrow{tours} string \equiv Excursion \leftrightarrow Itinerary \xrightarrow{tours} string$$

Now, suppose that the attributes *tours* and *stops* of $Excursion_{TMF}$ evolve to a new class *Tour*. This modification affects the set of correspondences between both local schemas. The new correspondences are:

$$Excursion \leftrightarrow Tour \xrightarrow{stops} string \equiv Excursion \leftrightarrow Itinerary \xrightarrow{stops} string$$
$$Excursion \leftrightarrow Tour \xrightarrow{tours} string \equiv Excursion \leftrightarrow Itinerary \xrightarrow{tours} string$$

Traditional schema integration methodologies can not propagate this change automatically due the following ambiguity: Is the class *Tour* corresponding to the class *Itinerary*? Interaction with the user is necessary to solve this ambiguity. However, the main problem is to identify the correspondences affected by the ambiguity.

Modifications that lead to inconsistency: Consider now the evolution of Easy Travel presented in Figure 1. The class *TrainExc* is moved through the hierarchy of classes to appear as a subclass of *SpecialExc*. In this case there is no possible propagation of the local change because of an inconsistency between the correspondences that represent the modification and the initial ones, see Figure 1. The reason of the inconsistency is that for the new set of correspondences:

$$Excursion \leftarrow IndivExc \leftarrow AirExc \equiv Excursion \leftarrow AirExc$$
$$Excursion \leftarrow IndivExc \leftarrow TrainExc \equiv Excursion \leftarrow SpecialExc \leftarrow TrainExc$$
$$Excursion \leftarrow FluvialExc \equiv Excursion \leftarrow SpecialExc \leftarrow FluvialExc$$

it is not possible to fulfill all of them simultaneously. The direct propagation of such a schema change is usually rejected by most methodologies because they maintain previous decisions taken by the user.

Our methodology, in contrast, supplies the user the set of correspondences that lead to the inconsistency in order to eliminate one of them, obtaining in that way a consistent set of correspondences. In the next section we describe how to identify the set of correspondences that lead to the ambiguity or inconsistency.

4   Dynamic Maintenance

A key characteristic of the maintenance of an integrated schema is the fact that a local schema evolution may invalidate correspondences established in some previous integration steps. Our solution to this problem is to identify the augmentations affected by the

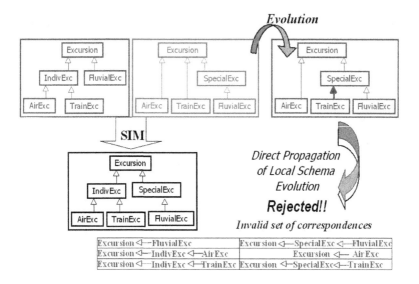

Fig. 1. Structural Modification that leads to inconsistency

local structural modification, and either modify them directly or deduce from them the involved corresponding subschemas where re-integration is required.

Schema changes may produce the addition or deletion of correspondences between local subschemas. In this sense we can regard the propagation of local schema changes as a form of *incremental schema integration*. To achieve this, we provide SIM with a mechanism able to treat ambiguities or inconsistencies incrementally. Such a mechanism essentially consists of two phases: first, it identifies the subschema of the integrated schema that has been affected by a given set of correspondences, and second, it manipulates this subschema so that it becomes consistent.

Semantic modifications are regarded as semantic correspondences between local schemas. As mentioned previously, semantic correspondences can in turn be expressed as structural modifications plus a set of equivalence correspondences. Given a vertex or path correspondence $p_1 \star p_2$ between two local schemas G_1 and G_2, with $\star \in \{\equiv, \subset, \odot, \gg\}$, $p_1 \in G_1$ and $p_2 \in G_2$, we define a structural transformation $\mathcal{T}(p_1 \star p_2) = (\mathcal{T}_1, \mathcal{T}_2, EC)$ given by structural mappings $\mathcal{T}_1 : p_1 \to G'_1$ and $\mathcal{T}_2 : p_2 \to G'_2$, and a set of equivalence correspondences EC between the modified schemas G'_1 and G'_2. The new set of equivalence correspondences are then handled using the techniques developed to the propagation of structural modifications.

The propagation of structural modifications is performed by our methodology as follows. Given two local schemas G_1 and G_2 and a local schema change in G_1 represented as a subschema C_1, we identify the corresponding portions of the local schemas as well as of the integrated schema affected by the schema change. We start finding the image of C_1 in the integrated schema by applying the augmentation mapping $\mathcal{A}_1$, $IC_1 = \mathcal{A}_1(C_1)$.

Then, by applying the inverse of the other augmentation[1] on that image, we obtain a sub-schema of G_2, $C_2 = \mathcal{A}_2^{-1}(IC_1)$. The subschema of G_1 that is in correspondence with C_2 is obtained by applying the mappings in the other direction, i.e. $C_3 = \mathcal{A}_1^{-1}(\mathcal{A}_2(C_2))$. Finally, we have found the corresponding subschemas affected by the schema change. It is worth mentioning that the correspondence between the subschemas is expressed as a set of equivalence vertex/path correspondences.

The local structural modifications we handle are within the following categories:

1. Modifications that extend an edge to a path
   (a) *Refinement of a specialization hierarchy*
       An edge $x \Leftarrow y \in S_i$ evolves to a path : $x \Leftarrow z \Leftarrow y$.
   (b) *Generalization of multiple classes*
       Edges $x \Leftarrow y_j \in S_i$ evolve to paths: $x \Leftarrow z \Leftarrow y_j$ with $j = 1 \cdots n$.
   (c) *Objectification of attributes/relationships*
       An edge $x{=\!=\!}y_j \in E_i$ evolves to a path: $x{=\!=\!}z{=\!=\!}y$ with $j = 1 \cdots n$.
   (d) *Generalization of relationships*
       An edge $x \overset{r}{\longleftrightarrow} y \in E_i$ evolves to a path:
   (e) *Specialization of relationships*
       An edge $x \overset{r}{\leftrightarrow} y \in E_i$ evolves to a path:
2. Addition of a new vertex or edge
3. Deletion of an existing vertex or edge
4. Modifications that compress a path to an edge
   (a) *Flatting of a specialization hierarchy*
       A path $x \overset{+}{\Leftarrow} z \overset{+}{\Leftarrow} y \in G_i$ evolves to the edge $x \Leftarrow y$.
   (b) *De-Objectification of attributes/relationships*
       A path $x \overset{+}{=\!=} z \overset{+}{=\!=} y \in G_i$ evolves to the edge $x{=\!=\!}y$.

In modifications of type (1) and (4) the crucial point is how to identify path correspondences affected by an edge. Given an edge $x{=\!=\!}y \in G_1$, the path correspondences in the affected subschemas are given by the *proper extension* of the edge, which is calculated as the componentwise concatenation of the paths pairs belonging to the right and left extension of the edge. By *right extension* of an edge $x{=\!=\!}y$, we understand the set of path pairs (p_1, p_2), with $p_1 \in G_1$, $p_2 \in G_2$ and $p_1 = (x{=\!=\!}y) \cdot p_1'$, which are derived by simultaneously traversing the graphs G_1 and G_2 following those paths indicated by the augmentations $\mathcal{A}_1$ and $\mathcal{A}_2$. The *left extension* of $x{=\!=\!}y$ is defined analogously except that, instead of at the beginning, $x{=\!=\!}y$ appears at the end in all paths derived from G_1 in the extension, i.e. for each path pair (p_1, p_2), $p_1 = p_1' \cdot (x{=\!=\!}y)$. The existence of such a proper extension of an edge is ensured by construction of augmentations. In fact, augmentations $\mathcal{A}_1$ and $\mathcal{A}_2$ are built from sets of path correspondences, where each set can be regarded as a pair of corresponding trees with roots in vertex correspondences. When building the extension of an edge $x{=\!=\!}y$, we are essentially walking in parallel on such a pair of trees, determining those path pairs, connecting the root of the corresponding tree with a leaf, such that they contain the edge $x{=\!=\!}y$.

All path correspondences that overlap in some subpath may be regarded as forming a pair of trees, from which the integration process produces an augmentation tree in the

---

[1] The inverse always exists because augmentations are injective functions

integrated schema. By definition of augmentation, an edge may belong to at most one augmentation tree.[2] This means that we can derive those parts of the original local trees formed by the path correspondences that contain the given edge by "ideally" walking through the augmentation tree. However, in some cases the subschemas affected by an edge are formed by more path correspondences than only those in the extension of the given edge. This leads us to consider the whole augmentation tree —or, equivalently, to consider the local trees completely— in order to include also those path correspondences that do not contain the given edge. Let us see this with an example.

Consider the following corresponding schemas:

with these initial path correspondences:

$$A \xleftrightarrow{r} B \xrightarrow{c} C \equiv A \xrightarrow{c} C \qquad A \xleftrightarrow{r} B \xrightarrow{d} D \equiv A \xrightarrow{d} D$$

Vertices with equal name are in vertex correspondence. The integrated schema is then given by G_1. Suppose we perform the following local schema modification: $A \xrightarrow{c} C$ of G_2 evolves to the path $A \xleftrightarrow{m} M \xrightarrow{c'} C$. Let us consider that the subschema affected by $A \xrightarrow{c} C$ is only formed by the extension of the edge, i.e. by the path correspondence: $A \xleftrightarrow{r} B \xrightarrow{c} C \equiv A \xrightarrow{c} C$.

If we now integrate on the updated version of this path correspondence, namely

$$A \xleftrightarrow{r} B \xrightarrow{c} C \equiv A \xleftrightarrow{m} M \xrightarrow{c'} C$$

an ambiguity arises, because all these alternatives are equally valid:

$$\mathcal{A}_1(A) = A \xleftrightarrow{m} M \qquad \mathcal{A}_2(A) = A \xleftrightarrow{r} B \qquad B \equiv M$$

On the contrary, if we consider that the subschemas affected are formed by the complete augmentation tree to which belongs the given edge $A \xrightarrow{c} C$, then no ambiguity arises and it can be automatically deduced that $\mathcal{A}_2(A) = A \xleftrightarrow{r} B$.

To derive the whole local trees, we need to determine which vertex is the root of the calculated extension of the given edge. After having the root, we can calculate the extension of the edge starting at the root, obtaining the whole local trees, since all paths correspondences from the root towards the leaves necessarily traverse this edge. The problem then reduces to finding the root. When the extension of the given edge is formed by several path correspondences, it reduces to finding the overlapping parts of the paths at hand. On the other hand, when the extension is formed by a single path correspondence we need to test all four begin/end edges of the paths in the path correspondence in order to determine the desired root.

The description of the corresponding algorithms can be found in [14].

---

[2] This is not the case with a vertex in vertex correspondence, as it may belong to several trees.

5   Related Work

Our framework for the dynamic maintenance of an integrated schema permits the propagation of local schema changes in tightly coupled federated databases. It manages the impact of structural as well as semantic local changes by means of a semi-automatic mechanism that propagates the changes to the integrated schema without information loss and with a minimal amount of re-integration steps. Our work shares common subgoals with areas like *schema evolution* [5,9], *schema impact analysis* [2,3], and *federated view update mechanisms* [1]. The FEvoS project [15] uses ontologies combined with a fuzzy logic approach to identify the discrepancies produced by structural as well as semantic local schema changes. FEvoS shares with our work the interest in identifying the subschemas affected by a local schema change, but it does not proceed to re-establish the discrepancies as we do.

Schönhoff *et. al* [16] propose to use version management in the integrated schema. For each local schema change, the proposed service makes a new local version "visible" at the global layer of the federation, and vice-versa. It tries to identify automatically properties like a new version's history and predecessor. The service requires user assistance to propagate completely the information to the new version.

Recent works [11,13] follow a schema transformation approach to both schema integration and schema evolution. Source schemas are integrated into a global one by applying a sequence of primitive transformations to them. The same set of primitive transformations are used to specify the evolution of a source schema. In our work we also follow a schema transformation approach in which integration and evolution are treated uniformly. However, while [11] and [13] resolve local schema evolution in a loosely-coupled federation, we resolve the problem in a tightly-coupled federation. Another relevant difference with [11,13] is the fact that our framework is declarative, whereas theirs is operational.

6   Conclusions and Further Work

We presented a methodology for the dynamic maintenance of an integrated schema based on an *incremental schema integration* approach. This means that we avoid as much as possible re-integration steps in the propagation process. An essential aspect of this process is that, from the augmentation mappings for the already integrated schema and the local schema changes, we semi-automatically derive a new state for the augmentations. The user is guided in the process of propagating the schema changes, only requiring his assistance in case of ambiguity or inconsistency in the set of given correspondences.

To propagate a semantic modification, we first transform the respective semantic correspondence into appropriate structural modifications on the local schemas and a set of equivalence correspondences. Then we identify the subschemas affected by the semantic correspondence (deriving the equivalence correspondences that originate the affected subschemas), and finally we re-integrate using the derived equivalence correspondences plus those obtained by the transformation of the semantic correspondences [14].

One issue that still remains open is that of updating. Future work will consider the update problem, with the corresponding definition of a *write semantics*. Another promising direction for further research is to study the application of our techniques to evolutionary environments, such as electronic commerce or data warehouses built from Internet data repositories. In [10] and [4], we report experiences in this direction.

References

1. M. Castellanos. View mechanism for schema evolution in object oriented DBMS. In *14th British National Conference on Databases (BNCOD14)*, July 1996.
2. L. Deruelle, G. Goncalves, and J.C. Nicolas. Local and Federated Database Schemas Evolution. An Impact propagation Model. In *Databases and Expert Systems Applications (DEXA)*, 1999.
3. L. Deruelle, G. Goncalves, and J.C. Nicolas. A change impact analysis approach for corba-based feerated databases. . In *Databases and Expert Systems Applications (DEXA)*, 2000.
4. A. do Carmo and R. Motz. Propuesta para integrar bases de datos que contienen información de la Web. In *Proceedings of the 4to. Workshop Iberoamericano de Ingeniería de Requisitos y Ambientes de Software (IDEAS'2001), Costa Rica*, April 2001.
5. K. Claypool et. al. SERF: A Schema Evolution through an extensible, re-usable and flexible framework. In *CIMK98*, 1998.
6. Peter Fankhauser. *Methodology for Knowledge-Based Schema Integration*. PhD thesis, University of Vienna, Austria, December 1997.
7. Richard Hull. Relative Information Capacity of Simple Relational Database Schemata. *SIAM Journal of Computation*, 15(3), August 1986.
8. Anthony Kosky, Susan Davidson, and Peter Bunemann. Semantics of Database Transformations. Technical report, MS-CIS-95-25, University of Pennsylvania, USA, 1995.
9. X. Li. A survey of schema evolution in object-oriented databases. In *Technology of Object Oriented Languages and Systems, IEEE Comp. Soc., Los Alamitos, CA, USA*, 1999.
10. A. Marotta, R. Motz, and R. Ruggia. Managing Source Schema Evolution in Web Warehouses. *Journal of the Brazilian Computer Society, Special Issue on Information Integration on the Web.*, 8(2), November 2002.
11. P. Mc.Brien and A. Poulovassilis. Schema Evolution in Heterogeneous Database Architectures, A Schema Transformation Approach. In A. Banks Pidduck et. al., editor, *14th International Conference on Advanced Information Systems Engineering (CAiSE 2002), Lectures Notes in Computer Science vol. 2348*, pages 484–499. Springer Verlag, 2002.
12. R. J. Miller, Y. E. Ioannidis, and R. Ramakrishnan. The use of Information Capacity in Schema Integration and Translation. In *Proc. of the 19th. VLDB Conf. Dublin, Ireland.*, 1993.
13. R.J. Miller, M.A. Hernández, L.M. Haas, L. Yan, C.T.H. Ho, R. Fagin, and L. Popa. The Clio Project: Managing Heterogeneity. *SIGMOD Record*, 30(1), March 2001.
14. Regina Motz. *Dynamic Maintenance of an Integrated Schema*. PhD thesis, Darmstadt University of Technology, January 2004.
15. N. Pittas, A. C. Jones, and W. A. Gray. Conceptual Concistency Management in Multi-databases: The FEvoS Framework. In *18th British National Conference on Databases (BNCOD18), Oxfordshire*, July 2001.
16. Martin Schönhoff, Markus Strässler, and Klaus R. Dittrich. Version Propagation in Federated Database Systems. In *Proc. Int. Databases and Applications Symposium (IDEAS'01), Grenoble, France*, July 2001.

Efficient Evaluation of Nearest-Neighbor Queries in Content-Addressable Networks

Erik Buchmann[1] and Klemens Böhm[2]

[1] University of Magdeburg, Germany
buchmann@iti.cs.uni-magdeburg.de
[2] University of Karlsruhe, Germany
klemens.boehm@ipd.uni-karlsruhe.de

Abstract. Content-Addressable Networks (CAN) are able to manage huge sets of (key,value)-pairs and cope with very high workloads. They follow the peer-to-peer (P2P) paradigm in order to build scalable, distributed data structures on top of the Internet. CAN are designed to drive Internet-scale applications like distributed search engines, multimedia retrieval systems and more. In these scenarios, the nearest-neighbor (NN) query model is very natural: the user specifies a query key, and the engine responds with the set of query results closest to the key. Implementing NN queries in CAN is challenging. As with any P2P system, global knowledge about the peers responsible for parts of the query result is not available, and the communication overhead is the most critical factor. In this paper, we present our approach to realize efficient NN queries in CAN. We evaluate our NN query processing scheme by experiments with a CAN implementation in a setting derived from web applications. The results of our experiments with 10.000 peers are positive: even large result sets with a precision of 75% can be obtained by invoking less than 1.6 peers on average. In addition, our NN protocol is suitable for prefetching in settings with sequences of consecutive queries for similar keys.

1 Introduction

A Content-Addressable Network (CAN, [1]) is a distributed hashtable (DHT) that follows the peer-to-peer (P2P) paradigm: on the one hand, it offers features of P2P systems, such as scalability up to Internet-scale, self-organization, the absence of single points of failure and the distribution of infrastructure costs among its users. On the other hand, it provides the abilities of a common hashtable, i.e., it offers simple exact-match queries like $v = get(k)$ API on sets of (key,value)-pairs. In general, CAN are used as dictionaries for object lookup. Other applications like distributed search engines or multimedia retrieval systems usually need some more exhaustive search capabilities like nearest-neighbor (NN) queries. In addition, in scenarios where users issue successive queries with sequences of related query keys, NN query processing may be a helpful prefetching strategy. Here, the peer responds an exact-match query with the query result, and some additional (key,value)-pairs the issuer may request as next.

In this paper we present a protocol for NN query processing in a CAN. While a simple $get(key)$ query returns a single result value or $null$, a NN query returns a number of (key,value)-pairs closest to the query key. Fragmentation scheme and query processing

M. Hemmje et al. (Eds.): E.J. Neuhold Festschrift, LNCS 3379, pp. 31–40, 2005.

in CAN is based on Euclidean distances between keys in the key space. Therefore, the distances between the query key and the (key,value)-pairs used to determine the NN query result have to be Euclidean as well. Thus, NN query processing in CAN has the following aspects:

- A few additional API primitives are used to determine all (key,value)-pairs within a certain radius from a given key.
- An extension to the CAN protocol forwards NN queries to nodes which might be able to add (key,value)-pairs to the result set.
- A certain neighborhood-preserving hash function guarantees that similar keys are mapped on adjacent positions in the key space of the CAN.

It is challenging to realize NN queries in CAN. The query result can be distributed over multiple peers. Without any global knowledge, peers have to estimate the distribution of (key,value)-pairs managed by other peers in order to decide which nodes are queried first. Thus, the communication overhead is the most critical factor. Our protocol exploits the fragmentation scheme of the CAN in order to provide resource-efficient query processing. We evaluate our NN query processing scheme by experiments with a CAN implementation in a setting with real-world (key,value)-pairs and access patterns from web applications. The results of our experiments with 10.000 peers are positive: we show that NN queries could be used in search engines at moderate costs, and could be used for prefetching in locality-aware data sets as well. The remainder of this article has the following structure: After reviewing CAN in Section 2, Section 3 describes our NN query protocol. Section 4 evaluates our protocol by means of extensive experiments. Related work is discussed in Section 5, and Section 6 concludes.

2   Content-Addressable Networks

Content-Addressable Networks (CAN [1]) are a variant of *Distributed Hash Tables (DHT)*. CAN, as well as any other hashtable, manage (key,value)-pairs whereby a certain hash function maps the keys of the application to the key space of the hashtable, and the values are arbitrary items of unstructured data. CAN are primary used as dictionaries. In a distributed search engine scenario, the keys would be keywords or parts of them [2], and the values are URLs. Other applications are annotation services which allow users to rate and comment web pages, push services for event notification or web recommendation systems which would suggest similar web pages.

The CAN uses a d-dimensional Cartesian key space $K \subset \mathbb{N}^d$ on a d-torus. Thus, keys are described by a list of d coordinates: $k = \{c_1, c_2, \cdots c_d\}, c_i \in \mathbb{N}$. Each peer $p \in P$ in the CAN is responsible for a certain part of the key space, its *zone* $(k_{p,min}, k_{p,max})$, forming a d-hypercube. The key space is entirely independent from the underlying physical network topology. In other words, a CAN is a virtual overlay network on top of a large physical network. A peer stores all (key, value)-pairs whose keys fall into its zone. Thus, each peer maintains the data set $D_p = \{(k, v)|v = f(k), k \in (k_{p,min}, k_{p,max})\}$. In addition to its (key, value)-pairs, each peer keeps a list of contact peers which are neighbors of its zone. All distances in CAN are the Euclidean[1] distances

---

[1] Note that we have a torus, so there are two distances in each dimension. Here, we always use the smaller distances.

between coordinates in the key space. The distance between two peers is the smallest distance between the borders of their zones. So the list of the neighbors of node p is $L_p = \{l | dist(p, l) = 0, l \in P\}$.

A query in CAN is simply a key $k \in K$, its result is the corresponding value v. In detail, the CAN implements a query as a message addressed by the query key. A node answers a query if the key fits in its zone: $k_{p,min} \leq k \leq k_{p,max}$ in all dimensions of k. Otherwise, the node forwards the query to another node, the *target peer* p_t. To do so, the peer uses *Greedy Forwarding*: given a query that it cannot answer, the peer chooses p_t from its neighbors so that the Euclidean distance of the key to the peer p_t in question is minimal, $\forall i \in L_p : dist(k, p_t) \leq dist(k, i)$. For a small d and a network of n peers this results in a number of routing hops of $O(dn^{\frac{1}{d}})$.

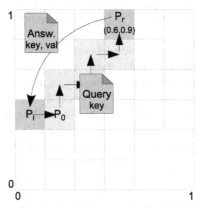

Fig. 1. Greedy Forwarding in CAN

Figure 1 shows a CAN, together with a query. The key space has two dimensions and is the unit space. Peer P_i has issued a query with key $(0.6, 0.9)$, i.e., it wants to retrieve the corresponding value. Since it does not know the peer which is responsible for this key, P_i searches for the peer that is closest to key $(0.6, 0.9)$ in its list of neighbors, and sends it the message. In the example, the query is forwarded to P_o. If that peer is not responsible for the query key either, it forwards the message in the same manner. This goes on until the right peer is reached, P_r in our example. P_r then sends the result of the query to P_i.

3   Evaluation of NN Queries in CAN

This section describes our protocol for realizing NN queries in CAN. We start with an overview of our protocol, followed by an outline of our implementation.

3.1   Overview

A CAN is a variant of a distributed hashtable. In order to be able to process NN queries, the keys of the stored (key, value)-pairs have to be generated with a hash function that preserves the relationships between the keys. I.e., neighboring application keys are mapped to adjacent keys in the key space of the CAN. The type of relationship which have to be supported by the hash function depends on the application. For example, in a setting based on URLs, all URLs addressing the same server would have adjacent keys in the key space of the CAN. Thus, the NN query processing is specialized to the relationships between the keys. In CAN, the data structures managed by each node are comparatively small, but distributed over a large number of nodes. Here, the most expensive part of the protocol is to ask other nodes. Because of the P2P nature of the CAN, query processing should be an successive process which displays the results from the most suitable peers first, and refines the result set with fragments from other nodes if needed. Thus, our protocol works as follows:

1. Route the query to the node responsible for the query key.
2. Determine the s (key,value)-pairs closest to the query key from the local data set, and return it to the issuer of the query. In addition, return a set of relevant neighbors as well.
3. Estimate the precision of the returned data set. If the precision satisfies the demand, return the result set to the user and stop.
4. Order the result set by the distances of its (key,value)-pairs to the query key. Send the query key and the distance between the key and the s-th element in the result set to a node obtained in Step 2 whose zone is close to the query key.
5. Return the set of at most s (key,value)-pairs whose keys are in the given distance to the query key, and a set of relevant neighbors. Continue with Step 3.

3.2 Protocol Description

Our protocol comes with a few new data structures and methods. The node which issues the query keeps the intermediate result in a list R. Its entries are sorted by the distance of their (key, value)-pairs to the query key k. Then the peer needs two sets S_p, S_q in order to distinguish between the peers it knows beyond its neighbors, and the ones it has already queried. In conjunction with the methods coming with the original CAN protocol, we require the methods dist(key, key) and dist(key, peer) which return the Euclidean distance between two keys or a key and the zone of a certain peer in units of the key space. At last, we introduce the method vol(peer, key, radius) to estimate the intersected volume of a zone and a hypersphere defined by center and radius.

Assume that a peer – the *issuer* – wants to release a NN query relating to a given query key k, asking for a result set R of the size s. I.e., it asks for a set containing the s (key, value)-pairs closest to k, ordered by the distance of its entries to k. Then it initiates the protocol by sending[2] a message containing k and s to the peer responsible for k. In the following, we name that peer the *responder r*.

The responder now generates a set S_t of s (key,value)-pairs closest to k from its own zone. I.e., it answers the query from its own scope, without taking into account the zones of its neighbors. More formally, $S_t = \{(k_0, v_0), (k_1, v_1), \cdots, (k_{s-1}, v_{s-1})\}$ with

---

[2] Routing a message to a peer that manages a certain zone of the key space is a basic functionality of the underlying CAN protocol (cf. Section 2).

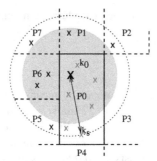

Fig. 2. Fragmented NN result set

$|S_t| = s$, $(k_i, v_i) \in D_r$ and $\forall (k_i, v_i) \in (D_r - S_t) : dist(k, k_i) \geq dist(k, k_s)$. Having obtained the answer, the issuer adds the new data to the result set, $R' = R \cup S_t$.

Of course, the correct result set may come from the zones of adjacent peers as well. Consider the example in Figure 2. Here, the query key k is depicted as a cross, and $P0$ is responsible for its zone. Given $s = 6$, all points in the scope of $P0$ are returned, but the points on the gray circle are the result set which was requested by the issuer of the query. In order to allow to refine the query result, the responder determines a set S_p of possibly helpful other peers. The original CAN protocol demands that each peer maintains meta-data about the nodes with adjacent zones. Here we exploit these information: the responder adds all neighbors whose zones are closer to k than the distance between k_s and k. Thus, $S_p = \{p | dist(k, p) \leq dist(k, k_s), p \in L_r\}$. Both the collected (key,value)-pairs of the intermediate result set S_t and the set of other peers S_p are returned to the issuer.

Now the issuer has two options: it may decide that the result is 'good enough' and stop processing the NN query. On the other hand, it may refine the result set by asking the returned other peers. Tangible strategies depend on the applications which make use of the CAN. However, a general approach is to estimate the precision of the returned set of (key,value)-pairs. Because there is no global knowledge that tells us the distribution of keys, the peer has to assume uniformly distributed keys. In our settings, the estimated precision is the volume of the part of the data space that is already queried, divided by the volume of a field with center k and radius $dist(k, k_s)$. In Figure 2, this is the surface area of $P0$ which is surrounded by the dotted circle, divided by the whole surface area of the dotted circle. If the responder returned less than s keys, the precision is set to 0.

In the case the issuer wants to refine the result set, it has to choose the next peer to send the query to. In our protocol, the issuer selects a peer which was not queried before, and whose zone has the largest overlapping with the relevant field (the dotted circle in Figure 2). Thus $p' \in S_p$, $p' \notin S_q$ and $\forall p_i \in S_p : vol(p', k, dist(k, k_s)) \geq vol(p_i, k, dist(k, k_s))$ The issuer now sends k, s and $dist(k, k_s)$ directly to p' and adds p' to S_q. Peer p' in turn answers with (key,value)-pairs and promising other peers as described above, except that it returns a number of s (key,value)-pairs only if their keys fit into the bounding field described by k and $dist(k, k_s)$. Because the issuer got the meta data of p' from the last responder, the query can be sent to p' immediately without any further lookup operations. Now the procedure recurs until the result set satisfies the needs of the query issuer.

4 Experimental Evaluation

We have evaluated our NN query protocol by means of extensive experiments. The experiments are performed on a cluster of 32 Linux workstations, with a CAN prototype that was stripped from all unessential methods like joining the CAN, repair methods etc. (see [3] for an exhaustive description of our experimental setup.) The CAN manages a key space of 4 dimensions. It consists of 10.000 peers that issue a number of 2.000.000 queries.

We use two different data sets. The first set consists of 10.000.000 uniformly distributed random (key,value)-pairs and reproduces a general worst-case scenario. Two dimensions of the keys are shown in the upper right part of Figure 3. The second set (the lower left part in Figure 3) is a substitute for a web-based application. The URLs are obtained from a Web-crawler, and are mapped to the key space of the CAN by a locality-aware hash function. The hash function splits the URL into d pieces and preserves the locality of adjacent web pages by weighting the first characters (the server part of the URL) higher than the latter ones (the path and filename part): Let u be the list of characters of an URL $u = \{u_0, u_1, \cdots, u_{length-1}\}$ and d the dimensionality of the key space. Then the key is $k = \{f_u(0), f_u(1), \cdots, f_u(d-1)\}$ with $f_u(n) = \sum_{i=0}^{length/d} u_{(i \cdot d + n)} \cdot 1/v^i$. The extent of v is a tuning parameter that adjusts the distance of adjacent URLs.

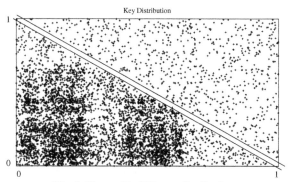

Fig. 3. Keys with different distributions

Now we simulate two different applications on the data sets. The first application processes NN queries with different sizes of the result sets and different precisions desired. The second one tries to employ the NN queries as a prefetching strategy for data sets addressed by URLs.

4.1 Issuing NN Queries

The most important question arising from our protocol regards to the cost of processing NN queries. Because the costs of processing fragments of the whole data set are comparably small, e.g. by using a grid-file to store the data tuples, we use the number of nodes (hops) involved in the processing of a query. Now we wonder: How many peers have to be queried in order to satisfy a given precision of the NN result set, by different data distributions and different extents of the result set? What is the relation between the precision and the number of peers queried?

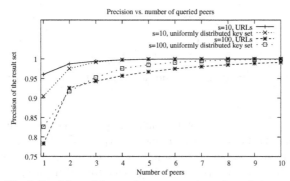

Fig. 4. Precision of the result set vs. number of queried peers

To evaluate this, we ran queries for 10 and 100 NN results on the randomly distributed key set, and the key set consisting of URLs as well. Figure 4 faces the average precision of the resulting NN set to the number of peers queried. It shows that – even for large result sets – more than 90% of all (key,value)-pairs in the exact result set come from two peers on average. But to be eager for a correct result set, i.e., demanding a precision of 100%, involves a rapidly increasing number of peers. Especially for large result sets on data sets containing fields with sparse keys as well as "hot spots", such as URLs, a large number of peers have to participate in the processing of a single query.

But what is the trade-off between the precision on the one hand and the effort to ask many peers on the other hand? To answer this query, we varied the size of the requested NN set, and monitored the number of peers which are invoked to satisfy precisions of 75% and 100% respectively. Figure 5 shows that even for large results sets a precision of 75% can be met by asking less than 1.6 peers on average. In contrast, requiring a precision of 100% leads to a number of invoked peers that is doubled in comparison to the 75% case.

4.2   Prefetching by NN Queries

In application scenarios where the query result is small and consecutive queries on adjacent keys may occur, it can be useful to employ our NN protocol as a kind of prefetching. The idea is that the query returns not only the requested result, but also a few additional (key,value)-pairs which may be requested in the following. The issuer then caches the additional tuples and uses this information in order to speed up the next queries.

Here we use a model for web applications in order to evaluate NN based prefetching. URLs are used as keys and queries as well. Related applications are backlink-services,

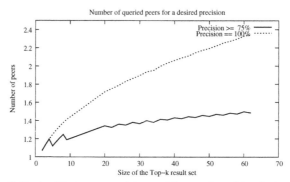

Fig. 5. Tradeoff between precision and the number of invoked peers

web annotation systems or web recommendation systems. The rationale behind locality in web-based requests is that web surfer request web pages (URLs) in certain sequences. In order to experiment with our protocol in that setting, we generated an artifical web surfer that issues successive queries according to the following probabilities:

34%	Repeat the last query (back-button).
23%	Start new sequence (external link / keyboard input).
16%	Query a URL with a different directory on the same server.
14%	Query a URL with the same directory on the same server.
6%	Query the first key (home-button).
4%	Query a URL that was already visited (history/bookmarks).
3%	Repeat the current query (reload-button).

The probabilities for the different actions released by the surfer are taken from [4]; the URLs come from our web crawler. The questions that arise now are: How useful is the prefetching strategy? What is the relation between the number of cache hits and size of the returned data set? We anticipate that the relation between the size of the NN result set and the probability to answer a query from the cache follows a logarithmic curve. This holds because the volume of a hypersphere – the part of the key space containing relevant (key,value)-pairs – grows exponential by increasing the radius $(dist(k, k_s))$, but it is not feasible increase the size of the returned query result by the same rate.

Figure 6 graphs the size of the returned result set on the x-axis and the probability to answer the query from the preceding result set on the y-axis. One may wonder why the graph begins by 4.5% in a setting with result set size = 0: this is the accumulated probability for pressing the reload-button or re-querying the current key from bookmarks, history etc. The figure tells us that in our virtual application 11% of all queries could be answered from cache, if the responder returns not only the query result, but also at least 20 additional (key,value)-pairs. In other words, if it is cheaper to transmit 181 (key,value)-pairs than routing a query to the proper peer which answers it then, our NN caching strategy would be able to save infrastructure costs. Clearly, the measures presented are hardly comparable to any web application. But we could show that the NN protocol is working, and is useful in many situations.

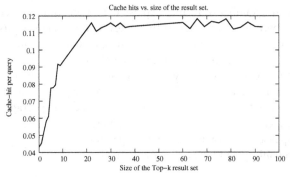

Fig. 6. Cache hits vs. size of the returned result set

5   Related Work

The variants of Distributed Hash Tables next to CAN differ primarily in the topology of the key space. *LH** [5] determines nodes responsible for a certain key statically by its hash function. *Chord* [6] organizes the data in a circular one-dimensional data space. Messages travel from peer to peer in one direction through the cycle, until the peer whose ID is closest to the key of the query has been found. *Pastry* [7] uses a Plaxton Mesh to store and locate its data. The forwarding algorithm is similar to the one of Chord. Pastry forwards to peers such that the common prefix of the ID and the query key becomes longer with each hop. Our NN query protocol could be easily adapted to variants of DHT, if each peer maintains a list of nodes with adjacent zones, and if there a locality-aware fragmentation scheme can be used. From the DHT outlined here, this is true for LH* and Chord.

Locality-preserving hashing in multiple dimensions is a common problem. [8] investigates in proofs for collision probabilities and time complexity for a family of hash functions based on d-dimensional cubes, and [9] shows that this kind of hash functions can be used to perform similarity queries on multimedia documents.

One of the biggest obstacles of all kinds of DHT is the limited query capability. However, there are some approaches to exploit the hash-based nature of the CAN in order to perform extended queries. One idea is to decompose keywords into trigrams ("hello" → "hel", "ell", "llo"), which allows for substring searches [2]. Another idea is to introduce a relational schema whose tuples are stored in the CAN [10]. Complex hash-based query plan operators are a preliminary stage to a SQL-like query processing in CANs. Our NN query protocol is orthogonal to both of the approaches. For example, it could be used to search for phonetic similarity in triplets by using a soundex-based hash. In the other scenario, our protocol could be exploited for extended range operations on tuples stored in the CAN.

6   Conclusions

This article has presented a protocol that enables Content-Addressable Networks to perform Nearest-Neighbor queries. Processing NN queries means that the user specifies the query key and the number of results requested, and one or more peers in the CAN answer with the (key,value)-pairs closest to the key. Our protocol consists of measures to estimate the precision of intermediate result sets, and contains methods to forward queries to all peers which are likely to have parts of the query result. We have evaluated the protocol by the means of extensive experiments. The experiments show that NN queries can be performed at moderate costs: in settings such as ours, a result set with a precision of 75% can be obtained from less than 1.6 peers on average. In addition, in scenarios with sequences of consecutive queries, NN-based prefetching is suitable for saving routing expenses. Several topics remain open for future research. We for our part want to address reliability and load balancing issues.

References

1. Ratnasamy, S., Francis, P., Handley, M., Karp, R., Shenker, S.: A Scalable Content-Addressable Network. In: Proceedings of the ACM SIGCOMM 2001 Conference, New York, ACM Press (2001)
2. Harren, M., Hellerstein, J., Huebsch, R., Loo, B., Shenker, S., Stoica, I.: Complex Queries in DHT-based Peer-to-Peer Networks, in: Proceedings of IPTPS02 (2002)
3. Buchmann, E., Böhm, K.: How to Run Experiments with Large Peer-to-Peer Data Structures. In: Proceedings of the 18th International Parallel and Distributed Processing Symposium, Santa Fe, USA. (2004)
4. Tauscher, L., Greenberg, S.: How people revisit web pages: empirical findings and implications for the design of history systems. International Journal of Human-Computer Studies (1997)
5. Litwin, W., Neimat, M.A., Schneider, D.A.: LH* - Linear Hashing for Distributed Files. In Buneman, P., Jajodia, S., eds.: Proceedings of the 1993 ACM SIGMOD International Conference on Management of Data, Washington, D.C., May 26-28, 1993, ACM Press (1993)
6. Stoica, I., Morris, R., Karger, D., Kaashoek, M.F., Balakrishnan, H.: Chord: A Scalable Peer-To-Peer Lookup Service for Internet Applications. In: Proceedings of the ACM SIGCOMM 2001 Conference. (2001)
7. Rowstron, A., Druschel, P.: Pastry: Scalable, Decentralized Object Location, and Routing for Large-Scale Peer-to-Peer Systems. In: IFIP/ACM International Conference on Distributed Systems Platforms. (2001)
8. Indyk, P., Motwani, R., Raghavan, P., Vempala, S.: Locality-Preserving Hashing in Multidimensional Spaces. In: Proceedings of the Twenty-Ninth Annual ACM Symposium on Theory of Computing, El Paso, Texas (1997)
9. Gionis, A., Indyk, P., Motwani, R.: Similarity search in high dimensions via hashing. In: Proceedings of the VLDB'99, San Francisco, Morgan Kaufmann (1999)
10. Sattler, K.U., Rösch, P., Buchmann, E., Böhm, K.: A Physical Query Algebra for DHT-based P2P Systems. In: Proceedings of the 6th Workshop on Distributed Data and Structures, Lausanne, Switzerland. (2004)

Ontology-Based Query Refinement
for Semantic Portals

Jens Hartmann[1], Nenad Stojanovic[1], Rudi Studer[1], and Lars Schmidt-Thieme[1,2]

[1] Institute AIFB
University of Karlsruhe
{hartmann, stojanovic, studer}@aifb.uni-karlsruhe.de

[2] Computer Based New Media Group
Institute for Computer Science, University of Freiburg
lst@informatik.uni-freiburg.de

Abstract. The Semantic Web aims to provide access to information for humansand machines. Practical implementations of Semantic Web technologies need to consider aspects such as scalability and reliability to be attractive for industrial practitioners. Our approach shows a portal infrastructure which benefits on the one hand from the access facilities provided by Semantic Web technologies and on the other hand from the applicability of current Web technologies for industrial strength applications. The main achievement of the approach is an up-and-running network of content-interchanging portals. Accompanying tools and methods are provided for setting up such networks from scratch or to put them on top of existing information sources. In the paper, special attention is given to the ontology-supported query refinement service that enables a user to find the relevant results even if his query does not match his information need ideally.

1 Introduction

Identifying and presenting useful information for a given context is an interesting area for current research activities and developments of web technologies (cf., e.g., [2]). We present an architecture which realizes semantic-based search and access facilities to information represented by **SEmantic portALs (SEALs)**. Such portals typically provide knowledge about a specific domain relying on ontologies to structure and exchange this knowledge. Ontologies are being exploited in Computer Science to enhance knowledge sharing and re-use (cf., e.g., [8]). Firstly, they provide a shared and common understanding of knowledge in a domain of interest. Secondly, they capture and formalize knowledge by connecting human understanding of symbols with their semantic interpretability for machines.

The basic conceptual architecture on which our approach relies is presented in [9]. Here, we provide an extension of the SEAL architecture which is aiming towards the usage of semantic technologies in real world scenarios, viz. a semantic *query refinement approach*. This approach is based on the Librarian Agent Refinement Process, which

M. Hemmje et al. (Eds.): E.J. Neuhold Festschrift, LNCS 3379, pp. 41–50, 2005.
© Springer-Verlag Berlin Heidelberg 2005

enables a user to navigate through the information content incrementally and interactively. In each refinement step a user is provided with a complete but minimal set of refinements, which enables him to develop/express his information need in a step-by-step fashion.

2   Related Work

Several approaches previously being developed are using ontologies to support the access of content via web technologies. Within Ontobroker-based web portals [5], a Hyperbolic View Applet allows for graphical access to an ontology and its knowledge base. Another related work is KAON Portal[1] which provides access to an ontology via a standard Web interface e.g. the KM-Vision.org[2] portal.

OntoWebber [10] is another tool which generates web interfaces based on ontologies. It actually is a Web site management system, which facilitates the creation, generation and maintenance of Web sites. Using OntoWebber, site engineers can build site models for domain-specific Web sites. The site models are based on explicit ontologies including the domain ontology and four distinct site modeling ontologies. In contrast to our approach OntoWebber mainly aims to support the creation of a single web portal, but does not so much focus on the creation of an interconnected infrastructure of portals.

Given the difficulties with managing complex Web content, several papers tackled the problem of facilitating database technology to simplify the creation and maintenance of data-intensive web-sites. OntoWeb[3] implements our framework for a SEmantic portAL, viz. SEAL, that relies on standard Semantic Web technologies. Other systems, such as Araneus [11] and AutoWeb [3], take a declarative approach, i.e. they introduce their own data models and query languages, although all approaches share the idea to provide high-level descriptions of web-sites by distinct orthogonal dimensions. The idea of leveraging mediation technologies for the acquisition of data is also found in approaches like Strudel [7] and Tiramisu [1], they propose a separation according to the aforementioned task profiles as well. Strudel does not concern the aspects of site maintenance and personalization. It is actually only an implementation tool, not a management system.

Similar to SEAL, the ODESeW approach [4] uses ontologies for creating and managing knowledge portals whereby the surrounding technology does not allow interconnecting and integrating exiting knowledge sources as in SEAL.

3   The SEAL Approach

SEAL (cf. [9]) has been developed to use ontologies as key elements for managing community web sites and web portals. The ontology supports queries to multiple sources, but beyond that it also includes the intensive use of the schema information

---

[1]   cf. http://kaon.semanticweb.org/Portal
[2]   http://km-vision.org
[3]   http://www.OntoWeb.org

itself allowing for automatic generation of navigational views[4] and mixed ontology and content-based presentation. In order to reduce engineering and maintenance efforts SEAL uses an ontology for semantic integration of existing data sources as well as for web site management and presentation to the outside world. SEAL exploits the ontology to offer mechanisms for acquiring, structuring and sharing information by means of semantic annotations between human and/or machine agents. The SEAL architecture consists of several conceptual layers: Knowledge Integration, Processing, Representation, Organisation and Access of Knowledge, as shown in figure 1. The depicted layers can be seen as knowledge workflows from the bottom, viz. integration, towards the top, viz. the final visualization of knowledge e.g. in a web browser.

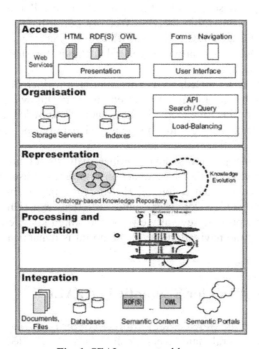

Fig. 1. SEAL conceptual layers

The **Knowledge Integration** layer holds a set of modules, each module being able to handle a specific information source. The knowledge integration is divided into three main parts. We speak of (i) *Interconnected Integration* of knowledge when the data sources are closely technically and semantically interconnected. On the other hand, we use the term of (ii) *Bounded Integration* when the information sources (as the case may be: other portals) are *semantically bounded* and may technically diverge. Nevertheless, to share and integrate knowledge from previously unknown information sources or single (small) sources, we use the generic (iii) *Knowledge Integration* module providing integration facilities for several formats like the widely accepted

---

[4] Examples are navigation hierarchies that appear as has-part-trees or has-subtopic trees in the ontology.

RDF(S) and the Semantic Web language OWL. On one hand, one can keep using existing information sources and its infrastructure and, on the other hand, easily setting up a Semantic Portal without a time and cost consuming transformation process.

The **Knowledge Processing** layer creates content instances and provides a set of knowledge processing methods, e.g. publishing workflows.

The representation of knowledge is handled in the **Knowledge Representation** layer by using ontologies and associated knowledge representation languages such as RDF(S) or OWL. Ontologies are shared conceptualizations of a domain, which can be seen as an agreed view of a domain for affiliated persons. We use an Ontology describing technically objects in the portal as also the knowledge of a portal. Further, we support the usage of several Ontologies in a Semantic Portal. Exemplary, such domain ontology[5] is used within the OntoWeb.org portal modelling the knowledge stored in the knowledge base. The knowledge is kept in an *Ontology-based Knowledge Repository* which provides general methods for storing the knowledge through a generic interface.

The next layer is the **Knowledge Organisation** layer, which provides methods for indexing and search functionalities. Based on the knowledge representation mechanism several continuative methods for organizing knowledge are developed to provide fast and effective access to knowledge. Generally, indexes are created for concepts, relations and full-text search ability.

Finally, the **Knowledge Access** layer defines methods for presenting content in different output formats and defines interaction interfaces. Presenting knowledge to users is not one generic generation of HTML files rather than a sophisticated visualization of knowledge for users with different experiences. Therefore, a Semantic Portal must provide several views on the stored knowledge. The browsing interface respectively the navigation bar of the portal is dynamically generated from the Ontology.

4   Semantic Services for SEmantic PortaALs

The presented architecture provides an infrastructure for managing knowledge within a portal separated in several main layers. Each layer uses so-called SEmantic PortAL Services. Exemplary, to capture and integrate knowledge the developed Web Crawler METIS[6] can be used to identify and extract knowledge from the Web. Therefore, METIS uses a domain ontology to identify related content found in the Web. Having already a running SEAL portal usage mining methods might be applied on the usage log files to improve the amount and structure of particular knowledge items. Therefore, we developed the tool ONTOMANAGER[7] to support the organisation of knowledge. Providing semantic driven access to knowledge used within the Knowledge Access layer of a SEAL we developed a query-refinement mechanism which we will present in more detail. The access layer of the portal architecture offers several search and query functionalities to the user like standard full-text search forms

---

[5]   http://ontoweb.aifb.uni-karlsruhe.de/Ontology/ and http://ontoweb.aifb.uni-karlsruhe.de/CMI/
[6]   http://ontoware.org/projects/metis
[7]   http://ontoware.org/projects/ontomanager

as well as complex query forms, e.g. allowing to query for specific concepts or a set of them by using a simple query logic. We focus on a novel feature that enables a user to satisfy his information need in a more efficient way – semantic-enabled query refinement. Existing methods for query refinement seem to be quite unsuccessfully for real-world usage since they try to refine a query primarily on a syntactic basis, i.e. not considering the meaning of query terms, and in a non-personalized way, i.e. not taking into account the current information need of a user[14]. We present here a comprehensive approach for the refinement of ontology-based queries, the so-called Librarian Agent Refinement Process that takes into account these problems. In the following, we give the basic terminology used in this paper. More details can be found in [13].

Definition 1: An ontology is a structure $O := (C, \leq_c, R, \sigma)$ consisting of:

- two disjoint sets C and R whose elements are called concept identifiers and relation identifiers, resp.,
- a partial order $\leq_c$ on C, called concept hierarchy or taxonomy (without cycles)
- a function $\sigma : R \to C^+$, called signature

Definition 2: A Knowledge Base is a structure $KB := (C_{KB}, R_{KB}, I, l_c, l_r)$ consisting of:

- two disjoint sets C_{KB} and R_{KB}
- a set I whose elements are called instance identifiers (or instances shortly)
- a function $l_C : C_{KB} \to I$ called concept instantiation
- a function $l_r : R_{KB} \to I^+$ called relation instantiation

A relation instance can be depicted as $r(I_1, I_2, ..., I_n)$, where $r \in R_{KB}, I_i \in I$.

Definition 3: A conjunctive query is of the form or can be rewritten into the form: $Q(\overline{X}) \equiv forall \ \overline{X} \ \overline{P}(\overline{X}, \overline{k})$, with $\overline{X}$ being a vector of variables $(X_1, ..., X_n)$, $\overline{k}$ being a vector of constants (concept instances), $\overline{P}$ being a vector of conjoined predicates.

Query Refinement Process

The goal of the Librarian Agent Query Refinement process is to enable a user to efficiently find results relevant for his information need in an ontology-based information repository, even if his query does not match ideally his information need, so that either a lot of irrelevant results and/or only a few relevant results are retrieved. The process consists of three phases, described in the following three subsections.

Phase 1: Ambiguity Discovery

We define query ambiguity as an indicator of the gap between the user's information need and the query that results from that need. If a query is more ambiguous, then it follows that there are more (mis)interpretations of that query. We define two types of the ambiguity that can arise in interpreting a query: (i) the *semantic ambiguity*, as the characteristic of the used ontology and (ii) the *content-related ambiguity*, as the characteristic of the repository. The second type of the ambiguity is related to the comparison of results of the given query with the results of other queries and it is out of the scope of this paper.

Semantic Ambiguity: In an ontology-based query the constraints are applied on the *query variables*. For example in the query: $\forall$ x $\leftarrow$ Book(x) and hasKeyword(x, "Optimization")

x is a *query variable* and hasKeyword(x,"Optimization") is a *query constraint*. The stronger these constraints are, the more relevant the retrieved instances are for the user's information need. Since an instance in an ontology is described through (i) the concept it belongs to and (ii) the relations to other instances, we see two factors which determine thesemantic ambiguity of a query variable:

- the concept hierarchy: How general is the concept the variable belongs to.

- the relation-instantiation: How strong are constraints applied to that variable.

Definition 4: *VariableGenerality*

$$VariableGenerality(X) = Subconcepts(Type(X)) + 1,$$

where *Type(X)* is the concept the variable *X* belongs to, *Subconcepts(C)* is the number of direct subconcepts of the concept *C*. Note that our query model does not allow multiple inheritance.

Definition 5: *VariableAmbiguity*

$$VariableAmbiguity(X,Q) = \frac{\dfrac{|Relation(Type(X))| + 1}{|Assigned Relations(Type(X),Q)| + 1}}{\dfrac{1}{|AssignedConstraints(X,Q)| - |Assigned Relations(Type(X),Q)| + 1}},$$

where *Relation(C)* is the set of all relations defined for the concept *C* in the ontology, *AssignedRelations(C,Q)* is the set of all relations defined in the set *Relation(C)* and which also appear in the query *Q*. *AssignedConstraints(X,Q)* is the set of all constraints related to the variable *X* that appear in the query *Q*.

We now define the ambiguity as follows:

$$Ambiguity(X,Q) = VariableGenerality(X) \cdot VariableAmbiguity(X,Q)$$

Finally, the *Semantic Ambiguity* for the query Q is calculated as follows:

$$SemanticAmbiguity(Q) = \sum_{X \in Var(Q)} Ambiguity(x,Q)$$

where *Var(Q)* represents the set of variables that appear in the query *Q*. By analysing these ambiguity parameters it is possible to discover which of the query variables introduces the highest ambiguity in a query.

Phase 2: Refinement Generation

The goal of a *query refinement operator* is to transform a query Q to a query Q' so that the latter is acceptable according to an acceptance test. For our purpose the acceptance test is related to the number of results: $Q \rightarrow_{ref} Q'$, if in the context of the given knowledge base *KB* and the ontology *O* holds $R(Q') \subseteq R(Q)$. It is clear that a refinement operator ($\rightarrow_{ref}$) derives a set of refinements for a query Q, or more formally: $Q \rightarrow_{ref} \{Q' | R(Q') \subseteq R(Q)\}$. (1)

If we consider a query Q as a logical formula, then the results of the query, $R(Q)$, can be treated as a Herbrand interpretation I which is a model for the formula Q. Further, the condition $R(Q') \subseteq R(Q)$ from (1) can be treated as a definition of the logic implication, i.e. a query Q' implies another query Q (Q logically entails Q'). Since the ontology and the schema are the only constraints used for driving the refinement process, then $(Q \rightarrow_{ref} Q') \equiv (KB,O \vdash Q' \rightarrow Q)$, (2)

where $\vdash$ depicts the derivation (inference) process.

Therefore, the process of query refinement can be mapped onto subsumption reasoning, i.e. for a query Q we can find/calculate all queries which logically implies it – this set is the set of valid query refinements. However, due to undecidability of the subsumption reasoning in the general case, we need an alternative subsumption order, which introduces more tractability by the minimal lost in the quality of the subsumption. We choose the θ-subsumption, a frequently used subsumption order in inductive logic programming tasks [6].

Moreover, if a model M is not a model for query Q then M will not be a model for any logical refinement Q' of Q. Therefore, it is sufficient to analyse the answers of a query Q in order to find all constraints that are relevant for the refinement. Let us assume that $X = R(Q)$. For each variable from Q, we get a set of instances related to the variable x and retrieved for the query Q as:

$$OccuringInstances(x,Q) = \bigcup_{a \in R(Q)} Projection(x,a) ,$$

where *Projection* retrieves, from an answer tuple a, the instance that corresponds to the variable x. From each of these relevant sets a new pattern set is generated by replacing each element with all its relation instances (facts) from the knowledge base:

$$RelevantInstances(x,Q) = \{r(a,b) \mid a \in OccuringInstances(x,Q), r(a,b) = true\} ,$$

where $r(x, y)$ is a relation instance from the given ontology.

Finally, this set is analysed in order to find pattern that can be used for the refinement. We find two types of patterns:
- *Substitutions*(y, Q) by counting only those relation instances from *RelevantInstances* whose predicate matches with a constraint from query.
- *Literals*(y, Q) by treating the rest of the *RelevantInstances*.

For each pattern *pat* we define its confidence and specificity as follows:

$$Confidence(pat,x,Q) = \frac{\left|\{l \mid l \in RelaventInstances(x,Q) \wedge Predicate(l) = pat\}\right|}{\left|OccuringInstances(x,Q)\right|}$$

where *Predicate* returns the predicate of a relation instance.

$$Specificity(pat,x,Q) = \frac{\left|R(Query(pat))\right|}{\{l \mid l \in RelevantInstances(x,Q) \wedge Predicate(l) = pat\}} ,$$

where *Query*(pat) returns an elementary query that contains *pat* as the single constraint and *Predicate*(l) returns the relation contained in the relation instance *l*.

Now, we can define a refinement operator in the following manner.

Definition 6: Refinement from closed observations under θ-subsumption
The closed-refinement of a query Q, denoted $\rho_{closed}(Q)$ is a query obtained as:

a) $\rho_{closed}(Q) = Q\theta$, where θ is a substitution from the set *Substitutions*(x, Q) in the case that θ correspond to the variable x from Q;

b) $\rho_{closed}(Q) = (Q \wedge L)$, where L is a ground literal contained in the set *Literals*(x, Q) for any variable x from the query Q;

In both cases, a) and b):

1.- equ refinements, $R(\rho_{closed}(Q)) = R(Q)$, are aggregated to the initial query (i.e. they are treated as equivalent queries to the initial query) and

2.- non-minimal refinements, refinements which are subsumed by another (but not equ-) refinement A, $R(\rho_{closed}(Q)) \subset R(A)$, are filtered.

Phase 3: Ranking

In order to determine the relevance of a refinement for a user's need, we use two sources of information: (a) user's preferences for such a refinement and (b) informativeness of a refinement. We sketch these approaches here:

a) Since the users are reluctant to provide an explicit information about the relevance of a result, the ranking has to be based on the implicit information that are captured by observing user's behaviour. We define three types of implicit relevance feedback:

Actuality, which reflects the phenomena that a user may change the criteria about the relevance of a query term, when encountering newly retrieved results,

ImplicitRelevance, which postulates that if a user selects a resource from the list of retrieved results, then this resource corresponds, to some extent, to the user's information need and

ImplicitIrrelevance, that is opposite to the previous type of relevance

b) *Informativeness* defines the capability of a refinement regarding the underyling information repository. The parameters *Confidence* and *Specificity* are used for these ranking: higher value for *Confidence*(*Specificity*) means higher rank of a refinement.

Finally, the total relevance of the constraint c for the refinement of the query Q_i is a function of all these four parameters. Moreover, this relevance includes the impact of the refinement process on the ambiguity of query variables (*Variable Ambiguity*).

5   Applications

In this section we present very briefly the application of the previously described approach for refining queries against a traditional bibliographic database, we have done in the scope of the project SemIPort (http://km.aifb.uni-karlsruhe.de/semiport/). The goal was to enhance the standard searching process in a bibliographic database, by using ontologies. Since the bibliographic data is structured according to a schema defined by a database provider, we migrated this schema into an ontology. By using this ontology the content of the database is translated into a knowledge base. Figure 2 presents the simplified integration architecture. A user's query is executed against a full-text search engine. In the case that a user requires refinement of his query, the query string is transformed into an ontology based query (the task of the "conceptualisation" module in Figure 1) and processed using the approach presented in this paper (the task of the "query refinement" module in Figure 2). The generated refinements are translated into a set of query strings, ranked according to their informativeness and retrieved to the user. For testing purposes, the developed approaches will be evaluated on data from the online bibliography DBLP, and the tools are planned to be integrated into the competency and service network portal of the German Informatics Society (GI), which is currently under construction (www.io-port.net). SEAL has been also successfully applied within the EU project OntoWeb (www.OntoWeb.org) and the portal of the EU project SEKT – Semantically Enabled Knowledge Technologies (www.Sekt-Project.org).

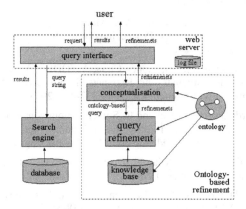

Fig. 2. The integration of the logic-based refinement in a traditional information portal

6   Conclusion and Outlook

We presented a scalable and reliable portal infrastructure for creating and maintaining portals based on our SEAL approach. We demonstrated a real-world infrastructure having a large number of users and a large volume of content. The framework can either be applied on existing information sources while the sources are kept in their original state or be used to set up new portals from scratch. In order to support searching facilities in the portal, we have developed a method for query refinement that enables a user to develop/express his information need interactively, in a step-by-step fashion. Consequently, a user to find the relevant results even if his query does not match his information need ideally. In the future, we plan to improve the surrounding SEAL infrastructure by interconnecting client applications e.g. an ontology editor to a SEAL portal (server). Further, to improve the content quality within a SEAL we are currently working on machine learning techniques[8] to learn resp. build up an ontology.

Regarding the query refinement service, we will investigate in the future the methods for dealing with light-weight ontologies, that can emerge, using ontology learning techniques, from a text corpus automatically.

Acknowledgements: Research reported in this paper has been partially funded by EU in the IST project SEKT (IST-2003-506826), the network of excellence Knowledge Web (IST-2004-507482) and by the german BMBF (federal ministry of education and research) project SemIPort.

---

[8]   See the ARTEMIS project for details: ontoware.org/projects/artemis

References

[1] C. R. Anderson , A. Y. Levy and D. S. Weld, Declarative Web Site Management with Tiramisu, ACM SIGMOD Workshop on the Web and Databases - WebDB99, pages 19-24, 1999

[2] S. Chakrabarti, Mining the Web: Discovering knowledge from hypertext data, Morgan Kaufmann, San Francisco, 2003

[3] S. Ceri, P. Fraternali and A. Bongio, Web Modeling Language (WebML): a modeling language for designing Web sites, Proceedings of the 9th World Wide Web Conference (WWW9), pages 137-157, 2000

[4] O. Corcho, A. Gómez-Pérez, A. López-Cima, V. ODESeW Automatic Generation of Knowledge Portals for Intranets and Extranets. López-García, M.C. Suárez-Figueroa. International Semantic Web Conference, pages 802-817, 2003.

[5] S. Decker, M. Erdmann, D. Fensel and R. Studer, Ontobroker: Ontology Based Access to Distributed and Semi-Structured Information, in Database Semantics: Semantic Issues in Multimedia Systems, Kluwer Academic Publisher, Boston, pages 351-369, 1999

[6] De Raedt, L., Dehaspe, L. "Clausal Discovery", Report CW 238, Department of Computing Science, K.U.Leuven, 1996

[7] M. F. Fernandez, D. Florescu, A. Y. Levy and D. Suciu, Declarative Specification of Web Sites with Strudel, VLDB Journal, volume 9, pages 38-55, 2000

[8] T. R. Gruber, Towards principles for the design of ontologies used for knowledge sharing, International Journal of Human-Computer Studies, volume 43, pages 907-928, 1995

[9] J. Hartmann and Y. Sure, An Infrastructure for Scalable, Reliable Semantic Portals, IEEE Intelligent Systems 19 (3): 58-65. May 2004

[10] Yuhui Jin, Stefan Decker and Gio Wiederhold, OntoWebber: Building Web Sites Using Semantic Web Technologies, Twelfth International World Wide Web Conference in Budapest, Hungary, May 2003

[11] G. Mecca, P. Merialdo, P. Atzeni and V. Crescenzi, The (Short) Araneus Guide to Web-Site Development, Second Intern. Workshop on the Web and Databases (WebDB'99) in conjunction with SIGMOD'99, pages 13-18, May 1999

[12] S. Staab, J. Angele, S. Decker, M. Erdmann, A. Hotho, A. Maedche, H.-P. Schnurr, R. Studer and Y. Sure, Semantic Community Web Portals, Proceedings of the 9th International World Wide Web Conference, Amsterdam, The Netherlands, volume 33, pages 473-491, 2000

[13] Stojanovic, N., Stojanovic, Lj. A Logic-based Approach for Query Refinement in Ontology-based Information Retrieval Systems, IEEE ICTAI 2004, 2004

[14] Voorhees, E. Query expansion using lexical-semantic relations, 17th ACM/SIGIR, Dublin, 1994

Towards Supporting Annotation for Existing Web Pages Enabling Hyperstructure-Based Searching

Zhanzi Qiu[*] and Matthias Hemmje

FernUniversitaet Hagen
Universitaetsstrasse 1
D-58087 Hagen, Germany
Matthias.Hemmje@fernuni-hagen.de
zhanzi@yahoo.com

Abstract. This paper discusses the requirements and tasks in annotating existing Web pages with additional structural and semantic information. It suggests annotating existing Web pages with the concepts of a domain model, and annotating the links between the Web pages with the relations between these concepts. It also suggests explicitly representing high-level hypermedia structures, so-called hypertext composites and contexts, and annotating the corresponding composite and context pages with such structures. RDF and RDF Schema are adopted to represent the domain models and the resulting annotations. The architecture of a prototype annotation tool is outlined and corresponding requirements for automatic annotation support are discussed.

1 Introduction

In the traditional Web, nodes and links are not typed, and there is no link-based composition mechanism. Thus the Web lacks structure [14]. Semantic Web is about adding formal structural and semantic information to Web content for the purpose of more efficient management and access. Due to the efforts of W3C, this kind of information can now be represented in standard ways, but annotating the huge amount of existing Web pages with such information imposes a major challenge to the implementation of the Semantic Web.

This paper introduces the types of structural and semantic information that can be applied in several hyperstructure-based search methods we have already proposed before. Furthermore, the paper discusses the issues in annotating existing Web pages with this kind of information. These issues cover the annotation tasks, structure, and representation of the annotations, and tools that support the annotation tasks.

The remainder of the paper is structured as follows. Section 2 describes the types of structural and semantic information that can be embedded into hyperstructures. Section 3 and 4 defines the requirements and the tasks in annotating existing Web pages with additional structural and semantic information. Section 5 discusses the standard representation of the annotations and the domain models used for the annotation. Section 6 discusses tool issues by outlining a prototype annotation tool and presenting some primary considerations about automatic annotation. Section 7 reviews related work, while Section 8 summarizes the paper.

---

[*] Former Member of Research Staff at Fraunhofer-IPSI, Germany

M. Hemmje et al. (Eds.): E.J. Neuhold Festschrift, LNCS 3379, pp. 51–60, 2005.

2   Structural and Semantic Information in Hyperstructures

The concept of *hyperstructure* refers to an information structure that is not necessarily linear. More specifically, such a structure refers to a hierarchical and non-hierarchical structure composed by linking mechanisms [11]. The *structural and semantic information in hyperstructures* refers to machine understandable information about hypertext components and the overall structural characteristics of hypertext. Generally, such information (referred as *hyperstructural information* later) can be classified into three different categories. The first category is **basic hypermedia components** and the types of these components, the second category is **high-level hypermedia structures** formed by these basic hypermedia components, and the third category includes various **document models** and **domain models**.

Basic hypermedia components are *nodes*, *links* and *anchors*. A *node* is a unit of information. A *link* is a relationship between nodes. An *anchor* is an area within the content of a node that is the source or destination of a link. The anchor may be the whole of the node content [16].

The main semantic information about hypermedia components is *node types* and *link types*. A node type specifies a concept, or in other words, is the specification of the kind of information contained in the node. A link type identifies the meaning of a link. The meaning can be semantic or structural. A link with a specific semantic type is a semantic link. A link with a structural type is a structural link, which often identifies containment (e.g. partOf, hasPart) relations between nodes.

In most cases, node types and semantic link types are detailed and domain-specific. They usually exist in certain domain models.

High-level hypermedia structures are structures formed by basic hypermedia components. Two of the major high-level hypermedia structures are *hypertext contexts* and *hypertext composites*. They are both groups of nodes and links, however, the first without structural constraints, and the second with structural constraints (e.g. tree or a directed acyclic graph).

A *hypertext context* is a generic high-level hypermedia structure that groups together a set of nodes and links into a logical whole. However, a *hypertext context* is usually said to be a container for a group of nodes, while the links between the nodes are thought to be included implicitly in the context.

In practice, *hypertext contexts* can be used to support configuration, private workspaces, and version history trees [13]. They can be used as a mechanism to describe different context views of the same hyperdocuments, tuned to different applications or classes of users of the documents [2]. A simple hypertext context A is shown in Figure 1.

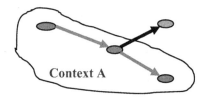

Fig. 1. A simple hypertext context

Hypertext composites are often used to support the logical structures in hypertexts. A *link-based hypertext composite* is a special kind of node that is constructed out of other nodes and composites [5]. These nodes and composites are *components* of the composite. They are linked from the composite or the other components in the composite with containment (or part-of) relations. By means of embedding other composites, the composite organizes its components in different levels of the structure. A simple hypertext composite "HTML User Guide" with 2 structural levels is shown in Figure 2.

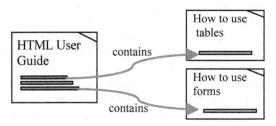

Fig. 2. A simple composite "HTML User Guide"

Domain models and **document models** are two kinds of hyperstructures that have domain specific semantics. From the structural point of view, they can be either hypertext composites or hypertext contexts as described above.

A *domain model* specifies the concepts and their relationships in a specific application domain. In a link-based or graph-based representation of a *domain model*, the nodes represent the domain concepts and the links represent the relationships between the concepts. Each concept may still have internal structure, which can be represented as a set of attributes where different kinds of topics usually have different sets of values. A simple exemplary domain model is displayed in Figure 3.

A *document model* specifies the allowed elements and the relationships between the elements in a kind of documents. Traditionally, a document model refers to a hierarchical structure specified by a SGML DTD, or a XML DTD, or a XML Schema, for a structured document. For link-based hypertext documents, their document models can be seen as a kind of domain models, as the document elements all get names that represent various concepts.

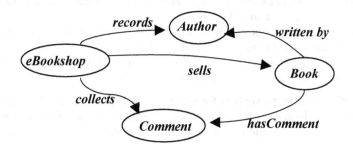

Fig. 3. A simple domain model

3   Hyperstructure-Based Search Methods and the Current Web

Our research has revealed that all above mentioned categories of hyperstructural information can be represented with emerging Web standards mainly XML, RDF, and related standards[1], and can therefore be applied in new search methods to improve Web search quality [11]. For instance, semantic link types, along with the node types in a domain can play an important role in improving Web search, especially for ranking and filtering purpose. Hypertext contexts can be used as a mechanism to specify the information space to be examined in a search activity. Composite structures can be applied in query and search facilities to enable users to query different levels of the structures with the same or different keywords and get search hits that are set of inter-linked nodes rather than separate nodes. Finally, in a domain, domain concepts can be used to index document nodes and the relations between concepts can be applied in constructing structured queries so that users may get better and more specific search results that are relevant to some specific information needs.

However, concerning the current state of the Web, it will be a long way to make these hyperstructure-based search methods practically usable and beneficial to users, as it is a fact that the current Web does not provide rich hyperstructural information that is explicitly represented and can be taken advantage of. During our work, we have not even been able to find a large collection for an in depth evaluation of the above mentioned methods and the related prototype system implementing these methods.

We believe that as the new Web standards become more and more widely adopted, information producers will provide more metadata information along with their new Web documents. However, in any search systems dealing with such information, we cannot ignore the huge amount of existing Web pages. Annotating these pages and the relations between them stands as a major challenge to the Semantic Web community.

4   Supporting the Annotation of Existing Web Pages with Additional Structural and Semantic Information

As outlined above, large collections of rich structural and semantic information are essential for applying hyperstructure-based search methods. These can only be achieved by properly supporting the following basic tasks:

1. Supporting the annotation of pages and relations between them with certain semantic node types and link types
2. Supporting the annotation of structural relations between composite pages with structural link types
3. Supporting the annotation of pages with high-level hypermedia structures – composites and contexts – attached to them

A precondition to achieve support for the first task is that various domain models are developed and adopted, as the node types and link types used for the annotation are usually domain specific and thus should be defined in certain domain models for

---

[1] Actually the Web standards have been partly developed for this purpose.

sharing and reuse purpose. Such a domain model can be as broad as being adaptable to the whole Web, or as specific as being adaptable only to one site, only that it is commonly accepted in the domain of interest. In the annotations, the domain concepts are used to type the Web pages, while the links in the domain model are used to identify the relations between the pages.

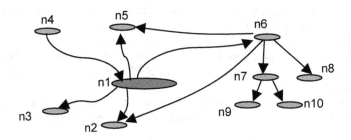

Fig. 4. Part of an E-Commerce Site Before Annotation

For instance, Figure 4 shows a part of a traditional E-Commerce site, in which pages and relations between them are not typed (but humans can recognize them). Figure 5 shows the part of the E-Commerce site after annotation with the simple domain model shown in Figure 3. For simplification purposes we use, e.g. in Figure 5, *(Book)n6* to denote that the page *n6* is annotated with the domain concept *Book*[2]. Further, *(Book)n6 [written by] (Author)n2* will be used to denote that the relation between the page *n6* and *n2* is *written by*. In the context of our work, this kind of relational annotations are considered as an important part of semantic annotations to already existing Web pages.

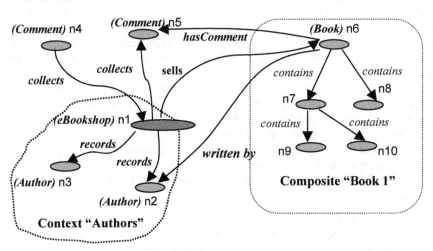

Fig. 5. Part of an E-Commerce Site After Annotation

---

[2] In practice, a page may be annotated with more than 1 domain concept.

The second task is to support explicit representation of relations between composite pages. This is the part of structural annotations to already existing Web pages. For instance, as shown in Figure 5, a structural link type "contains" has been used to annotate the containment relations between the page *n6* and its following pages. Based on these annotated relationships, the composite *"Book1"* can be computed.

The third task is to support the annotation of already existing Web pages with high-level hypermedia structures attached to them. For instance, in Figure 5, the *eBookshop n1* can be annotated with the context *"Authors"* which is computed with the relationship *"records"*, and the node types *"Author"* and *"eBookshop"*. The page *n6* can be annotated with the composite *"Book1"* which is computed with the containment relationships.

To summarize shortly, assuming the achievement of support for the three above mentioned tasks, already existing Web pages will have annotations for their

1. types or categories, which are domain concepts,
2. relations to other pages, and
3. attached high-level hypermedia structures, i.e., hypertext composites and contexts.

5   Annotation Representation

In this section, we are discussing the structure and representation of the annotations defined in last section. The first important issue to be clarified in the context of this work is that, as any interested parties may annotate existing Web pages provided by other parties, we are considering mainly the annotations which are kept separate from the content of the pages annotated, i.e., we are not considering embedded annotations.

For representing and encoding such annotations and the related domain models, there is no better choice than RDF and RDF Schema language [12]. This is because RDF Schema is well established in the Semantic Web community as a knowledge representation and interchange language. Within the Semantic Web Community there is already a rich diversity of RDF schema repositories, APIs, and tools so that systems to deal with (e.g. generate, store, etc.) RDF representations are easily to be developed. Comparatively, the new OWL standard [10] still lacks a sufficient tool support. According to our experience, RDF and RDF Schema provide sufficient expressiveness for the representation of domain models and the resulting annotations we intent to achieve in this work. They enable the wide reuse and shared access of the represented domain models and annotations.

The following exemplary RDF schema describes a simple domain model: "A book is written by an author":

```
<rdf:RDF xml:lang="en"
   xmlns:rdf="http://www.w3.org/1999/02/22-rdf-syntax-ns#"
   xmlns:rdfs="http://www.w3.org/2000/01/rdf-schema#">
      <rdfs:Class rdf:ID="book">
          <rdfs:subClassOf rdf:resource="http://www.w3.org/2000/01/rdf-
   schema#Resource"/>
```

```
        </rdfs:Class>
        <rdfs:Class rdf:ID="author">
            <rdfs:subClassOf rdf:resource="http://www.w3.org/2000/01/rdf-
    schema#Resource"/>
        </rdfs:Class>
        <rdf:Property ID="writtenBy">
            <rdfs:domain rdf:resource="#book"/>
            <rdfs:range rdf:resource="#author"/>
        </rdf:Property>
    </rdf:RDF>
```

Suppose the above schema is labeled as *"booksite"*, the following example RDF encoding describes the annotations for a page with URL *"http://books/maths.html"*. This page is annotated with the domain concept "Book", and its relation to the page *"http://authors/Smith.html"* is "writtenby".

```
    <rdf:RDF xmlns:rdf="http://www.w3.org/1999/02/22-rdf-syntax-ns#"
            xmlns:booksite="http://descriptions/domainmodels/booksite/">
    <rdf:Description about="http://books/maths.html">
            <rdf:type
            rdf:resource="http://descriptions/domainmodels/booksite/Book"/>
            <booksite:writtenby rdf:resource="http://authos/Smith.html"/>
    </rdf:Description>
    </rdf:RDF>
```

If there is more than one author for the book, an RDF bag can be inserted into the above encoding to represent a hypertext context attached to the book, such as, e.g.

```
    <booksite:writtenby>
        <rdf:Bag>
            <rdf:li resource="http://authos/Smith.html">
            <rdf:li resource="http://authos/Bush.html">
        </rdf:Bag>
    </booksite:writtenby>
```

Finally, if the page has some following composite pages, the following RDF descriptions can be inserted into the encoding to annotate the containment relationships between the pages:

```
    <dcterms:hasPart rdf: resource="maths1.html"/>
    <dcterms:hasPart rdf:resource="maths2.html"/>
```

Here *dcterms* labels the schema for Dublin Core [3] vocabularies. The namespace description *xmlns:dcterms=http://purl.org/dc/terms/* needs to be inserted into the <rdf:RDF> description.

By now, we have explained how annotations for already existing Web pages can be described within a RDF document with a pair of <rdf:Description> and </rdf:Description>.

6   Annotation Tool – From Manual to Automatic

Because of the popular acceptance of RDF, there are a number of commercial and non-commercial groups who are designing RDF software (as shown at http://www.w3.org/RDF/). There should be no problem for information providers to choose an available RDF authoring/editing system to create RDF descriptions for representing domain models and annotations as defined above. The described relationship information between domain model concepts and Web pages, the composite information and context information can then be extracted and processed by other systems.

However, considering the variety of Web users, specific interactive tools that support the generation of annotations with no need of knowing the representation format (in this work, RDF) are still needed. Such tools will enable any interested parties to provide explicit structural and semantic information via annotations. And such information can be stored in a relational database in an efficient way, and can be represented in other formats when necessary.

Thus, accompanying our research on hyperstructure-based search methods, we have developed a primary interactive tool that supports the annotations as defined in this paper to help us to build the test collection for our evaluations for the methods. The tool consists of

1. an extractor module,
2. a domain model processor,
3. an annotation module, and
4. storage for basic page and link information, domain models and resulting annotations.

The extractor is responsible for handling existing Web pages. It downloads the pages that own URIs specified by users, extracts the link information from the pages, and then stores the link information in the relational database in the system. The domain model processor is used to generate domain models interactively, or extract from RDF schemas the data about domain models, and store the domain models, including concepts and relationships, in the database. The annotation module provides a user interface to display the list of links from a page and enable users to annotate the page and the links with a domain model stored in the database, or annotate the structural links to represent composite structure, or annotate a hypertext context by specifying the components pages. The annotation results are also stored in the database. The issues about how to store domain models, links, nodes and their types, as well as hypertext composites and contexts have been discussed in our earlier papers [11].

We are now on the way to research methods for automatic annotation, as we are aware that, annotating totally manually for the huge number of existing Web pages is not considered a feasible approach, though this approach is needed in some cases. This is to say that tools that support automatic annotation should be developed. Only when such tools get wide acceptance and usage, we will then have rich structural and semantic information in the Web space and search methods taking advantage of such information will really help users to receive better search results.

In our context, a tool that supports automatic annotation should be able to extract the implicit structural and semantic information from the current Web space and make such information explicitly represented. Currently, we regard the kinds of Web pages, such as site maps, tables of contents, guided tours, and focused WWW resource lists related to a particular topic or subject domain, as the important sources for the extraction. Appropriate extraction technologies for this purpose are under exploration.

7   Related Work

An ontology provides an explicit specification of a conceptualization [4]. In the context of our work, we view ontologies as typical examples of domain models. An ontology is a super domain model, or a large general-purpose domain model for a community. An application-oriented domain model in the community can be the whole or part of the ontology for the domain, or is an instance of the ontology. Any kinds of such domain models can be applied in hyperstructure-based search methods that support domain-specific searching. This is why we adopt the term domain model in our work, while most of the related work uses ontology in their context.

The semantic annotation of documents with respect to an ontology is discussed in a number of work. For instance, [9] presents a metadata model allowing ontology-based named entity annotation, indexing and retrieval. Especially, it claims that light-weight upper level ontologies are likely to be more suitable for semantic annotation. [7] presents SHOE Knowledge Annotator, which allows users to mark up pages in SHOE guided by ontologies available locally or via a URL. [15] presents an annotation tool MnM that provides both automated and semi-automated support for annotating Web pages with semantic contents. [6] presents an approach to automatically extracting relations between the entities that are annotated by involving heavily machine learning technologies. [8] focuses on manual semantic annotation for authoring Web content, while [1] targets on the creation of a Web-based, open hypermedia linking service, backed by a conceptual model of document terminology.

Our work is different from all the above related work with regards to the annotation purpose and tasks. As claimed, our work focuses on providing annotation support for existing Web pages with well-defined types of structural and semantic information, in order that hyperstructure-based search methods can be actually applied to improve Web search quality. In this sense, our annotation model is more target-oriented than most of the other models.

8   Summary

This paper describes the structural and semantic information that can be embedded in hyperstructures and discusses the demands of annotating existing Web pages with additional structural and semantic information. These requirements result from the potential of hyperstructure-based search methods in improving Web search and the lack of such information explicitly represented and recognizable by search systems.

To meet the demands, we suggest annotating existing Web pages with the concepts in a domain model, and annotating the links between the Web pages with the relations between the concepts. We also suggest explicitly representing the high-level hypermedia structures, mainly hypertext composites and contexts, and annotating the corresponding composite and context pages with such structures. Furthermore, all resulting annotations should be represented in a standard way so that they can be widely shared and processed. For this purpose, RDF Schema is chosen to represent domain models, while RDF is used to represent the annotations.

Finally, the paper discusses tool issues by outlining a prototype interactive tool that implements our annotation vision described in the paper and presenting some of our primary considerations for supporting automatic annotation.

References

1. Carr L., Bechhofer S., Goble C., Hall W., "Conceptual Linking: Ontology-Based Open Hypermedia," in Proc. WWW 10, Hong Kong, May 2001, pp. 334-342.
2. Casanova M. A. and Tucherman L., "The nested context model for hyperdocuments," Proc. of Hypertext'91, pp. 193-201.
3. Dublin Core: http://purl.oclc.org/dc
4. Gruber, T.R., "A translation approach to portable ontologies", *Knowledge Acquisition*, 5(2): 199-220, 1993.
5. Halasz F. and Schwartz M., "The Dexter Hypertext Reference Model," Communications of the ACM, 37(2), pp.30-39, February 1994.
6. Handschuh S., Staab S., Ciravegna F., "S-CREAM – Semi-automatic CREAtion of Metadata," in Proc. of EKAW 2002 (LNCS 2473), pp. 358-372, Springer Verlag, 2002.
7. Heflin J. And Hendler J., "A Portrait of the Semantic Web in Action," IEEE Intelligent Systems, 16(2), 2001.
8. Kahan J., Koivunen M., Prud'Hommeaux E., Swick R., "Annotea: An Open RDF Infrastructure for Shared Web Annotations," in Proc. WWW 10, Hong Kong, May 2001, pp. 623-632.
9. Kiryakov A., Popov B., Terziev I., Manov D., Ognyanoff D., "Semantic Annotation, Indexing, and Retrieval, " Elevier's Journal of Web Semantics, Vol. 1, ISWC 2003 Special Issue (2), 2004.
10. Dean M., Connolly D., van Harmelen F., Hendler J., Horrocks I., Mcguinness D., Patel-Schneider P. F., Stein L. A., "Web Ontology Language (OWL) Reference Version 1.0," W3C Working Draft 12 November 2002, at: http://w3.org/TR/2002/WD-owl-ref-20021112/.
11. Qiu Z., "Hyperstructure-based search methods for the World Wide Web," Ph.D. thesis, Department of Computer Science, Technische Universitaet Darmstadt, Darmstadt, Germany, 2004.
12. Manola F., Miller E., eds. RDF Primer (W3C Recommendation 10 February 2004). At: http://www.w3.org/TR/rdf-primer/.
13. Schwartz M., Delisle N., "Contexts – A partitioning concept for hypertext," ACMTransactions on Office Information Systems, 5 (2), April 1987, pp. 168-186.
14. Trigg R. H., "Hypermedia as integration: Recollections, reflections and exhortations," Keynote Address in Hypertext'96 Conference. Xerox Palo Alto Research Center.
15. Vargas-Vera M., Motta E., Domingue J., Lanzoni, Stutt A., and Ciravegna F., "MnM: Ontology Driven Semi-automatic and Automatic Support for Semantic Markup," Proc. of EKAW 2002 (LNCS 2473), pp. 379-391, Springer, 2002.
16. Hypertext Terms. At: http://www.w3c.org/Terms.html.

Maintaining Dublin Core
as a Semantic Web Vocabulary

Thomas Baker[1]

Institutszentrum Birlinghoven, Fraunhofer-Gesellschaft
53754 Sankt Augustin, Germany
thomas.baker@izb.fraunhofer.de

Abstract. The Dublin Core Metadata Initiative (DCMI) maintains a
vocabulary of several dozen metadata terms, notably the fifteen-element
"Dublin Core." These terms (and their historical versions) are identified with URI references, described in Web documents and machine-
processable schemas, indexed in registries, cited in application profiles,
and of course used in metadata records. Within DCMI, however, the emphasis has been less on growing this small vocabulary than on clarifying
how the DCMI vocabulary can "play well" with other, complementary
vocabularies in a Semantic Web that recombines semantics from multiple
sources for specialized purposes. This priority has led DCMI to examine models for referencing other vocabularies and to clarify the modeling
bases for interoperability among heterogeneous systems.

1 Maintaining a Small Vocabulary

Since the publication of Version 1.0 and RFC 2413 in September 1998, the fifteen
elements of the "Dublin Core" — Title, Description, Date, and the rest — have
become a familiar feature of the digital landscape [11]. They have been printed on
tee shirts, used in millions of metadata records, and enshrined in an international
standard, ISO 15836 [7]. Its user community, the Dublin Core Metadata Initiative
(DCMI), has evolved from a workshop series into a maintenance network with
an increasingly global basis of institutional stakeholders [8].

Since the publication of Version 1.1 in 1999 there has been little discussion
in the Initiative about the Core itself. The fifteen elements have some long-
recognized and well-understood flaws, but none so serious as to justify the dis-
ruption of a full-scale revision. Rather, discussion has focused more on the policies, processes, metadata principles, and data models that provide a context for
the Core.

The problem as initially posed in 1994 — that of agreeing on a simple set of
descriptors for embedding in Web pages — has evolved into a cluster of issues
ranging from technical architecture to naming policies and maintenance procedures. Much of this discussion has aimed at clarifying how the elements can be
used with an ever-evolving array of Web technologies, from the simple HTML
of the early years through XML and XML Schemas to Resource Description

M. Hemmje et al. (Eds.): E.J. Neuhold Festschrift, LNCS 3379, pp. 61–68, 2005.
© Springer-Verlag Berlin Heidelberg 2005

Framework and OWL Web Ontology Language. Much of the effort has been motivated by the vague but powerful vision of a Semantic Web in which well-defined data and metadata underpin applications that are increasingly automated and intelligent.

This paper summarizes the state of discussion as of October 2004 regarding the identification and referencing of metadata terms in DCMI– and related non-DCMI–maintained vocabularies. The paper reduces the problem of maintaining a vocabulary for the Semantic Web to its essence: the declaration of terms with persistent identifiers and the maintenance of assertions about those terms — i.e., about what they mean, how they change over time, and how they relate to terms in other vocabularies. Specifically, the paper examines several areas in which practical problems reveal issues relevant to the more fundamental problem of maintaining and using metadata vocabularies in a Semantic Web environment:

- persistence and semantic stability policies for term identifiers,
- the historical versioning of terms,
- namespace hosting,
- the identification of controlled vocabularies of values,
- the "re-use" of terms in application profiles,
- the etiquette of assertions about terms in other vocabularies.

Taking each of these areas in turn, this paper will reveal a basic tension between the need to solve problems in the short term and the sustainability of solutions for the long term. The question of when to create new metadata terms and when to cite or re-use existing terms maintained by others depends on the sustainability of the social and institutional processes by which the vocabularies are maintained. Section Two will lay the groundwork for this discussion by describing how DCMI forms identifiers for its own metadata terms and what social commitment is thereby implied. Section Three will then describe how practices for referencing terms in other, complementary vocabularies have emerged in response to various practical problems.

None of these issues are unique to Dublin Core, so the solutions devised for the DCMI context should be of interest to other vocabulary maintainers, especially as the solutions are tested over time in an evolving landscape of Semantic Web vocabularies.

2   Identifying Metadata Terms

2.1   DCMI Namespace Policy

The Internet was revolutionary because it made the resources of any connected server accessible via a single global address space. The vision of a future Semantic Web further generalizes this notion of a global space of addresses to that of a global space of identifiers. According to Tim Berners-Lee, "The most fundamental specification of Web architecture, while one of the simpler, is that of the Uniform Resource Identifier, or URI. The principle that anything, absolutely anything 'on the Web' should be identified distinctly by an otherwise opaque string of characters... is core" [1].

URIs can provide unique identity not just to "information resources" — Web pages, scientific pre-prints, satellite photos, video clips, and the like — but also to any metadata terms used to describe those resources. As compact character strings associated with known institutional domain authorities, URIs can stand alone as self-contained references to metadata terms. While relevant to all data technologies, they are usable most directly in Web-based description technologies such as XLink, Topic Maps, and RDF.

DCMI began to experiment with URIs in 1997, which led to the formulation in 2001 of a formal Namespace Policy [4]. This policy declares URI references for three DCMI namespaces:

- `http://purl.org/dc/elements/1.1/`
- `http://purl.org/dc/terms/`
- `http://purl.org/dc/dcmitype/`

to designate (respectively) the fifteen-element Dublin Core, all other DCMI elements and qualifiers, and a controlled vocabulary of values for the Dublin Core element Type. A URI reference is constructed for a DCMI term by appending its character-string "name" to the URI of a DCMI namespace. For example, the URIs

- `http://purl.org/dc/elements/1.1/title`
- `http://purl.org/dc/terms/extent`
- `http://purl.org/dc/dcmitype/Image`

respectively identify Title (one of the fifteen "core" elements), Extent (an element refinement) and Image (a term in the DCMI Type Vocabulary).

Through normal processes of editorial review and revision, terms can and will change over time — a bibliographic reference may be added, usage comments may be updated, the status assigned to a term may change, or a new term may be created. The Namespace Policy describes possible types of change and specifies the consequences of those changes for identifiers. A term may be subject to "minor" or "substantive" change of an editorial nature — the correction of errors, the addition or update of a bibliographic reference, or changes of wording to clarify a meaning — without consequence for its URI reference. Proposed changes of a semantic nature, however — changes with significant impact on the meaning of term — must trigger the creation of a new term with a new URI reference. To support the future interpretation of legacy metadata, the Namespace Policy commits DCMI to maintaining formal documentation for all terms assigned URI references — even for terms that might some day be assigned a status of "obsolete."

2.2   Historical Versions of Metadata Terms

The fifteen-element Dublin Core was initially versioned as a set — Version 1.0 of 1998 was followed by Version 1.1 of 1999. Since July 2000, however, new terms have been added to a vocabulary that is no longer versioned as a whole. The decision to do this was taken because the model of periodic, batched releases seemed a bad fit to a vocabulary that was expected to grow by continual increment. Apart from the DCMI namespace for the fifteen core elements, which includes the version-number string "1.1" — a legacy URI from before the Namespace Policy — the URI references for DCMI namespaces do not show versioning information.

At the same time, it was recognized that the ability to reference a term or term set as of a specific historical date would be important in a number of contexts, such as library automation contracts, translations of DCMI terms into other languages, and the future interpretation of legacy metadata. The pragmatic solution to this problem has been to version both individual terms (which evolve at different rates) and Web pages which document batches of terms as of a particular date (which are updated whenever a term is added or anything else in the term set changes).

Individual terms are versioned by saving a snapshot of their attributes whenever any one of their attributes changes and assigning to that snapshot a URI such as the following:

- `http://dublincore.org/usage/terms/history/#Image-002`
- `http://dublincore.org/usage/terms/history/#Image-001`

Although such URIs are currently outside the scope of the DCMI Namespace Policy, they effectively function as identifiers for successive versions of a term (in this case Image). In practice, URIs currently resolve to anchors in a Web document which holds a periodically updated snapshot of all past and present versions of all DCMI terms. In modeling terms, a distinction is made between the URI references for the "term" as a notion or concept, and opposed to the "term description" — a cluster of descriptive attributes captured at a specific moment in time.

Following W3C practice for versioning specifications, the Web pages documenting DCMI terms are versioned with a URI for the specific historical version (using a directory name as a time stamp) and a URI for a generic "latest version," along with pointers to prior and successive versions. For example, the March 2003 version of the DCMI Metadata Terms document has the following Identifier, Latest Version, and Replaced By attributes (respectively):

- `http://dublincore.org/documents/2003/03/04/dcmi-terms/`
- `http://dublincore.org/documents/dcmi-terms/`
- `http://dublincore.org/documents/2003/11/19/dcmi-terms/`

where the Identifier resolves to the permanently archived and unchanging version of the document displayed, Replaced By resolves to the next historical version, and Latest Version resolves to a continually updated pointer on the DCMI Web site to the most up-to-date version of DCMI Metadata Terms.

In DCMI practice, then, the method for versioning metadata terms is analogous to that for Web documents: in each case, identifiers are assigned both for the resource in a generic sense (the namespace-policy-supported URI for a term or Latest Version for a document) and for a specific historical version.

3   A Bias Towards Re-use

In its evolution from a workshop series into a maintenance agency, the Dublin Core Metadata Initiative has instituted formal processes of editorial control. Since 2001, proposals for extensions or clarifications to the standard are evaluated for conformance to grammatical principle and usefulness by a nine-member Usage Board [5] Each decision of the Usage Board is assigned a URI reference, and links are created to supporting documentation, decision texts, and to the historical term declarations of any metadata terms affected by the decisions [6]. The URI-identified Decision, then, is an event point linking the creation of a new term description with all supporting documentation in an audit trail.

Over the past two years, the Usage Board has shown a bias towards keeping the vocabularies maintained by DCMI relatively small and generic. This bias has been motivated in part by a desire to avoid the slippery slope of complexification. Adding ever more-specialized terms to meet the perceived needs of particular communities would sacrifice the generic simplicity that constitutes much of Dublin Core's appeal. The criteria by which the Usage Board has delimited its scope are those of usefulness "across domains" and for "resource discovery."

3.1   Namespace Hosting

Given the conservative approach of the Usage Board towards expanding the DCMI vocabularies, user communities with pressing needs for citable metadata terms have occasionally proposed that DCMI provide services as a "namespace host" — i.e., as a home for a maintained namespace with known URI policies where metadata terms coined by ad-hoc user groups might be published without any sort of review or implied approval on the part of DCMI. In principle, this could enable communities of practice to use or reference new metadata terms as soon as they are created while ensuring that they remain documented and citable over time. This idea is associated with the appealing notion that a "vocabulary marketplace" might operate more efficiently if freed from the strictures of formal review.

However, discussions of these proposals have always reached the same conclusion. Opening a hosted namespace to the unrestricted creation of terms would by definition be "out of control" — the namespace would quickly expand into sprawling incoherence. Despite disclaimers to the contrary, hosted terms would inevitably be perceived as having some form of DCMI branding or approval. Requests would be made to change this or that definition, implying maintenance responsibility. The task is clearly beyond the capacity of a light-weight, networked maintenance organization.

3.2   Identifying Controlled Vocabularies of Values

In DCMI terminology, a Vocabulary Encoding Scheme is a metadata term used to indicate that a value in a metadata record is a term from a controlled vocabulary — for example, that "China — History" is from Library of Congress Subject Headings (LCSH). The set of qualifiers approved in July 2000 included eleven Vocabulary Encoding Schemes, such as LCSH, Dewey Decimal Classification, and the Getty Thesaurus of Historical Names. Metadata creators have long requested that DCMI provide a streamlined process for the "registration" of several dozen more vocabularies in common use.

To meet this need, DCMI tested a fast-track process for moving a proposal from submission via a Web form through to the creation of a URI reference in a DCMI namespace. However, the test revealed a wide range of problems and risks: uncertainty about the need to obtain permission from vocabulary owners and requirements for archiving such permissions; the sustainability both of initial reviews and of the longer-term maintenance of links and descriptions; and issues around the construction of unique names in the face of clashing acronyms, translations or other derivative works, and generic "works" (such as "Dewey Decimal Classification") as opposed to specific versions ("DDC 16th Edition of 1958"). In the end, DCMI decided not to implement the registration procedure.

Rather, DCMI is now developing a process designed to encourage the creation of Vocabulary Encoding Schemes — to be precise, of URI references usable as Vocabulary Encoding Schemes — by maintainers of the vocabularies themselves. Guidelines describing four simple strategies for assigning URI references to metadata terms are currently under review in DCMI working groups [9]. What remains to be specified is a procedure whereby vocabulary maintainers can "register" their own URI references for inclusion in DCMI Registry, in DCMI Web documents, and in RDF schemas. The intent is not just to avoid creating an unsustainably large, centralized set of URI references, but to shift the burden of maintaining those URI references to their most appropriate owners through promoting guidelines of good practice.

3.3   Re-use of Terms in Application Profiles

In the context of DCMI, the notion of an Application Profile arose from the recognition that implementers often use Dublin Core elements together with elements specific to a particular application. The Application Profile was seen as a form of documentation for sharing or converging on particular "Dublin-Core-based" metadata models within communities of use. It is worth noting that roughly analogous concepts for "profiles" developed in metadata communities as different from each other as DCMI, DOI (for publishers' metadata), MARC21 (in the library world), and IEEE/LOM (for e-learning), suggesting that the impulse to customize, constrain, or extend a standard vocabulary for a specific purpose may be a universal linguistic need.

Dublin Core Application Profiles (DCAPs) have been developed for purposes ranging from the description of existing record structures to the development of good-practice guidelines for formats yet to be implemented. Application Profiles have also helped identify emerging semantics "around the edges" as proposals to the DCMI Usage Board for inclusion in the officially maintained vocabularies. In 2003, a Workshop on Dublin Core Metadata in the European Committee for Standardization (CEN) put forward guidelines for a consistent documentary format for Dublin Core Application Profiles (DCAPs) [2], and work in 2004 has focused on developing a formal expression of DCAPs in RDF [3].

The RDF model makes clear a distinction between the "declaration" of terms in metadata vocabularies versus their "usage" in application profiles. Meeting the formal requirements of a DCAP compels an application designer to ensure that terms are assigned URI references and properly cited and that the metadata design fits the DCMI Abstract Model. In principle, this analytical effort improves interoperability by specifying a model for metadata statements that are formally coherent and precise. Further potential uses of formal DCAPs for mapping or querying conceptual spaces spanning multiple data providers is a topic for ongoing research.

3.4 Assertions About Terms in Other Vocabularies

To keep its own vocabularies small, the DCMI Usage Board has put effort into clarifying how DCMI-maintained vocabularies can be used in conjunction with more detailed or domain-specific vocabularies declared and maintained by specialised communities of expertise outside of DCMI. This has involved discussion with maintainers of other vocabularies and standards on forms of mutual recognition and support.

As of October 2004, DCMI is finalizing an agreement with the US Library of Congress on the mechanics of formally declaring MARC Relator terms — roles of agents with respect to a resource, such as Adaptor, Artist, and Translator — to be refinements of the Dublin Core element Contributor. Working with the Library of Congress, DCMI helped select roughly one hundred of the MARC Relator terms as sub-properties, logically speaking, of Contributor. This process involved discussion of whether the MARC Relator terms could indeed be considered and used as "properties" in an RDF modeling sense.

The Usage Board gave careful thought to the mechanism by which the relationship between the terms of these different vocabularies should be expressed, seeing this as a first test case for expressing relationships with other vocabularies. For each of this properties, Library of Congress will assert a sub-property relationship to Contributor. DCMI will then endorse each of these assertions. The assertions and the endorsements will be published on the Web in RDF — a form easily fed into metadata registries and publication workflows for dissemination. Library of Congress will include DCMI in routine announcements of additions to the MARC Relator vocabulary so that new terms can be reviewed and added as appropriate.

4   Conclusion

DCMI has evolved a set of principles and practices for declaring and maintaining metadata vocabularies in the historically new and rapidly evolving context of a Semantic Web. Its typology of terms and data model provide a conceptual foundation for metadata practice of the sort that a grammar provides for any other variety of human language.

DCMI's choices reflect a tension between building up a central vocabulary versus pushing maintenance responsibility out to more specialized communities. Distributing responsibility implies not just shared data models, but shared practices and conventions — essentially social in nature — regarding the identification, maintenance, and re-use of metadata terms. While specifics of DCMI practice may not be appropriate for all communities, models and conventions much like them are generally needed. Solutions may differ for other contexts, but the problems will surely be in large part the same

References

1. Berners-Lee, T., "Web architecture from 50,000 feet",
   http://www.w3.org/DesignIssues/Architecture.html.
2. CEN/ISSS MMI-DC Workshop, "Dublin Core Application Profile Guidelines" [CEN Workshop Agreement CWA 14855], European Committee for Standardization, ftp://ftp.cenorm.be/PUBLIC/CWAs/e-Europe/MMI-DC/cwa14855-00-2003-Nov.pdf.
3. CEN/ISSS MMI-DC Workshop, "Guidelines for Machine-Processable Representation of Dublin Core Application Profiles" [Draft CEN Workshop Agreement], European Committee for Standardization,
   ftp://ftp.cenorm.be/public/ws-mmi-dc/mmidc116.htm.
4. "DCMI Namespace Policy", http://dublincore.org/documents/dcmi-namespace/.
5. DCMI Usage Board, http://dublincore.org/usage/.
6. "DCMI Usage Board decisions", http://dublincore.org/usage/decisions/.
7. The Dublin Core Metadata Element Set [ISO 15836:2003(E)],
   http://www.niso.org/international/SC4/n515.pdf.
8. Dublin Core Metadata Initiative, http://dublincore.org/.
9. Powell, A., "Guidelines for assigning identifiers to metadata terms,"
   http://www.ukoln.ac.uk/metadata/dcmi/term-identifier-guidelines/.
10. Powell, A., Nilsson, M., Naeve, A., Johnston, P., "DCMI Abstract Model,"
    http://www.ukoln.ac.uk/metadata/dcmi/abstract-model/.
11. Weibel, S., Kunze, J., Lagoze, C., Wolf, M.: Dublin Core Metadata for Resource Discovery, RFC 2413 (September 1998), The Internet Society.

A Peer-to-Peer Content Distribution Network

Oliver Heckmann, Nicolas Liebau, Vasilios Darlagiannis,
Axel Bock, Andreas Mauthe, and Ralf Steinmetz

Multimedia Kommunikation (KOM)
Technische Universität Darmstadt
Merckstr. 25, 64293 Darmstadt
{heckmann, liebau, bdarla,
bock, mauthe, steinmetz}@kom.tu-darmstadt.de

Abstract. The distribution of large content files, like videos, over a large number of users is a demanding and costly operation if done using a traditional client/server architecture. Peer-to-peer based file-sharing systems can be used as an alternative for content distribution.

The eDonkey file-sharing network is one of the most successful peer-to-peer file-sharing networks, especially in Germany. eDonkey forms a hybrid network that capitalizes both on the client/server and peer-to-peer paradigms in the design of its architecture.

In this paper, we describe the eDonkey protocol, the constructed overlay network, the critical operations and their characteristics, as well as the results of measurements of the network and transport layer and of the user behavior. The measurements were made with the client software and with an open-source eDonkey server we extended explicitly for these measurements. Our study shows that eDonkey is particularly well suited for content distribution and not surprisingly also intensively used for the distribution of large files, mainly videos.

1 Introduction

Content distribution realized either as inelastic media streams or as elastic downloadable files over a large number of users is a challenging and demanding service. In an idealistic solution, both the transport network and the deployed applications should collaborate to achieve an optimally operating service. However, with the currently best-effort deployed service of the Internet, the support of the network is limited to very basic delivery operations. In order to realize content distribution over a large number of users, application developers typically design virtual networks at the Application Layer, the so-called *overlay networks*.

A significant number of applications that employ overlay networks to interconnect a large number of users have been deployed and heavily operating lately over the Internet. Such applications harvest the resources of the end-systems and are called peer-to-peer (P2P) applications. To understand the influence of these applications and the characteristics of the traffic they produce as well as their impact on network design, capacity expansion, traffic engineering and shaping, it is important to empirically analyze the dominant file-sharing applications.

M. Hemmje et al. (Eds.): E.J. Neuhold Festschrift, LNCS 3379, pp. 69–78, 2005.

The eDonkey file-sharing protocol is one of these file-sharing protocols. It is used by the original eDonkey2000 client [eDonkey] and additionally by some advanced open-source clients like mldonkey [mlDonkey] and eMule [eMule]. According to [San03], the eDonkey protocol is the most successful P2P file-sharing protocol in Germany (52% of the generated file-sharing traffic). It is more successful than the FastTrack [FTrack] protocol used by KaZaa [KaZaa] (that contributes to 44% of the traffic). Contrary to other P2P file-sharing applications, such as Gnutella [Gnut], that are widely discussed in literature, the eDonkey protocol is not well analyzed yet. In this work, we shed light on this protocol and its suitability for content distribution with a measurement study of the observed traffic, the user behavior, and the topological characteristics of the constructed overlay network.

In the next section, we give an overview of related work. Then, in Section 3 we describe the eDonkey protocol. In Section 4, our measurements are presented. They were gathered with the eMule client software and with an open-source eDonkey server we extended for the purpose of this paper. We also present the results of the measurements before we give a summary and draw the conclusions in Section 5.

2   Related Work

P2P file sharing applications received a considerable attention after the wide deployment of Napster [Napster]. Though Napster did not follow a pure P2P architecture since it required centralized infrastructure for indexing of published documents, file exchange itself was taking place in a P2P manner. However, Napster was mostly appropriate for exchanging relatively small files such as compressed music files (mp3) since each file could be requested and downloaded from a single user only. Legal issues caused by the exchange of copyright protected content forced Napster to cease its operation, mainly due to Napster's centralized infrastructure. However, the Napster protocol is still active and utilized by OpenNap, an open-source implementation of the Napster network. Here, instead of one single server location, multiple servers exist to help coordinate the search queries of connected users. While the network is still structured around central servers, the abundance of them would make it harder to target than the original Napster. OpenNap is still targeting on music files.

Gnutella [Gnut] became the most popular P2P file sharing application after Napster's operation discontinued. Gnutella was the first file sharing application with pure P2P architecture deployed in such a large scale. However, the flooding mechanism, which was used for searching, made its operation very costly in terms of network overhead. Again, Gnutella users were focusing on small music files, however, video exchange started to appear. Gnutella's exchange mechanisms did not allow for downloading from multiple peers in parallel, so large content files exchange could not be efficiently supported. In addition, the aforementioned high network overhead motivated the design of a new architecture that used

UltraPeers [Gnut2] to perform common overlay operations such as indexing and searching.

The KaZaa [KaZaa] client followed Gnutella in popularity almost synchronously with eDonkey2000. KaZaa uses the FastTrack [FTrack] protocol for its overlay operations. Its architecture introduces the term of "super-peers" to handle the common overlay operations. Peers are dynamically assigned the role of a super-peer. KaZaA enables parallel downloads of the same file from multiple users, so increasing its suitability to exchange large content files. However, KaZaa does not make optimal use of the available content since users can download only from remote peers that have complete copies of the files. Incomplete ones are simply ignored.

BitTorrent [BitTor] is a unique file distribution system different then traditional P2P systems. BitTorrent is used to distribute large files and its operation is as follows. Initially, peers must share and host the published source files. Other peers may start downloading from the original source, each a different part of the file. Shortly afterwards, they start downloading the parts they do not have from each other. The file transfer is therefore spread and distributed over the total number of peers downloading the file, who are forced to upload as well[1]. BitTorrent, however, is not a general purpose P2P network and its searching capabilities are not sufficient.

There is a large number of additional P2P file sharing applications with different characteristics. For example, MojoNation [Wil02] was an attempt to enforce micro-payment mechanisms to provide incentives for users to share documents and avoid free-riders. MNET [Mnet] is MojoNation's successor with reduced complexity. FreeNet [CSWH00] is another file sharing network that provides a significant degree of anonymity for anti-censorship reasons. DirectConnect [DirCon] follows a Hub-based architecture. A Hub is a server with indexing and searching capabilities which brings users with similar interests together.

In addition to the media exchange as a file downloading approach, there is an attempt lately to address streaming of media in Internet-deployed P2P applications. A significant effort is the Mercora [Mercora] network that supports real time audio streaming. Also, Skype [Skype] is a free IP-Telephony application that became very popular because of the good quality of speech encoders and the relatively small end-to-end delay. Skype uses FastTrack (such as KaZaa do) to find remote users and media transfer takes place directly between the endpoints (multiparty teleconferences are supported as well).

3   The eDonkey Network

The eDonkey network is a decentralized hybrid peer-to-peer file-sharing network with client applications running on the end-systems that are connected to a distributed network of dedicated servers.

---

[1] This same mechanism is implemented in the eDonkey2000 P2P network (and one of the reasons why eDonkey is so efficient at distributing large files).

Contrary to the original Gnutella protocol, it is not completely decentralized as it uses servers; contrary to the original Napster protocol it does not use a single server (or a farm of them), which is a single point of failure. Instead it uses servers that are run by power users and offers mechanisms for inter-server communication. Unlike super-peer protocols like KaZaa, or the modern UltraPeer-based Gnutella protocol, the eDonkey network has a dedicated client/server based structure. The servers are slightly similar to the KaZaa super-nodes, but they are a separate application and do not share any files. Their role is to manage the information distribution and to operate as several central dictionaries, which hold the information about the shared files and their respective client locations.

In the eDonkey network the clients are the only nodes sharing data. Their files are indexed by the servers. If a client wants to download a file or a part of a file, it first has to connect via TCP to a server or send a short search request via UDP to one or more servers to get the necessary information about other clients offering that file. Figure 1 illustrates the eDonkey network structure.

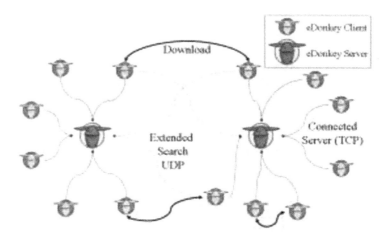

Fig. 1. eDonkey Network Structure

The eDonkey network uses 16 byte MD4 hashes to (with very high probability) uniquely identify a file independent of its filename. The implication for searching is that two steps are necessary before a file can be downloaded. First, a full text search is made at a server for the filename. The corresponding reply includes those file hashes that have an associated filename which matches the full text search. In a second step, the client requests the sources from the server for a certain file-hash. Finally, the client connects to some of these sources to download the file. File transfer takes place directly among the participating clients without involving the server entities to minimize the cost of the operation.

The eDonkey protocol supports the download of a single file from multiple sources. This can improve the download speed dramatically and reduces the risk of unfinished downloads. Files are downloaded in chunks of 9MB. Files that are downloaded even to a part are already shared by a client and can be downloaded by other clients. The MD4 hash allows to identify whether a certain shared file is the requested file or not. As individual chunks are also hashed, corrupted chunks can be identified. All these properties make the eDonkey protocol well suited for sharing large files like video files. Our measurement study below verifies that it is also being used for that.

4   Measurements

4.1   Experiments Setup

We ran two types of experiments to analyze the eDonkey protocol and to collect traffic samples:

In the first experiment, we measured the traffic at two clients connected to 768/128 kbps ADSL connection and a 10 MBit/sec at the TU Darmstadt, respectively. The most popular client of the network, eMule [eMule] under Windows XP, was used for this experiment. From the measurements, we derive traffic characteristics such as the protocol overhead, downloading behavior and message size distributions.

For the second experiment, we modified an open-source eDonkey server [Lus03] that was connected to the university network collecting application level information about the usage of the network, requested files, offered files and the overall size of the network[2].

A more detailed protocol analysis based on measurements with TCPDump can be found in our technical report [HB02].

4.2   Results

TCP/UDP summary. For the clients-focused experiments, the share of the TCP traffic of the overall network traffic was 94% (number of packets) or 99.8% (of the payload size), respectively. Those values do not differ significantly between ADSL and broadband connections. It should be noted that all TCP ACK packets with zero payload were counted, too. On the ADSL line the packet loss was approximately 5.5%, about 2.25 times higher than on the broadband line (2%).

The server-side measurements differ: TCP traffic only forms about 2,4% of the packets and 6% of the payload. The server is mainly busy with handling UDP requests from clients *not* directly connected: If a search of a client does not deliver enough results from the server it is connected to, further known servers can be searched. This behavior has implications on dial-up connections. If the dial-up IP address was assigned to an operating eDonkey server before, many clients all over the world still reference to that IP address as a server. Server

---

[2] The server proved to be quite popular and due to the sheer amount of flows was ranked on the second place of the traffic statistic of the whole TU Darmstadt network for the duration of the experiment.

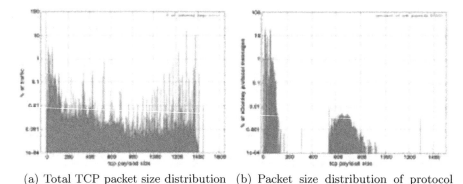

(a) Total TCP packet size distribution (b) Packet size distribution of protocol
                                             messages

Fig. 2. eDonkey traffic statistics

entries are typically kept 1 day or longer in most client implementations. These
clients will still send UDP based search queries to that IP address consuming
bandwidth[3] until the expiration of the corresponding entry.

The TCP packet sizes range greatly from header only to MTU size (see
Figure 2 a). Some characteristic peaks can be identified, e.g., for TCP messages
of payload size 24, which are typically used for the frequent *QUERY SOURCES*
messages. In most cases a TCP packet carries only a single protocol message.
Figure 2 shows the TCP packet size distribution for eDonkey protocol messages.
Protocol messages can be identified quite reliably as the payload starts with
"E3" (for details see [HB02]). The UDP packets are much less variable in size,
the size clearly indicating which kind of message is transported.

Protocol Messages. Looking at client's UDP traffic, the most observed protocol message type is by far *QUERY SOURCES* (approximately 65%). On the
other hand, TCP messages are distributed far more evenly where all common
message types have a percentaged share between one and ten percent. The only
surprising exception is TCP *QUERY SOURCES* message type, which appeared
approximately 0.008% only.

On the server side the most frequently seen messages types is the *QUERY
SOURCES* (approximately 36% for (TCP) and 95% for (UDP)).

Throughput. On the eMule/ADSL and eMule/broadband clients we observed an
average overall throughput of 30 kB/s respectively 45 kB/s while downloading,
which decreased to the preset maximum upload bandwidth (10 kB/s in our case)
after downloads were finished. UDP traffic is not very important in the client
scenario.

---

[3] This even led to a permanent entry in the FAQ section of the computer magazine
c't [ct04].

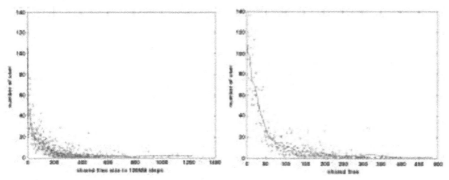

(a) Size of shared files by number of users (b) Number of shared files by number of users

Fig. 3. User Statistics

On the server side, the UDP in/out ratio was 16/2 kB/s after roughly a day (so we have 18 kB/s overall throughput), while TCP was about 0.75/0.25 kB/s after the same time. In the starting phase though, TCP throughput was approximately 1.5/1 kB/s. As the server popularity was increasing, the UDP throughput was increasing massively and the TCP throughput was decreasing significantly thus, suppressing it to the aforementioned rates.

Connection Statistics. We observed about 100 (eMule broadband), 85 (eMule ADSL) and 150 (server) connection requests per minute. The share of connections actually used for data exchange was 77%, 74% and 72%. The number of simultaneous connections was 30 to 50 for eMule/broadband, 30 to 45 for eMule/ADSL and approximately 700 for the server (gathered by TCP trace file analysis) (see Figure 5 (a)).

For getting the average bandwidth use per connection, we looked at all connections carrying more than 0.5 MB incoming payload. Of those the great majority (several hundred) utilized roughly two to four kB/s and some of them a higher bandwidth (about 40) ranging from 5 to 10 kB/s. About ten connections utilized bandwidth rates up to 55 KB/sec. Those values are connection independent.

Our measurements show that an average of roughly four MBytes of data was transferred per (TCP) connection. The maximum size transferred we encountered was 150 MBytes. The average TCP connection time was 30 minutes while the average idle time 875 seconds (for ADSL) and 2500 seconds (for broadband).

User Statistics. We concentrated on getting information about the amount of files the users share in terms of size (see Figure 3 a) and in terms of file numbers (see Figure 3 b), as well as what they search most (indicated by search terms and identified files, see Figure 4). Our research showed that the average eDonkey user shares 57.8 (max. 470) files with an average size of 217 MB (max 1.2 TByte).

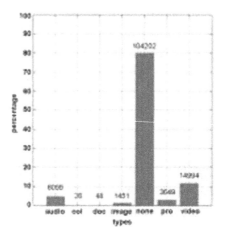

Fig. 4. Searched file types

Most searched-for keywords were media-related words like "MP3", "AVI" and "DVD" and a very high share of clearly recognizable words from current blockbuster movie titles.

Because all files are identified by their unique hash values we were able to identify the most wanted files by analyzing *QUERY SOURCES* messages. The corresponding filenames were extracted from the *PUBLISH FILES* messages. This showed that the vast majority of the identified files were movies just played in the cinemas at the time of the experiments.

Looking at these results we can state that eDonkey is mainly a movie distribution network.

Geographical Analysis and Network Size. The IP Addresses of all the clients connected to the broadband test client were reverse resolved to lookup their top-level domains for a rough geographical overview. Table 1 shows the results.

Table 1. Clients by region (Top 10)

Region	Number of addresses	Percentage(%)
.de	25,559	66.21%
.net	3,939	10.20
.com	2,038	5.28
.fr	2,491	6.45
.at	367	0.95
.br	365	0.95
.ch	562	1.46
.es	972	2.52
.il	470	1.22
.it	455	1.18

The .de domain dominates with 66.21%, followed by the "dot-net"-Domains (10%), then .fr (6%) and .at (1%). There is a tend towards higher interconnectivity among clients from a certain region, because they exchange movies in their spoken language. This is also an additional indication why the eDonkey network is more popular in Germany than in other countries. The latter is also supported by the study in [San03].

To estimate the network size we monitored the number of servers in a serverlist provided by "ocbmaurice" [Ocb04]. This showed that the average size shrunk down from roughly 220 servers in beginning of 2002, over 100 servers in 2003 down to 47 servers in 2004 (see Figure 5 (b)).

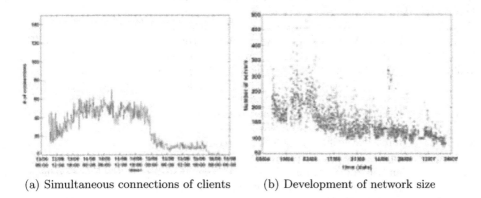

(a) Simultaneous connections of clients   (b) Development of network size

Fig. 5. Network statistics

This indicates that the eDonkey network as a whole is shrinking. One reason could be the release of the serverless eDonkey network called Overnet. Moreover, since the end of 2002 some people operating an eDonkey server faced accusations by authorities, since the exchanged material was copyrighted[4].

5   Conclusions

In this chapter, we presented results from two measurement experiments in the eDonkey network, which is the most successful peer-to-peer network in Germany. A protocol analysis shows that eDonkey supports parallel downloads by identifying files with hashes instead of file names and separates the full text search for files from the search for sources for actual downloads. These features are very useful for using eDonkey for the distribution of large content files like video files. In fact, our measurements show that the eDonkey network is primarily used for distributing movies. The ten most frequent downloads in our experiments were all current movie blockbusters. With respect to the generated network traffic,

---

[4] For example the operator of the Danish site http://www.siffan.dk

most traffic is caused by long-lived TCP connections and therefore very different
from the web traffic, which is mostly short-lived TCP traffic and was dominating
the Internet traffic only a few years ago.

References

BitTor.   BitTorrent Homepage. http://bittorrent.com/
CSWH00.   Ian Clarke, Oskar Sandberg, Brandon Wiley and Theodore W. Hong.
             Freenet: A Distributed Anonymous Information Storage and Retrieval Sys-
             tem. ICSI Workshop on Design Issues in Anonymity and Unobservability,
             2000, Berkeley, CA, USA
DirCon.   DirectConnect Website. http://www.neo-modus.com/
DirCon++.   DirectConnect++ Website. http://dcplusplus.sourceforge.net/
FTrack.   FastTrack Website. http://www.fasttrack.nu
Gnut.   Gnutella Website. http://www.gnutella.com
Gnut2.   Gnutella 2 Website. http://www.gnutella2.com
Wil02.   Bryce Wilcox-O'Hearn. *Experiences Deploying a Large-Scale Emergent*
             Network. Proceedings of the 1st International Workshop on Peer-to-Peer
             Systems (IPTPS02), March 2002
Mnet.   MNET Website. http://mnet.sourceforge.net/
Skype.   Skype Website. http://www.skype.com/
Mercora.   Mercora Website http://www.mercora.com/
Napster.   Napster Website http://www.napster.com/
San03.   Sandvine Incorporated. *Regional Characteristics of P2P - File Sharing as*
             a Multi-Application, Multinational Phenomenon. White Paper, 2003.
eDonkey.   eDonkey2000 Original Client Homepage. http://www.edonkey2000.com.
eMule.   eMule Project Homepage. http://www.emule-project.net.
mlDonkey.   mlDonkey Homepage. http://savannah.nongnu.org/projects/mldonkey/.
KaZaa.   Sharman Networks. *The KaZaa application for the FastTrack network.*
             Official Homepage. http://www.kazaa.com.
Kli02.   Alexey Klimkin. *pDonkey, an eDonkey Protocol Library.*
             http://pdonkey.sourceforge.net.
Lug04.   "Lugdunum". *Building an Efficient eDonkey Server on Linux/FreeBSD/*
             Win32.
             http://lugdunum2k.free.fr/kiten.html 2004.
Lus03.   Thomas Lussnig. *cDonkey, an Open-Source eDonkey Server with Overnet*
             and eMule Extensions. http://cdonkey.suche.org. 2003.
Mul02.   Tim-Philip Muller. *eDonkey2000 tools.* http://ed2k-tools.sourceforge.net.
Ocb04.   "Ocbmaurice". *eDonkey2000 Server-lists and Statistics.*
             http://ocbmaurice.dyndns.org 2004.
HB02.   Oliver Heckmann, Axel Bock. *The eDonkey2000 protocol.* KOM technical
             report.
             http://www.kom.e-technik.tu-darmstadt.de/publications/abstracts/
             HB02-1.html
ct04.   c't - Magazin für computer technik. *FAQ Section Entry - "Nervige Port*
             Scans" ("Annoying Port Scans"). Heise Verlag.
             http://www.heise.de/ct/faq/qna/nervige-port-scans.shtml

Secure Production of Digital Media

Martin Steinebach[1] and Jana Dittmann[2]

[1] Fraunhofer IPSI, Dolivostrasse 15, 64293 Darmstadt, Germany
69042 Heidelberg, Germany
martin.steinebach@ipsi.fraunhofer.de
[2] Otto-von-Guericke-University Magdeburg, Germany
Jana.Dittmann@iti.cs.uni-magdeburg.de

Abstract. Today more and more media data is produced completely in the digital domain without the need of analogue input. This brings an increase of flexibility and efficiency in media handling, as distributed access, duplication and modification are possible without the need to move or touch physical data carriers. But this also reduces the security of the process: Without physical originals to refer to, changes in the material can remain unnoticed, at the end making the manipulated data the new original. Theft and illegal copies in the digital domain can happen without notice and loss of quality. We therefore see the need of setting up secure media production environments, where access control, integrity and copyright protection as well as traceability of individual copies are enabled. Addressing this need, we design a framework for media production environments, where mechanisms like encryption, digital signatures and digital watermarking help to enable a flexible yet secure handling and processing of the content.

1   Motivation

The media industry today suffers from a massive decrease of e.g. audio CD sales or movie theatre visitors. One reason for this decrease is claimed to be the early availability of illegal copies in the Internet. These copies are often found in file sharing networks before they are available to the legal customer. In some cases, draft versions of movies or albums enter these networks months before their official release date.

Therefore it is obvious that a strict access control must not start at the delivery of the media products to the public or to distributors. With the occurrence of copies, which can only be taken directly from the production stage, the protection of this stage is needed to be able to prevent further theft of pre-release material.

This is only one example of multimedia security challenges coming with modern digital media production. The carrier medium, which was needed in the analogue production process, is transformed into an exchangeable memory device where a digital representation of the media product is stored on. Two examples: A digital camera records on a chip, which later transfers the stored data to a computer. Here it is printed or stored on e.g. a CD. The original data on the chip is erased. The same is the case with a hard disk recorder in a musical production. After the recording session the audio material is transferred to cheaper storage devices.

With respect to the security of the produced media data, this has several impacts:

M. Hemmje et al. (Eds.): E.J. Neuhold Festschrift, LNCS 3379, pp. 79–86, 2005.

- There is no actual original anymore. With the habit of erasing the initial recording stored on expensive memory after copying it to cheaper storage space, what is left is an environment where only copies exist. The best example of our daily life is the advance of digital cameras ending the need of film negatives. But without an original, it will obviously become hard to prove the originality and integrity of recorded material.
- There is no reduction of quality by the copy process. In analogue production environments, only one master copy of maximal quality could exist. Each subsequent copy's quality was reduced by a certain degree. When copying a digital original, two copies of the original quality are the result. This makes it easy to steal produced media without notice as nothing is missing after the theft, only a second original exists. On the other hand, when there is no provable original and the copy process does not reduce two distinguishable versions of a media, it is hard to decide which the true original is when one copy is modified.

In the further sections we show how these challenges can be solved by applying existing security mechanisms especially developed for multimedia applications. In section we give an overview on various security mechanisms, mainly based on cryptography and data hiding. Object recognition and perceptual hashes are also discussed as they are commonly used in integrity protection or verification. Section 3 describes a typical media production scenario and the different roles and objects in it. We identify security challenges which can be derived from the scenario and show how the mechanisms from section 2 address these challenges. In section 4 we briefly summarize and conclude our work.

2   Available Security Mechanisms

Various mechanisms for protecting multimedia data exist, coming from the wide domain of cryptology. These mechanisms can be divided into cryptography and data hiding.

2.1   Cryptography

The best-known example of cryptography is the encryption of data to ensure confidentiality. Encryption can be done with various algorithms, which differ in complexity, key length and security. There are symmetric and asymmetric approaches, as well as hybrid protocols applying the advantages of both to achieve further security aspects like authenticity and integrity. For example cryptographic hash functions can produce a collision-free one-way identification code of fixed length from media data of arbitrary length for integrity validation. By combining encryption and hashing we can built comprehensive security protocols, an important example is the use of asymmetric encryption and hash functions in digital or electronic signatures [Sch1996], [B1999].

   There are also encryption methods especially dedicated to multimedia to improve the efficiency. Partial encryption was introduced to identify vital portions of the semantic content of media data and only encrypts this comparatively small part of the data, see for example [DiSt97] or [SZ2004]. Furthermore Robust hash functions are designed similarly to traditional hash functions but use a derived feature of the multimedia content as input. Thereby they do not validate the integrity of the binary representation of the medium, but the content-based representation of it.

2.2   Data Hiding

Data hiding enables concealing information and is used for example in the field of of steganography and digital watermarking.

Steganography offers mechanisms to undetectably hide information into media data, also called cover. Usually there is no correspondence between embedded information and the cover it is written into. Steganography therefore does not protect the cover, but aims at the confidential delivery of the embedded content.

Digital watermarking invisibly embeds information into a cover. This information refers to the cover, like e.g. a copyright notice. It is often seen as a means of copy protection or an alternative to digital rights management. But the function of the watermark only depends on the nature of embedded information. There are watermarking-based approaches for multimedia content integrity protection called fragile, semi-fragile or content-fragile watermarking While the first two approaches apply an optimized parameter set to show integrity violations of the marked content, the last one uses a semantic content description as the embedded information.

2.3   Additional Tools

Other mechanisms can be used as supplements when protecting multimedia data known as passive fingerprinting or perceptual hashing for content authentication, object recognition or time stamping.

In the field passive fingerprinting there is no direct modification or transformation of the content to add or embed security features. The ideas here is to generate a fingerprint or also called perceptual hash from the original source and store this unique and content describing fingerprint in a database, see for example in [KHO01]. Based on the stored identification features all monitored content is now processed in the same manner und the actual retrieved perceptual hash can be compared with the fingerprint database. Applications are related to content monitoring or royalty tracking for Digital Rights Management and commercial verification, but also to added-value services like intelligent and content aware p2p networks or mobile music recognition, enhanced radio, music management. Furthermore the technology can be used for authentication and tamper detection by embedding fingerprints in watermark as alternative to fragile watermarks. Main challenges derived from [KHO01] are:

a)   how to define of perceptual equality by using discrimination and ambiguity thresholds,

b)   how to quantify and achieve good error rates for False Rejection Rates (FRR) and False Acceptance Rates (FAR),

c)   how to scale the robustness of the hash for example in respect to time stretching and shrinking , pitch invariant scaling, different code like GSM codec, background noise or synchronization,

d) Which granularity is useful, like the appropriate time interval for the hash, the number of successive frames or the decision of using the full song or video,

e) Which complexity is appropriate for each application during fingerprint extraction, fingerprint comparison (verification) and which fingerprint size would be the best,

f) Which scalability can be achieved in respect to complexity to handle of large fingerprint database, obtaining songs and meta-data for fingerprint generation, request rate and versatility (same database for different applications)

Very little known are security issues like the ability to fool the fingerprinting extraction or to attack the robustness of the hash generation during verification.

Object recognition can also help on the one hand to identify and describe content and on the other hand it can be used in combination with forensic techniques for integrity verification. Approaches in the first area can be found for example in publications of [Dit01] where object recognition is based on edge maps and additionally used in combination with watermarking by using object features as watermark itself.

To ensure data authenticity very often time stamps are used in combination with other security techniques. The main issue here is to determine the time of creation, capturing, modification, transmission or receipt of material. Approaches here can be found for example in [DDSV01]. The general problem is to produce a trustworthy, synchronized and source independent time.

3   Strategies

The protection of digital media requires more than the application of security mechanisms. Only a complete scalable strategy for the media production process can ensure the security of the media. Such a strategy can be of surprising complexity. To show this, we make the following assumptions:

- The creation of the media data takes place on a computer, like animation software or a virtual music studio, or a digital device, like a digital camera. We call the digitally produced media "work". A work consists of "elements", like sounds, music, speech or image and video sequences.
- The editing of the work takes place in an environment where different persons need to have access to the medium. We call the persons who have access to the work "players".
- The players remotely access the work or elements, maybe even worldwide like in movie native language dubbing. We call the distributed access points "nodes" and the distribution system "web". Players at nodes can access the work or elements via the web. Nodes are usually computers.
- The different production stages require specialized software not part of the web, like sound editors or video cutting systems. We call the specialized software "tools". Players edit the work or elements with tools.

A promising security strategy is to limit the number of players and nodes. As soon as a work or an element of it is created, it is moved into a central secure storage with access to the web. The players can only access the work or its elements via their nodes after a successful strong authentication using secure connections. The tools are certified to be secure and run on trustworthy computers. As soon as a player has edited the work or its elements, he moves the result to the central storage and deletes all copies from his local node.

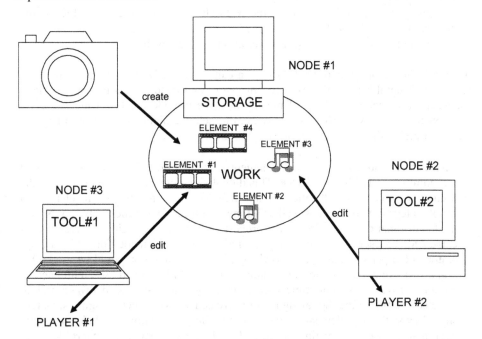

Fig. 1. Players access the media storage via their nodes and edit elements of the work with their tools

Obliviously practice looks different: the access rules are more fuzzy and the environment more complex. Copies of the work are not only accessible by players, but also by their colleagues or service personal. Each player prefers his individual set of tools and nodes feature different operating systems, causing the overall system to be vulnerable to a huge number of attacks. After editing the work, players keep copies on their computers or make backups on media like CD or DVD which a stored in insecure places.

In addition to these risks, players will tend to involve third parties in the process. They may ask co-workers to assist them in editing the work or some elements. They also may take the work to other places to show the work on computers, DVD players or home stereo systems for a third party opinion.

All this leads to a situation where the work could easily accessed by pirates and attackers, could be modified or stolen. Theft is especially hard to trace in this case, as it will be unclear how the work got in the hands of pirates. At least the following possibilities exist:

- The player has given away the work to a pirate directly.
- The player has given the work to a third party, which passed it to a pirate indirectly.

- Trojan software on the node of the player made the copy available to the pirate.
- The tools of the player feature a backdoor the pirate can use.
- The players' authentication code was captured and used by a pirate to access the storage of the work via the web.
- The pirate get hold of a backup of the work stored somewhere accessible via the internet or the real world.
- The pirate found a way to capture material send via the web.

A digital rights management (DRM) system can help to solve some but not all problems. Only a combination of most mechanisms for multimedia security may be able to enable a more secure handling of media data. We provide the following examples how existing security mechanisms may help to achieve higher security in a production, post-processing and distribution environment.

- **Element creation:** As soon as an element is created on a digital device, a digital signature is created by the device. This digital signature can only generated by the used device to ensure authenticity and it includes a hash function of the element to enable integrity validation as well as a time stamp for data authenticity too. Now a trusted original exists as long as the process of creating the digital signature is not corrupted. To trace the person who captured the material, an additional binding operator to the persons based on knowledge, being or possesion could be used. One major challenge may be the time stamp, which could be solved by satellite access modules providing a secure time signal. The device can also embed a watermark in the element before the digital signature is created showing such a digital signature should exist for this element. Embedding the time of creation will help to disable later attacks based on creating a second digital signature. By using invertible or reversible watermarking, the captured material could also be reduced in his original quality to provide access protection to the original too.
- **Element transportation to secure storage:** The element together with the digital signature now needs to be transported securely (confidential) to the storage device. Known asymmetric or session key protocols can help to ensure that only one or a group of possible destination of the element exists. It is encrypted with the public key of the storage system. Only after placing the element in the storage device, it will become accessible, as only here the fitting private key is present.
- **Element exchange:** When a player wants to access an element via the web, he or she must identify the tool he or she plans to use to edit the element. The central storage then encrypts the element with the public key of the tool and sends it to the node of the player. A successful attack on the node will still not help to access the element as it is encrypted. Only the tool is able to load the element, decrypt, process it and then encrypt it again with the public key of the central storage.
- **Element modification:** It would be possible to limit the possible edit steps and applied filters of the tool by sending a certificate together with the element identifying the allowed procedures. An example could be not to allow the removal and addition of objects to an image, while blurring, color modifications or luminance changes may be allowed. A more decent approach would be to calculate a robust hash of the original element when the tool accesses it. After each edit step, the current robust hash is calculated and compare to the original. When both differ too

much, either a warning for the player can be prompted or the edition is disallowed. This could disable changes of the original content which may be of interest for news agencies or similar organizations.

- **Element copies to third parties**: In some cases it may be necessary to leave the secured web and provide copies accessible by insecure devices. The tools can feature an export mechanism where the element is not encrypted but saved in an open file format, for example an MPEG system stream. The protection of the element is now in the hand of the player. Therefore a watermark with the players ID should be embedded by the tool during the export for further identification. When a copy of the element is stolen by a pirate and is distributed, the associated player can be made responsible.

These are only a few selected examples, but it obvious that, when designing a distributed media production system, security can be included in many ways. The earlier the security mechanisms are included, the easier it will be to provide a dependable protection against attackers. When security becomes a transparent yet omnipresent part of media production and not an additional layer, users will accept and apply the features. Compared to a DRM system where rights management usually means hindrances and restrictions, an embedded security system should enable easy and secure creation, handling and editing of multimedia data.

The Open Mobile Alliance is an actual example for integrated security features in the field of DRM. The OMA "Digital Rights Management" (DRM) is designed to enable the distribution and consumption of digital content in a controlled manner. The approach of OMA is to distribute and consume content on authenticated devices per the usage rights expressed by the content owners. OMA DRM work addresses the various technical aspects of this system by providing appropriate specifications for content formats, protocols, and a rights expression language, see for example OMA-ERELD-DRM-V2 on URL:http://www.openmobilealliance.org/.

4   Summary and Conclusion

Security must be all-embracing to ensure the protection of media data from production until consumption. Only then leakage and manipulation can be prevented. The integration of security mechanisms in tools for creation, transportation and post-processing are therefore necessary, as this is the only way to enable secure handling of digital media without gaps and frustrating overhead for the user.

We provide an overview of existing mechanism which can help to protect digital media as well as its transportation. Applying these we also show how a media production scenario can look like if security is integrated in its design. This includes the exchange of encrypted multimedia files as well as export functions to insecure environments protected by digital watermarking.

The threat of piracy and content-changing manipulations increases steadily for the producers of multimedia material. We are therefore confident that the future will bring media production environments featuring at least DRM mechanisms to protect the created values.

References

[B1999]   Buchmann; Einführung in die Kryptographie, Springer, Berlin, ISBN 3-540-66059-3, 1999

[DDSV01]   Dittmann, Jana; Dappa, Artur; Steinebach, Martin; Vielhauer, Claus: Eine Sicherheitsarchitektur auf Basis digitaler Wasserzeichen und kryptographischer Ansätze, In: Verlässliche IT-Systeme 2001, Sicherheit in komplexen IT-Infrastrukturen, Vieweg & Sohn Verlagsgesellschaft mbH, Braunschweig/Wiesbaden, pp. 209-224, ISBN 3-528-05782-3, 2001

[DiSt97]   Dittmann, Jana; Steinmetz, Arnd: *A Technical Approach to the Transparent Encryption of MPEG-2 Video*, in Katsikas, Sokratis (Ed.), Communications and Multimedia Security, Vol.3, pp. 215-226, London, Weinheim, New York: Chapman & Hall, 1997

[Dit01]   Dittmann, Jana: Content-fragile Watermarking for Image Authentication, In: Security and Watermarking of Multimedia Contents III, Ping Wah Wong, Edward J. Delp III, Editors, Proceedings of SPIE Vol. 4314, pp. 175-184, ISBN 0-8194-3992-4, 2001

[KHO01]   Kalker, T.; Haitsma, J.; Oostveen, J.: Issues with digital watermarking and perceptual hashing; Proceeding SPIE Vol. 4518, p. 189-197, Multimedia Systems and Applications IV, 2001

[Sch1996] Schneier; Angewandte Kryptographie: Protokolle, Algorithmen und Sourcecode in C, Addison-Wesley, Bonn, ISBN 3-89319-854-7, 1996

[SZ2004]   Steinebach, Zmudzinski; Partielle Verschlüsselung von MPEG Audio, D•A•CH Security 2004, Syssec - IT Security & IT Management, Patrick Horster (Hrsg.), ISBN 3-00-013137-X, pp 470-484, 2004

Data Communication Between the German NBC Reconnaissance Vehicle and Its Control Center Unit

Andreas Meissner and Wolfgang Schönfeld

Fraunhofer IPSI
Dolivostrasse 15, 64293 Darmstadt, Germany
{Andreas.Meissner, Wolfgang.Schoenfeld}@ipsi.fraunhofer.de

Abstract. In Germany, the public safety system is largely organized by the German Federal States, which operate, among other equipment, a fleet of Nuclear, Biological and Chemical Reconnaissance Vehicles (NBC RVs) to take measurements in contaminated areas. Currently, NBC RV staff verbally report measured data to a Control Center Unit (CCU) over the assigned Public Safety Organization (PSO) analog voice radio channel. This procedure has several disadvantages. The channel is not secure and its capacity is wasted, which places a limit on the achievable throughput and thus on the number of NBC RVs that can be operational simultaneously. Also, while data is being reported, other PSO members are blocked from sending, and operating personnel is distracted from other work. To overcome these problems, we propose a heterogeneous and flexible communication platform that complies with reliability and coverage requirements for PSO. More specifically, our proposed system is designed to replace current ways of communicating between NBC RVs and the CCU. A drastically higher amount of data can then be transmitted to the CCU, and it can be processed in a much more effective manner in the CCU as well as in cooperating PSO units. Ultimately, this will improve NBC RV missions and consequently shorten PSO response time when dealing with NBC disasters.

1   Introduction

The German Federal Government has, in recent years, designed, procured and deployed a considerable number of advanced Nuclear, Biological and Chemical Reconnaissance Vehicles (NBC RV) [1] that allow fire departments to detect and report various kinds of nuclear and chemical threats. The sensor data are communicated to a Control Center Unit (CCU) where they are recorded and analyzed by experts. Currently, analog voice radio transmission is used to report readings to the CCU. Clearly, this is time consuming and error-prone. Moreover, it is a waste of scarce radio frequency resources since one simple voice message occupies the radio channel for several seconds. Another drawback is that the channel is also blocked for other (possibly mission critical) messages, and encryption is hard to achieve.

Based on a recent study Fraunhofer IPSI conducted on behalf of the German Center for Civil Defense, now known as BBK, this paper presents new ways for data communication and data exchange, intended to replace the traditional way of having personnel read sensor data from the vehicle computer display and transmit them by

M. Hemmje et al. (Eds.): E.J. Neuhold Festschrift, LNCS 3379, pp. 87–95, 2005.

voice radio. In order to ensure interoperability of the NBC RVs in case of large-scale cross-border disaster response operations involving several units, the solution is designed to be extensible for adoption by all German Federal States. Traditionally, they have come up with individual solutions in the area of emergency management due to their constitutional responsibilities.

In the remainder of the paper, we first summarize in Section 2 what kind of operations NBC RVs are deployed in, and which limitations the current equipment has. Next, in Section 3 we propose new communication strategies and a system architecture for more effective NBC RV operations, addressing in particular how the NBC RV and the CCU interoperate. Finally, in Section 4 we conclude our findings and give an outlook.

Fig. 1. Nuclear, Biological and Chemical Reconnaissance Vehicle (NBC RV)

2 Reconnaissance Vehicle Operations

The NBC RV (Figure 1) is a high-tech vehicle used for measuring, detecting and reporting radioactive and chemical substances as well as for recognizing and reporting biological contamination, e.g. following an accident. Other missions include the search for scattered radioactive fragments and the marking and monitoring of contaminated areas using measuring techniques, ground, water and air sampling as well as the acquisition and reporting of weather data.

2.1 On-board Equipment

For emergency response operations, NBC RV staff make use of some or all of the vehicle's on-board equipment: Besides the instrumentation container which accommodates the radiological and chemical sensors, the NBC RV contains a PSO analog radio set, a set for solid, liquid or gas sampling, a meteorological measurement set, a location system, a marking set, respiratory protective equipment as well as a gas-tight and semi-permeable NBC protection system.

The radiological and chemical sensors are computer assisted. The system is capable of archiving sensor data, representing them graphically, in tabular form or visualizing and printing them on a geographic map. Moreover, the instrumentation container is fitted with a location tracking system for positioning purposes. The measured values are always linked with data from the location system. Assisted by standard GPS satellite navigation and supported by a differential GPS system, a location error of less than 5m is obtained. In addition, the location system is equipped with a dead-reckoning navigation component (self-sufficient navigation), which is only used when no GPS information is available. This may be due to nearby high buildings, tunnel passages, satellite breakdowns etc. To protect the operating personnel, the system generates visual and audible alarms whenever measured values exceed adjustable thresholds.

2.2   Current Practice

Various sensors onboard the NBC RV generate a large amount of data. For example, the radiological device typically generates one readout per second. These values are collected, visualized, and stored by the NBC RV software. The staff of the NBC vehicles analyze the measured values only for self-protection purposes to avoid stays in contaminated areas. Since it is the responsibility of the staff at the CCU to evaluate the overall situation and make judgments, they need to receive a continuous stream of sensor data from all deployed NBC RVs under their guidance. The current practice is, as stated above, to read this information from a computer display in the vehicle and to transmit it via the onboard PSO analog voice radio system to the CCU. Obviously, this stream has to be set up, controlled and terminated by verbal orders also transmitted via voice radio communication.

2.3   Major Problems

Upstream data transmission capacity is clearly the bottleneck due to the usage of analog voice radio. A large amount of data is collected during the measuring process. As their transmission according to a „human dialogue protocol" is a time-consuming task and since the channel is blocked for other PSO usage during a radio message exchange, only few selected measured values are transmitted to the CCU.

The drawbacks of the current solution were well recognized by practitioners. Partial solutions were developed in some German Federal States. But problems still persist for middle- to large-scale operations and, in particular, inter-state cooperation. There is no established standard for work processes and communication protocols.

Existing alternative communication technologies like GSM or GPRS are either not reliable enough or have too bad a coverage and availability for PSO purposes, if used in a stand-alone manner. TETRA or other digital PSO communication systems can be expected to be partly suitable, but such technology is still to be deployed in Germany, and due to cost reasons, it is not even sure that 100% coverage will be attainable.

3   Towards a New NBC Vehicle ICT System

To overcome these problems, we propose to use existing communication infrastructures by integrating the different technologies into one platform and using them flexibly and interchangeably according to prevailing radio conditions. In this way, the various communication alternatives can complement each other, and an acceptable level of reliability and coverage can be guaranteed. We evaluate in which way our proposed solution could improve the organization and coordination (i.e. the workflow) of NBC RV operations. The subsequent sections address these issues in more detail.

First, none of the existing data communication technologies fulfills all of the requirements that we determined in close contact with practitioners. The challenge is thus to integrate various alternatives in a „fallback" arrangement, so that at least a low-level, nevertheless reliable communication between the NBC RVs and the CCU is enabled. The solution should complement the currently used analog voice radio transmissions, have high reliability and coverage, and be inexpensive.

Second, only a small subset of measured values is (currently) transmitted to the CCU. To provide a better overview about potentially critical situations to the staff at the CCU, as much sensor data as possible should be transmitted to the CCU, while critical data must obtain priority if the communication channel suddenly deteriorates.

Third, control communication is also done via voice radio, so it suffers from the same inefficiencies as data communication. Workflow communication specifies e.g., the start, eventual modifications, and the termination of operations. There is no suitable operation control model defined that specifies message exchange between NBC RVs and CCU for small-, medium-, and large-sized operations. Such a model must also be adaptable to varying communication channel restrictions (e.g., bandwidth, latency, etc.).

3.1   Communication Infrastructure Requirements and Alternatives

There are several requirements placed on the communication infrastructure. The CCU should receive data from the NBC RV in near real time, or at the latest 5 seconds after taking the measurement. Therefore, it is interesting to compare the *latency* and *connection setup time* for each communication technology. Regarding the *data rate*, the data structure used for the measurement data is relatively compact, so that no more than 4 kbit/s is needed (on average). Additionally, the workflow messages will require some small capacity, bringing the total data rate up to 6 kbit/s.

Operations over long distances (here, „*roaming*") are currently problematic, since each Federal State follows its own PSO frequency allotment plan. Consequently, a moving sender must bring and consult a radio frequency table in order to switch to the correct PSO frequency when entering a new county area. At that point, direct communication with the HQ „at home" is no longer possible over the PSO radio channel. To solve this problem, any alternative communication technology should support seamless roaming, i.e. operations over Federal State borders should be possible without user action. More generally, long-distance operations should be supported by very good outdoor *coverage*, if possible even within tunnels etc.

An at least rudimentary level of *encryption* is important to ensure confidentiality of sensitive PSO data. TETRA-25, TETRAPOL, GSM-BOS seem promising for PSO purposes, but in this context they are only *operational* in very limited testing areas in Germany (we have refrained from assessing TETRAPOL in this work). Similarly, UMTS has only recently been launched and it will take some time before it is fully operational. One of the most important questions in this scenario is whether the communication technology is *reliable* or not. Experiences from the 2002 flooding in eastern Germany, where GSM base stations were rendered inoperable, show that a land-based communication system for PSO purposes must have a support organization that can bring failing equipment back online quickly. Finally, it is interesting to know if the technology has good *prospects* or not, since the investment decision is influenced by the expected lifetime of the technology.

In order to comply with the requirements mentioned above, we have evaluated existing and forthcoming wireless WAN (Wide Area Network) alternatives for communication between NBC RVs and CCUs. We focused on the technologies GSM (Global System for Mobile Communications), GPRS (General Packet Radio Service), TETRA (Terrestrial Trunked Radio, more specifically: ETSI TETRA-25), GSM-BOS (GSM adapted for PSO requirements, as proposed by Vodafone), data communication over the PSO 4m radio band currently used (mainly) for voice communication, LEO (Low Earth Orbit) and GEO (Geostationary Earth Orbit) satellite systems, and UMTS (Universal Mobile Telecommunications System) (see Table 1).

Table 1. Evaluation of communication technologies (where applicable, estimated maximum values are given)

	GSM	GPRS	TETRA	GSM-BOS	4m-Band	LEO	GEO	UMTS
Latency (s)	1	Netw. dep.	N/A	Netw. dep.	0	1	1	Netw. dep.
Conn. setup time	5 s	2 s	2 s	2 s	0 s	Min-utes	Min-utes	2 s
Data rate (kbit/s)	9,6	111	28,8	111	1,2	10	64	2000
Roaming	EU	EU	DE	DE	No	Glob	Glob	EU
Coverage	Fair	Fair	Good	Good	Good	Good	Good	Bad
Encryption	Yes	Yes	Yes	Yes	No	Yes	Yes	Yes
Operational	Yes	Yes	N/A	N/A	Yes	Yes	Yes	Yes
Reliability	No	No	Yes	Yes	Yes	Yes	No	No
Prospect	Good	Good	N/A	N/A	Bad	Good	Good	Good

TETRA [3] or GSM-BOS [4] are interesting for general PSO needs, since these technologies have additional features like group calling and direct (walkie-talkie type) connectivity. But, in this scenario we are only interested in their data transferring qualities. Besides, it is still to be decided if, when, and to which extent a new PSO digital technology is to be deployed in Germany. Therefore, in some cases no precise information was available. The PSO analog radio channel on the 4m band is used mainly for voice communication, but experimental modems exist that can achieve a data rate of 1,2 kbit/s over the channel.

The remaining alternatives do unfortunately not meet the reliability and coverage requirements. High elevation angle systems like Low Earth Orbit (LEO) satellite systems (e.g., Iridium) have very good outdoor coverage and are not affected by local disasters, but have poor indoor (e.g., tunnels) coverage. LEO satellite signals can be picked up with small omni-directional antennas, but the data rate is very limited. Geostationary Earth Orbit (GEO) satellite systems like Inmarsat, offer ISDN-type data rates, but bigger antennas must be used, since the distance to the satellite is much longer. Also, the antenna must be precisely aimed at the satellite at all times, which makes it impractical for this scenario, since NBC RVs must be able to stay online even while on the move. Recently, Inmarsat antennas that address this problem have appeared on the market (see e.g., [5]), but they are rather expensive, and the need for a clear line-of-sight to the satellite positioned only a few degrees above the horizon renders operation in cities or mountainous areas difficult. Promising research indicates that a solution for vehicular satellite-based mobile applications can be expected in the near future, where the antenna not only automatically adjusts for best signal reception, but is also able to utilize both LEO and GEO satellite systems [2].

Commercial systems like GSM/GPRS/UMTS position their infrastructure according to cost-benefit calculations and not PSO considerations, i.e. good coverage in all areas cannot be guaranteed. However, some major tunnels do have GSM and GPRS coverage. The technical support organization around PSO-based technologies is also expected to be much better, so that for example mobile base stations are deployed on-site within short time when needed for an operation. This translates into higher reliability for the system, since there is a lower probability of communication failure.

For a survey of technologies and initiatives for disaster response communication in areas with underdeveloped or non-existing infrastructure, we refer to [7], where, in particular, ad-hoc technology is discussed. Rapidly deployable networks, which might be considered for NBC RV operations in a very limited geographical area, are investigated in [8].

3.2   System Architecture and Message Exchange

As mentioned, we propose to use multiple communication options (see Figure 2) in a fallback solution setup. When one option is unavailable, the system can switch to another infrastructure, as proposed in [9] where vertical handoffs are discussed. The last resort is to send a messenger with an appropriate storage device. As examples, PSO radio data communication, GPRS and satellite communication are incorporated in the figure. In the end, it is up to the system designer and the customer to decide which and how many fallback technologies should be used. Each option adds coverage and reliability but increases the costs.

The system needs to monitor and control the transmission so that it fits the underlying communication technology that is being used. It adapts the data stream generated from the onboard sensors to the current communication conditions. For example, if only PSO 4m band data communication is available, the data rate is too low to send all data. In this case, only the most essential data is sent to the CCU, according to a preset filter. Feedback from the CCU (i.e. acknowledgements) will help to manage the system. Moreover, the inherent unreliability of radio links will cause frequent data traffic jams. It is an important question for how long such jammed data have to be kept by the system. This shows that simple Internet transport protocols such as TCP will not suffice. Instead, proprietary transport protocols have to be supported for greater flexibility. In any case, all generated data is stored in the NBC RV even if it is not sent to the CCU during an operation. In this way, the data can be used for later simulations and personnel training. For the same reasons, operation events are logged in the NBC RV and in the CCU.

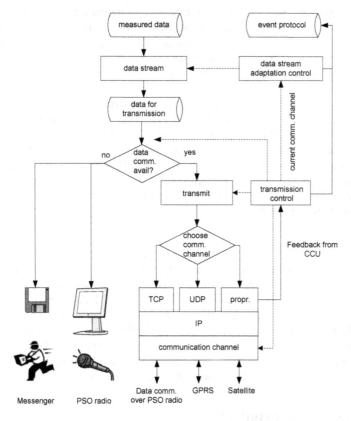

Fig. 2. Proposed Communication Architecture

Obvious advantages of our proposed architecture are increased reliability and coverage while using existing infrastructure. Also, the system is flexible both during operation and with regard to communication technology development. If, for example, a PSO TETRA system were deployed in Germany, it would not be difficult to integrate it in the system described above. The drawbacks are increased system complexity and cost.

We do not discuss the format of the communicated data here and refer to [10] for more details on data modeling alternatives, including XML representation for sensor data. Control messages to be exchanged between the NBC RV and the CCU include orders to the NBC TV to

- start operations, i.e. to examine potentially contaminated areas. This also includes modifications of the ongoing operations and their termination.
- start, modify or stop transmission of sensor data from the vehicle to the CCU. By default, all measured values are transmitted.
- switch to fallback communication solutions. In such situations, the data volume is typically reduced, and only a fraction of the measured values are sent to the control center.

Appropriate formats for these control messages and robust protocols have to be developed – this was however not part of the work we carried out for BBK. Most probably, such commands will be issued in the traditional way also in the future. But even then, they will be accompanied by commands concerning the communication system. For instance, alerting additional NBC RVs will require the setup of the corresponding communication links.

The above questions on data transmission have to be seen in context with data processing in the CCU. In particular, the transmission cycle must fit both to the generation cycle at the NBC RV and the processing cycle at the CCU. In turn, the latter has to respect the physical environment conditions. If their prospective change is slow, processing speed at the CCU may be reduced. This may e.g. be the case for a chemical pollution under quiet weather conditions. On the contrary, high speed processing may be required on the occasion of a large explosion when sudden changes in the environment are expected.

3.3   Cost Considerations

Our evaluation, which we can only partially report here, shows that for now, GPRS is the most cost-effective solution, since investment costs, operational costs, and maintenance costs are all comparably low. PSO systems like TETRA are likely to incur huge investment costs, and a model for service provisioning still has to be chosen. This may add to operation expenses. Satellite technology is promising due to its robustness, but very expensive, at least if GEO systems are used. In the end, the user has to make a choice according to his preferences on which communication technologies and how many fallback levels to integrate into the system.

4   Conclusions and Outlook

In this paper, we have reviewed the issue of enabling the German NBC Reconnaissance Vehicle for data communication, in order to allow measured values to be transmitted to a Control Center Unit and to provide a means for sending operational messages to the vehicle. We have compiled recommendations for appropriate communication technology, arguing that fallback solutions must be provided in order to ensure reliability in the presence of possible network failures. There are still some uncertainties due to, in particular, the pending decision on the selection of a new country-wide digital radio system for German Public Safety Organizations, and the fact that establishing a „federal" data communication solution for the NBC vehicle stands in some contrast to the German Federal States' constitutional role of making the decisions in the field of fire department equipment and policies.

The use of mobile data communication to support emergency response field operations is still a relatively new concept for German PSOs, and so we feel that our results may have significance beyond the individual case. However, apart from network connectivity issues, a lot of work remains to be done in order to ensure proper integration of mobile nodes into established back-end PSO information systems [6]. Thus, this paper (and the study it is based on) can be seen as a building block for our contributions in the field we refer to as „e-Emergency".

Acknowledgements

We thank Diego Klappenbach and Silvia von Stackelberg for their contributions to both the *ABC/DataCom* study, including the technology survey in section 3.1 and data modeling considerations, and to a previous version of this paper [10]. Stefan Wilbert (BBK) provided valuable help with the description of NBC RV on-board equipment as well as operation tactics.

References

1. The NBC Reconnaissance Vehicle – a brief technical description, Federal Office of Administration, Center for Civil Defense, http://www.bva.bund.de/zivilschutz
2. Tiezzi, F.: „Multiband multibeam conformal antennas for vehicular mobile satellite systems", European Space Agency (ESA) project, http://www.telecom.esa.int/telecom/www/object/index.cfm?fobjectid=9249#1
3. Terrestrial Trunked Radio (TETRA): http://www.tetramou.com/
4. Vodafone GSM-BOS: http://www.vodafone.de/bos/
5. NERA World Communicator Voyager: http://www.nera.de/nwcv.en.html
6. Meissner, A.; Luckenbach, T.; Risse, T.; Kirste, T.; Kirchner, H. (2002). „Design Challenges for an Integrated Disaster Management Communication and In-formation System." The First IEEE Workshop on Disaster Recovery Networks (DIREN 2002), June 24, 2002, New York City, USA, co-located IEEE INFOCOM 2002, http://comet.columbia.edu/~aurel/workshops/diren02/IEEE_DIREN2002_Meissner_DesignChallenges.pdf
7. Panchard, J.; Hubaux, J.-P. (2003). „Mobile Communications for Emergencies and Disaster Recovery in Developing Countries", EPFL Technical Report, Lausanne, Switzerland, March 2003, http://icawww.epfl.ch/panchard/Files/ Docs/Article.pdf
8. Midkiff, S. F.; Bostian, C. W. (2002): „Rapidly-Deployable Broadband Wireless Networks for Disaster and Emergency Response", Proc. The First IEEE Workshop on Disaster Recovery Networks (DIREN 2002), June 24, 2002, New York City, USA, co-located IEEE INFOCOM 2002 http://comet.columbia.edu/~aurel/workshops/diren02/Midkiff_Bostian_DIREN02.pdf
9. Brewer, E. et al.: „A Network Architecture for Heterogeneous Mobile Computing", IEEE Personal Communications Magazine, Oct. 1998, http://citeseer.ist.psu.edu/brewer98network.html
10. Klappenbach, D.; Hollfelder, S.; Meissner, A.; Wilbert, S. (2004). "From Analog Voice Radio to ICT: Data Communication and Data Modeling for the German NBC Reconnaissance Vehicle". ISCRAM 2004: International Workshop on Information Systems for Crisis Response and Management, Brussels, May 3-4 2004; proceedings; Carle, Benny [eds.]; Van de Walle, Bartel [eds.]; ISBN 9076971080.

The Role of Digital Libraries in Moving Toward Knowledge Environments

Edward A. Fox, Marcos André Gonçalves, and Rao Shen

Virginia Tech Dept. of Computer Science, 660 McBryde Hall, Blacksburg, VA 24061 USA
{fox, mgoncalv, rshen}@vt.edu
http://www.dlib.vt.edu

Abstract. For thousands of years, libraries have allowed humanity to collect and organize data and information, and to support the discovery and communication of knowledge, across time and space. Coming together in this Internet Age, the world's societies have extended this process to span from the personal to the global, as the concepts, practices, systems, and services related to Library and Information Science unfold through digital libraries. Scientists, scholars, teachers, learners, and practitioners of all kinds benefit from the distributed and collaborative knowledge environments that are at the heart of the digital library movement. Digital libraries thus encompass the dimensions in the 5S Framework: Societies, Scenarios, Spaces, Streams, and Structures. To clarify this approach, we explain the role of meta-models, such as of a minimal digital library (DL), and of more specialized (discipline-oriented) DLs, such as archeological DLs. We illustrate how suitable knowledge environments can be more easily prepared as instances of these meta-models, resulting in usable and useful DLs, including for education, computing, and archaeology.

1 Introduction

People need information. Libraries help us satisfy this requirement, playing a key role in the Information Life Cycle [3]. Today, Digital Libraries (DLs [2, 6, 18]) provide essential cyberinfrastructure, moving us toward knowledge environments geared toward individual needs, as well as helping us address global concerns.

Figure 1 provides perspective on our work. DLs typically focus on some domain, so that interested patrons (actors) interact with a running system, built according to some architectural approach. Underlying this is a model of the "real world", which fits into a meta-model (encoded using a suitable language) tuned to the domain of interest. "5S" (Table 1) provides fundamental abstractions for this process. Streams, Structures, Spaces, Scenarios, and Societies are easy to understand, addressing key objectives of DLs. Column 2 of Table 1 highlights commonly found examples of these constructs. Then, Section 2, on 5S, helps situate the field of DLs in the world of (computer/library/information) science, considering formalisms, models, minimalist meta-models, and (semi)automatic approaches. Section 3 briefly illustrates application of our framework to representative domains. Section 4 concludes the discussion.

M. Hemmje et al. (Eds.): E.J. Neuhold Festschrift, LNCS 3379, pp. 96–106, 2005.
© Springer-Verlag Berlin Heidelberg 2005

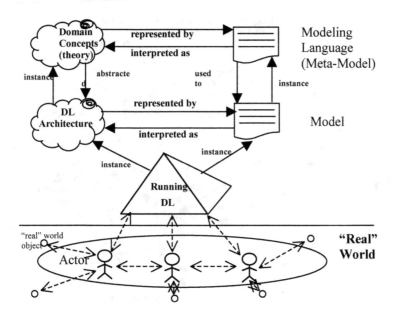

Fig. 1. Perspective underlying the 5S framework

2 5S Framework

Building upon the five constructs explained in Table 1, we have developed a formal framework for the DL field [9, 10], summarized in Figure 2. We aim to define a minimal digital library (definition 24 of [9], shown at the bottom right), representing the culmination of the network of definitions portrayed. Thus we cover exactly those concepts that, after careful study of the DL literature, seem to be at the core of the field; without any of these one does not have a DL. Figure 2 can be viewed as made of five layers: mathematical foundations, 5Ss, key concepts of a DL, and the minimal DL.

Table 1. 5S fundamental abstractions

Models	Examples	Objectives
Streams	Text; video; audio; image	Describes properties of the DL content such as encoding and language for textual material or particular forms of multimedia data
Structures	Collection; catalog; hypertext; document; metadata; organizational tools	Specifies organizational aspects of the DL content
Spaces	Measure; measurable, topological, vector, probabilistic	Defines logical and presentational views of several DL components
Scenarios	Searching, browsing, recommending	Details the behavior of DL services
Societies	Service managers, learners, teachers, etc.	Defines managers responsible for running DL services; actors that use those; and relationships among them

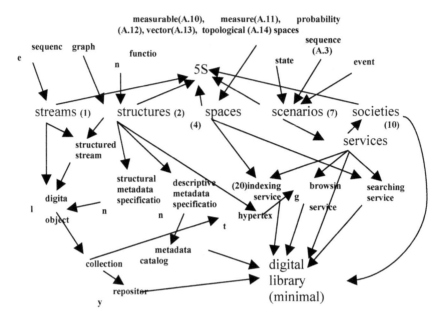

Fig. 2. 5S definitional structure

Figure 3 illustrates how we define additional elements, e.g., for a minimal archaeological DL [20]. In particular, we go beyond the foundation of *digital object (do)* and include *ArchDO* that refers to a real world *ArchObj*. Our minimalist *ArchDL* includes a digital collection *(ArchDColl)* and digital repository *(ArchDR)*. The metadata in our catalog makes use of a stratigraphic diagram *(StraDia)* which builds upon space-time organization *(SpaTemOrg)*. We argue that Figure 3 conveys the essence of a meta-model for archaeological DLs.

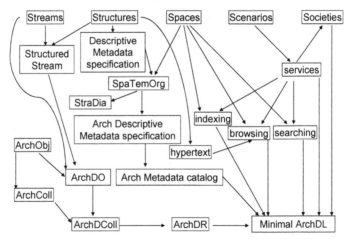

Fig. 3. Minimal archaeological DL in the 5S framework

Moving toward a theory, we developed a minimal DL ontology, summarized in Figure 4 [10]. We note that Streams, Structures, and Spaces are highly interrelated dimensions, as are Scenarios and Societies. We note that though most concepts fit into a particular S (e.g., text viewed as a Stream), some important concepts, like *digital object*, are defined using two Ss (e.g., structured stream), while some key concepts, like *index*, are defined using three Ss. Our ontology also shows relationships, including those inside a particular S, such as that *video* contains both *images* and *audio*. More complex relationships cross S boundaries, such as that a *Service Manager* runs a *Service*, or that an *Actor* participates in a *Scenario*, which in turn contains *events*.

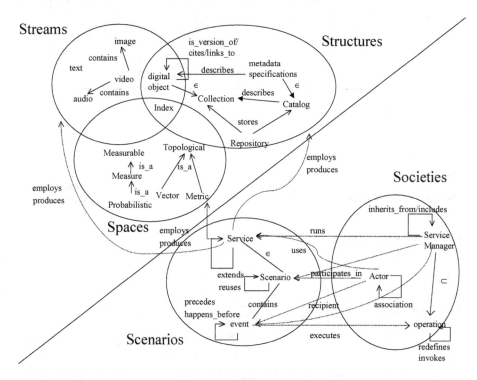

Fig. 4. DL ontology

An application of the ontology is a taxonomy of DL services and activities (Table 2). This was developed through careful analysis and bottom up clustering of services that are found in common DLs, each of which we have carefully defined in terms of abovementioned definitions. We believe this taxonomy provides not only a checklist for developers of DLs, but also a novel yet intuitive overview of the field. Further, this formalism (where e=employs, p=produces) enables reasoning about composition of services (Figure 5). Such reasoning might guide design of code and facilitate reuse and enhance modular development, as well as semi-automatic development approaches, as explained in the next section.

Table 2. DL services/activities taxonomy

Infrastructure Services			Information Satisfaction Services
Repository-Building		**Add Value**	
Creational	Preservational		
Acquiring	Conserving	Annotating	Browsing
Cataloging	Converting	Classifying	Collaborating
Crawling (focused)	Copying/Replicating	Clustering	Customizing
Describing	Emulating	Evaluating	Filtering
Digitizing	Renewing	Extracting	Providing access
Federating	Translating (format)	Indexing	Recommending
Harvesting		Measuring	Requesting
Purchasing		Publicizing	Searching
Submitting		Rating	Visualizing
		Reviewing (peer)	
		Surveying	
		Translating (language)	

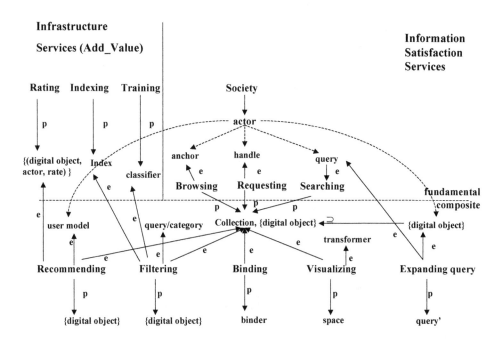

Fig. 5. Example of composition of DL services (Keys: e=employs; p=produces)

3   Applications of 5S

The 5S framework allows a new approach to DL development (Figure 6). 5SGraph [23] supports analysis and specification, while 5SLGen [15] melds together suitable components from a large software pool to yield a running system (Figure 7). Key to the success of this semi-automatic approach to DL construction is separating the roles of the domain expert, who builds the meta-model for a class of DLs, and of the DL designer, who develops a model of a particular DL. We expect that this latter role will be filled by next-generation digital librarians, who will rely upon powerful tools like 5SGraph and 5SLGen.

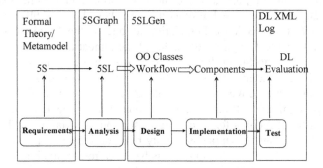

Fig. 6. 5S framework and DL development

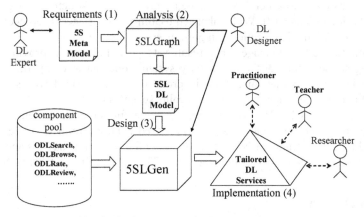

Fig. 7. 5SLGen: automatic DL generation

Figure 8 illustrates the use of 5SGraph to specify the CITIDEL system (see collections in top right); the minimal DL meta-model is shown in the bottom portion. Our preliminary experiments have shown that a knowledgeable librarian can undertake such a specification task in less than an hour. Figure 9 illustrates this same process for the Nimrin archaeological site, focusing on Space, drawing upon a meta-model for archaeology that we have built for ETANA-DL [20]. The current interface for the ETANA-DL system is shown in Figure 10. The heart of the ETANA-DL approach is to leverage 5S to develop a union digital library, deploying methods of metadata harvesting [17]. Our initial prototype has demonstrated significant code reuse as a result of our approach [20]. We believe that 5S will help us formalize key concepts of interoperability of DLs, and allow both archaeologists and the general public to have integrated access to the results of a number of archaeological digs.

Further, we argue that 5S allows formalization of quality issues [10] in the Information Life Cycle [3]. In particular, we have shown that key indicators of quality can be defined using 5S concepts, and can be computed based on simple characterizations of these indicators, suitably contextualized.

In addition to ongoing work on 5S in the context of archaeology, we have applied it to education and computing. Thus, the Computing and Information Technology Interactive Digital Educational Library [4] was launched in 2001 through support from the US National Science Foundation as one of the National Science Digital Library (NSDL) collection projects. Included are almost a million metadata records. We balanced including broad digital libraries from professional societies (ACM [1] and IEEE-CS [13]), large collections obtained by web crawling (CiteSeer [8]), and curated bibliographies covering key conferences and journals (DBLP). Using the Open Archives Initiative Protocol for Metadata Harvesting [17], we were able to gather the subset of records for electronic theses and dissertations (ETDs) relating to computing [22] or PlanetMath (a community-build online math encyclopedia.

Another goal of NSDL collection efforts has been to provide improved support for targeted communities, such as through portals. In the latter regard, the VIADUCT portion of CITIDEL [5] helps with the creation of lesson plans built around learning resources, extending earlier NSDL-funded work on the Instructional Architect [21] and on Walden's Paths [7]. With enhanced usability, such systems can become easier to use [19]. With visualization support, users can more quickly learn about the collection as well as manage large result sets [14]. Further, to provide enhanced browsing support, four different category systems relevant to computing have been mapped by hand so that an automatic process has categorized works, previously indexed in only one scheme, into all applicable schemes [16].

Assessment of CITIDEL is ongoing, to guide further enhancements. Our main emphasis has been on using logs. We proposed [11] and refined [12] a suggested standard for DL logging, based on 5S, covering all important behaviors and activities. Indeed, 5S has guided much of the work on CITIDEL as well as ETANA-DL.

4   Conclusion

Digital libraries have evolved since their inception in the early 1990s. Our work on the 5S framework aims to guide a movement toward knowledge environments, as has been illustrated by our applications of 5S to education, computing, and archaeology. We believe that the 5S framework may provide a firm foundation for advanced DLs.

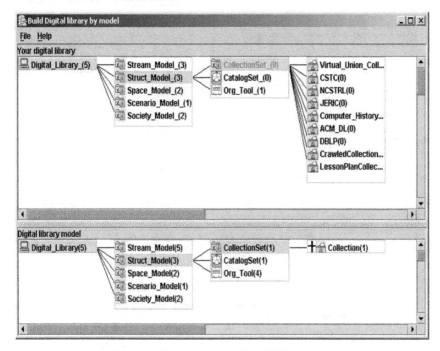

Fig. 8. 5SGraph, minimal DL, CITIDEL model

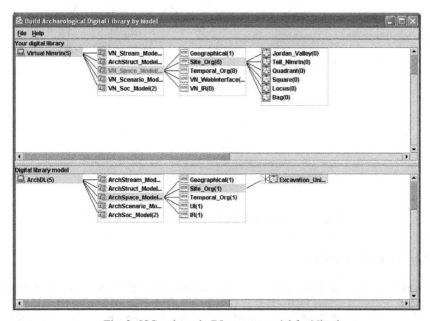

Fig. 9. 5SGraph, arch. DL, space model for Nimrin

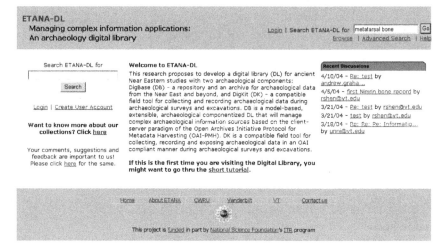

Fig.10. ETANA-DL searching service

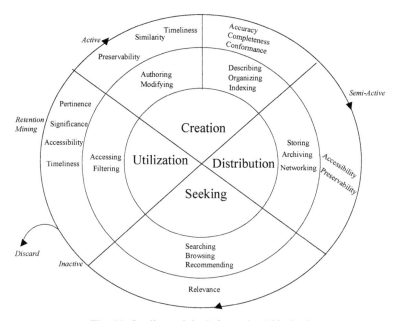

Fig. 11. Quality and the Information Life Cycle

5   Acknowledgements

The work discussed in this paper was funded in part by the US National Science Foundation through grants DUE-0333531, 0121741, 0136690, 0121679; IIS-0325579, 0086227, 0080748, 0002935, and 9986089. Additional support has been provided by AOL, CAPES, OCLC, Sun, and VTLS. Special thanks go to the many faculty, students, staff, and others who have collaborated or assisted in our work.

References

[1]   ACM. "ACM Digital Library", 2000. *http://www.acm.org/dl/*.
[2]   Arms, W. Y. *Digital Libraries*. Cambridge, MA, MIT Press, 2000.
[3]   Borgman, C. "Social Aspects of Digital Libraries", UCLA, Los Angeles, NSF Workshop Report, Feb. 16-17 1996. *http://www-lis.gseis.ucla.edu/DL/*.
[4]   CITIDEL. "CITIDEL: Computing and Information Technology Interactive Digital Educational Library", E. A. Fox, D. Knox, L. Cassel, J. A. N. Lee, M. Pérez-Quiñones, J. Impagliazzo, and C. L. Giles, Eds. Blacksburg, VA: Virginia Tech, 2002. *http://www.citidel.org*.
[5]   CITIDEL. Virginia Instructional Architect for Digital Undergraduate Computing Teaching (VIADUCT), 2004. *http://www.citidel.org/?op=viaduct_front*.
[6]   Fox, E. A. and Urs, S. "Digital Libraries", in *Annual Review of Information Science and Technology*, vol. 36, Ch. 12, B. Cronin, Ed., 2002, pp. 503-589.
[7]   Furuta, R. Walden's Paths, 2004. *http://csdl.cs.tamu.edu/walden/*.
[8]   Giles, C. L., Bollacker, K., and Lawrence, S. "CiteSeer: An Automatic Citation Indexing System", in *Proc. Third ACM Conf. Digital Libraries, DL'98 (Pittsburgh)*, I. Witten, R. Akscyn, and F. M. Shipman III, Eds. ACM Press: ACM, 1998, pp. 89-98. *http://www.neci.nj.nec.com/homepages/lawrence/papers/cs-dl98/*.
[9]   Gonçalves, M., Fox, E., Watson, L., and Kipp, N. *Streams, Structures, Spaces, Scenarios, Societies (5S): A Formal Model for Digital Libraries*. ACM Transactions on Information Systems, vol. 22(2), pp. 270-312, April, 2004.
[10] Gonçalves, M. A. *Streams, Structures, Spaces, Scenarios, and Societies (5S): A Formal Digital Library Framework and Its Applications*. Doctoral dissertation. Computer Science, Virginia Tech, Blacksburg, VA, 2004. *http://scholar.lib.vt.edu/theses/available/etd-12052004-135923/unrestricted/MarcosDissertation.pdf*.
[11] Gonçalves, M. A., Luo, M., Shen, R., Farooq, M., and Fox, E. A. *An XML Log Standard and Tool for Digital Library Logging Analysis*. Presented at Sixth European Conference on Research and Advanced Technology for Digital Libraries, Rome, Italy, 2002.
[12] Gonçalves, M. A., Panchanathan, G., Ravindranathan, U., Krowne, A., Fox, E., Jagodzinski, F., and Cassel, L. *Standards, mark-up, and metadata: The XML log standard for digital libraries: analysis, evolution, and deployment*. Presented at 3rd ACM/IEEE-CS joint conference on digital libraries, IEEE Computer Society, 2003.
[13] IEEE-CS. IEEE Computer Society Digital Library, 2004. *http://www.computer.org/publications/dlib/*.
[14] Kampanya, N., Shen, R., Kim, S., North, C., and Fox, E. A. "Citiviz: A Visual User Interface to the CITIDEL System", in *Proc. European Conference on Digital Libraries (ECDL) 2004, September 12-17, University of Bath, UK*, 2004.
[15] Kelapure, R. *Scenario-Based Generation of Digital Library Services*. MS thesis. Computer Science, Virginia Tech, Blacksburg, VA, 2003. *http://scholar.lib.vt.edu/theses/available/etd-06182003-055012/unrestricted/Thesis_etd_changes.pdf*.
[16] Krowne, A. and Fox, E. A. "An Architecture for Multischeming in Digital Libraries", in *Proceedings 6th International Conference on Asian Digital Libraries, ICADL 2003, Digital Libraries: Technology and Management of Indigenous Knowledge for Global Access;Kuala Lumpur, Malaysia, Dec.; Springer, Lecture Notes in Computer Science 2911*, T. Mohd, T. Sembok, H. B. Zaman, H. Chen, S. R. Urs, and S. H. Myaeng, Eds., 2003, pp. 563-577.
[17] Lagoze, C., Van de Sompel, H., Nelson, M., and Warner, S. "The Open Archives Initiative Protocol for Metadata Harvesting - Version 2.0, Open Archives Initiative", 2002. *http://www.openarchives.org/OAI/2.0/openarchivesprotocol.htm*.

[18] Lesk, M. *Practical Digital Libraries: Books, Bytes and Bucks*. San Francisco, Morgan Kaufmann Publishers, 1997.
[19] Perugini, S., McDevitt, K., Richardson, R., Perez-Quinones, M., Shen, R., Ramakrishnan, N., Williams, C., and Fox, E. A. "Enhancing Usability in CITIDEL: Multimodal, Multilingual, and Interactive Visualization Interfaces", in *Proceedings Fourth ACM/IEEE-CS Joint Conference on Digital Libraries (JCDL2004), Tucson, AZ, June 7-11*, 2004, pp. 315-324.
[20] Ravindranathan, U., Shen, R., Gonçalves, M. A., Fan, W., Fox, E. A., and Flanagan, J. W. "Prototyping Digital Libraries Handling Heterogeneous Data Sources – The ETANA-DL Case Study", in *Proc. European Conference on Digital Libraries (ECDL) 2004, ECDL2004, September 12-17, 2004, U. Bath, UK*, 2004, pp. 186-197.
[21] Rucker, M. Instructional Architect, 2004. *http://ia.usu.edu/*.
[22] Zhang, B., Gonçalves, M. A., and Fox, E. A. "An OAI-Based Filtering Service for CITIDEL from NDLTD", in *Proceedings 6th International Conference on Asian Digital Libraries, ICADL 2003, Digital Libraries: Technology and Management of Indigenous Knowledge for Global Access; Kuala Lumpur, Malaysia, Dec.; Springer, Lecture Notes in Computer Science 2911*, T. Mohd, T. Sembok, H. B. Zaman, H. Chen, S. R. Urs, and S. H. Myaeng, Eds., 2003, pp. 590-601.
[23] Zhu, Q. *5SGraph: A Modeling Tool for Digital Libraries*. Masters thesis. Department of Computer Science, Virginia Tech, Blacksburg, 2002. *http://scholar.lib.vt.edu/theses/available/etd-11272002-210531/*.

Scientific Work and the Usage of Digital Scientific Information – Some Notes on Structures, Discrepancies, Tendencies, and Strategies

Rudi Schmiede

Darmstadt University of Technology
Dept. of Sociology
Residenzschloss
DE-64283 Darmstadt
schmiede@ifs.tu-darmstadt.de

Abstract. The article discusses changes in scientific work (academic and applied) associated with new potentials, but also coercions of information technologies. Background for this interest is the experience gained in several digital library projects that inclinations and willingness to use these technical possibilities is much less common than the developers of these systems, and we all, tended to think in recent years. This seems to be true even in those scientific disciplines which were and are at the forefront of the development, e.g. physics, mathematics, etc. The background for this observation is discussed looking at general economic and social changes, viewing the environments of work in the scientific sphere, the contents and their quantity and quality of supply in scientific IT systems, the user side in their communities of practice, and the technological and organizational basis of scientific information. Some strategic issues to improve the situation are discussed in the final part of the paper.

Economic and Social Background

In the last thirty years the role of knowledge, and especially of scientific knowledge and its information basis, has changed dramatically in the international economy and society. The new "Informational Capitalism" (Castells 1996) or "Digital Capitalism" (Schiller 1999) is characterized by a new stage of globalization, implying new forms of markets and organization, and by a dramatic take-off and intensification of overall informatization. In general, the new capacity of informational capitalism is the development of socio-technical systems which generate, communicate and process information around the globe in real-time. For society and organizations, the "network society" (Castells 1996) entails an increasing role of network forms of cooperation and organization, characterized by the creation of "horizontal" organizations with flat hierarchies, decentralized structures, focussed on continuous re-engineering of their resources with the concentration on their key competences and continuous rationalization along the value creation chain (cf. Knoke 2001, ch. 1). The new type of network or virtual organization brings the market as close as possible to every department, project, work group, and individual – it implies a "new immediacy" of

M. Hemmje et al. (Eds.): E.J. Neuhold Festschrift, LNCS 3379, pp. 107–116, 2005.

the economy, an increased directness of economic forces shaping the conditions of the single economic unit (cf. Schmiede 2003; Benner 2002).

Network structures play an increasing role on various levels. The new forms of network cooperation depend more or less on the digital information and communication media spread in the last thirty years. It was on this economic and social basis that IC technologies could enter their expansive and revolutionizing career which led theorists to coin the phrase of the "information society" (cf. Lyon 1988; Schmiede 1996b). Furthermore, information has become reflexive: Processing information creates new information. Information is a formalized abstraction of reality. In this world of abstract information – quasi in a second reality – one can combine informations, process them, model information-led systems, and simulate their working in reality. Then, the desired result is transferred back into the (first) reality and given a real material form: Information changes and shapes reality. (Probably, one of the most impressive examples to understand these processes in two worlds of reality is the virtual construction of a car by processing information sets delivered from engineers of the assembling firm and many suppliers and subsidiaries, up to the simulation of certain properties of the future car in the computer.) Innovation is generated by processing information, and it is used in a cumulative feedback-loop to generate new innovation. In other words: The technical form of knowledge, its information form, is the step from conventional technification and automatization to informatization (Schmiede 1996a; Spinner 1998, p. 75).

This is the economic and social background for scientific work and its use of digital scientific information to have become and still being in the process of developing towards a crucial resource of economic growth and social dynamics. The usage of digitized scientific information is in no way confined to the academic sphere: It is estimated by the Central Statistical Office that in Germany about 70% of national expenditure on research and development is spent in the private sector of the economy, only the remaining 30% in universities and research institutions outside the universities. So, in our discussion of some moments of structure, problems and perspectives in the usage of digital scientific information below it has to be kept in mind that we are talking as well on academic tendencies as on structural changes in industry and administration.

Scientific Work and Digital Libraries

As for the internet in general, for many years it was physics and some parts of mathematics who initiated building and using the largest digital scientific database, the reknowned Ginsparg or Los Alamos server (since a couple of years "ArXiv" database). With the American Digital Library Initiatives and parallel activities in many European nations since the mid-nineties, a new phase of dissemination, popularization and technological progress in DL development took off which led to a multitude of new digital libraries and many scientific disciplines joining into the process as well as new kinds of information and objects being included.

In Germany a combined initiative developed to get the different scientific disciplines and learned societies to cooperate on the one hand, to include the commercial database providers and publishers on the other hand. The so-called IuK-Initiative of Learned Societies was founded in 1995 by the societies for informations science, physics, mathematics, and chemistry and in the years to follow attracted not only the traditionally technology-oriented disciplines, but also sociology, pedagogics, biology, sport science and others. Web-based information networks in mathematics, physics, and later in sociology and special digital information services in other areas had a considerable impetus towards the dissemination of the usage of scientific digital information not only in universities, but also in industry. In the Global Info program from 1997 to 2000 the interdisciplinary cooperation and the collaboration with the commercial suppliers were consciously advanced; a whole bunch of joint projects, some of them working until 2002, emerged, and German activities opened much more than before to international developments (cf. Schmiede 1999).

Since, however, the dynamic momentum of these initiatives has to a considerable extent disappeared. Not, that DL activities generally have come to a halt: There are numerous digital library projects nationally and internationally; the scope of research and development activities has rather been enlarged including in recent years new areas like museums, films, and archives, extending the scope of technological development to questions like long-term preservation, integrated desktop services and, most recently, designing new open architectures on the basis of web services technologies (cf. Payette/Staples 2002; Stoll et al. 2004). The Open Archive Initiative has substantially enlarged and improved availability and access to digital resources in various areas. And the provision of digital content today belongs to the standard tasks of most scientific libraries with a number of innovative activities.

In contrast, the IuK initiative of learned societies mentioned above is in a bad state. The web-based information networks in physics, mathematics and sociology advance slowly, but they have not developed to become a central communication and cooperation medium in their respective disciplines. In the German Research Association (DFG) led projects creating virtual subject libraries in various disciplines and in the Federal Education and Research Ministry (bmb+f) led projects heading towards a national digital scientific library (vascoda) with interdisciplinary sub-branches in medicine, economics, technology and social sciences, the DL development is re-concentrated with the traditional scientific database information providers and a number of leading libraries in Germany. And the cooperation with the commercial publishing world once envisaged in Global Info did not evolve to be stable but was confined to the projects in the course of this program; it has dissolved to close to zero since.

In sum, at least looking at the situation in Germany, digital library activities – used as a synonym for the systematic usage of digital scientific information in the work of scientists – did not succeed to overcome their fringe status in sciences and humanities hitherto. Although, to a certain extent, using the internet and its resources has become part of everyday work of many people doing scientific work, the vision of the DL movement, condensed in the general Global Info aim of providing "world-wide information at the indvidual scientist's desktop", is far from having become reality.

Changes in Scientific Work

One might list a number of political or contingent reasons to explain this development. They account for one or the other special feature of the situation in Germany; they are not, however, a sufficient explanation for the problems mentioned.

My impression is, first, that this state of affairs is by no way limited to Germany; even if DL movements are more vivid in the USA or UK, the inroad into everyday work of researchers, teachers and students as well as researchers and developpers in industry has not been found yet there, either. Secondly, I doubt whether this reflects principal differences between sciences and humanities; rather, the same deficiencies (albeit with gradual differences) seem to be true also in those scientific disciplines which were and are at the forefront of the development, implementation and usage of advanced systems of science information, e.g. physics, mathematics, medicine, biology; they are the more prominent in social sciences and humanities which are traditionally more framed into their national cultures, languages and habits.

As a consequence, I am convinced that an analysis has to look a bit deeper into the relation between changes and continuities in scientific work on the one hand, the use of resources and instruments of digital information on the other one. Unfortunately, there is not yet any systematic research on this relation available. There are studies on media usage in special environments (e.g. Berker 2001; Goll 2002). On the other hand, there is research to identify and describe communities of practice, but mostly without special attention to the use of digital information and related work practices (cf. the case studies in Huysmann et al. 2003). So, in the following paragraphs, I will present rather questions and theses than results. This might raise awareness that there are hidden problems and emphasize the necessity to deal with them in the future.

A very simple economic model may help to specify the possible factors contributing to the differences between supply and usage of scientific information: There seems to be a more or less pronounced divergence between the supply of scientific information facilities based on information technologies and the demand of acting scientists for IT-based scientific information. The theoretical options to explain this mismatch are limited: (1) Supply exceeds demand quantitatively, or (2) does not meet the demand qualitatively, with its contents, or, as a special case, (2a) it is primarily technology-, not content-driven; (3) demand is sluggish because there are no measurable or sufficiently susceptible advantages in using the supply, or (4) because supply is too expensive (in terms of workload: it demands too much effort to be traded). These options describe analytic categories to approach the problem described, but they have to be translated into real questions concerning the field of scientific information, knowledge and work.

In this paragraph I want to deal with some of the characterstic moments of the demand side, i.e. of scientific work itself and the scientists. A first group of questions and theses which I want to go through concerns the *environment of work* in the scientific sphere. (1) Have *contents* of sciences and humanities changed because of the introduction of informatized objects and methods into most scientific disciplines? The answer is a cautious, but definite Yes. In the *quantitative* dimension facts, relations and structures can be modelled because of informatization which so far could not be treated due to their sheer size. The terabytes of information which are delivered day per day in the big international geological and geospatial projects; the modelling and calculation of properties of substances in chemistry; the calculation of properties of free forms by systems of infinite equations in mechanics; the modelling and visualization of energetic processes in thermodynamics or in construction engineering physics; the recognition of patterns and the numerical comparison of gene sequences in biogenetics; but also the voluminous statistical calculation of cluster structures in the sociological analysis of social structures or in the economic investigation of input-output-matrices which allow for new insights and dimensions of analysis, are but some examples for the enormous potential of informatized procedures in science in general. Methods and technologies of *simulation* today are playing a central role in what Daniel Bell thirty years ago called "intellectual technologies" (Bell 1973). In the humanities, new methods of analysis of texts, symbols, figures and pictures, i.e. in the more *qualitative dimension*, are imminent; however, computer philology is still in its beginnnings. Informatization in scientific work goes along with *new objects, new standards and norms*: Virtual construction processes in mechanical engineering are based upon massive efforts of formal or de-facto-standardization ob technical objects; and the normed definition of diseases by ICD 10 (the International Classification of Diseases) has enormous scientific and practical consequences in medicine, e.g. in form of acceptance or rejection by health insurance institutions. So, my answer to the question posed above is: The examples listed show substantial changes in the contents of sciences and humanities, but we do not really have a systematic overview on their dimensions and extent, yet.

These changes are mainly on the content side of scientific information. Are there correlates on the user side? More specific: (2) Have *working habits* and *conditions* undergone a change due to the omnipresence of IC technologies? Have *communication and cooperation styles* of scientific communities come up to the expectations the technological possibilities of IT seemed and still seem to promise? These are the questions to which I know only few answers so far. We know that networks of peers are a common structure in various scientific spheres; we also know that network structures in the working of scientists are on the increase; we are also familiar with the traditional ways of networking of scientists via conferences, workshops, journals etc. But we have hardly any indications – apart from personal experience and impressions from colleagues – of how this working together is done, and especially, how it is conducted as far as the ICT is concerned. So to deal with the above questions I can only express my guess that neither working habits and conditions nor communication and cooperation styles have really undergone comparably dramatic changes as the environmental conditions certainly have. My hypothesis for the necessary studies in this sphere would be that by and large communication between scientists who cooperate is essentially conducted by exchange of papers and the use of telephone and mail; adequate collaboration systems seem to be absent – be it because of their own inadequacy, be it because of conventionality or ignorance on the side of the acting scientists.

A third group of questions (3) complementing the *user side* of digital scientific information arises from these deliberations: What are the *relevant communities* in the respective fields? Does electronic communication and collaboration offer significant *advantages* to them? Is there a *tradition* to exchange working papers, data etc. in printed or digital form? Is the *single scientist* supported or discouraged by his or her environment to systematically use electronic facilities and publish and communicate in digital form? One often neglected dimension of publishing has to be recalled at this point of the argument: Publishing is not just the technical multiplication and dissemination of a text or other contents, its more or less successful bringing into the market; to solve this task organizationally and technically, is the easier part of the problem. The more difficult one is dealing with publication as part of the working mode of the scientific social system. Publication plays a crucial role in demonstrating and allocating acknowledgement, status, functions, jobs and remuneration in the world of institutionalized science. Journals, series, and scientific publishing companies in general are sources of honour and reward, of power and influence, and – last but not least – of income for learned societies. My impression is that electronic publishing so far has not provided a functional substitute for this system. The well-known guess that around 90% of scientific papers on the ArXiv server are later published in a printed journal suggests that the excellent solution for the quick and cheap dissemination of scientific innovation which this service is providing does not seriously impede the working of the second crucial social process of publishing as allocation mechanism in the scientific system.

There is one additional consideration to be mentioned concerning the consequences of the availability and use of world-wide scientific information systems. These facilities might help to increase national and international competition in scientific fields for they help to create world-wide markets for scientific information. Strongly canonized scientific disciplines as e.g. large parts of physics or mathematics are familiar with working in the context of a global presence of their respective community. So, it is probably not accidental that the first world-wide scientific information system (the mentioned Los Alamos server) originated in these sciences. In contrast, in many fields of social science and humanities the reference space is by tradition rather culturally or nationally defined. Here the advantages of the new systems might be more difficult to see and be counteracted by possible real or alleged threats to the own position in the scientific context associated with the anticipated increased transparency of global information systems in science.

To sum up the argument of this paragraph: In terms of the economic model sketched above, we seem to have a combination of options 2 and 3. The supply of electronic tool systems does not seem to meet the demand qualitatively; obviously, changed contents are important, but they don't seem to be processed within the new available electronic communication and cooperation facilities. Turned the other way around: Available systems do not seem to offer advantages substantial enough to use them instead of conventional ways of information, communication and cooperation.

Technological Advances, Organization, and Business Models

To round up the picture we have to add a closer look at the supply side of changed scientific work, i.e. information supply in the various sciences. A first group of questions and theses (1) in this field aims at the *technical characteristics* of scientific information systems: Is supply of electronic information in the respective fields organized in a *centralized* manner, usually as one or few central databases, administered and kept by some central agency? (This usually implies more or less severe selections of contents.) Or do *decentralized* information structures exist in the field which are apt to react to the continuously changing information and communication modes in the sciences? This has consequences for the access possibilities of the single scientist as a user and as a producer: For the *user*, centralized database structures usually go along with more or less specialized retrieval languages and routines, so that in the worst case I have to learn and keep in continuous usage a special language for every source. The alternative is the *web-based* (i.e. browser-based) access common to decentralised web oriented information structures; here many attempts are made (and considerable progress has been achieved) to incorporate advanced *retrieval options* into user-friendly *interfaces*. In the role as *producer* (in science, most users are producers at the same time), the question is how I get my products into the publishing system. Do I have to deliver special formats, specialized metadata etc.? Do I receive *support* by the system to publish, to mark up the publication and to get it into review systems? The open character of the information and publication system depends on technological preconditions in the form of the support of current *standards* (DC, XML/rdf, OWL, WSDL, OAI-MHP etc.). Are they adhered to, how far are they implemented? Is the system's *architecture* adaptable to changing needs (e.g. to SODA-like structures)? The alternative of centralized vs. decentralized information systems is not only a question of competing technologies; rather these are adapted according to social circumstances and interests. Centralized systems are usually run by centralized service institutions, often employing hundreds of scientific and administrative staff. So changes in organizational structures, especially by introducing elements of bottom-up activity by scientists, considered to be lay people in terms of information technology and documentation by the professionals, tend to entail bureaucratic counteraction by the latter ones. On the other hand, their attitude is often supported and justified by the complementary disinterest of working scientists concerning questions of publication and documentation. It is especially difficult to turn this vicious circle into a virtuous one.

A second group of questions and considerations (2) in this paragraph relates to the *contents* of scientific information systems and their *availability*; it has to deal with their *organizational and economic conditions*: To which extent are contents *publicly*, to which extent only via the *market* available? E.g. in physics most contents seem to be easily and early accessible via ArXiv and complementary ways, whereas in chemistry most important contents are published first and exclusively in journals of the leading publishers. How far do relevant contents exist in *digitized* form? In the more canonic sciences (mathematics, natural sciences) most contents are available in digital form, whereas in humanities and social sciences only unsystematically selected contents seem to be available electronically. A good measure to evaluate this situation is to answer the question whether a scientist in his or her everyday working environment is able to do this work without repeated *media breaks* (this will prevent him or her from using systematically IT sources). Another question of this group aims at the *quality* of electronic information: Is the available information structured by metadata accepted in the community and eventually evaluated as to its reliability and relevance, or is it just any web content which I have googled according to ratings not transparent for me as a scientist? Finally the question of *conditions of access* are important: Are electronic sources in the fields of research and teaching in the respective scientific disciplines accessible free or for fees (option 4 above)? The well discussed journals' or libraries' crisis has its roots here, and it is especially virulent in the fields dominated by large academic publishers.

To sum up the argument in this paragraph: We find some evidence that in many fields of scientific information supply does not fit demand in its quality (option 2 in the model above), quality in this context having a twofold meaning: Quality concerns on the one hand the quality of contents, discussed in the second group; on the other hand, it means quality of the supply mode as described in the first group of questions and considerations. Finally, we have many cases where supply is too expensive in time or in money terms.

Some Strategic Consequences

Seen in the context of the evolving new informational capitalism and the accompagning network society sketched at the beginning of this article scientific work based on digital sources and a respective instrumentarium is of vital importance for the future of science and of work, in the academic sphere as well as in the private economy and administration. Science is conducted in more or less competitive contexts. Since digital networking is a condition of productivity in both areas it will be enforced on or adopted by acting scientists increasingly. Growing parts of scientific work can be conducted – because of the character of its objects and its methods – only in informatized form. So, dealing with the development of scientific work and the usage of digital scientific information is discussing the future of science and of work in a changing society, their conditions and their chances.

We have found several instances of a mismatch between the supply of scientific information services and the needs and working habits of users and producers. It is worthwile to improve the motivation and quality on both sides. As a general rule for the development of information systems one should proclaim the formula "picking the user up where he is". This is not just shrewd tactics to find support for a system but a responsibility of developers and providers of information services deciding on success or failure of their work, i.e. on the quality of their product.

One more specific consequence of this general formula is to adjust information systems to their respective user communities. This presupposes knowledge on these communities, especially on their way of communicating and cooperating and their use of technologies in doing so. One the one hand serious research is needed to gain information on this unknown area on the map of science. But on the other hand, below that research level, every systems' designer should explore the community to secure success and quality of his or her work. In their recent programmatic statement on "Rethinking Scholarly Communication. Building the System that Scholars Deserve" Herbert Van de Sompel and his colleagues (Van de Sompel et al. 2004) formulate this principle. Since working within an electronic environment is a social setting and not just a question of improving technological efficiency, collaboration with the user (and also the user als producer) is essential. User orientation has two complementary meanings: First to let the user take influence to shape systems according to his or her work needs; second to make working with scientific information systems a necessary and useful part of everyday scientific work, beginning with school and study practices.

To allow the user to influence your system it has to contain bottom-up structures because that is the only way to have a built-in reaction to changes in user's work habits and needs and, furthermore, to make information work as part of his or her everyday business. One should avoid erecting a wall of abstract contradictions between centralized and decentralized tasks and structures. On one hand the acting scientist will best know his environment and what he needs to optimally work in it. So bottom-up structures are not just in the user's interest but in the interest of the efficiency of the whole system (cf. Meier et al. 2003). On the other hand, professional information and documentation does not belong to the normal education of any scientist; so he or she will need assistance in the information area, e.g. advice in getting to know all the world-wide information resources in their field, help in quality assurance of contents, let alone technical assistance.

Most curricula in higher education are not yet up to the new role of electronic scientific information, or to put it a bit more dramatic: The vast majority of curricula is adequate only to a past world of information and in this sense partly obsolete. Formulated positively: It should be an obligatory part of every scientific study to teach and be taught the information dimensions of your respective scientific disciplines. Getting to know resources and services, learning to handle the modern instrumentarium, and becoming able to deal with the heterogeneity of information sources, especially the side-by-side of printed and electronic material, but also of high-quality and googled contents, is an essential qualification for today's scientific work.

Last, but not least: There have to be found new complementary forms of access to scientific contents. Neither the "free-for-all" approach nor the monopolization of whole scientific areas by few academic publishers are a long-term viable future. In practice, the approach of electronic free pre-print and later publication in a printed journal, increasingly paralleled by e-versions of the publication, has evolved to be a model frequently used. Besides, publishers are experimenting with new regulations for parallel print and electronic publication. On the other hand, on-line publications and new models for their organization are spreading. This field seems to become today rather one of experimental projects than one of principal controversies (cf. Henry 2003).

Digital scientific information, its sources, its tools, its services, and especially its relationship to acting scientists' work is an area of experiments and tentative developments. It is to a certain extent neglected by scientific research because it is still considered by most scientists as an area of minor interest, as a sphere of instruments, service and background technology. It is time for all sides to realize that it has become an integral part of original scientific work and has to be taken as serious as the theoretical, methodological and applied dimensions of any scientific discipline. If scientists themselves do not understand these fundamental changes in their work economy and society will force them in probably rather unsubtle ways to realize and to comply with these basic changes.

References

Bell, Daniel (1973): The Coming of Post-Industrial Society. A Venture in Social Forecasting, New York, 1973

Benner, Chris (2002): Work in the New Economy. Flexible Labor Markets in Silicon Valley, Malden/Mass.: Blackwell Publishers Ltd., 2002

Berker, Thomas (2001): Internetnutzung in den 90er Jahren. Wie ein junges Medium alltäglich wurde, Frankfurt am Main/New York: Campus Verlag, 2001

Castells, Manuel (1996): The Rise of the Network Society (The Information Age: Economy, Society and Culture, Vol. I), Malden/Mass.; Oxford/UK: Blackwell Publishers Ltd., 1996

Goll, Michaela (2002): Arbeiten im Netz. Kommunikationsstrukturen, Arbeitsabläufe und Wissensmanagement, Wiesbaden: Westdeutscher Verlag 2002

Henry, Geneva (2003): On-line Publishing in the 21st Century. Challenges and Opportunities, in: D-Lib Magazine, vol. 9, no. 10, Okt. 2003; also via: doi:10.1045/october2003-henry

Huysmann, Marleen; Wenger, Etienne; Wulf, Volker (eds.) (2003): Communities and Technologies, Dordrecht/Boston/London: Kluwer Academic Publishers, 2003

Knoke, David (2001): Changing Organizations. Business Networks in the New Political Economy, Boulder/Co: Westview Press, 2001

Lyon, David (1988): The Information Society. Issues and Illusions, Cambridge: Polity Press, 1988

Meier, Wolfgang/Schumann, Natascha/Heise, Sue/Schmiede, Rudi (2003): SozioNet: Networking Social Science Ressources, in: Traugott Koch/Ingeborg Torvik Sølvberg (eds.): Research and Advanced Technology for Digital Libraries. 7th European Conference, ECDL 2003, Trondheim, Norway, August 17-22, 2003. Proceedings, Berlin etc.: Springer Lecture Notes in Computer Science 2769, pp. 245-256

Payette, Sandra/Staples, Thornton (2002): The Mellon Fedora Project. Digital Library Architecture Meets XML and Web Services. European Conference on Research and Advanced Technology for Digital Libraries, Rome, Italy, September 2002. accessible via: http://www.fedora.info/documents/ecdl2002final.pdf

Schiller, Dan (1999): Digital Capitalism. Networking the Global Market System, Boston/Mass.: MIT Press, 1999

Schmiede, Rudi (1996a): Informatisierung, Formalisierung und kapitalistische Produktionsweise. Entstehung der Informationstechnik und Wandel der gesellschaftlichen Arbeit, in: ders. (Hg.) Virtuelle Arbeitswelten. Arbeit, Produktion und Subjekt in der „Informationsgesellschaft", Berlin: edition sigma, 1996, pp. 15-47

Schmiede, Rudi (1996b): Informatisierung und gesellschaftliche Arbeit. Strukturveränderungen von Arbeit und Gesellschaft, in: ders. (Hg.) Virtuelle Arbeitswelten. Arbeit, Produktion und Subjekt in der „Informationsgesellschaft", Berlin: edition sigma, 1996, pp. 107-128

Schmiede, Rudi (1999): Digital Library Activities in Germany. The German Digital Library Program GLOBAL INFO, in: IEEE Forum on Research and Technology Advances in Digital Libraries. IEEE ADL '99, Proceedings, May 19-21, 1999, Baltimore, MD, pp. 73-83; also accessible via http://www.global-info.org/doc/990413-schmiede.pdf

Schmiede, Rudi (2003): Informationstechnik im gegenwärtigen Kapitalismus, in: Gernot Böhme/Alexandra Manzei (Hg.): Kritische Theorie der Technik und der Natur, München: Wilhelm Fink Verlag 2003, pp. 173-183

Sompel, Herbert van de /Payette, Sandy/Erickson, John/Lagoze, Carl/Warner, Simeon (2004): Rethinking Scholarly Communication. Building the System that Scholars Deserve, in: D-Lib Magazine, vol. 10, no. 9, Sept. 2004; also via http://www.dlib.org/dlib/september04/vandesompel/09vandesompel.html

Spinner, Helmut F. (1998): Die Architektur der Informationsgesellschaft. Entwurf eines wissensorientierten Gesamtkonzepts, Bodenheim: Philo Verlagsgesellschaft, 1998

Stoll, Julia/Körnig, Stephan/Schmiede, Rudi (2004): Towards the Integration of Digital Library Applications via Web Services for Use in a Scientific Workspace, in: Annemarie Nase/Geert Van Grootel (eds.): Putting the Sparkle in the Knowledge Society: 7th International Conference on Current Research Information Systems, Antwerpen, 13-15.5.2004, Leuven: Leuven Univ. Press, pp. 125-137

Queries in Context: Access to Digitized Historic Documents in a Collaboratory for the Humanities

Ulrich Thiel, Holger Brocks, Andrea Dirsch-Weigand, André Everts,
Ingo Frommholz, and Adelheit Stein

Fraunhofer IPSI
Dolivostr. 15, 64293 Darmstadt, Germany
{thiel, brocks, dirsch, everts, frommholz,
stein}@ipsi.fraunhofer.de

Abstract. In contrast to standard digital libraries, systems addressing the specific requirements of cultural heritage need to deal with digitized material like scanned documents instead of borne digital items. Such systems aim at providing the means for domain experts, e.g. historians, to collaboratively work with the given material. To support their work, automatic indexing mechanisms for both textual and pictorial digitized documents need to be combined with retrieval methods exploiting the content as well as the context of information items for precise searches. In the COLLATE project we devised several access methods using textual contents, feature extraction from images, metadata, and annotations provided by the users.

1   Creating Context by Interpretative Metadata and Annotations

In most contemporary digital library (DL) systems the tools which allow users to access the collection restrict themselves to classical search criteria, e.g. topical and bibliographic relevance.

However, this is not sufficient for coping with embedded usages, where access to the contents is not seen as an isolated activity but as part of a larger work process, where interaction with other users, indexing and annotating documents need to be integrated. Especially for cultural heritage experts – the specific user group we consider in this paper – much of their work is devoted to reconstructing the past from historic sources by assembling facts and assumptions which help the contemporary public to understand the documents' contents. Therefore, systems dealing with digital copies of historic material need to provide the means for users in different usage scenarios to collaboratively work with the given material, which will be identified, catalogued and interpreted as part of a research project. This feature enables system designers to conceive highly precise and versatile access facilities, which take into account both the contents of the source document as well as what is known about this document, i.e. its related metadata or existing annotations provided during earlier phases of the interpretation process. In the following, we will refer to this body of additional data and knowledge as the *'context' of the document* (see also *Figure 1*). We will outline how it was created and used in the COLLATE project, in which we

M. Hemmje et al. (Eds.): E.J. Neuhold Festschrift, LNCS 3379, pp. 117–127, 2005.

designed and implemented a working collaboratory for the Humanities, supporting interpretative work on historic documents.

As a part of this project, appropriate indexing and retrieval procedures have been developed, allowing for content-oriented access to the material in order to support the users' work. Most of the in-depth indexing was to be done manually; therefore, we devoted much effort to adequate indexing vocabularies and tools, which were developed in close cooperation with the user community (film researchers and historians). To a certain degree, the indexing process can be supported by automatic procedures, even if the documents are not machine-readable texts but images. We will illustrate this by sketching a method for indexing images with semantic features, which enables the users to search on a conceptual level. Thus, each document is embedded in a metadata context, which facilitates highly precise searches.

A second way of accessing a historic source document is more indirect. Annotations may contain concepts which are relevant for the document, but are for some reason not contained in the document itself. Therefore, we added an access facility which also takes into account the annotation context of a document.

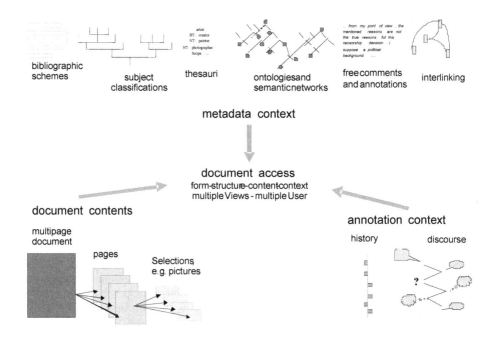

Fig. 1. Document access in COLLATE based on contents, metadata, and annotations

In the following, we will first give a brief introduction to the COLLATE system and its architecture. After an outline of the measures taken to improve the manual indexing, we discuss the requirements for the automatic image indexing approach. Then, the collaborative annotation facility is presented. Finally, we will show how the different contexts are used while accessing documents in COLLATE.

2 System Overview

Various Web-based collaboratories for the Natural Sciences have been employed since the early 1990s, but only few similar efforts exist in the Arts and Humanities (e.g. [6]). Work processes in the interpreting sciences are different and need to be supported by appropriate technologies. Especially the process of compiling arguments, counterarguments, examples and references to other historic sources – the prevailing method in the Humanities – may profit from a collaborative work environment that enhances the capacity of the individual knowledge worker.

The EU-funded project *"COLLATE – Collaboratory for Annotation, Indexing and Retrieval of Digitized Historical Archive Material"* (http://www.collate.de) started in fall 2000 (IST-1999-20882) and ran for three years. An international team of content providers, film domain experts, and technology providers worked together to develop a new type of collaboratory in the domain of cultural heritage (cf. [7]). The implemented system offers access to a digital repository of text archive material documenting film censorship practices for several thousands of European films from the 1920s and 1930s. For a subset of significant films it provides enriched documentation including press articles, film advertising material, photos and some film fragments. Major film archives from Germany, Austria and the Czech Republic provided the sources and worked as pilot users with the COLLATE system.

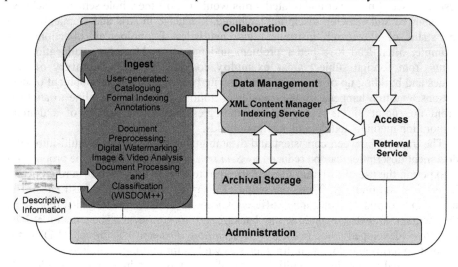

Fig. 2. COLLATE system architecture

The architecture of the system (see *Figure 2*) developed during the COLLATE project can be seen as a variant of the OAIS standard architecture (see [2]), with an additional layer for handling the collaboration among the users. Main modules are:
- Three *document pre-processing modules* for digital watermarking (copyright and integrity watermarks), automatic document structure analysis and classification, and automatic, concept-based image indexing and retrieval.

- A *distributed multimedia data repository* comprising digitized text material, pictorial material like photos and posters and digital video fragments.
- Tools for the *representation and management of metadata*, the XML-based content manager incorporating an ontology manager and a retrieval engine (see [3]).
- A *collaborative task manager* for complex individual and collaborative tasks, such as indexing, annotation, comparison, interlinking and information retrieval, including tools for online communication and collaborative discourse between the domain experts and other system users (see [1]).
- The *Web-based user interface* of COLLATE comprises several workspaces for various tasks performed by distributed user groups, offering different access rights and interface functions to different types of users.

3   Integrating Complementary Domain-Specific Vocabularies

The COLLATE project unites specialists with different expert views on the film domain using various expert vocabularies and idioms for their scientific statements. Every partial discipline in Arts and Humanities, every theory and paradigm school has developed its own language with often subtle but significant nuances in the semantics of the same notation. Reducing these subtle differences to preferred descriptors with a restricted set of narrower and related terms would cut off the whole semantic richness of a spirited and growing discipline language. Language in Arts and Humanities has the status of a research instrument and heuristics. Etymological reflections, for example, often lead to a better problem understanding. Metaphoric allocations of terms from foreign subject areas exemplify complex theories. Discovery of new issues and building up of new hypothesis is intertwined with the development of new notions, or often happens by the transfer of notions from one discipline to another. From this point of view, explicit terminologies have the character of a domain exploration medium and domain navigation aids.

The tradeoff between consistent and disambiguous indexing and a multi-idiomatic document description can be reduced by *Semantic Web* technologies. One proposition is to permit the use of different vocabularies but to qualify each term by a reference to its original terminology. Thus, the scope of every term could be reconstructed. The next step is to combine or bundle different vocabularies in an ontology that represents the domain knowledge and is the background for retrieval. The *Semantic Web Initiative* developed the *Resource Description Framework* format (RDF) for annotating terms and document fragments as well as for ontology building.

Conceptual integration of multiple vocabularies aims at an indexing terminology as a unified whole that could be applied as well on film censorship documents, film related pictures, film press or any other literature on films. On the conceptual level, a taxonomic layer model was developed to integrate multiple vocabularies for controlled keyword indexing in a background ontology (see *Figure 3*).

The integration was effected top-down from the generic concepts over domain-specific notions to application-specific concepts. The generic *ABC Model* and *Ontology* presents the top level; at the same time, the ABC Model provides the domain-specific cultural heritage concepts (that were originally adopted from the *CIDOC Conceptual Reference Model*). The specific concepts for the film archive sub-domain come from the *FIAF Subject Classification* and the *Library of Congress Thesaurus for Graphical Material I and II* (LOC TGM I, II). Finally, the *specific COLLATE vocabulary* covers the film censorship concepts on the application level.

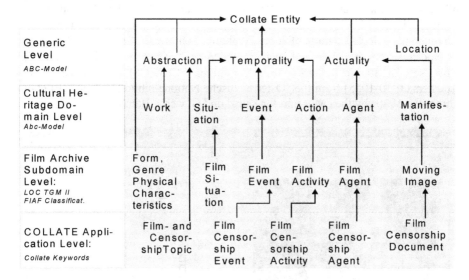

Fig. 3. Conceptual integration of COLLATE indexing vocabularies

Thus, a compromise was achieved between the requirements of using a standardized vocabulary whenever this is feasible, and enriching the vocabulary with specific terms used by a certain community when this is needed. The vocabulary serves as a comprehensive conceptual framework allowing indexers to assign domain-specific keywords which contribute to the interpretation of the document w.r.t. its function in the processes of film making, censoring and distributing.

The COLLATE collection, however, also comprises pictorial documents, mostly stills from films or photographs from the set during the making of a film, as well as digitized video fragments. These items need to be formally catalogued by bibliographical metadata, but it is also useful to characterize them by visual features such as the type of object shown, light conditions etc. The latter task can be supported by automatic indexing mechanisms we employed in COLLATE.

4   Automatic Image Indexing with Semantic Features

As image indexing as well as text indexing require appropriate vocabularies, we first had to develop – based on empirical analyses of a sample set of pictures – a rough classification of the picture document types and a subject matter indexing scheme that is domain-specific but extensible to a other picture types and creation times.

This scheme was used for the manual indexing of a training set, which was needed for the automatic image analysis and rule generation. It should not be confused with the subject matter vocabulary developed for the intellectual indexing work of professional domain/film experts, which is included in the COLLATE prototype for the archive users' indexing and annotation. The latter allows standard keyword search of the indexed pictures, whereas the automatic, rule-based indexing method supports to some degree concept-based searches of not yet (manually) indexed larger collections, e.g. keyframes extracted from videos, or picture collections added after the end of the COLLATE project. The initial picture set analyzed consisted of

- a randomly selected sample of about 50 photos from the COLLATE collection;
- 20 posters from the 1950s and 1960s provided by the German film institute, DIF;
- two sets of 30 pictures each from commercial CD-ROM collections: (a) film posters (1910-1955) from the "Österreichische Nationalbibliothek", and (b) photos from the 1920s by the "Museum für Kunst und Gewerbe Hamburg".

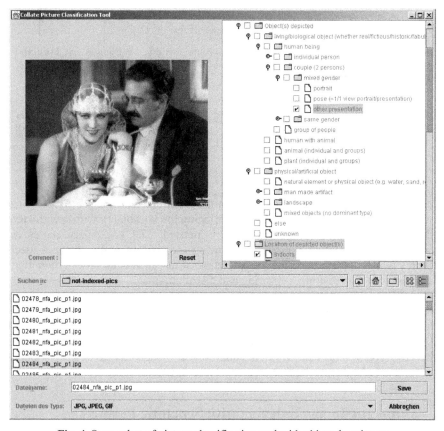

Fig. 4. Screenshot of picture classification tool with object descriptors

First, free index terms (keywords or brief free-text descriptions) were collected for given samples, which were then grouped and structured into the two schemata for objects and topics. Whereas the first is a quite rough – but complete – classification scheme, the second is an open-ended structured keyword list, both being highly domain-specific, reflecting the characteristics of our image collection. The resulting scheme was used within the classification/indexing tool we developed for indexing a training set (comprising 500 images from the COLLATE collection) as a structured list of index terms (see right-hand side of *Figure 4*).

For rule generation we employed an empirical approach in which manually indexed images are used as a training set. Generated rules and extracted feature values are stored in a metadata database. Note that the latter feature values are not restricted to the original sample set used for the rule generation process. Instead, feature analysis results obtained from the many times larger picture collection are now used as the basis for semantic access. If the user poses a conceptual query, the retrieval engine analyses the query and maps it to a set of rules which are requested from the metadata database. The rules are interpreted by an appropriate rule interpreter yielding specification of features extraction values to be searched for. If feature values matching the constraints can be found, the associated video parts are retrieved. The result is returned to the user as a ranked list of items.

In the image retrieval system we combined 17 algorithms based on the PBM format (portable bitmap) to calculate such characteristics as the color distribution within an image, the surface texture of objects in an image, or values which express the degree of similarity in color distribution between two pictures.

The association between feature values and manually assigned index terms, i.e. the descriptors chosen from the classification scheme above, can now be accomplished using algorithmic statistical methods, ranging from exhaustive exploration to complex stochastic computation. Which method is applicable depends on the degree of aggregation applied to the original feature values. We start with p-dimensional vectors containing the results from p different feature extraction methods applied to the image. In the next step, the feature-extraction values may be aggregated to dynamically built constraints, e.g., ranges, or linear combinations of the feature values.

In our experiments, we used the Quadratic Classification Function (QCF) – a standard method in statistics – to calculate the probability that an image matches a classification item. The QCF gives a measure for the distance of the feature extraction values of an image and the mean values of a set of manually classified images.

Let C be a classification attribute (e.g., source of light), $c_j \in C$ be a descriptor (e.g., source of light: natural). For an image represented by a feature vector x_m the QCF method determines the distance measure χ^2_{jm} between the feature-extraction values and the c_j-classified images of the training set based on a co-variance analysis of the feature vectors. With this measure we can compare the degrees of association of different pictures with a given descriptor c_j.

However, the values of χ^2_{jm} are not comparable over the attributes C, so we now calculate the probability $p(c_j \mid x_m)$ that an image with the feature-extraction values x_m belongs to a descriptor c_j as

$$p(c_j \mid x_m) = \frac{e^{-(\chi^2_{jm}/2)}}{\sum_k e^{-(\chi^2_{km}/2)}}, \text{ where } \sum_k e^{-(\chi^2_{km}/2)} \text{ is the sum over all descriptors of the}$$

attribute C. This probability value can be used to rank the images in descending order. In the retrieval process, conceptual queries consisting of single descriptors can now be translated into search criteria on the feature level which can be executed in the metadata DBMS.

5   Collaborative Annotation

Digital libraries offer new opportunities for collaboration and communication that were unfeasible in traditional libraries (cf. [6]). This holds especially true for the cultural domain where indexing, annotation and information seeking can be considered as key activities within a digital library system.

In COLLATE we employ a simple, but general collaboration model and use discourse structure relations to introduce collaborative discourses within a cultural digital library (see [7]). Ranging from factual to more interpersonal levels they describe the intended relations between domain objects, especially annotations. Pragmatic aspects are covered by communicative acts, which complement the discourse structure relations by providing means for meta-communication. The resulting interrelations between the various domain objects can be employed to perform advanced context-based retrieval.

Interpretation is an incremental process which involves domain-specific knowledge. It becomes quite obvious that within a collaborative environment several users cooperate in pursuing a particular goal, which might be too complex to be accomplished by a single user alone. In COLLATE we support for asynchronous collaboration in indexing for non-technical users. In our understanding the domain objects (scanned documents, metadata) represent the main focus of collaborative work, i.e. collaboration is performed through annotating the digitized artifacts or their associated metadata objects.

We devised a comprehensive model of annotation reference types between a) binary image versions of the original document and annotations and b) discussion threads realized as annotations on annotations. Our model is loosely based on concepts taken from discourse theory developed within computational linguistics. Particularly, we adopt the concept of discourse structure relations (or rhetorical relations as defined within the Rhetorical Structure Theory (RST), cf. [5]). For detailed reviews on other existing approaches and a meta-taxonomy see [4].

We employ a specific subset of relations that are relevant in the COLLATE context, ranging from factual to more interpersonal levels, i.e. focusing on certain qualities of the participants of a discourse. In the following we just briefly exemplify the relations used in COLLATE (cf. [4] for exact definitions of the relations):

- *Elaboration* – Providing additional, e.g. more detailed information (see *Figure 5*).
- *Comparison* – Comparative relations can be further sub-structured to emphasize semantic similarities or contrasts between two elements of a discourse.
- *Cause* – To state a specific cause for a certain circumstance.
- Background information – Using information about the background of the author (e.g., "As a psychologist the author does not consider the political aspects.").
- *Interpretation* – Interpretation of a statement (e.g., "He actually means…").
- *Argumentation* – The statement or argument of the other author is either supported, or a counterargument/antithesis is formulated here.

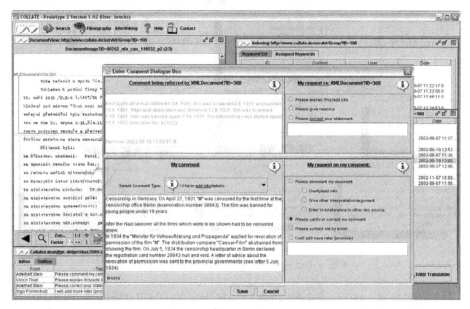

Fig. 5. Screenshot: Elaboration

While the film experts involved in the discussion successively enter a growing body of annotations over time – *Figure 6* shows a simplified example – they can use the context-oriented retrieval methods provided by the COLLATE system to access historic documents in their interpretation context.

6   Retrieval Options

The access facilities designed for users of the COLLATE collaboratory aim at exploiting the contents as well as the context of a document during the retrieval process. Several query forms with increasingly complex choice options allow to pose queries on different levels of expressiveness. For advanced search we exploit the annotations created by the COLLATE users. There are two ways of involving annotations into the retrieval process:

- Perform a full-text search on the annotations belonging to a document (i.e. annotations and annotations of annotations). With this, additional keywords which help identifying the content of an annotated document can be found. A document, its metadata and its annotations are seen as one global document where the search is performed on. For this global document, a weight is being calculated.
- Exploit the discourse context of an annotation. The relationship between two linked domain objects can be categorized into one of the discourse structure relations introduced above. With this information, we know if an annotation is an elaboration, an example, a counter-example, etc.

We will now discuss how this discourse context is used to improve the retrieval quality (for details on our approach to context-based retrieval see [3]). Let us have a look at the fictitious discourse example in *Figure 6*.

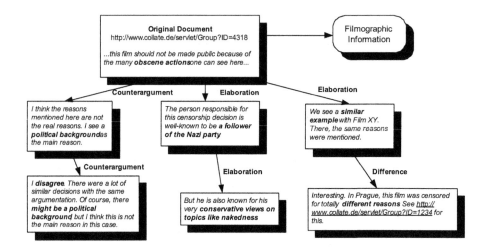

Fig. 6. Example of a discourse in COLLATE

Here, we have a censorship document where the censorship reason seems to be the occurrence of obscene actions in the film. Suppose the user asks for all films that were censored or banned for political reasons. Without using the annotations, this film would not be retrieved, because at the first glance, there was no political decision involved. But there is one annotation that states that the real reason were political considerations. This way, we have a hint that this film might be relevant to the query. But the statement that political reasons were the main reasons for the censorship decision is weakened by another annotator who disagrees with the opinion of the first.

Original documents, annotations, and discourse structure relations are used to create a ranking of documents, films, etc. with respect to the user's query. For this, a retrieval weight is calculated for every object to be retrieved. Annotations and discourse structure relations have a direct influence on this weight. In the example given above, the original document itself might contribute a weight of zero with respect to the query for films which were censored for political reasons, because it seems that this document has nothing to do with politics. But the fact that one annotator believes that the real reasons were political reasons could possibly raise the contributing weight of the original document to the film this document is about. On the other hand, the remarks of the annotator who disagrees with the opinion of his ancestor could lower this weight again. So, if we know to which extent an annotation is about a certain topic or concept, and if we know in which context of the discourse this annotation was made, one can try to calculate a specific influence of this annotation on the overall retrieval weight.

7   Conclusions

In the COLLATE collaboratory, content-based indexing denotes interpretative work on binary image representations of historic material supported by a rich term vocabulary. Pictorial documents are automatically classified w.r.t. semantic features concerning visual cues. In the collaborative environment, several users cooperate in order to achieve an interpretation of a historic document or the historic process it refers to. The collaboration process is implemented by threaded annotations. The links between annotations are classified to reflect argumentation patterns. The annotation context is being used to derive additional evidence that a document is relevant for a certain information need.

References

1. Brocks, H. Thiel, U. & Stein, A. Agent-Based User Interface Customization in a System-Mediated Collaboration Environment. In: Harris, D. et al. (Eds.), *Human-Centred Computing. Cognitive, Social and Ergonomic Aspects. Vol. 3 of the Proceedings of HCI International 2003*. Mahwah, NJ: Erlbaum, 2003, pp. 664-669.
2. CCSDS 650.0-B-1. *Reference Model for an Open Archival Information System (OAIS)*. Blue Book (Standard). Issue 1, January 2002.
   (http://ssdoo.gsfc.nasa.gov/nost/wwwclassic/documents/pdf/CCSDS-650.0-B-1.pdf)
3. Frommholz, I., Brocks, H., Thiel, U., Neuhold, E.J., Iannone, L., Semeraro, G., Berardi M. & Ceci, M. Document-Centered Collaboration for Scholars in the Humanities – The COLLATE System. In: Koch, T. & Sølvberg, I.T. (Eds.), *Research and Advanced Technology for Digital Libraries. Proceedings of the 7th European Conference (ECDL 2003)*. Berlin: Springer, 2003, pp. 434-445.
4. Maier, E. & Hovy, E.H. Organising Discourse Structure Relations Using Metafunctions. In: Horacek, H. & Zock, M. (Eds.), *New Concepts in Natural Language Processing*. London: Pinter, 1993, pp. 69-86.
5. Mann, W.C. & Thompson, S.A. Rhetorical Structure Theory: A Theory of Text Organization. In: Polanyi, L. (Ed.), *Discourse Structure*. Norwood: Ablex, 1987, pp. 85-96.
6. Nichols, D.M., Pemberton, D., Dalhoumi, S. , Larouk, O., Belisle, C. & Twindale M.B. DEBORA: Developing an Interface to Support Collaboration in a Digital Library. In: Borbinha, J.L. & Baker, T. (Eds.), *Research and Advanced Technology for Digital Libraries. Proceedings of the 4th European Conference (ECDL 2000)*. Berlin: Springer, 2000, pp. 239 ff.
7. Stein, A., Keiper, J., Bezerra, L., Brocks, H. & Thiel, U. Collaborative Research and Documentation of European Film History: The COLLATE Collaboratory. *International Journal of Digital Information Management (JDIM)*, 2004, 2(1): 30-39.

Separation of Concerns in Hypertext: Articulation Points That Increase Flexibility

Richard Furuta

Texas A&M University, College Station TX 77843-3112, USA,
furuta@cs.tamu.edu

Abstract. The benefits of separating document structure from presentation have long been understood—e.g., the distinction between the SGML and DSSSL standards as well as the ODA standard's separation of layout and logical structure. More recently, the breadth of applications incorporating XML specifications have provided further evidence in the context of the World-Wide Web of the strength of the abstraction that this separation provides. The structure/presentation separation, focused on describing the characteristics of documents, usefully can be extended to encompass the additional characteristics of interactive hypertextual documents, such as the Web's—for example, specifying the hypertext's responses to the reader's actions remains outside of the scope of the structure/presentation representation. We have explored one such family of models in which the hypertext is modeled by an automaton structure rather than a graph structure. In this paper, I will discuss how these new articulation points have lead to investigations into novel and flexible hypertext/hypermedia system implementations.

1 Introduction

The realization, over 30 years ago, that a document's structure could be separated from its presentation [1] revolutionized the view of document specifications, opening up applications that took advantage of the generality, flexibility, and reusability of the separated document specification form [2]. In the 1990's, the Web community discovered that the power of this approach was not the syntax of these representations (i.e., the SGML-like syntax adopted in HTML), but instead the inherent separation of specification, definition, and presentation embodied in these approaches (e.g., XML).

Even these notations capture only part of the significant hypertextual characteristics. Hypertext's dynamic characteristics largely are not specified but instead occur as implied side effects of other specifications. A key missing element is identification of the hypertext's behavior when read—its *browsing semantics*. In this paper, I assert that seeking the relevant conceptual separations in the hypertext model provides an opportunity for identifying leverage points that allow separation of hypertext from specific presentation.

Hypertext often is viewed as being modeled by a directed graph—graph nodes represent the content and graph arcs the links between content items. A natural

M. Hemmje et al. (Eds.): E.J. Neuhold Festschrift, LNCS 3379, pp. 128–137, 2005.

extension to incorporate a notion of dynamic behavior would be to model the hypertext as an automation rather than a graph. The automaton's semantics, then, would define the permissible behaviors of the hypertext during reading. For example, a finite state automaton could replace the directed graph with the automaton's state representing the current and state change representing link following. Using more complex kinds of automata would result in the potential for more complex hypertext behaviors—an investigation that could yield further insights into the future of hypertext [3].

In the late 1980s, Dave Stotts and I began working on Trellis, an automaton-centered hypertext model based on the Petri net [4,5,6]. In this paper, I will review this work, the research articulation points it provides, and the research explorations that it has enabled. Influenced by SGML's separation of structure, content, and presentation, the Trellis model distinguishes:

- Link structure (represented by the formal model)
- Content (represented abstractly by the formal model with the specific content instance mapped by the implementation)
- Presentation (provided, in implementation, by browser programs)
- Browsing semantics (represented by the model's automaton semantics and the instance's initial state)

As a further point that enables research explorations, the Trellis-based hypertext system implementation architecture is a client-server one in which hypertext engine and browsing programs are separate processes. The hypertext engine, the server in the architecture, interprets the hypertext's specification based on the model's automaton semantics and its initial state. The automaton-centered view is visible only within the context of the server, which instead presents a hypertext-centered view to the browsing programs (the client programs).

The implementation architecture has several interesting characteristics when compared to today's Web implementation:

1. Multiple clients can be active and communicating simultaneously with a single server.
2. The browsing state is defined by the automaton's state and consequently is associated with the server.
3. Client programs determine what content to show and how.
4. With the exception of clients used to edit the hypertext's specification, the semantics of the automaton that defines the model are revealed only within the context of the server. The browser's view of the world is based on a hypertext-oriented model of active/inactive nodes and associated active/inactive links.

Interpreting the first two of the characteristics in the context of a hypertext implementation means that several browser windows can be open on the same hypertext simultaneously *and* that the state of the browsing session in each of these windows is interlinked. Adding the third characteristic means that browsers can be customized for particular content types, that different browsers may be showing different interpretations of the content simultaneously, and that, indeed, a multimedia presentation may be realized for a particular reader through the coordinated, simultaneous efforts of multiple browsers. The fourth characteristic means that model semantics and browser behaviors can be investigated independently—in other words, the same set of browsers can be used with different clients based on different automaton semantics and browsers can be changed at will without affecting the state of the model. Thus the first and fourth characteristics mean that the state of the hypertext will persist across browsing sessions—i.e., the hypertext retains its state as long as the server is active even if no clients are active.

The client-server implementation architecture and its separate, simultaneously active browsers, also enables hypertextual applications involving multiple users. Hypertext browsing can be a collaborative activity, with each reader's activities affecting the information displayed to all.

The Trellis model and implementation architecture enable multiple independent investigation points:

- The underlying automaton **model** can be extended or different models can be substituted, supporting investigation of the nuances associated with different concepts of browsing semantics, and of the tradeoffs in different ways of specifying similar browsing behaviors. These investigations are primarily contextualized in the implementation architecture's server.
- Aspects of **presentation** can be articulated. New presentation modalities can be investigated as can coordination mechanisms among separate browsers. These investigations are primarily contextualized in the implementation architecture's clients.
- **External influences** can be incorporated; i.e., investigating how the hypertext's state can reflect potentially changing environmental characteristics. These investigations may affect both server and clients.

The Trellis hypertext model is described next. Section 3 presents examples from our subsequent investigations illustrating the reflection of the articulation points. Section 4's discussion of further implications concludes the paper.

2   The Trellis Model

This section contains an informal introduction to Trellis' Petri-net-based hypertext model. A formal description of the extended version we use at present can be found in [7].

A Petri net (see, e.g., [8,9]) is represented graphically as a bipartite directed graph, in which the circular nodes are called places and the bar nodes are called transitions. A dot in a place represents a token, and a place containing one or more tokens is said to be marked. When each place incident on a transition is marked that transition is enabled. An enabled transition may fire by removing one token from each of its input places and putting one token into each of its output places.

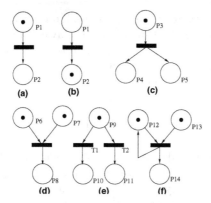

Fig. 1. Petri net examples

Figure 1 gives some Petri net examples. Net (a) shows a simple case of a single place, which is marked, incident on a transition. When the transition is fired, the result is net (b). When the transition in net (c) is fired, the token in place P3 is removed and one token is deposited into each of the places P4 and P5; hence this can be thought of as a fork. The transition in net (d) will not become enabled until both places P6 and P7 are marked; this is a join. On firing, the net will contain a single token in place P8. Net (e) encodes a choice. Both transitions T1 and T2 are enabled, but only one can fire, since firing will consume the token in place P9. Finally, net (f) presents a slightly more complex example. Firing the transition will remove the tokens in places P12 and P13, depositing tokens into P12 and P14. Thus after firing, place P12 remains marked.

Petri nets are mapped to hypertexts by associating content elements (i.e., a self-contained unit of content) with places and links with transitions. When a place is marked, the corresponding content is displayed, and when a transition is enabled, the corresponding link can be selected. Thus the token distribution encodes the hypertext's browsing state. Nets (a) and (b) correspond to the display of a sequence of content elements, net (c) to two content elements following in parallel from a single element, net (d) to a single content element replacing two predecessors, net (e) to two links, either of which may be selected, and net (f) to a case in which one content element remains visible while the second is replaced by a new content element.

The actual form of Petri net used is a stochastic colored Petri Net [10]. As a notational convenience, tokens have a "color", and predicates on the arcs specify what color (or colors) must be present before the transition is enabled as well as the color that is produced once the transition is fired. In addition to allow dynamic net behaviors, transitions are augmented with non-negative timing values, (τ_r, τ_m), $\tau_r \leq \tau_m$. τ_r, the release time, represents the amount of time that must elapse after the transition is enabled before the system permits its firing. τ_m, the maximum latency time, represents the maximum amount of time that the transition will be permitted to be enabled; the system fires the transition automatically after time τ_m passes. Time values can be thought of as defining a range, a delay and a timeout, for the availability of an event. $(0, \infty)$ is the common case (available for firing immediately and never fired by the system). Other interesting values include $(0, 0)$, which fires itself immediately on enabling, and (∞, ∞), which can never be fired.

3   Extensions and Investigations

In the initial section I argued that the Trellis model provides articulation points in the hypertext model that are useful in enabling investigations into the nature of hypertext and hypertext systems. The investigations that we have carried out to date fall into three categories: investigations involving the underlying automaton model, investigations involving aspects of the presentation, and investigations involving the effect of external influences as modifications to the model's browsing semantics. In this section, I will review examples of the investigations that have been enabled by these articulation points.

3.1   caT: Underlying Automaton Model and Effect of External Influences

An extension to Trellis called caT, whose acronym stands for "Context-Aware Trellis," investigated the addition of hierarchy to the Trellis Petri-net model and the encoding of responses to characteristics of the external environment in the hypertext's specification [11,7,12].

caT expands the Trellis definition in several ways. In the caT model, a token has optional local variables in addition to its color value. In addition, global variables are found in a user profile. Conditional predicates, referring to the local and global variables, are associated with the transitions and must be satisfied before the transition is permitted to fire. Assignment statements, associated with the arcs from transition to place, set and modify the variables' values.

caT incorporates a form of hierarchical Petri net [10]—essentially the specification is built as a collection of subnets, tied together in a hierarchy. In caT's representation, a transition in a higher-level net may be mapped to a separate subnet. The transition that is expanded to the subnet is called the *substitution transition*. Additionally, places in the higher-level net are mapped to places in the subnet—generally, the input to the subnet corresponds to places that lead into the substitution transition, and the output from the subnet corresponds to places that come from the substitution transition. When a token arrives in a mapped place, it appears simultaneously in both nets. Consequently, tokens in the higher-level net are first conveyed to the subnet, and then back from the subnet to the higher-level net. Variables passed from the higher-level net to the subnet can be used to specify the mapping of content to place, so the same subnet definition can be used multiple times in a single hypertext.

The caT extensions to the hypertext model illustrate how the separation of client and server enables investigation of the characteristics of hypertext model

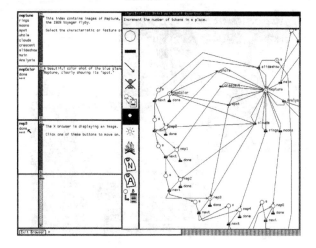

Fig. 2. An αTrellis display with text windows on the left and Petri net editor on the right

without involving implementation changes to the browsers used by readers. The hierarchical extensions to the Trellis model provide features that are visible and relevant to authors but not to readers—in other words, these modifications enable authoring of more complex hypertexts without changing the expressive power or reader-visible behaviors of the hypertexts. On the other hand, the additional of conditional predicates affects the runtime behavior of the hypertexts, perhaps modifying the reader's view of the hypertext's browsing semantics. Additionally, the predicates provide an alternate means for achieving some browsing behaviors, perhaps at the expense of adding a degree of non-directness to the specification; a relevant evaluation question is to examine the authoring tradeoffs between the power and the clarity of the specification mechanisms.

The Trellis architecture also enables experiments that focus on different kinds of browser behaviors without affecting the model. Some of our activities in this area will be described in the next section.

3.2   New Browsers: Presentation

Multiple Trellis content items may be available for simultaneous display. The initial prototype,αTrellis, divided a single window, into four panes to show textual content and links (the left-hand side window in figure 2). We realized at this time that the Trellis architecture enabled simultaneous use of specialized browsers, and so included a separate browser whose sole function was to display images (see figure 3). χTrellis, a reimplementation completed in the early 1990's by Stotts and students, replaced the single display with a separate window for each visible textual content element.

The caT prototype was built by Jin-Cheon Na in the late 1990's starting with the χTrellis code base. A major factor in the browsing environment not present

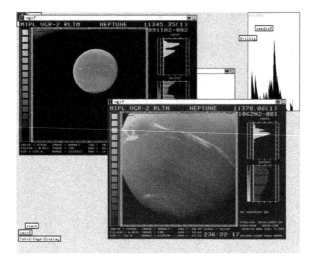

Fig. 3. Browser on a separate workstation displaying images in conjunction with the previous figure's browsing session

in the early 1990's but ubiquitous today is the World-Wide Web. Consequently, caT supported composition of individual active content elements into a single World-Wide Web page through a special-purpose browser without direct display connection that consults a template file to determine which of the active content elements to display, how to arrange them, and where to embed links within the Web display. The template file is actually just another hypertext element whose type is not displayed by most browsers. Consequently, different template files can be active at different times during a browsing session, allowing differing displays.

More recently, we have implemented a number of browsers that go beyond a purely textual rendition in one way or another. An audio browser [13] converts

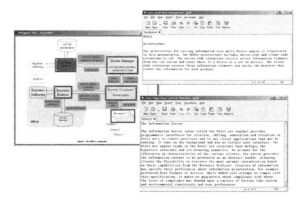

Fig. 4. A browser that presents a spatial view of the hypertext

text into synthetic speech. It also can renders an audio/video file when one is provided. Interactions are entirely through the keyboard, and audio prompts/ feedback is provided for operations.

We also have investigated browsers that are not limited to presenting a literal representation of the hypertext's content. For example, figure 4 shows a screen-shot of a spatial browser, implemented by Tolga Cifci, that shows a graphical overview of a hypertext that describes a system's architectural framework (see the next section for its details). Nodes with active links are highlighted. Select-ing any of them causes a corresponding link to be selected in the hypertext, which adds a textual description to the display (two descriptions may be seen in the figure). Thus this browser presents a graphical abstraction of the hypertext space while remaining within the context of that space.

It is relevant to repeat that the content and browsing semantics of each of these browsers is controlled by the same net-based specification. As before, mul-tiple browsers can be in use simultaneously. The user can select among different browsers to compensate for a variety of factors: the user's physical limitations, the characteristics of different display devices, the characteristics of the user's location (e.g., public or private), and characteristics of the user's task. In the next section, we describe our current efforts to providing automatic assistance to the user in managing the browsing environment.

3.3 MIDAS: Presentation

The modern computing environment is marked by increasingly universal net-work access and by widespread device diversity. A hypertext reader may have multiple networked displays available at any point in time—traditional com-puter workstations and their display or displays, small-sized hand-held devices such as Palms, even smaller-screened devices such as cellular telephones that also provide an integrated audio environment, and large-sized displays such as Plasma panels. The increasing availability of wireless networks means that the reader may be in motion—perhaps walking between locations or driving. The Trellis/caT separation of hypertext from display seems potentially well-suited for supporting readers in a multi-device and changing display environment. Yet a requirement that the reader be expected to manage the display characteristics of the environment manually greatly restricts the potential for usability gain from the flexibility provided by separating hypertext from display.

Management of the complexity and provision of the flexibility afforded by today's complex browser environment is the goal of a current project named MIDAS (Multi-device Integrated Dynamic Activity Spaces), being carried out by Unmil Karadkar [14]. MIDAS has six primary objectives:

- To ensure that all information content associated with the current browsing state is presented (completeness).
- To ensure consistency of the presented information (coherence).
- To coordinate the information rendered over all available browsers.
- To support browsing from multiple browsers on a set of diverse client devices.

  – To allow clients and browsers to dynamically join or leave a browsing session, and to handle the implications of this on maintaining coherence.

In essence, MIDAS's purpose is to move concerns about the information's rendering outside of the scope of the hypertext system. In doing so, MIDAS must cope with diversity in device characteristics, in environmental constraints, and in user preferences.

The MIDAS architecture interposes an additional layer between hypertext specification and browsers, with the intent of managing the browser display to achieve its goals. Success in this enterprise requires not only management of browser displays, but also guidance to hypertext authors. MIDAS includes authoring support to advise authors of the information formats needed to support the anticipated use environment. In some cases, separate information representations can be created automatically (e.g., different resolutions for an image), but in others, author input is required. For example, transforming the aspect ratio of an image can be carried out semi-automatically, perhaps requiring assistance from the author in determing whether to clip the image and how. However, providing a textual version of an image will always require that the author provide additional content and automatic assistance likely cannot be provided.

Developing MIDAS requires understanding of how readers view information and studies directed to this purpose are underway. More broadly, MIDAS illustrates the system and research opportunities enabled by separating hypertext content from its presentation.

4   Conclusions

As the sophistication of our computing and information environments evolves, creation of effective content becomes an increasingly complex task. Separating the job of hypertext authoring into a collection of independent concerns enhances the utility and reusability of the resulting hypertexts. However, the separation of the formerly monolithic task into subtasks requires identification of and understanding of the articulation points that support task subdivision. The thesis of this paper has been that the approach initiated in Trellis provides that segmentation and provides a framework on which to experiment with and to understand better the characteristics of each of the subdivisions. Our ongoing research seeks to point the way towards a new generation of hypertext, in which the message, its organization, its presentation, and its behavior are all independently-developable and customizable elements.

5   Acknowledgments

The Trellis project was a joint development by David Stotts and myself, and has benefited from the help of many others. I would like, in particular, to acknowledge some of the recent activities that are reflected in this paper. caT was developed as a component of Jin-Cheon Na's PhD dissertation [15]. Unmil Karadkar is designing, implementing, and evaluating the MIDAS architecture. Selen Ustun created the audio browser for her MS thesis [13]. Vivek Gupta created the first implementation of the graphical browser [16], and Tolga Cifci has extended, redefined, and improved the implementation. Yungah Park is investigating automated discovery of hierarchical model components and applications of such components in authoring. Youngjoo Park has created support for categorization of characteristics of display environments and for using the characterizations in guiding authors.

References

1. Goldfarb, C.F.: A generalized approach to document markup. Proceedings of the ACM SIGPLAN SIGOA Symposium on Text Manipulation, SIGPLAN Notices **16** (1981) and *SIGOA Newsletter* 2(1&2), (Spring/Summer 1981) 68–73

2. Furuta, R., Scofield, J., Shaw, A.: Document formatting systems: Survey, concepts, and issues. ACM Computing Surveys **14** (1982) 417–472

3. Stotts, D., Furuta, R.: Language-theoretic classification of hypermedia paths. In: Proc. 15th ACM Conf. Hypertext and Hypermedia, ACM Press (2004) 40–41

4. Stotts, P.D., Furuta, R.: Adding browsing semantics to the hypertext model. In: Proceedings of ACM Conference on Document Processing Systems (December 5–9, 1988, Santa Fe, New Mexico), ACM, New York (1988) 43–50

5. Furuta, R., Stotts, P.D.: Programmable browsing semantics in Trellis. In: Hypertext '89 Proceedings, ACM, New York (1989) 27–42

6. Stotts, P.D., Furuta, R.: Petri-net-based hypertext: Document structure with browsing semantics. ACM Transactions on Information Systems **7** (1989) 3–29

7. Na, J.C., Furuta, R.: Dynamic documents: Authoring, browsing, and analysis using a high-level Petri net-based hypermedia system. In: Proceedings of the ACM Symposium on Document Engineering (DocEng '01), ACM (2001) 38–47

8. Peterson, J.L.: Petri Net Theory and the Modeling of Systems. Prentice-Hall, Inc. (1981)

9. Reisig, W.: Petri Nets: An Introduction. Springer-Verlag (1985)

10. Jensen, K.: Coloured Petri Nets: Basic Concepts, Analysis Methods and Practical Use. Springer-Verlag (1992)

11. Na, J.C., Furuta, R.: Context-aware digital documents described in a high-level Petri-net-based hypermedia system. In: Digital Documents and Electronic Publishing (DDEP00). (2000) Munich, September 13–15, 2000.

12. Furuta, R., Na, J.C.: Applying caT's programmable browsing semanitcs to specify World-Wide Web documents that reflect place, time, reader, and community. In: Proc. 2002 ACM Symp. Document Engineering, ACM Press (2002) 10–17

13. Ustun, S.: Audio browsing of automaton-based hypermedia. Master's thesis, Department of Computer Science, Texas A&M University (2003)

14. Karadkar, U.P., Furuta, R., Ustun, S., Park, Y., Na, J.C., Gupta, V., Ciftci, T., Park, Y.: Display-agnostic hypermedia. In: Proceedings of the fifteenth ACM Conference on Hypertext and Hypermedia, ACM Press (2004) 58–67

15. Na, J.C.: Context-Aware Hypermedia in a Dynamically-Changing Environment, Supported by a High-Level Petri Net. PhD thesis, Texas A&M University, Department of Computer Science, College Station, TX (2001)

16. Gupta, V.: Graphical browser for Context Aware Trellis. Master of computer science project, Department of Computer Science, Texas A&M University (2003)

Towards a Common Framework for Peer-to-Peer Web Retrieval[*]

Karl Aberer and Jie Wu

School of Computer and Communication Sciences
EPFL, Lausanne
1015 Lausanne, Switzerland
{karl.aberer, jie.wu}@epfl.ch

Abstract. Search engines are among the most important services on the Web. Due to the scale of the ever-growing Web, classic centralized models and algorithms can no longer meet the requirements of a search system for the whole Web. Decentralization seems to be an attractive alternative. Consequently Web retrieval has received growing attention in the area of peer-to-peer systems. Decentralization of Web retrieval methods, in particular of text-based retrieval and link-based ranking as used in standard Web search engines have become subject of intensive research. This allows both to distribute the computational effort for more scalable solutions and to share different interpretations of the Web content to support personalized and context-dependent search. In this paper we first review existing studies about the algorithmic feasibility of realizing peer-to-peer Web search using text and link-based retrieval methods. From our perspective realizing peer-to-peer Web retrieval also requires a common framework that enables interoperability of peers using different peer-to-peer search methods. Therefore in the second part we introduce a common framework consisting of an architecture for peer-to-peer information retrieval and a logical framework for distributed ranking computation.

Keywords: search engine, information retrieval, peer-to-peer computing, distributed system, link analysis

1 Introduction

Search engines have been among the most important services since the very beginning of the World Wide Web. The different search engine providers have always been competing in terms of Web coverage measured by index size [2]. Google has claimed to index over 4 billion Web documents. However, this number is no more than 10-20% of the available surface Web pages according to a recent

[*] The work presented in this paper was carried out in the framework of the EPFL Center for Global Computing and supported by the Swiss National Funding Agency OFES as part of the European FP 6 STREP project ALVIS (002068).

M. Hemmje et al. (Eds.): E.J. Neuhold Festschrift, LNCS 3379, pp. 138–151, 2005.

conservative estimation [3]. Moreover, deep or hidden Web pages, which are not accessible for traditional Web crawlers, account for another 550 billion [5] Web pages. Due to such an ever-growing scale of the Web, it is increasingly difficult to meet the requirements of Web search with classic centralized models and algorithms. An attractive alternative is therefore decentralization. Consequently Web information retrieval has received growing attention in the area of peer-to-peer systems.

Recently the application of the peer-to-peer architectural paradigm to Web search engines has become a subject of intensive research. Most proposals address the decentralization of content-based retrieval techniques, such as classical text-based vector space retrieval or latent semantic indexing [19,34,33]. To a lesser extent the decentralization of ranking methods based on the link structure of the Web has been addressed. To fill this gap, we have devised in [42] an inherently distributed multi-layer Markov model for Web ranking computation in a decentralized fashion.

In this paper we will first review existing studies about the algorithmic feasibility of realizing peer-to-peer Web search using text and link-based retrieval methods. From our perspective realizing peer-to-peer Web retrieval also requires a common framework that enables interoperability of peers using different peer-to-peer search methods. Therefore in the second part we introduce a common framework consisting of an architecture for peer-to-peer information retrieval and a logical framework for distributed ranking computation.

2   Feasibility of P2P Web Indexing and Search

Applying the peer-to-peer paradigm to decentralized Web search aims at distributing the workload of a centralized Web search engine over many communicating peers. Thus a central bottleneck is eliminated at the cost of increasing the bandwidth consumption induced by communication among peers. The feasibility of Web search has been studied under this aspect in [25]. The authors find that a peer-to-peer network does not have enough bandwidth to support typical keyword searches on the Web document collection, both using unstructured and structured peer-to-peer networks. In unstructured networks the high bandwidth is induced by flooding queries over the whole network, whereas in structured overlay networks using distributed hash tables for the implementation of distributed inverted files, the extremely large size of posting lists that need to be transferred among peers, is identified as a limiting factor.

In this analysis, the authors first estimate the size of the Web index and the rate of users' submitting Web searches. They consider the two fundamental resource constraints, namely the available bandwidth of the Internet and the amount of disk space available on peers. It is shown that the communication costs of naive implementations of peer-to-peer Web search are at orders of magnitudes higher than the available resources. However, the authors also show that using several known optimization techniques, e.g. Bloom filters, and some design compromises, the gap between communication cost and available resources in orders of magnitude could be almost closed.

In short, naive implementations of peer-to-peer Web search are not feasible, but with some widely-used optimizations and a few design compromises they are becoming a realistic option. In particular the use of distributed hash tables opens many design options beyond simple exchange and intersection of posting lists for multiple keyword queries which were not examined. [33] is one example of a technique for substantially improving performance by distributing posting lists and search on them.

3   Text-Based Search

Text-based search has been intensively studied both for unstructured and structured peer-to-peer networks. In unstructured networks [27] like Gnutella [1] and KaZaA [4], peers typically flood search queries by forwarding them to neighboring peers to locate information. While flooding-based approaches are effective for finding highly replicated items, their performance is very poor for finding rare items. In contrast, many structured peer-to-peer networks [6,29,32,45,30] have been proposed recently based on the distributed hash table abstraction. Structured networks are good at finding rare items, but for frequent items they tend to introduce higher costs than unstructured networks. To address this dilemma, hybrid search solution have been proposed to use structured search methods to index and find rare items, and use flooding methods to find highly replicated content. We discuss some of the proposed approaches in the following.

3.1   Unstructured Networks

Improving the scalability of content-based searches in unstructured peer-to-peer networks has been a topic of intensive research. In [44], several techniques are developed to reduce the number of peers that are visited while broadcasting a keyword query. The aggregate bandwidth consumption and processing cost are thus reduced. The techniques include:

- Iterative deepening, where the requesting peer iteratively sends a query to growing number of peers until the query is answered.
- Directed breadth-first traversal, where peers maintain statistics on past interactions with their neighbors and select during searches those neighbors could potentially return more results and do that more quickly.
- Local indices, where peers may also maintain simple indices over other peers' data, usually the neighbors in the range of a given hop radius. Thus a peer could answer a query on behalf of some others without forwarding the query to them.

The approach of *compound routing indices* (CRI) in [13] can be considered as an extension of local indices. Documents are assumed to be on zero or more topics, using a pre-defined topic hierarchy and queries request documents on particular topics. A CRI contains the number of documents along each network path and the number of documents on each topic of interest. Such a CRI provides a coarse summary of the documents found in the network. Experimental results show that under given assumptions CRIs can improve the performance of content-based searches in unstructured peer-to-peer networks.

In [26], the authors use content-based search in a hybrid peer-to-peer network, where in an unstructured network some special peers provide local directory services. For determining content-based similarity the authors use the Kullback-Leibler (K-L) divergence [43]. In this approach, the directory peers construct the content models of neighbors and use them to determine the routing path for a query. The content models consist of the information on terms and term frequency of a peer's document collection. By using this technique, the average number of messages per query is greatly reduced, and the precision is increased while causing little degradation in recall.

To summarize, approaches to improve search performance while decreasing message traffic in unstructured peer-to-peer networks require the maintenance of some statistical summaries of document contents of peer neighbors, such as, local indices, routing indices, term statistics, Bloom filters, etc. within a certain graph neighborhood to guide query forwarding. From another perspective these approaches can be interpreted as strategies to impose some additional structure on the a priori unstructured networks.

3.2 Structured Networks

The fundamental limitation of unstructured peer-to-peer network is that documents are distributed randomly over peers and obtaining query results requires contacting a large number of peers. In [34] this problem is directly addressed by reassigning documents to peers that cluster semantically related documents. The peers are organized in a content-addressable network (CAN) [29] which is used to partition a logical document space into zones. Using LSI (Latent Semantic Indexing) [14] and some subsequent transformation of the resulting document vectors, documents are mapped into a low-dimensional space that is used as the logical document space used by CAN for partitioning. By this approach documents relevant to a given query tend to cluster on a small number of neighboring peers. Initial results show that the approach is fairly promising. However, the problem of distributed LSI computation using SVD (Singular Vector Decomposition) was not addressed in this approach and the low retrieval quality of LSI for large and heterogeneous corpora remains a critical issue. Enhancements addressing these issues were made in [33].

Solutions to text-based search in structured peer-to-peer networks have to address the fundamental problem of establishing a reasonable mapping between the network distance in a peer-to-peer network and semantic similarity of documents. The solution outlined above is one example of how to achieve this. We can expect many similar proposal to appear in the near future. Thus a common architectural framework for the modular implementation of such approaches and supporting interoperability has been proposed recently by us [8].

In this architecture we differentiate between concepts related to the construction and maintenance of a peer-to-peer overlay network, and those related to the application of a specific information retrieval technique. With respect to information retrieval techniques we further distinguish the issue of efficient implementation of structural queries (e.g. using distributed inverted files) and the semantic processing in a specific retrieval model. In the architecture we propose to decompose the information retrieval process in a peer-to-peer environment into four different layers:

1. Transport Layer Communications. Transport communications are handled at this layer.
2. Structured Overlay Networks. The purpose of this layer is to provide a logical network that is responsible for efficient routing of resource requests. Such a service is usually referred to as *key-based routing* (KBR). By mapping keys of the next-higher layer to *identifiers* of this layer, we associate certain document management tasks to specific peers.
3. Document and Content Management. The main objects handled at this layer are the basic document abstractions for text-based retrieval, namely the term sets and term statistics extracted from documents. They serve as the basis for determining semantic similarity of documents which is handled as the next-higher layer.
4. Retrieval Models. Here the objects are documents. Different retrieval models define different semantic distance functions for documents and resulting ranking functions for query answering. The ranking algorithms are typically based on computations performed on keys, but consider link-based methods as well.

In this way, we separate different concerns and allow different solutions at the higher layers to take advantage of the same infrastructure provided at the lower layers. This separation of concerns increases modularity of design and thus reusability of components offering basic services. Furthermore, it provides a step towards making different P2P-IR solutions interoperable, as it is unlikely that a single approach will prevail.

3.3   Top-k Query Processing

Recently the problem of text-based search has also been tackled from a slightly different angle using top-k query processing. Different from the previous approaches these works do not attempt to obtain complete query answers as efficiently as possible, but to retrieve the most relevant answers as fast as possible. These techniques are based on a well-known, centralized algorithm presented in Fagin's papers on the Threshold Algorithm (TA) [16,17].

In [10] this approach is applied to peer-to-peer networks. In a super-peer backbone organized in the HyperCuP topology [31], another variant of a distributed hash table, a distributed top-k retrieval algorithm is proposed to use sophisticated local indexes for query routing optimization and process intermediate query results at the earliest possible time. Only dynamically collected query statistics is used in the approach avoiding continuous updating of index information.

In [35], the authors argue that hardly any end-user would be interested in having the exact k best matches to a similarity query. Instead, occasional errors such as false positives or false negatives would be definitely tolerated. Thus they introduce a family of *approximative* top-k algorithms based on probabilistic algorithms. The basic idea underlying these algorithms is to calculate the probability that the total score exceeds a threshold, when we know a partial score of one or several but not all dimensions. When the total score is bigger than the threshold, the object would be among the top-k result with high probability. This work is still assuming a centralized system, however, we expect the principles could be conveniently extended and applied to peer-to-peer settings.

4 Link-Based Ranking

A large part of the success of Google is contributed to its introduction of link-based ranking methods into Web retrieval. Using contextual knowledge on documents extracted from the link graph allowed for the first time to assess not only the relevance of documents by analyzing their contents, but also to assess the authority or quality of documents and thus to greatly improve the quality of search results. At the time that PageRank [28], Google's link-based ranking method, was developed, the Web was still comparably small and using a centralized algorithm was not a critical issue [11]. In the meantime the situation has changed forcing Google to invest heavily into computing infrastructure to keep up with the Web growth. As a consequence, eventually link analysis of the complete Web graph will be performed in a distributed approach. This problem has recently also been investigated in the context of P2P IR.

4.1 Centralized Models

We first briefly review the two most prominent link-based ranking algorithms - HITS [24] and PageRank, and then describe our main contribution towards enabling link-based ranking in Peer-to-Peer Web search systems.

HITS is a query-dependent link-analysis approach, which first obtains a sub-graph of the Web relevant to a query result, and then applies the algorithm to this sub-graph. On the other hand, PageRank is query-independent and operates on the whole Web graph directly. Disregarding this difference, both rely on the same principles of linear algebra to generate a ranking vector, by using a principal Eigenvector of a matrix generated from the (sub) Web graph to be studied.

It has been shown [18] that HITS is often instable such that the returned Eigenvectors depend on variations of the initial seed vector and that the resulting Eigenvectors inappropriately assign zero weights to parts of the graph. In short,

HITS lacks strong theoretical basis assuring certain desirable properties of the resulting rankings.

In PageRank the process of surfing the Web is used as an intuitive model for assessing importance of Web pages and is modeled as a random walker on the Web graph. As the Web is not fully connected in practice, the process is complemented by random jumps such that transitions among non-connected pages are possible. The resulting transition matrix defines a stochastic process with a unique stationary distribution for the states, i.e. the Web pages, which is used to generate their ranking.

The computation of PageRank (and similarly of HITS if it were applied to the complete Web graph) is performed on a matrix representation of the complete Web graph and inherently difficult to decompose. However such decomposition would definitely be required for a distributed computation in a Peer-to-Peer architecture.

4.2   Trials of Distributed PageRank Computations

Various methods [20,21,22] have been proposed to speed up the computation of PageRank by either more efficient implementations or the application of optimized numerical algorithms. However, all these attempts have a limited potential of keeping up with the Web growth, as the complexity of centralized computation of PageRank is inherently related to the size of the link matrix of the Web, which is extremely large and growing. A different direction has been taken in [12,23], where structural features of the Web graph related to the hierarchical organization of the Web are used to simplify the link matrix and thus the computation of PageRank. In [12] the Web graph is aggregated at the Web site level in order to improve the efficiency of PageRank computation. Even though these algorithms make use of the internal structure of the Web in ranking computation, they are typically designed to be centralized.

4.3   A Layered Markov Model for Distributed Ranking Computation

Recently several research groups, including ours, have thus investigated the possibility to compute PageRank in a distributed fashion [36,40,41]. Common to these approaches is an idea similar to the one used in [12]: the Web graph is aggregated at the Web site level and a ranking is computed at this granularity, which we will call *SiteRank*. For each Web site independently rankings are computed for the local document collection, which we will call *DocRank*. The different DocRanks are then aggregated by using the SiteRank to weight the relative importance of the Web sites. Apparently this computation can be performed in a distributed manner since all DocRanks can be computed independently. The computation of SiteRank is of a comparably low complexity and can be either performed centrally or in a distributed fashion, depending on the architectural requirements. First experimental studies provide empirical evidence that link-based rankings computed in this way, not only allow a widely distributed and thus scalable computation, but also produce ranking results comparable (and sometimes even more reasonable) than applying global PageRank. However, as opposed to the standard PageRank method, a solid theoretical foundation for this approach has not yet been provided. This is the gap that we have tried to close [42].

While PageRank assumes that the Web is a flat graph of documents and the surfers move among them without exploiting the hierarchical structure, we consider the Layered Markov Model as a suitable replacement for the flat Markov Model to analyze the Web link structure for the following reasons:

- The logical structure of the Web graph is inherently hierarchical. No matter, whether the Web pages are grouped by Internet domain names, by geographical distribution, or by Web sites, the resulting organization is hierarchical. Such a hierarchical structure does definitely influence the patterns of user behavior.
- The Web is shown to be self-similar [15] in the sense that interestingly, part of it demonstrates properties similar to those of the whole Web. Thus instead of obtaining a snapshot of the whole Web graph, introducing substantial latency, and performing costly computations on it, bottom-up approaches, which deal only with part of the Web graph and then integrate the partial results in a decentralized way to obtain the final result, seem to be a very promising and scalable alternative for approaching such a large-scale problem.

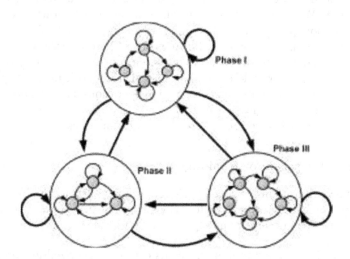

Fig. 1. Phases and sub-states in Layered Markov Model

Figure 1 illustrates a LMM (Layered Markov Model) structure. The model consists of 12 sub-states (small circles) and 3 super-states (big circles), which are referred to as *phases* in [9]. There exists a transition process at the upper layer among phases and there are three independent transition processes among the sub-states belonging to the three super-states.

Based on this hierarchical model for the Web graph, we propose a centralized and a decentralized approach for the computation of a link-based ranking of Web documents. Both are shown to produce a well-defined ranking for a given Web graph. The centralized approach is given to clarify the relationship of this method to other centralized link-based ranking methods, such as PageRank. The two approaches are formally proven to be equivalent [39,42]. Thus we show of how a well-understood centralized, link-based ranking method can be equivalently computed in a decentralized fashion, such as required for Web search engines having a peer-to-peer architecture. Furthermore, personalized rankings can be included when using this approach by adapting the computation at both the local layer and the global layer.

We performed preliminary experiments with data crawled at our campus Web, and the empirical results show that the ranking generated by our model is qualitatively comparable to or even better than the ranking produced by PageRank [39,42].

5   A Common Logical Framework for P2P IR

We have shown that decentralization of Web retrieval methods bears the potential of providing a wide range of solutions addressing both the issues of better scalability and improved ranking quality in web search. Having different methods for ranking Web contents allows sharing different interpretations of the Web content to support personalized and context-dependent search. We have already argued that a common architectural framework will be essential in enabling interoperability and sharing of resources in such a context. We believe that it will be important to also provide a common logical framework in which peers can represent the various outputs and composition operations used in a decentralized ranking scenario. This logical framework provides a common model to be used at the retrieval models layer of our architectural framework.

5.1   Characterization of Rankings

In our framework, rankings are the basic, underlying abstraction. To characterize rankings we associate them with various types of metadata. The metadata identifies the following important aspects of a ranking:

- The type of a ranking: ranking methods can be categorized in various ways, e.g., according to the structural information they used, such as text-based vs. link-based, or according to the algorithmic approach taken, such as vector-space models, LSI models, or biology-inspired algorithms [37]. The categorization would be based on a shared ontology.
- The operations applicable to a ranking: the specification contains the operations together with their interface type that are applicable to a ranking,

e.g. in order to restrict it to a specific context or to combine it with other rankings.

- The scope of a ranking: rankings or not necessarily provided for the complete Web contents, but for certain subsets of it, such as Web sites or peers' document collections.
- The quality of a ranking: this characterizes aspects such as the freshness of a ranking, i.e., when it was computed, and a characterization for how long the quality of a ranking may be considered as being high, or in other words when a ranking expires.

More details on the characterization of rankings can be found in [38].

5.2   Ranking Composition in P2P IR

Once different rankings, text-based or link-based or other types of rankings, are being generated by individual peers or cooperatively by multiple peers connected in a peer-to-peer network, a consistent framework for their composition is required. This allows the production of rankings matching specific requirements of users and applications.

We illustrate this by means of an example. Suppose in a peer-to-peer Web search system each participating peer is free to choose its own algorithm to rank the local document collection, such as the vector space model (VSM), the HITS algorithm or a biology-inspired algorithm [37]. In addition, different rankings for assessing the quality or authority of the rankings produced by different peers are available, producing a *PeerRank*. This could be achieved using a distributed link-based ranking algorithm such as the algorithm based on our LMM model [42]. Furthermore, different overlay networks exist to actively manage documents by semantically clustering them at peers using an approach similar to the one from [34,33].

With such a system setting, no uniform global ranking exists. Rather, the rankings can be combined in different ways for satisfying different information needs. In order to specify, manipulate and compare such combinations of rankings a formal framework is required. As in the case of relational databases, an algebraic framework seems to be an adequate approach to that end.

5.3   Ranking Algebra

We sketch here some of the operations that would be expressed in a ranking algebra. A formal specification of a ranking algebra has been given in [38]. Assume rankings as described in the previous section are provided, their composition could proceed as follows.

1. The individual peers apply their local ranking methods (e.g. VSM, HITS) to their local document collections. They create the corresponding metadata for the rankings and share it through a structured peer-to-peer network. These rankings are the basic operands for the subsequent application of ranking algebra operations.

2. A global PeerRank based on the LMM model is computed. Each peer includes into the metadata associated with it's locally computed ranking the weight it receives from PeerRank.
3. When a query is received by the peer-to-peer Web search system, it is first forwarded, using the structured peer-to-peer network that has been used to cluster documents, to a peer holding documents relevant to the query. This can be used to create a first, content-based ranking of results. Using the weights obtained from 2 and considering the intermediate result obtained so far, peers having relevant ranking information on result documents are selected. The local rankings of these peers obtained in step 1 are then factored in, in order to produce the final result ranking.

This scenario shows that the algebra has to include a number of basic operations, such as standard set-operations (e.g. selection, projection) as well as ranking specific operations, such as weighted combination of rankings or normalization of rankings. Details of such operators have been described in [38]. Such a ranking algebra together with a common architectural framework provides a foundation for a both logically and physically decentralized approach Web retrieval, a true P2P IR system.

6   Conclusion and Outlook

In this paper we have reviewed state-of-the-art technologies and approaches in peer-to-peer Web retrieval, including keyword-based retrieval and decentralized link-based ranking computation. We then stated the necessity of having a solid framework for the sharing of the available ranking resources in a peer-to-peer Web search system consisting of an architectural framework and a common algebraic model.

The framework we outlined is under continuous development. An important aspect in peer-to-peer networks is the issue of trust. Mechanisms to provide incentives for peers to behave cooperatively and honestly are essential to maintain the integrity of such a system. Results from work on managing trust in peer-to-peer systems need thus to be taken into account [7]. Interestingly, they carry many similarities with link-based methods for assessing the authority of Web resources.

Though research on peer-to-peer approaches to Web search has fully taken off, it remains to be seen in which way this approach will compete with or complement existing centralized search engines. Certain important characteristics of centralized approaches, in particular the very short latency in query answering, seem to be very hard to achieve in a fully decentralized approach. Thus it seems likely that standard, keyword based searches for quickly addressing Web contents (containing characteristic terms) will remain a domain for centralized engines, whereas semantically more sophisticated searches, requiring specialized search techniques and in-depth content analysis bear a huge potential for decentralized approaches.

References

1. Gnutella protocol development website. http://rfc-gnutella.sourceforge.net/, visited on 27th of Oct. 2004.
2. How big are the search engines?
   http://searchenginewatch.com/sereport/article.php/2165301, visited on 26th of Oct. 2004.
3. How many pages estimated on the internet?
   http://www.webmasterworld.com/forum10/5219-2-10.htm, visited on 26th of Oct. 2004.
4. Kazaa. http://www.kazza.com/, visited on 27th of Oct. 2004.
5. How much information, 2000.
   http://www.sims.berkeley.edu/research/projects/how-much-info/internet.html, visited on 26th of Oct. 2004.
6. Karl Aberer. P-grid: A self-organizing access structure for p2p information systems. In *Proceedings of the Sixth International Conference on Cooperative Information Systems (CoopIS 2001)*, Trento, Italy, 2001.
7. Karl Aberer and Zoran Despotovic. Managing trust in a peer-2-peer information system. In *Proceedings of the Ninth International Conference on Information and Knowledge Management (CIKM 2001)*, 2001.
8. Karl Aberer, Fabius Klemm, Martin Rajman, and Jie Wu. An architecture for peer-to-peer information retrieval. In *Proceedings of the SIGIR 2004 Workshop on P2P IR*, Sheffield, UK, July 2004.
9. Jafar Adibi and Wei-Min Shen. Self-similar layered hidden Markov models. *Lecture Notes in Computer Science*, 2168:1–15, 2001.
10. Wolf-Tilo Balke, Wolfgang Nejdl, Wolf Siberski, and Uwe Thaden. Progressive distributed top k retrieval in peer-to-peer networks. In *Proceedings of the 21st International Conference on Data Engineering (ICDE 2005)*, April 2005.
11. Sergey Brin, Rajeev Motwani, Lawrence Page, and Terry Winograd. What can you do with a web in your pocket? *Data Engineering Bulletin*, 21(2):37–47, 1998.
12. Andrei Z. Broder, Ronny Lempel, Farzin Maghoul, and Jan Pedersen. Efficient pagerank approximation via graph aggregation. In *Proceedings of the 13th international World Wide Web conference on Alternate track papers & posters*, pages 484–485. ACM Press, 2004.
13. A. Crespo and H. Garcia-Molina. Routing indices for peer-to-peer systems, 2002.
14. Scott C. Deerwester, Susan T. Dumais, Thomas K. Landauer, George W. Furnas, and Richard A. Harshman. Indexing by latent semantic analysis. *Journal of the American Society of Information Science*, 41(6):391–407, 1990.
15. Stephen Dill, S. Ravi Kumar, Kevin S. McCurley, Sridhar Rajagopalan, D. Sivakumar, and Andrew Tomkins. Self-similarity in the web. In *The VLDB Journal*, pages 69–78, 2001.
16. Ronald Fagin. Combining fuzzy information from multiple systems (extended abstract). In *Proceedings of the fifteenth ACM SIGACT-SIGMOD-SIGART symposium on Principles of database systems*, pages 216–226. ACM Press, 1996.
17. Ronald Fagin, Amnon Lotem, and Moni Naor. Optimal aggregation algorithms for middleware. In *Proceedings of the twentieth ACM SIGMOD-SIGACT-SIGART symposium on Principles of database systems*, pages 102–113. ACM Press, 2001.
18. A. Farahat, T. LoFaro, J. C. Miller, G. Rae, and L. A. Ward. Existence and Uniqueness of Ranking Vectors for Linear Link Analysis Algorithms. *SIAM Journal on Scientific Computing*, (submitted), 2003.

19. Omprakash D Gnawali. A keyword-set search system for peer-to-peer networks. Master's thesis, Department of Electrical Engineering and Computer Science, MIT, May 2002.
20. Taher Haveliwala. Efficient computation of pageRank. Technical Report 1999-31, Stanford University, September 1999.
21. S. Kamvar, T. Haveliwala, C. Manning, and G. Golub. Extrapolation methods for accelerating pagerank computations. In *Proceedings of the Twelfth International World Wide Web Conference*, 2003.
22. Sepandar Kamvar, Taher Haveliwala, and Gene Golub. Adaptive methods for the computation of pagerank. Technical report, 2003.
23. Sepandar D. Kamvar, Taher H. Haveliwala, Christopher D. Manning, and Gene H. Golub. Exploiting the block structure of the web for computing pagerank. Technical report, Stanford University, March 2003. Submitted on 4th of March 2003.
24. Jon Kleinberg. Authoritative sources in a hyperlinked environment. In *Proceedings of the ACM-SIAM Symposium on Discrete Algorithms*, 1998.
25. Jinyang Li, Boon Thau Loo, Joseph M. Hellerstein, M. Frans Kaashoek, David R. Karger, and Robert Morris. On the feasibility of peer-to-peer web indexing and search. In *Proceedings of the 2nd International Workshop on Peer-to-Peer Systems*, Berkeley, California, USA, 2003.
26. Jie Lu and Jamie Callan. Content-based retrieval in hybrid peer-to-peer networks. In *Proceedings of the twelfth international conference on Information and knowledge management*, pages 199–206. ACM Press, 2003.
27. Qin Lv, Pei Cao, Edith Cohen, Kai Li, and Scott Shenker. Search and replication in unstructured peer-to-peer networks. In *Proceedings of the 16th international conference on Supercomputing*, pages 84–95. ACM Press, 2002.
28. Larry Page, Sergey Brin, Rajeev Motwani, and Terry Winograd. The pagerank citation ranking: Bringing order to the web. Technical report, Stanford University, January 1998.
29. Sylvia Ratnasamy, Paul Francis, Mark Handley, Richard Karp, and Scott Shenker. A scalable content addressable network. Technical Report TR-00-010, Berkeley, CA, 2000.
30. Antony Rowstron and Peter Druschel. Pastry: Scalable, distributed object location and routing for large-scale peer-to-peer systems. In *IFIP/ACM International Conference on Distributed Systems Platforms (Middleware)*, pages 329–350, November 2001.
31. Mario Schlosser, Michael Sintek, Stefan Decker, and Wolfgang Nejdl. HyperCuP – hypercubes, ontologies and efficient search on peer-to-peer networks, May 2003. http://www-db.stanford.edu/ schloss/docs/HyperCuP-LNCS2530.ps.
32. Ion Stoica, Robert Morris, David Karger, Frans Kaashoek, and Hari Balakrishnan. Chord: A scalable Peer-To-Peer lookup service for internet applications. In *Proceedings of the 2001 ACM SIGCOMM Conference*, pages 149–160, 2001.
33. Chunqiang Tang, Sandhya Dwarkadas, and Zhichen Xu. On scaling latent semantic indexing for large peer-to-peer systems. In *Proceedings of the 27th Annual International ACM SIGIR Conference*, Sheffield, UK, July 2004.
34. Chunqiang Tang, Zhichen Xu, and Sandhya Dwarkadas. Peer-to-peer information retrieval using self-organizing semantic overlay networks. In *Proceedings of the 2003 conference on Applications, technologies, architectures, and protocols for computer communications*, pages 175–186, Karlsruhe, Germany, 2003. ACM Press.
35. Martin Theobald, Gerhard Weikum, and Ralf Schenkel. Top-k query evaluation with probabilistic guarantees. In *Proceedings of the Thirtieth International Conference on Very Large Data Bases*. Morgan Kaufmann, August 2004.

36. Yuan Wang and David J. DeWitt. Computing pagerank in a distributed internet search system. In *Proceedings of the 30th International Conference on Very Large Data Bases*, pages 420–431. Morgan Kaufmann Publishers Inc., 2004.

37. Jie Wu and Karl Aberer. Swarm intelligent surfing in the web. In *Proceedings of the Third International Conference on Web Engineering, ICWE'03*, Oviedo, Asturias, Spain, July 2003. July 14-18, 2003.

38. Jie Wu and Karl Aberer. Foundation model for semantic p2p retrieval. *In preparation for submission*, 2004.

39. Jie Wu and Karl Aberer. Using a layered markov model for decentralized web ranking. Technical Report IC/2004/70, Swiss Federal Institute of Technology, Lausanne, Switzerland, Auguest 2004.

40. Jie Wu and Karl Aberer. Using siterank for decentralized computation of web document ranking. In *Proceedings of the third International Conference on Adaptive Hypermedia and Adaptive Web-Based Systems*, Eindhoven, The Netherlands, August 2004.

41. Jie Wu and Karl Aberer. Using siterank in p2p information retrieval. Technical Report IC/2004/31, Swiss Federal Institute of Technology, Lausanne, Switzerland, March 2004.

42. Jie Wu and Karl Aberer. Using a layered markov model for distributed web rank computation. In *Submitted to ICDCS 2005*, Columbus, Ohio, U.S.A., June 2005.

43. Jinxi Xu and W. Bruce Croft. Cluster-based language models for distributed retrieval. In *Proceedings of the 22nd annual international ACM SIGIR conference on Research and development in information retrieval*, pages 254–261. ACM Press, 1999.

44. Beverly Yang and Hector Garcia-Molina. Improving search in peer-to-peer networks. In *Proceedings of the 22 nd International Conference on Distributed Computing Systems (ICDCS'02)*, page 5. IEEE Computer Society, 2002.

45. B. Y. Zhao, J. D. Kubiatowicz, and A. D. Joseph. Tapestry: An infrastructure for fault-tolerant wide-area location and routing. Technical Report UCB/CSD-01-1141, UC Berkeley, April 2001.

Comparative Evaluation of Cross-language Information Retrieval Systems

Carol Peters

ISTI-CNR, Area di Ricerca CNR, Via Moruzzi, 1
56124 Pisa, Italy
carol.peters@isti.cnr.it

Abstract: With the increasing importance of the "Global Information Society" and as the world's depositories of online collections proliferate, there is a growing need for systems that enable access to information of interest wherever and however it is stored, regardless of form or language. In recognition of this, five years ago, the DELOS Network for Digital Libraries launched the Cross-Language Evaluation Forum (CLEF), with the objective of promoting multilingual information access by providing the research community with an infrastructure for testing and evaluating systems operating in multilingual contexts and a common platform for the comparison of methodologies and results. In this paper, we outline the various activities initiated by CLEF over the years in order to meet the emerging needs of the application communities, and trace the impact of these activities on advances in multilingual system development.

1   Introduction

In recognition of the fact that "multilinguality" is of particular relevance for European digital collections, although a frequently neglected issue in European digital library (DL) projects, in 2000 DELOS decided to sponsor the work of the Cross-Language Evaluation Forum (CLEF) as part of its DL evaluation activity. CLEF was given the mandate to promote cross-language information retrieval (CLIR) system development by providing the research community with an infrastructure for testing and evaluating systems operating in both monolingual and cross-language contexts and by encouraging take-up of the R&D results by the application communities. In order to achieve these objectives, CLEF organises annual system evaluation campaigns, which culminate each year in a workshop where the participants present and discuss their experiments. In this paper, we will describe the main achievements of CLEF so far and will discuss the efforts that are being made to ensure that CLEF continues to meet the emerging needs of system developers and application communities.

M. Hemmje et al. (Eds.): E.J. Neuhold Festschrift, LNCS 3379, pp. 152–161, 2005.

2   Consolidating Multilingual Document Retrieval

Over the last decade, with the increasing globalization of the information society, the interest in the potential of multilingual[1] information access functionality has grown considerably. However, when the first CLIR system evaluation activity began in 1997 at TREC[2], very little IR system testing work had been done for languages other than English and almost all existing cross-language systems were designed to handle no more than two languages: searching from query language to target language. Since its beginnings, CLEF[3] has worked hard to change this situation and to promote the development of systems capable of searching over multiple languages, with the focus on European languages. For this reason, each year the CLEF ad-hoc track has proposed a set of core evaluation tasks designed to test monolingual, bilingual (queries in one language against a target collection in another) and multilingual (queries in one language against target collections in many languages) text retrieval systems. The aim has been to encourage groups to work their way up gradually from mono- to multilingual retrieval, providing them with facilities to test and compare search and access techniques over languages and pushing them to investigate the issues involved in simultaneously processing a number of languages with different characteristics. Over the years, the language combinations provided have increased and the tasks offered have grown in complexity. The CLEF 2003 multilingual track included a task which entailed searching a collection in eight languages. In 2000, the main CLEF multilingual corpus consisted of approximately 360,000 newspaper and news agency documents for four languages; by 2004 it included nearly two million documents and ten languages[4].

The evaluation environment for this track adopted an automatic scoring method, based on the well-known Cranfield methodology [2]. The test collection consists of a set of "topics" describing information needs and a set of documents to be searched to find those documents that satisfy the information needs. Evaluation is then done for each ranking of documents with respect to a topic by the usual computation of recall and precision. The distinguishing feature of CLEF is that it applies this evaluation

---

[1]   We use "multilingual" to denote both cross-language and multiple language information processing activities.

[2]   TREC – the Text REtrieval Conference series, co-sponsored by the National Institute of Standards and Technology (NIST) and the US Department of Defense, was started in 1992 to support research within the information retrieval community by providing the infrastructure necessary for large-scale evaluation of text retrieval methodologies. See http://trec.nist.gov/

[3]   CLEF was launched when it was decided to move the coordination of the CLIR track at TREC to Europe. CLEF 2000 and 2001 were sponsored by the 5FP DELOS Network of Excellence for Digital Libraries; CLEF 2002 and 2003 were funded as an independent project by the European Commission under the IST programme. CLEF 2004 was again organized as an activity of the DELOS Network of Excellence, under the Sixth Framework Programme of the European Commission.

[4]   The CLEF comparable corpus currently contains news documents for the same time period (1994-95) in ten languages: Dutch, English, Finnish, French, German, Italian, Portuguese, Russian, Spanish, and Swedish; we are now working on adding some central European languages: Bulgarian, Czech and Hungarian.

paradigm in a multilingual setting. This means that the criteria normally adopted to create a test collection, consisting of suitable documents, sample queries and relevance assessments, have been adapted to satisfy the particular requirements of the multilingual context. All language dependent tasks such as topic creation and relevance judgments are performed in a distributed setting by native speakers. Rules are established and a tight central coordination is maintained in order to ensure consistency and coherency of topic and relevance judgment sets over the different collections, languages and tracks.

The results of this track in terms of participation and of the different approaches and techniques tested have been impressive. Regular CLEF participants, i.e. groups that have participated several years running, have shown improvements in performance and flexibility in advancing to more complex tasks. Much work has been done on fine-tuning for individual languages, while other efforts have concentrated on developing language-independent strategies. The issues involved in cross-language text retrieval have been investigated in depth and are now well understood. Recent work at CLEF has shown that what can be called a "blueprint" for a successful multilingual system is now emerging, although the merging of results over collections can still be considered as a largely unsolved problem. At the same time, a clear improvement in system performance has been demonstrated for bilingual information retrieval. At the CLIR track in TREC in 1977, bilingual retrieval averaged at about 50% of monolingual retrieval on the same collection; the figures for both CLEF 2003 and 2004 show the best bilingual system performance at more than 80% of monolingual retrieval. A detailed discussion of these results can be found in [1].

3   Towards Multilingual Information Access

As described in the previous section, in the beginning CLEF focused mainly on testing performance of off-line text retrieval systems, where good system performance is equated with good retrieval effectiveness (in terms of returning lists of documents). However, it became obvious that this was only one part of the CLIR problem. A multilingual system evaluation activity that meets the needs of the application communities must also provide facilities to investigate many other aspects including:

- not just retrieval on news documents but also on other genres which may have their own specific access and retrieval problems;
- not just system performance but also wider usability issues that affect the users' ability to recognize relevant information and refine search results even when documents are written in an unfamiliar language;
- not just document retrieval, but also targeted information location and extraction;
- not just text but also mixed-media data, e.g. collections containing images or spoken documents.

With these requirements in mind, CLEF has gradually extended its range of interests and increased the number of evaluation tracks offered. Over the years, the focus in CLEF has shifted from straight document retrieval and has diversified to include different kinds of text retrieval across languages (from documents to exact answers) and retrieval on different kinds of media (not just text but image and speech as well).

By designing and offering new and challenging tasks, our intention has been to stimulate advances in system development. In this section, we describe what has been done so far and our plans for the next years. As will be seen, in order to be able to run so many diverse evaluation tracks (six in 2004, eight tracks are planned for 2005), the expertise and the efforts of a large number of research groups have been mobilized.

3.1   Cross-Language System Evaluation for Different Genres

The main CLEF collection is the multilingual comparable corpus of news documents described above. However, news media have characteristics which may not hold true for other genres: wide use of proper nouns (names and places), association of date stamps, particular style of writing and a rapid evolution of general-purpose vocabulary. Certain features may facilitate access and retrieval, others may hinder it. [3]. For this reason, CLEF has also included a mono- and cross-language domain-specific retrieval track each year, mainly based on the GIRT corpus of structured social science data which has an associated social science thesaurus in German-English and German-Russian[5]. Since the first CLEF campaign in 2000 the GIRT corpus has been enlarged several times, and is now presented as a pseudo-parallel corpus[6], with about 150,000 identical documents in German and English. In this way, we have provided the opportunity for developers to test their CLIR systems on domain-specific data, with domain related vocabulary. In 2005 we intend to enlarge the existing social science collection with Russian sociology data. However, a severe problem with offering domain-specific collections in a CLEF-type evaluation campaign is that you need domain-specific experts willing to perform the relevance assessment task. Cross-lingual patent retrieval is already offered as an evaluation task by the Asian initiative, NTICIR[7], and CLEF is now considering offering a similar task; contacts are now under way with the European patent office. Although there is much industrial interest in such a tasks but its realization depends heavily on the availability and willingness of experts to do the relevance assessments.

Another document type will be included in CLEF 2005 with the introduction of a web task. The World Wide Web is, of course, a natural setting for cross-language retrieval activities and many issues for which people consult the Web are essentially issues that cross over language boundaries, e.g. news, education, travel, leisure. As web pages normally contain information in mixed media, searchers not familiar with the language of a page are often able to extract useful information, such as names, maps, timetables, etc. However, current web search engines do not offer truly multilingual search functionality. We believe CLEF could provide a real service to the research community by providing a multilingual Web test collection and testing

---

[5]   A German-English Social Science Thesaurus and the German-Russian wordlist are provided and made available in machine readable formats by IZ-Bonn, Germany. UC Berkeley made an XML version available.

[6]   The GIRT4 corpus is called pseudo-parallel because the original documents are in German and the English part consists of translations of these German documents into English; the English part is actually considerably smaller than the German.

[7]   NTCIR (NII-NACSIS Test Collection for IR Systems) organized by the Institute of Informatics, Tokyo: http://research.nii.ac.jp/ntcir/. There is an ongoing collaboration and sharing of ideas between NTCIR and CLEF.

systems with respect to different issues, eg results presentation, user interaction. Unfortunately, the building of a Web corpus for multilingual access is not a trivial task; the basic snapshot data of the Web and the evaluation metrics will have to be defined very carefully [4, 5]. A multilingual Web corpus should include carefully calculated representative samples for less commonly used languages plus random samples for the most dominant ones. Questions of intellectual property rights must also be considered.

The first step in 2005 will be to start work on building such a collection. A group from the University of Amsterdam is responsible for developing a pilot WebCLEF track. They intend to build on insights gained while building the W10G and the .gov collections at TREC [6]. Their aim for the first year is to have a collection of between one and two million pages with a minimum of 50,000 documents per language for at least ten languages; html, pdf and txt type documents will be included. Queries will be generated in many languages and will be created in two ways: partly artificially by participants and partly by extraction from log files.

There will also be a pilot experiment in CLEF 2005 in cross-language geographic information retrieval (GeoCLEF). This track will provide a framework in which to evaluate GIR systems for search tasks involving both spatial and multilingual aspects and is the first evaluation exercise of this type to be attempted.

3.2   Considering the Users' Perspective

Of course, the user is at the centre of any information retrieval system and the system functionality must be designed with the user requirements in the forefront. This is especially true when users are searching for relevant information contained in documents written in languages that are unfamiliar to them. In this case, they may need assistance in recognizing which of a ranked list of documents are relevant for their purposes. They also may need help in refining their original query taking these results into account, and they need to understand how information contained in documents in an unfamiliar language can be exploited. These problems are crucial questions for the users of a CLIR system. The default assumptions for a cross-language search engine are that a) commercial Machine Translation (MT) systems can be used to translate documents into the native language of the user, and b) document selection and query refinement can be done using such translations. In order to challenge such (untested) assumptions, the University of Maryland, USA, and UNED, Spain, decided to organize an interactive track – iCLEF – within CLEF. The goal was comparative studies of user interaction issues in CLIR.

The first pilot interactive track at CLEF, known as iCLEF, was held in 2001 [7], and focused on document selection questions, i.e. approaches to facilitate fast and accurate relevance judgments for documents that the user could not read without assistance. The iCLEF experimental design combined insights from the interactive TREC track with the distributed multilingual assessment process of CLEF. The experience led to non-trivial empirical conclusions; for instance, full MT performed better than word-by-word translation, but cross-language pseudo-summaries (allowing faster relevance judgments without loss of precision) outperformed full MT. The success of this experiment led to the iCLEF track being included as a regular event in CLEF.

*i*CLEF tracks in CLEF 2002 and 2003 studied support mechanisms for interactive query formulation and refinement [8, 9], and included experiments such as user-assisted term translation (via inverse dictionaries, translation definitions, etc), which was shown to outperform automatic query translation, and user-assisted query reformulation by selection of relevant noun-phrases, which was shown to outperform user-assisted term translation.

In the 2004 track, five participating teams used a common evaluation design to assess the ability of interactive systems of their own design to support the task of finding specific answers to narrowly focused questions in collections of documents in a language different from that of the language in which the questions were expressed. This task was the interactive counterpoint to the fully automatic cross-language question-answering task in CLEF 2003 and 2004 [10]. Overall, *i*CLEF experiences so far have involved more than one thousand interactive cross-language searches in several languages (English, Spanish, Finnish, German and Swedish), constituting the largest set of empirical data about multilingual information access from the user perspective known to us.

The connection with the question-answering (QA) track (see next section) will be continued in 2005 where *i*CLEF will study the problem of cross-language question answering from a user-inclusive perspective. The challenge is twofold: from the point of view of QA as a machine task, interaction with the user may help a QA engine to retrieve better answers; from the point of view of QA as a user task, a search assistant may help the user to locate the answer more easily, more quickly and more accurately. The participating groups will share a common experiment design in which users explore different aspects of the above research challenges. *i*CLEF also intends to organize an interactive image retrieval task in coordination with the ImageCLEF track (see section 3.4 below).

3.3   Multilingual Information Extraction

Multilinguality has been identified as one of the major challenges for QA systems [11]. However, little is yet known about cross-language QA, i.e. when the question is not written in the same language as the documents. It is certainly a harder problem than CLIR: while, for document retrieval purposes, finding appropriate candidate translations for the query words can lead to good performance, questions demand a careful linguistic analysis (in the source language) which is not trivially translated into the target language; and a (possibly noisy) machine-translated question may produce errors in the linguistic analysis.

In order to study these issues, in 2003, three research groups from Italy, Spain and the Netherlands (ITC-irst, UNED and ILLC) organized a pilot Cross-Language QA track under the auspices of CLEF. This track, known as QA@CLEF, evaluated monolingual QA systems in Dutch, Italian and Spanish, and cross-language QA systems searching an English target collection with Spanish, Italian, Dutch, French or German questions [12]. It was a pilot experiment, just 200 simple fact-based questions were provided and participants were allowed to provide up to three responses per question, either exact or 50-byte answer strings. Although only limited comparisons between systems could be made (there was only one participating system per monolingual task) and just 6 groups participated in the bilingual experiment, the experience was considered a success, generating the first cross-language QA test suite and attracting a lot of interest from CLEF participants.

In 2004, the QA track was one of the most popular tracks at CLEF with 18 groups submitting mono- and/or cross-language runs using any of nine possible source languages against target collections in seven languages. New types of questions (how-questions and definition type questions) were given as input to the participating systems, while just one exact answer per question was allowed as output. A disadvantage of the wide range of language combinations means that for the cross-language tasks there were no real comparable results. However, much is being learnt about language-dependent factors for monolingual QA systems and the issues to be considered when working on cross-language QA. It is interesting to note that the average performance achieved by the monolingual systems in 2004 compared very favourably with the results generally obtained at TREC for English QA systems [13].

Following the positive outcome of the 2003 and 2004 QA@CLEF evaluation campaigns, in CLEF 2005, monolingual (non English) and cross-language QA systems will again be tested. All the combinations between nine or more source languages and eight target languages (Bulgarian, Dutch, English, French, German, Italian, Portuguese and Spanish) will be explored. The track will include a main task, where factoid and definition questions are given as input, and pilot tasks, that will explore other facets of QA, proposing both context oriented and more difficult types of questions. In addition, as reported above, experiments will be conducted in collaboration with the *i*CLEF track.

3.4   Cross-Language Retrieval in Mixed Media Collections

Of course, text is not the only media in which information is stored. Today's digital collections frequently tend to be in multi-media, text being accompanied or replaced by image, speech, or video. In recent years, CLEF has begun to examine the issues involved in multilingual information access in collections of mixed media.

Cross-Language Spoken Document Retrieval. CLEF began to pay attention to the issues involved in cross-language spoken document retrieval in 2002 when a pilot experiment was organized within the DELOS Network of Excellence by two groups (ITC-irst and University of Exeter) and the results were reported at the CLEF workshop that year [14]. The experiment was continued on a slightly larger scale as a regular track in CLEF 2003 with four participating groups. The track ran with very limited resources, using data from the TREC 8 and 9 English monolingual SDR tracks, made available by NIST. The results are closer to a benchmark rather than a real evaluation. The TREC collections were extended to a CL-SDR task by manually translating the short topics into five European languages: Dutch, French, German, Italian and Spanish. In 2003 the track aimed at evaluating CLIR systems on noisy automatic transcripts of spoken documents with known story boundaries. The results of the experiments showed that, as expected, bilingual performance was lower for all participants than the comparative English monolingual run. However, the degree of degraded performance was shown to depend on the translation resources used. It was also shown that it can be effective to use different indexing units for monolingual and bilingual retrieval on the data set [15]. The track was repeated in CLEF 2004 but with only two groups finally submitting runs and no conclusive results.

It was felt that one of the reasons for the lack of enthusiasm for the track in 2004 was the fact that the resources were so limited and the test collection not particularly appropriate for tasks focused on multilinguality. It is expected that there will be much more interest next year as a very new collection with immense potential for research is being introduced in the CLEF 2005 speech track. Both mono- and cross-language retrieval will be assessed on the Malach collection of spontaneous conversational speech from the archives of the Shoah foundation. The collection that will be used in 2005 is in English and will consist of 625 hours in 10,000 segments in ASR form plus ~5 keywords and a 3 sentence summary. A thesaurus, an in-domain expansion collection, and a word lattice should also be available. 25 topics in six languages (Czech, English, French, German, Russian and Spanish) will be prepared. Training topics will also be available. In future years, parts of the Malach collection in Russian and in Czech will be made available. This track is being coordinated by Dublin City University and the University of Maryland.

Cross-Language Retrieval in Image Collections. A cross-language image retrieval task, known as ImageCLEF, was first introduced into CLEF in 2003 [16]. Research in cross-language image retrieval is not just of academic interest, there is also a particularly strong commercial potential. Retrieval from an image collection is quite different than from a text collection. For example, the way in which a query is formulated, the methods used for retrieval (e.g. based on low-level features derived from an image, or based on associated textual information such as a caption), the types of query, how relevance is assessed, the involvement of the user during the search process, and fundamental cognitive differences between the interpretation of visual versus textual media are all issues that need careful consideration. Within CLEF, the problem is further complicated by user queries being expressed in a language different to that of the document collection. This requires crossing the language barrier by translating the collection, the queries, or both into the same language. ImageCLEF aims to provide the necessary collection(s) and framework in which to analyze the link between image and text and promote the discovery of alternate methods for cross-language image retrieval. The goal is thus to provide a test-bed that can be used to evaluate different retrieval methods and to analyze user behaviour during the search process, e.g. query formulation in both cross-language and visual environments, iterative searching and query reformulation.

The first ImageCLEF was set up as a pilot experiment: just four groups participated in an ad-hoc retrieval task. Participants were free to use either content-based or text-based retrieval methods, relevance feedback and any translation method. The search requests were first produced in English and then prepared in Dutch, French, German, Italian and Spanish and consisted of both visual examples and text descriptions of the user need. The image collection of approximately 30,000 historical photographs of Scotland complete with short captions was made available by St Andrews University Library. Although all groups chose to use the information derived from captions only, there was much interest in the potential of this exercise at the CLEF 2003 workshop and it was thus decided to expand it in CLEF 2004, adding another collection: the Casimage medical images of the University Hospitals Geneva.

Eighteen groups participated in ImageCLEF 2004. Three tasks were offered: ad-hoc type retrieval on the St Andrews and the Casimage collections and a user-centred evaluation task. Topics were offered in twelve languages and participating groups could use text-based and/or content-based retrieval methods. In general, it was found that for the two retrieval tasks across very different domains a combination of visual and textual features provided a retrieval effectiveness that was higher than retrieval based on text or visual features alone. It was also shown that, like cross-language retrieval on text collections, query expansion and relevance feedback improved performance. The high participation showed that there was a need for this type of evaluation event and the results proved that further research into the combination of visual and textual retrieval techniques should lead to optimal results on image collections containing some kind of caption or annotation text in the future [17].

The success of 2004 has led to the ImageCLEF track being further extended for CLEF 2005. Four tasks are offered: bilingual ad-hoc retrieval (collection in English, queries in several languages); interactive search; medical image retrieval (collection in English and French, images as queries); an automatic annotation task for medical images (a fully categorized collection with categories available in English and German). The tasks offer different and challenging retrieval problems for cross-language image retrieval. Three test collections will be made available: the St Andrews University historical photographic collection, the Casimage medical collection, enlarged for this year's CLEF by other teaching files, and the IRMA medical image collection for automatic image annotation created jointly by University Hospitals Geneva and the University of Aachen. The track will be coordinated jointly by University of Sheffield, University Hospitals Geneva and Oregon Health and Science University.

4   Conclusions

In this paper, we have shown how the activity of the Cross-Language Evaluation Forum has expanded and widened its range of activities over the years. The main objective of the CLEF initiative has been to stimulate and advance multilingual information retrieval system development. Our challenge has been to encourage the building of systems that will allow real people to find the information they need in languages that they have not mastered and in collections of diverse types and diverse media, and then to measure how well representative users are able to use these systems. For this reason, we have encouraged R&D work on multilingual system development in many different directions and have concentrated on developing appropriate evaluation infrastructures and methodologies in order to assess the results obtained in an objective setting.

We feel that our main results can be summarized in the following points:

- the building of a strong multidisciplinary research community, focused on improving and expanding multilingual system development;
- documented improvement in cross-language text retrieval system performance;
- the creation of a large set of empirical data about multilingual information access from the user perspective;

- the promotion of in-depth studies in previously uninvestigated areas, such as cross-language speech and image retrieval and multilingual question answering;
- the development of appropriate evaluation methodologies to assess new multilingual information access systems and/or new system components;
- the creation of a set of immensely valuable, reusable multilingual test collections, complete with documentation on how to use them.

Further information on the CLEF activities can be found at http://clef-campaign.org/.

References

1. Braschler, M., Peters, C.: Cross-Language Evaluation Forum: Objectives, Results, Achievements. Information Retrieval, 7, Nos 1-2 (2004) 7-31.
2. Cleverdon, C.: The Cranfield Tests on Index Language Devices. In: Spärck-Jones, K., Willett, P. (eds.): Readings in Information Retrieval, Morgan Kaufmann (1997) 47-59.
3. Gey, F., Kando, N., Peters, C.: Cross-Language Information Retrieval: the Way Ahead. Information Processing and Management. 4 (3). Forthcoming.
4. Gurrin, C., Smeaton, A. F. : Improving Evaluation of Web Search Systems. In Sebastiani, F. (ed.) Advances in Information Retrieval. Springer LNCS 2633 (2003) 25-40
5. Kando, N.: Evaluation of Information Access Technologies at the NTCIR Workshop. In CLEF 2003 Proceedings, Springer LNCS 3237 (2004), in print.
6. Bailey, P., Craswell, N., Hawking, D.: Engineering a multi-purpose test collection for web retrieval experiments. Information Processing and Management, 39(6). (2003) 853-871.
7. Oard, D., Gonzalo, J.: The CLEF 2001 Interactive Track. In Proceedings of CLEF 2001, Springer LNCS 2406 (2002) 308-319.
8. Gonzalo, J., Oard, D.: The CLEF 2002 Interactive Track. In CLEF 2002 Proceedings, Springer LNCS 2785 (2003) 372-382.
9. Oard, D., Gonzalo, J.: The CLEF 2003 Interactive Track. In CLEF 2003 Proceedings, Springer LNCS 3237 (2004). In print.
10. Gonzalo, J., Oard, D.: In CLEF 2004 Working Notes. See http://clef.isti.cnr.it/2004/working_notes/CLEF2004WN-Contents.html
11. Maybury, M.: Toward a Question Answering Roadmap, MITRE Tech. Report (2002).
12. Magnini, B., Romagnoli, S., Vallin, A., Herrera, J., Peñas, A., Peinado, V., Verdejo, F., de Rijke, M.: The Multiple Language Question Answering Track at CLEF 2003. In CLEF 2003 Proceedings, Springer LNCS 3237 (2004). In print.
13. Magnini, B., Vallin, A., Ayache, C., Erbach, G., Peñas, A. de Rijke, M., Rocha, P., Simov, K., Sutcliffe, R.: Overview of the CLEF 2004 Multilingual Question Answering Track. In CLEF 2004 Working Notes. See http://clef.isti.cnr.it/2004/working_notes/CLEF2004WN-Contents.html
14. Jones, G.J.F., Federico, M.: CLEF 2002 Cross-Language Spoken Document Retrieval Pilot Track Report. In Proceedings of CLEF 2002, Springer LNCS 2785 (2003) 446-457.
15. Federico, M., Jones, G.J.F.: The CLEF 2003 Cross-Language Spoken Document Retrieval Track. In CLEF 2003 Proceedings, Springer LNCS 3237 (2004). In print.
16. Clough, P.D., Sanderson, M.: The CLEF 2003 Cross Language Image Retrieval Track. In CLEF 2003 Proceedings, Springer LNCS 3237 (2004). In print.
17. Clough, P.D., Sanderson, M., Müller, H.: The CLEF Cross Language Image Retrieval Track (ImageCLEF) 2004. In CLEF 2004 Working Notes. See http://clef.isti.cnr.it/2004/working_notes/ CLEF2004WN-Contents.html

Personalization for the Web: Learning User Preferences from Text

Giovanni Semeraro, Pasquale Lops, and Marco Degemmis

Dipartimento di Informatica
Università di Bari
Via E. Orabona, 4 - 70125 Bari - Italia
{semeraro,lops,degemmis}@di.uniba.it

Abstract. As more information becomes available electronically, tools for finding information of interest to users become increasingly important. Information preferences vary greatly across users, therefore, filtering systems must be highly personalized to serve the individual interests of the user. Our research deals with learning approaches to build user profiles that accurately capture user interests from content (documents) and that could be used for personalized information filtering. The learning mechanisms analyzed in this paper are relevance feedback and a naïve Bayes method. Experiments conducted in the context of a content-based profiling system for movies show the pros and cons of each method.

1 Introduction

Much of the information in science, engineering and business has been recorded in the form of text. Traditionally, this information would appear in journals or company reports, but increasingly it can be found online in the World-Wide Web. Users are swamped with information and have difficulty in separating relevant from irrelevant information. This *relevant information problem* leads to a clear demand for automated methods able to support users in searching large Web repositories in order to retrieve relevant information with respect to users' individual preferences. Machine Learning techniques are being used to recognize regularities in the behavior of customers and to infer a model of their interests, referred to as *user profile*. The paper presents a new method, based on the classical Rocchio algorithm for text categorization [1]. It is able to discover user preferences from the analysis of textual descriptions of items in the catalogue of an e-commerce Web site. The novelty of the method can be summarized as follows:

a) positive and negative examples are weighted differently for each user, according to the ratings given during the training phase. The classical Rocchio method uses fixed control parameters that allow setting the relative importance of *all* positive and negative examples;

b) the method is able to manage documents structured in different slots, each corresponding to a specific feature of an item. This strategy permits to give a different weight to words on the basis of the slot in which they appear;

M. Hemmje et al. (Eds.): E.J. Neuhold Festschrift, LNCS 3379, pp. 162–172, 2005.

c) the method learns two different profiles of the user: one profile, that is learned from positive examples of interesting items, represents the interests of the user; the other profile, learned from negative examples, represents things the user dislikes. When a new item has to be classified, it is compared with the two profiles and the classification with the highest similarity score is chosen. In order to evaluate the effectiveness of the proposed approach, a comparison with a naïve Bayes method has been carried out. Motivation behind our research is the realization that user profiling can be used to tackle the *relevant information problem* already described. Our experiments evaluated the effects of the afore-mentioned methods in learning user profiles. The experiments were conducted in the context of a content-based profiling system for movies on the World Wide Web. The paper is organized as follows: Section 2 describes the main princi-ples for learning user profiles from textual description. Section 3 describes the new Rocchio-based algorithm for inferring user profiles and gives an overview of the system used for comparison: Item Recommender. Section 4 presents the experimental work. Finally, some conclusions are drawn in Section 5.

2   Learning User Profiles from Textual Descriptions

The content-based information filtering paradigm exploits textual descriptions of the items and ratings given by users to infer a profile used for selecting items of interest [2]. Classical text categorization algorithms have been modified for adapting them to the problem of inducing a profile of documents liked by a user (Section 2.1). Fot this purpose, documents have to be transformed in a form suitable for the learning algorithms (Section 2.2).

2.1   Text Categorization for Learning User Preferences

Text categorization aims to automatically assign categories (classes) to unseen text documents. The task is commonly described as follows: given a set of classes $C = \{c_1, \ldots, c_n\}$ and a set of training documents labelled with the class the doc-ument belongs to, the problem consists in building a classifier able to assign to a new document the proper class. We consider the problem of learning user profiles as a binary classification task: each document has to be classified as inter-esting or not with respect to the user preferences. The set of classes is restricted to c_+, that represents the positive class (user-likes), and c_- the negative one (user-dislikes). The application of text categorization methods to the problem of learning user profiles is not new (see LIBRA system [3] and Syskill & Webert [4]). The experiments carried out by the authors have shown that the naïve Bayesian classifier offers several advantages over other learning algorithms (also in terms of accuracy and efficiency). Therefore, we have decided to compare the proposed Rocchio-based algorithm with the naïve Bayesian classifier implemented in our Item Recommender system.

2.2 Documents Representation

The representation that dominates the text classification literature is known as *bag of words* (BOW). In this approach each feature corresponds to a single word found in the training set. Usually a list of *stop words* (that are assumed to have no information content) is removed from the original text. In order to make the features statistically independent, typically a *stemming* algorithm is used to remove suffixes from words. In our application scenario, items to be suggested to users are movies. Each movie is represented by a set of *slots*, where each slot is a textual field corresponding to a specific feature of the movie: title, cast, director, summary and keywords. The text in each slot is represented using the *BOW* model taking into account the occurrences of words in the original text. Thus, each instance is represented by five BOWs, one for each slot. This strategy counts separately the occurrences of each word in the slots in which it appears. The approach could be a more effective way to find words useful for distinguishing relevant documents from irrelevant ones. For example, if the word *political* appears only once in the document, but in the slot keywords, probably it is more indicative of user preferences than if the same word appears in the slot summary. Stemming and stop words removal have been applied to the documents used in the experiments.

3 Learning Profiles Using the Modified Rocchio Method

Some linear classifiers consist of an explicit profile (or prototypical document) of the category [5]. The Rocchio algorithm is one of the most popular learning methods from Information Retrieval and document classification.

3.1 Documents Representation in the Vector Space Model

In the Rocchio algorithm, documents are represented with the vector space representation [6] and the major heuristic component is the TFIDF (Term Frequency/Inverse Document Frequency) word weighting scheme . The computation of the weights for terms reflects empirical observations regarding text. Terms that appear frequently in one document (term frequency), but rarely on the outside (inverse document frequency), are more likely to be relevant to the topic of the document. Let N be the total number of documents in the training set and n_i be the number of documents in which the term t_i appears. Let $freq_{i,j}$ be the raw frequency of term t_i in the document d_j (i.e. the number of times the term is mentioned in the text of the document). The normalized frequency $f_{i,j}$ of term t_i in document d_j is given by

$$f_{i,j} = \frac{freq_{i,j}}{max_l freq_{l,j}} \qquad (1)$$

where the maximum is computed over all terms which are mentioned in the text of document d_j. If the term t_i does not appear in the document d_j then $freq_{i,j} = 0$. Further, let idf_i, inverse document frequency for t_i, be given by

$$idf_i = log\frac{N}{n_i} \qquad (2)$$

The best known term-weighting schemes, called TFIDF, use weights given by the product of term frequency and the inverse document frequency. Learning is achieved by combining document vectors (of positive and negative examples) into a prototype vector $\vec{c}$ for each class in the set of classes C. Items within a certain distance from the prototype (for example determined by the cosine similarity measure) are considered interesting. Formally, Rocchio's method computes a classifier $\vec{c_i} = \langle \omega_{1i}, \dots, \omega_{|T|i} \rangle$ ($|T|$ is the cardinality of the vocabulary, that is the number of distinct terms in the training set) for category c_i using the formula:

$$\omega_{ki} = \beta \cdot \sum_{\{d_j \in POS_i\}} \frac{\omega_{kj}}{|POS_i|} - \gamma \cdot \sum_{\{d_j \in NEG_i\}} \frac{\omega_{kj}}{|NEG_i|} \qquad (3)$$

where ω_{kj} is the tfidf weight of the term t_k in document d_j, POS_i and NEG_i are respectively the set of positive and negative examples in the training set for the specific class. β and γ are control parameters that allow setting the relative importance of all positive and negative examples. The vector model gives the possibility to evaluate the degree of similarity between two vectors using the concept of correlation. This correlation can be quantified, for instance, by the *cosine of the angle* between these two vectors. In order to assign a class $\tilde{c}$ to a document d_j, the similarity between each prototype vector $\vec{c_i}$ and the document vector $\vec{d_j}$ is computed and $\tilde{c}$ will be the c_i with the highest value of similarity. We propose a modified version of this method, that is able to manage documents represented using different slots. As described in the Section 2.2, a document is represented by a set of five slots: title, director, cast, summary and keywords. More formally, if m is the index of the slot ($m = 1, 2, 3, 4, 5$), a movie is represented by the concatenation of the five bag of words:

$$d_j = \langle w_{1j}^m, \dots, w_{|T_m|j}^m \rangle$$

where $|T_m|$ is the cardinality of the vocabulary for the slot s_m and w_{ij}^m is the weight of the term t_i in the document d_j, in the slot s_m. Each weight w_{ij}^m is computed as follows:

$$w_{ij}^m = f_{ij}^m \cdot idf_i^m \qquad (4)$$

where f_{ij}^m is the frequency of term t_i in the document d_j in the slot s_m computed according to the equation (1) and idf_i^m is the inverse document frequency of the term t_i in the slot s_m, computed according to the equation (2) as the logarithm of the ratio between the total number of documents N and the number of documents containing the term t_i in the slot s_m.

3.2   Extended Rocchio Algorithm

In on-line catalogues, items are often grouped in a fixed number of categories: movies, for example, are often grouped by genre. Our goal is to learn a profile of items preferred by a user in a specific category. Thus, given a user u and a set of rated movies in a specific category of interest (for example *Action*), the goal is to learn a profile able to recognize movies liked by the user in that category. The learning process consists in inducing a prototype vector for *each slot*: these five vectors will represent the user profile. The rationale of having distinct components of the profile is that words appearing in a 'heavy' slot such as the keywords could be more indicative of preferences than words appearing in other slots such as summary, having a low discriminatory power. For these reasons, each prototype vector of the profile could contribute in a different way to the calculation of the similarity between the vectors representing a movie and the vectors representing the user profile. Another key issue of our modified version of the Rocchio algorithm is that it separately exploits the training examples: it learns two different profiles $\vec{p_i} = \langle \omega_{1i}^m, \ldots, \omega_{|T|i}^m \rangle$ (T is the cardinality of the vocabulary), for a user u and a category c_i by taking into account the ratings given by the user on documents in that category. One profile is learned using the positive examples and corresponds to the class 'movies liked by the user u in the category c_i', while the other one represents the class 'movies disliked by the user u in the category c_i' and is learned from negative examples. To sum up, the profile of a user is composed by two profiles: the positive profile and the negative profile. The rating $r_{u,j}$ on the document d_j is a discrete judgement ranging from 0 to 5. It is used in order to compute the coordinates of the vectors in the positive and in the negative user profile. A coordinate ω_{ki}^m of the positive profile is computed as in equation (5), while a coordinate ω_{ki}^m of the negative profile is computed as shown in equation (6):

$$ \omega_{ki}^m = \sum_{\{d_j \in POS_i\}} \frac{\omega_{kj}^m \cdot r'_{u,j}}{|POS_i|} \quad (5) \qquad \omega_{ki}^m = \sum_{\{d_j \in NEG_i\}} \frac{\omega_{kj}^m \cdot r'_{u,j}}{|NEG_i|} \quad (6) $$

where $r'_{u,j}$ is the normalized value of $r_{u,j}$ ranging between 0 and 1 (respectively corresponding to $r_{u,j} = 0$ and 5), $POS_i = \{d_j \in T_r | r_{u,j} > 2\}$, $NEG_i = \{d_j \in T_r | r_{u,j} \leq 2\}$, and ω_{kj}^m is the weight of the term t_k in the document d_j in the slot s_m computed as in equation (4) where the idf_k^m factor is computed over POS_i or NEG_i depending on the fact that the term t_k is in the slot s_m of a movie rated as positive, or negative (if the term is present in both positive and negative movies two different values for idf_k^m will be computed). Equations (5) and (6) differ from the classical Rocchio formula reported in equation (3) in the fact that the parameters β and γ are substituted by the ratings $r'_{u,j}$ that allow to give a different weight to each document in the training set. As regards the computation of the similarity between a profile $\vec{p_i}$ and a movie $\vec{d_j}$, the idea is to compute five partial similarity values between each couple of corresponding vectors in $\vec{p_i}$ and $\vec{d_j}$. Then, a weighted average of the five values is computed, by assigning to the similarity for the slots *summary* and *keywords* an heavier weight than the ones assigned to *title*, *cast* and *director*.

$$sim(\overrightarrow{d_j}, \overrightarrow{p_i}) = \sum_{k=1}^{5} sim(\overrightarrow{d_j^k}, \overrightarrow{p_i^k}) \cdot \alpha_k \tag{7}$$

where α_k reflects the importance of a slot in classifying a movie. In our experiments we used $\alpha_1 = 0.1$ (title), $\alpha_2 = 0.15$ (director), $\alpha_3 = 0.15$ (cast), $\alpha_4 = 0.25$ (summary) and $\alpha_5 = 0.35$ (keywords). Since the user profile is composed by the positive and the negative profiles, we compute two similarity values $sim(\overrightarrow{d_j}, \overrightarrow{p_i})$, one for each profile. The document d_j is considered as interesting only if the similarity value of the positive profile is higher than the similarity of the negative one.

3.3   Item Recommender

ITR (ITem Recommender) implements a probabilistic learning algorithm to classify texts, the naïve Bayes classifier [7]. The prototype is able to classify text belonging to a specific category as interesting or uninteresting for a particular user.

According to the Bayesian approach to classify natural language text documents, given a set of classes $C = \{c_1, \ldots, c_{|C|}\}$, the conditional probability of a class c_j given a document d is calculated as follows:

$$P(c_j|d) = \frac{P(c_j)}{P(d)} P(d|c_j)$$

In our problem, we have only 2 classes: c_+ represents the positive class (user-likes, corresponding to ratings from 3 to 5), and c_- the negative one (user-dislikes, ratings from 0 to 2). Since instances are represented as a vector of documents (one for each BOW), and assumed that the probability of each word is independent of the word's context and position, the conditional probability of a category c_j given an instance d_i is computed using the formula:

$$P(c_j|d_i) = \frac{P(c_j)}{P(d_i)} \prod_{m=1}^{|S|} \prod_{k=1}^{|b_{im}|} P(t_k|c_j, s_m)^{n_{kim}} \tag{8}$$

where $S = \{s_1, s_2, \ldots, s_{|S|}\}$ is the set of slots, b_{im} is the BOW in the slot s_m of the instance d_i, n_{kim} is the number of occurrences of the token t_k in b_{im}.

In (8), since for any given document, the prior $P(d_i)$ is a constant, this factor can be ignored if the only interest concerns a ranking rather than a probability estimate. To calculate (8), we only need to estimate the terms $P(c_j)$ and $P(t_k|c_j, s_m)$, from the training set. Each instance is weighted according to the user rating r, normalized[1] in order to obtain values ranging between 0 and 1:

$$w_+^i = \frac{r-1}{5}; \qquad w_-^i = 1 - w_+^i \tag{9}$$

---

[1] In order to apply equations in (9), the voting scale has been shifted in the range 1-6

The weights in (9) are used for weighting the occurrences of a word in a document and to estimate the two probability terms from the training set TR according to the following equations:

$$\hat{P}(c_j) = \frac{\sum_{i=1}^{|TR|} w_j^i}{|TR|} \quad (10) \qquad \hat{P}(t_k|c_j, s_m) = \frac{\sum_{i=1}^{|TR|} w_j^i n_{kim}}{\sum_{i=1}^{|TR|} w_j^i |b_{im}|} \quad (11)$$

In (11), n_{kim} is the number of occurrences of the term t_k in the slot s_m of the ith instance, and the denominator denotes the total weighted length of the slot s_m in the class c_j. The length of b_{im} is computed by summing the occurrences of the words in the slot s_m of the ith instance. Therefore, $\hat{P}(t_k|c_j, s_m)$ is calculated as a ratio between the weighted occurrences of the term t_k in slot s_m of class c_j and the total weighted length of the slot. The final outcome of the learning process is a probabilistic model used to classify a new instance in the class c_+ or c_-. The model can be used to build a personal profile including those words that turn out to be most indicative of the user's preferences, according to the value of the conditional probabilities in (11).

4   Experimental Session

The goal of the experiment has been the comparison of the above described methods in terms of classification accuracy. The experiments have been carried out on a collection of textual descriptions of movies rated by real users, the EachMovie dataset.

The EachMovie project was conducted by the Compaq Systems Research Center[2] over an 18-month period from 1996-97. During this time, a large dataset of user-movie ratings was collected, consisting of 2,811,983 ratings for 1,628 movies from 72,916 users. The movies are rated on a 6-point scale (from 0 to 5). The zero-to-five star rating used externally on EachMovie is mapped linearly to the interval [0,1]. The content information for each movie was collected from the Internet Movie Database[3] using a simple crawler that gathers the *Title*, the *Director*, the *Genre*, that is the category of the movie, the list of *Keywords*, the *Summary* and the *Cast*. Movies are subdivided into different genres: Action, Animation, Art_Foreign, Classic, Comedy, Drama, Family, Horror, Romance, Thriller. For each genre or movie category, a set of 100 users was randomly selected among users that rated n items, $30 \leq n \leq 100$ in that movie category (only for genre 'animation', the number of users that rated n movies was 33). In this way, for each category, a dataset of at least 3000 triples (user,movie,rating) was obtained (at least 990 for 'animation'). Table 1 summarizes the data used for the experiments. The number of movies rated as positive and negative for each

---

[2] http://www.research.compaq.com/SRC/
[3] IMDb, http://www.imdb.com

genre is balanced in datasets 2, 5, 7, 8 (60-65 % positive, 35-40% negative), while is slightly unbalanced in datasets 1, 9, 10 (70-75 % positive, 25-30% negative), and is strongly unbalanced in datasets 3, 4, 6 (over 75% positive).

Table 1. 10 'Genre' datasets obtained from the original EachMovie dataset

Id Genre	Genre	Number of Movies rated	% POS	% NEG
1	Action	4474	72.05	27.95
2	Animation	1103	56.67	43.33
3	Art_Foreign	4246	76.21	23.79
4	Classic	5026	91.73	8.27
5	Comedy	4714	63.46	36.54
6	Drama	4880	76.24	23.76
7	Family	3808	63.71	36.29
8	Horror	3631	59.89	40.11
9	Romance	3707	72.97	27.03
10	Thriller	37.09	71.94	28.06
		39298	71.84	28.16

4.1   Design of the Experiment and Evaluation Measures

In the design of the experiment and the evaluation step, the concept of 'interesting item', that we call *relevant item* is central. Users adopted a 6-point (0-5) discrete scale for rating items: a movie in a specific category is considered as relevant by a user if the rating is greater or equal than 3. The Rocchio-based profiling algorithm classifies an item as relevant if the similarity score of the class *likes* is greater than the one for the class *dislikes*, while ITR considers an item d_i as relevant if $P(c_+|d_i) \geq 0.5$, calculated as in equation (8). Classification effectiveness is measured in terms of the classical Information Retrieval notions of *precision*, *recall* and *accuracy*, adapted to the case of text categorization [6]. *Precision* is the proportion of items classified as relevant that are really relevant, and *recall* is the proportion of relevant items that are classified as relevant; *accuracy* is the proportion of items that are correctly classified as relevant or not. We also adopted the Normalized Distance-based Performance Measure (NDPM) [8] to evaluate the goodness of the items' ranking calculated according to a certain relevance measure. Specifically, NDPM was exploited to measure the distance between the ranking imposed on items by the user ratings and the ranking predicted by the system.

Values range from 0 (agreement) to 1 (disagreement). In our experimental work, this measure was adopted in order to compare the ranking imposed by the user ratings and the classification scores given by the Rocchio algorithm (the similarity score for the class *likes*) and the ITR system (the a-posteriori probability of the class *likes*).

Table 2. Performance of the systems on 10 different datasets

Id Genre	Precision		Recall		F1		Accuracy		NDPM	
	ITR	New Rocchio	ITR	New Rocchio	ITR	New Rocchio	ITR	New Rocchio	ITR	New Rocchio
1	0.70	0.72	0.83	0.82	0.76	0.75	0.76	0.72	0.45	0.46
2	0.51	0.65	0.62	0.66	0.54	0.64	0.72	0.75	0.41	0.34
3	0.76	0.77	0.84	0.79	0.79	0.77	0.86	0.83	0.45	0.46
4	0.92	0.92	0.99	0.94	0.96	0.93	0.93	0.90	0.48	0.45
5	0.56	0.66	0.66	0.72	0.59	0.67	0.70	0.67	0.46	0.44
6	0.75	0.78	0.89	0.84	0.81	0.80	0.79	0.75	0.46	0.45
7	0.58	0.68	0.67	0.75	0.71	0.69	0.77	0.75	0.42	0.41
8	0.53	0.64	0.65	0.74	0.58	0.67	0.72	0.71	0.41	0.42
9	0.70	0.73	0.83	0.79	0.75	0.74	0.78	0.73	0.49	0.48
10	0.71	0.74	0.86	0.85	0.77	0.77	0.77	0.74	0.48	0.45
Mean	0.67	0.73	0.78	0.79	0.73	0.74	0.78	0.75	0.45	0.44

For each 'genre' dataset, we run n experiments, where n is the number of users in the dataset: the triples (user, movie, rating) of each specific user and the content of the rated movies have been used for learning the user profile and measuring its predictive accuracy, using the aforementioned measures.

Each experiment consisted in:

1. selecting the triples (user, movie, rating) of the user and the content of the movies rated by that user;
2. splitting the selected data into a training set *(Tr)* and a test set *(Ts)*;
3. using *Tr* for learning the corresponding user profile;
4. evaluating the predictive accuracy of the learned profile on the *Ts*, using the aforementioned measures.

The methodology adopted for obtaining *Tr* and *Ts* was the K-fold cross-validation, that works by partitioning the data into K equal-sized segments and holding out one segment at a time for test purposes. We fixed K=10, thus we run 10 experiments on each user, by averaging the evaluation measures computed in the test phase.

4.2   Results and Discussion

Table 2 shows the results of the experiment aimed at comparing the new Rocchio method with the one implemented by ITR in terms of average precision, recall, F1, accuracy and NDPM of the models learned in the 10 folds for each dataset. The last row of the table reports the mean values, averaged on all datasets. We have carried out a pairwise comparison of the results, using the nonparametric Wilcoxon signed rank test [9]. The most important result is that the the new Rocchio algorithm outperforms ITR in precision (significance level $p < 0.05$). As regards Recall, F1, Accuracy, NDPM, the difference between the two methods is not statistically significant, even if the results show that the new Rocchio algorithm is slightly better than ITR for all measures, except accuracy. Another remark worth noting is that the new Rocchio algorithm outperforms ITR for datasets 2, 5, 7, 8, where the number of movies rated as positive and negative is balanced. This could be due to the different representation of the profiles adopted by the systems: ITR exploits positive and negative examples to learn a unique profile, while the Rocchio algorithm uses in a separate way positive and negative examples for learning two different profiles, one for the class 'interesting movies' (positive class) and another one for the class 'not interesting movies' (negative class). The conclusion is that the Rocchio method takes into account in a better way the negative examples. This conclusion is supported by the fact that for the other datasets, in which the percentage of negative examples is lower (less than 30%), ITR surpasses the Rocchio method as regards Recall, F1 and Accuracy. Moreover, the two systems are equivalent in defining the ranking of the preferred movies with respect to the score for the 'interesting movies' class. Further investigations will be carried out in order to define a ranking score used for computing NDPM that takes into account the negative part of the profile as well. These results led us to conclude that the new Rocchio method is more effective than ITR, due to the fact that *trust* is a key word in giving recommendations: the systems should minimize false positive errors, in the sense that it is better to provide users with a few number of high quality recommendations (high precision) than to overload users with many recommendations that they have to filter manually (high recall, low precision).

5   Conclusions and Future Directions

The paper presented two different approaches for learning user profiles that capture user interests from the analysis of the documents evaluated by users. We proposed a naïve Bayes method and a new relevance feedback learning mechanism based on the classical Rocchio algorithm able to discover user preferences by analysing textual descriptions of items to be suggested to the user. An intensive experimental session in the context of a content-based profiling system for movies has been carried out. Results have shown that the method based on the relevance feedback learning technique exceeds the naïve Bayes method in precision, while there is not statistically significant difference between the methods as regards recall, F1, accuracy and NDPM.

Though many linguistic techniques have been employed, there are problems that still remain unsolved like polisemy, synonymy, etc. A possible solution for this kind of issues will be explored: the shift of the level of abstraction from words up to concepts. Profiles will not contain words anymore. They will contain references to concepts defined in lexicons or, in a further step, ontologies. A first advance in this direction will consist of employing WordNet [10] as a reference lexicon in substituting word forms with word meanings (semantics) into profiles.

References

1. Rocchio, J.:   Relevance feedback information retrieval.   In Salton, G., ed.:
   The SMART retrieval system - experiments in automated document processing,
   Prentice-Hall, Englewood Cliffs, NJ (1971) 313–323
2. Mladenic, D.: Text-learning and related intelligent agents: a survey. IEEE Intelligent Systems **14** (1999) 44–54
3. Mooney, R.J., Roy, L.: Content-based book recommending using learning for text
   categorization. In: Proceedings of the 5th ACM Conference on Digital Libraries,
   San Antonio, US, ACM Press, New York, US (2000) 195–204
4. Pazzani, M., Billsus, D.: Learning and revising user profiles: The identification of
   interesting web sites. Machine Learning **27** (1997) 313–331
5. Sebastiani, F.: Machine learning in automated text categorization. ACM Computing Surveys **34** (2002)
6. Salton, G., McGill, M.: Introduction to Modern Information Retrieval. McGraw-
   Hill, New York (1983)
7. Mitchell, T.: Machine Learning. McGraw-Hill, New York (1997)
8. Yao, Y.Y.: Measuring retrieval effectiveness based on user preference of documents.
   Journal of the American Society for Information Science **46** (1995) 133–145
9. Orkin, M., Drogin, R.: Vital Statistics. McGraw-Hill, New York (1990)
10. Miller, G.: WordNet: an online lexical database. International Journal of Lexicog-
    raphy **3** (1990)

Collaborative Machine Learning

Thomas Hofmann and Justin Basilico

Department of Computer Science, Brown University,
Providence, RI 02912, USA,
th@cs.brown.edu
http://www.cs.brown.edu/people/th

Abstract. In information retrieval, feedback provided by individual users is often very sparse. Consequently, machine learning algorithms for automatically retrieving documents or recommending items may not achieve satisfactory levels of accuracy. However, if one views users as members of a larger user community, then it should be possible to leverage similarities between different users to overcome the sparseness problem. The paper proposes a collaborative machine learning framework to exploit inter-user similarities. More specifically, we present a kernel-based learning architecture that generalizes the well-known Support Vector Machine learning approach by enriching content descriptors with inter-user correlations.

1 Introduction

Predicting ratings and preferences for users interacting with a computer system is a key challenge in application areas such as electronic commerce, information retrieval, information filtering, and user interface design. *Content-based filtering* is a common approach to automatically learn user interests based on a set of training examples such as observed user ratings. This paradigm is applicable, whenever informative content descriptors exist, for instance, in the case of books, web pages, news, etc., but with adequate feature extraction mechanisms may also be extended to music, movies, or other multimedia content. Generalization to new, unranked items relies on the capability of the employed learning algorithm to identify attributes and features that are indicative of user interest, e.g. the occurrence of certain keywords in documents. Standard machine learning methods like naive Bayes classification [10,13,12] or neural networks [9] have been used in this context.

In many scenarios, however, a straightforward application of machine learning methods for content-based filtering faces two problems that may prevent obtaining a sufficient degree of accuracy in predicting user interests: first, the content descriptors may simply be too weak in their predictive power, and, second, the amount of training data available for an individual user may be too small. One way to overcome these problems is to avoid treating users in isolation, but rather to put them in the context of a larger population or *community* of users, for which ratings or preference indications may also be available. The

M. Hemmje et al. (Eds.): E.J. Neuhold Festschrift, LNCS 3379, pp. 173–182, 2005.
© Springer-Verlag Berlin Heidelberg 2005

latter is often the case in practice, for instance, data may be available for the customers of an on-line store or for a user community accessing a specific information portal. It thus seems a reasonable and promising strategy to leverage the community as a whole to improve standard machine learning methods. We call this approach *collaborative machine learning*. Notice that we do not propose to foster any direct collaboration or interaction between users. Rather our approach only requires that users are willing to anonymously share their profiles with one another (or consent that this is done by the vendor or information service provider). The combination of data from different users is performed in a fully automatic manner by the machine learning algorithm.

Collaborative machine learning is closely related to an approach known as *collaborative filtering* or *social filtering* [7,14,17]. Collaborative filtering exploits correlations between ratings across a population of users, in its most popular incarnation by first finding users most similar to some active user and by then forming a weighted vote over these neighbors to predict unobserved ratings. This indeed leverages the data available for the user community and has been successful in some e-commerce applications, e.g. for product recommendation sites like amazon[1]. However, collaborative filtering has the downside that it cannot take advantage of item descriptors and attributes. Whereas content-based filtering ignores the community data, collaborative filtering ignores the content, which is apparently suboptimal in domains with content-rich item descriptors. In this paper, we pursue the philosophy that collaborative and content-based filtering are complementary views that should be unified in a collaborative machine learning architecture. In fact, it should also be possible to take into account other information such as demographic user data.

2   Collaborative Learning via Joint Feature Maps

2.1   Joint Feature Maps

The most common way of casting the present prediction problem as a standard classification problem – or more generally as an ordinal regression problem – is to treat every user u as an independent classification problem. Hence, every item x for which u has provided a rating $r(u, x)$ is considered as a training instance with the rating as its target value. As a representation of items x one may utilize item attributes (e.g. keywords) or encode known ratings provided by other users $u' \neq u$ as features [4]. Predictions for a specific user are then made by applying the learned classification rule to items with unknown ratings.

Yet, one can also take the opposite view and treat every item as a separate classification problem for which a user constitutes an instance. In the latter case, a user needs to be represented by some feature vector, for example, by encoding his/her ratings on other items or by utilizing demographic attributes. Interchanging the role of items and users is an alternative that is known as item-based collaborative filtering [15].

---

[1] www.amazon.com

We suggest to avoid this polarity of using a feature representation either over items or over users, by allowing features to be extracted jointly from user-item pairs (u, x). The crucial ingredient is a joint feature map $\Psi : (u, x) \mapsto \Psi(u, x) \in \Re^D$. For example, features may indicate that a pair (u, x) deals with a particular (type of) user *and* an item with a particular property (say, of a particular genre or category). One may also think of the inner product $\langle \Psi(u, x), \Psi(u', x') \rangle$ as a similarity measure that governs how generalization occurs over user-item pairs. Special cases on how to compute such similarities are, for example, to require that $u = u'$ and to use some similarity measure between items x and x', or to require that $x = x'$ and to use some similarity measure between users u and u', which yields the two extreme cases discussed above. However, as we will show, one can do better by defining joint feature maps that keep some middle ground and allow for simultaneous generalization along both dimensions.

2.2 Hypothesis Classes for Ordinal Regression

To state our modeling approach more formally, we denote by $\mathcal{U}$ a set of users and by $\mathcal{X}$ a set of items. A joint feature map is a mapping $\Psi : \mathcal{U} \times \mathcal{X} \to \Re^D$ which extracts features ψ_r, $1 \le r \le D$ from user-item pairs. We will define a family of functions F that are linear in the chosen feature map via $F(u, x; w) = \langle \Psi(u, x), w \rangle$, where $w \in \Re^D$ is a weight vector. In order to predict a rating for a pair (u, x), we use a set of adaptive thresholds θ to quantize F into bins. If there are k response levels (say a rating scale from 0 to $(k - 1)$ stars), then there will be thresholds $\theta_j \in \Re$ with $1 \le j \le k - 1$. For convenience we also define $\theta_0 = -\infty$ and $\theta_k = +\infty$. The prediction function simply picks the number of the bin the computed F-value falls into, formally:

$$f(u, x; w, \theta) = \min\{j \in \{1, \dots, k\} : F(u, x; w) < \theta_j\}. \tag{1}$$

The goal of learning now is to find an appropriate weight vector w and a set of thresholds θ. As we will show in the next section, the algorithm we propose for learning only depends on inner products $\langle \Psi(u, x), \Psi(u', x') \rangle$ for user-item pairs with observed ratings. This means that instead of specifying Ψ explicitly, we can also define kernels functions K over $\mathcal{U} \times \mathcal{X}$ which define a joint feature map implicitly, i.e. $K((u, x), (u', x')) \equiv \langle \Psi(u, x), \Psi(u', x') \rangle$. It will turn out that this is a very convenient way of designing appropriate representations over user-item pairs.

2.3 Joint Feature Maps via Tensor Products

In this paper, we restrict ourselves to joint feature maps that are generically constructed from feature maps for items and users via the tensor product. By this we mean a relatively simple operation of first defining $\Lambda : \mathcal{U} \to \Re^G$ and $\Phi : \mathcal{X} \to \Re^H$ and then combining every dimension of Λ multiplicatively with every dimension of Φ to define $\Psi(u, x) = \Lambda(u) \otimes \Phi(x) \in \Re^D$ where $D = G \cdot H$.

Notice that in the simplest case of binary features, the multiplicative combination corresponds to a logical conjunction. Explicitly computing feature maps Ψ constructed in this manner may be prohibitively expensive (i.e. in $\mathbf{O}(G \cdot H)$). However, the following simple lemma shows that inner products of this sort can be computed more efficiently (i.e. , namely in $\mathbf{O}(G + H)$).

Lemma 1. *If $\Psi(u, x) = \Lambda(u) \otimes \Phi(x)$ then the inner product of Ψ vectors can be expressed as the inner product between Λ and Φ vectors, respectively, as follows:*

$$\langle \Psi(u, x), \Psi(u', x') \rangle = \langle \Lambda(u), \Lambda(u') \rangle \langle \Phi(x), \Phi(x') \rangle .$$

This implies that we may design kernel functions K_U for users and K_X for items independently and combine them multiplicatively to define a joint kernel.

2.4   Designing Kernels

We propose to build kernels for users and items by additively combining elementary kernel functions, which are then combined multiplicatively to yield the joint kernel function.

Identity Kernel The simplest kernel function is the diagonal kernel, which is defined via the Kronecker delta $K^{\mathrm{id}}(z, z') = \delta_{z,z'}$. Interpreting K^{id} as an inner product, this corresponds to a feature map that encodes the identity of each object z by a separate Boolean feature. We will denote the diagonal kernel induced by the user and item identity by K_U^{id} and K_X^{id}, respectively.

Attribute Kernel The second type of kernel function is built from an explicit attribute representation for items or users. For users these attributes may correspond to demographic information such as gender, age, nationality, location, or income. For items such as documents this may encode a standard tf-idf vector space representation, whereas for movies it may include attributes such as genre or attributes extracted from cast, crew, or a synopsis of the plot. We will refer to the attribute-based kernels by K_U^{at} and K_X^{at}.

Correlation Kernel Collaborative filtering has demonstrated that predictions and recommendations can be learned based on correlations computed from a given matrix of ratings. The most popular correlation measure is the Pearson correlation coefficient, which corresponds to an inner product between normalized rating vectors. For instance, if applied to correlate users, one can define the so-called z-scores, by computing the user-specific mean $\mu(u)$ and variances $\sigma(u)$ and setting $z(u, x) = \frac{r(u,x) - \mu(u)}{\sigma(u)}$. However, since not all ratings are observed one needs to specify how to deal with missing values. We consider two *ad hoc* strategies for doing this: *mean imputation* and *pairwise deletion*. In the first case, unobserved values are identified with the mean value, i.e. their z-score is zero. In the second case, one computes the correlation between two users only from the subset of items that have been rated by both. While conceptually less preferable, mean imputation has the advantage to lead to positive semi-definite correlation matrices and hence can be directly used as a kernel K_U^{co}. A similar kernel K_X^{co} can be defined over items by interchanging the role of users and item in the above derivation.

Quadratic Correlation Kernels There are two disadvantages of the above correlation kernel. First of all, it is not possible to use the standard pairwise deletion, because this may result in an improper (i.e. not positive semi-definite) correlation matrix. Second, correlations between users that have very few items in common are often unreliable. One way to remedy these two problems is to define a kernel matrix by taking the square of the correlation matrix C obtained by pairwise deletion, $K^{qu} = C^2$. Notice that K^{qu} is positive semi-definite, since C is symmetric. Intuitively, K_U^{qu} measures user similarity in terms of how similar two users are correlated with other users. Again, a similar kernel K_X^{qu} can be derived for items.

Combining Kernels The above kernels can be combined by first additively combining kernel functions into a single kernel,

$$K_* = K_*^{id} + K_*^{at} + K_*^{co} + K_*^{qu}, \tag{2}$$

where $* \in \{U, X\}$. Then the joint kernel is obtained as the tensor product $K = K_U \otimes K_X$,

$$K((u, x), (u', x')) = K_U(u, u') K_X(x, x'). \tag{3}$$

Finally, we would like to stress that the joint kernel is perfectly symmetric in users and items. However, by making specific (asymmetric) choices with respect to the kernels K_U and K_X one can derive data representations used in previous work. In particular, the choice of $K_U = K_U^{id}$ orthogonalizes representations for different users, which implies that predictions for u and $u' \neq u$ are governed by different weights in the weight vector w. In this case, the weight vector can be thought of as a stacked version of these user-specific weights $w = (w_u)_{u \in \mathcal{U}}$.

Lemma 2. *Define $K = K_U^{id} \otimes K_X$ with $K_X(x, x') = \langle \Phi(x), \Phi(x') \rangle$ then there is a partition $w = (w_u)_{u \in \mathcal{U}}$ such that $F(u, x; w) = \langle w_u, \Phi(x) \rangle$.*

Obviously, there will be no generalization across users in this case. A similar observation holds for $K_X = K_X^{id}$.

3 Perceptron Algorithm

3.1 Design Goals

While most previous machine learning approaches decouple the learning problems associated with each user, our approach leads to a joint problem which couples learning across different users. In order to avoid an undue increase

---

Algorithm 1 JRank: joint kernel perceptron ranking.

1: input: number of iterations, training set of ratings
2: $\alpha(u, x) = 0$ for all training pairs (u, x, r)
3: **for** $s = 1, \ldots, k - 1$ **do** $\theta_s = 0$; $\theta_k = \infty$
4: **for** a fixed number of iterations **do**
5:     **for** all training ratings (u, x, r) **do**
6:         $\hat{r} = f(u, x; \alpha, \theta)$ from (1)
7:         **if** $\hat{r} > r$ **then**
8:             $\alpha(u, x) = \alpha(u, x) + (r - \hat{r})$
9:             **for** $s = r, \ldots, \hat{r} - 1$ **do** $\theta_s \leftarrow \theta_s + 1$
10:         **else if** $\hat{r} < r$ **then**
11:             $\alpha(u, x) = \alpha(u, x) + (r - \hat{r})$
12:             **for** $s = \hat{r}, \ldots, r - 1$ **do** $\theta_s \leftarrow \theta_s - 1$
13:         **end if**
14:     **end for**
15: **end for**
16: output: parameters α and θ

---

in complexity compared to other methods, we have investigated the use of a perceptron-like training algorithm, which has advantages due to its on-line nature (e.g. early stopping, fast re-training, small memory footprint).

Moreover we have identified two additional design goals. We would like to work with multi-level response variables on an *ordinal scale*, since this is appropriate for most applications. This means that we consider the total order among ratings, but avoid interpreting the rating as an absolute numeric value. The resulting problem is well-known as *ordinal regression*. Secondly, since we want to use implicit data representations via kernel functions, it is mandatory to work in a *dual representation* which only makes use of inner products between (joint) feature vectors. Putting all three aspects (on-line, ordinal, kernel) together, we propose to generalize the perceptron ranking algorithm of [6] as described in the sequel.

3.2   Joint Perceptron Ranking (JRank)

The generalization of perceptron learning to ordinal regression has been called perceptron ranking or *PRank* [6]. Here we use basically the same algorithm, with the key difference that the prediction problems for different users are coupled through the use of joint kernel functions. Moreover, in our model the thresholds that define the binning of the F-values are shared by all users. Similarly to the dual-form perceptron learning algorithm for binary classification, we introduce parameters $\alpha(u, x)$ for every training observation (u, x). The resulting algorithm is described in Algorithm 1. Updates occur if the predicted rating of an example (u, x) is incorrect (line 7 or 10). In w space, the updates are performed in direction of $\Psi(u, x)$ with a step size given by the (difference) between true and predicted rating. Notice that f is defined in terms of F, which is computed as

$$F(u, x; \alpha) = \sum_{(u', x')} \alpha(u', x') K((u, x), (u', x')), \qquad (4)$$

where the sum runs over all training ratings. Convergence proofs under suitable separability conditions and a mistake bound analysis can be found in [6]. Also, it is straightforward to verify that JRank reduces to binary perceptron learning when $k = 2$. In our experiments, we have actually used a more aggressive margin-sensitive update rule, which also updates if no sufficient margin is obtained, i.e. for (u, x, r) if $\langle w, \Psi(u, x) \rangle - \theta_{r-1} < \gamma$ or $\theta_r - \langle w, \Psi(u, x) \rangle < \gamma$ for some fixed constant $\gamma \geq 0$.

4   Related Work

Clearly, we are not the first ones to point out potential benefits of combining collaborative and content-based filtering techniques. The most popular family of methods are *hybrid* in nature. In the Fab system [1], content analysis is employed to generate user profiles from Web page ratings. The concept of filterbots was introduced in [16] to refer to fictive users (bots) who generate ratings based on content. This approach was further extended in [8] by including various user-specific filterbots propose a modular approach where independent predictions are computed by separate content filtering or collaborative filtering modules. [11] uses content-based predictors (naive Bayes) to impute missing values and create pseudo-user profiles.

A second family of approaches treat user rating prediction as a machine learning problem, where the prediction function is learned from labeled examples. In [3] this philosophy was implemented by constructing set-valued features that contain either a set of users who like a specific movie or a set of movies which are liked by a particular user. In addition, content features and hybrid features are defined and used as the input representation for a rule induction system. Similarly, the approaches of [4] and [6] described above can directly incorporate item features, if available.

5   Experiments

5.1   Data Sets and Experimental Setup

To evaluate the approach outlined above we use the EachMovie[2] data set that consists of 72,916 users and 2,811,983 recorded ratings on 1,628 different movies. We have scaled each rating to be on a zero to five star scale. The Internet Movie Database[3] was used to collect item attributes relating to genre, cast, crew, country, language, and keywords of a movie. The plot synopsis was utilized to

---

[2] courtesy of Digital Equipment Corporation
[3] http://www.imdb.com

generate a tf-idf representation. We also used demographic information about users in EachMovie about gender, age, and residence (zip-code, first two digits used). All multivariate attributes were encoded using a standard orthogonal (binary) feature representation.

The randomized generation of training and test data has been conducted as follows. First, we have eliminated users with incomplete attributes and with fewer than 10 ratings, leaving a total of 22,488 out of the initial 72,916 users. Items without ratings or with no valid attributes have also been removed; 1,613 out of the 1,628 items were retained. Second, we have randomly subsampled rows and columns of the rating matrix to produce a submatrix of user-item pairs. Third, we randomly divide the selected items into training and test items. In order to compute correlation matrices, we also make use of the users and items that are not part of the selected submatrix. Hence, these ratings only enter on the *input* side and do not contribute as training instances. The reported results are averaged over multiple trials of this procedure.

We have evaluated the JRank algorithm using various combinations of kernels, the details of which can be found in [2]. Here we report only a subset of these results. To show the competitiveness of our approach, we also compare JRank with a standard collaborative filtering algorithm based on the Pearson correlation coefficient [14]. In all our experiments JRank is trained on training instances presented in a random order for a maximum of 5 iterations with γ set to 1.

5.2   Evaluation Metrics

We have utilized three evaluation metrics which quantify the accuracy of predicted ratings $\hat{R} = (\hat{r}_1, ..., \hat{r}_n)$ with respect to true ratings $R = (r_1, ... r_n)$.

- *Mean average error (MAE)* - The mean average error is just the average deviation of the predicted rating from the actual rating $E(R, \hat{R}) = \|R - \hat{R}\|_1/n$.
- *Mean zero-one test error (0/1 Error)* - The zero-one error gives an error of 1 to every incorrect prediction $E(R, \hat{R}) = |\{i : r_i \neq \hat{r}_i\}|/n$.
- *Expected rank utility (ERU)* - In many applications, such as generating recommendations, correctly ranking items may be more important than predicting ratings for individual items. In particular, one would like to put more emphasis on the quality of the top ranked items. Thus, we have utilized the metric proposed in [5], which measures the expected utility of a proposed ranking by scoring items in a recommendation list from top to bottom using an exponential discounting factor.

5.3   Results and Discussion

In our evaluation of JRank we have systematically investigated various combinations of the four types of features described above [2]. The results indicate the identity features are very useful when the same set of users and/or items used

Table 1. Results for 100 training users, 5000 input users, and 1000 training/input items. Evaluation metrics used are Mean Absolute Error (MAE), Mean Zero-One Error and Expected Rank Utility (ERU).

K_u^{id}	K_u^{at}	K_u^{co}	K_u^{qu}	K_x^{id}	K_x^{at}	K_x^{co}	K_x^{qu}	MAE	0/1 Error	ERU
o		o				o	o	0.880	**0.621**	0.791
o		o	o			o	o	**0.877**	**0.621**	**0.793**
o	o	o	o	o	o	o	o	0.882	0.624	0.792
			Pearson					0.936	0.673	0.736
		Relative Improvement						6.3%	7.7%	7.7%

in training are used in testing. The collaborative information of the correlation and quadratic correlation kernels are also very useful, although there is only a minor improvement in combining the two. The least useful features are the ones that encode attributes, although the item attributes can be useful when little collaborative information is given. The user attributes are somewhat of a hindrance because they encode so little information, but in an application where more user attributes are available they could be useful. Our experiments also show that JRank converges to near optimal after a mere five iterations according to all three error metrics, it always has better performance than PRank, and does better than Pearson after only three iterations.

In evaluating the performance with regards to the amount of input data we have found that when more collaborative information given as input the performance of JRank improves when collaborative kernels are utilized. In addition, using more items for training also improves performance unilaterally. Increasing the number of training users, which is the number of users coupled together in learning, increased performance up until about 50 or 100 users at which point no additional gain is really seen. Table 1 shows the results of some good kernel combinations. The accuracy gains compared to the baseline collaborative filtering method are quite substantial: relative improvements are around 7% for all evaluation metrics. The performance of JRank also compares favorably to methods investigated with a slightly different experimental setup elsewhere [5].

6   Conclusion

We have presented a learning architecture for the problem of predicting ratings that can incorporate all available information based on the idea of defining joint kernel functions over user-item pairs. We have shown that using this method of coupling together learning problems can achieve substantial improvement in performance over state-of-the-art methods that treat each user individually.

Acknowledgments

We would like to thank the Compaq Equipment Corporation for making the EachMovie data set available. This work was sponsored by an NSF-ITR grant, award number IIS-0312401.

References

1. Marko Balabanovic and Yoav Shoham. Fab: Content-based, collaborative recommendation. *Communications of the ACM*, 40(3):66–72, March 1997.
2. J. Basilico and T. Hofmann. Unifying collaborative and content-based filtering. In *Proceedings of the 21th International Conference on Machine Learning*, 2004.
3. Chumki Basu, Haym Hirsh, and William W. Cohen. Recommendation as classification: Using social and content-based information in recommendation. In *Proceedings of the 15th National Conference on Artificial Intelligence*, pages 714–720, 1998.
4. Daniel Billsus and Michael J. Pazzani. Learning collaborative information filters. In *Proceedings of the 15th International Conference on Machine Learning*, pages 46–54, 1998.
5. J. S. Breese, D. Heckerman, and C. Kardie. Empiricial analysis of predictive algorithms for collaborative filtering. In *Proceedings of the 14th Conference on Uncertainty in Artificial Intelligence*, pages 43–52, 1998.
6. K. Crammer and Y. Singer. Pranking with ranking. In *Advances in Neural Information Processing Systems 14*, pages 641–647, 2002.
7. D. Goldberg, D. Nichols, B.M. Oki, and D. Terry. Using collabrorative filtering to weave an information tapestry. *Communications of the ACM*, 35(12):61–70, 1992.
8. Nathaniel Good, J. Ben Schafer, Joseph A. Konstan, Al Borchers, Badrul M. Sarwar, Jonathan L. Herlocker, and John Riedl. Combining collaborative filtering with personal agents for better recommendations. In *Proceedings of the 16th National Conference on Artificial Intelligence*, pages 439–446, 1999.
9. A. Jennings and H. Higuchi. A user model neural network for a personal news service. *User Modeling and User Adapted Interaction*, 3:1–25, 1993.
10. Ken Lang. NewsWeeder: Learning to filter netnews. In *Proceedings of the 12th International Conference on Machine Learning*, pages 331–339, 1995.
11. Prem Melville, Raymond J. Mooney, and Ramadass Nagarajan. Content-boosted collaborative filtering for improved recommendations. In *Proceedings of the 18th National Conference on Artificial Intelligence*, pages 187–192, 2002.
12. Raymond J. Mooney and Loriene Roy. Content-based book recommending using learning for text categorization. In *Proceedings of the 5th ACM Conference on Digital Libraries*, pages 195–204, 2000.
13. M. Pazzani, J. Muramatsu, and D. Billsus. Syskill & Webert: Identifying interesting web sites. In *Proceedings of the 13th National Conference on Artificial Intelligence*, pages 54–61, 1996.
14. P. Resnick, N. Iacovou, M. Suchak, P. Bergstrom, and J. Riedl. GroupLens: An open architecture for collaborative filtering of netnews. In *Proceedings of the ACM Conference on Computer Supported Cooperative Work*, pages 175–186, 1994.
15. B. M. Sarwar, G.e Karypis, J. A. Konstan, and J. Reidl. Item-based collaborative filtering recommendation algorithms. In *Proceedings of the 10th International World Wide Web Conference*, pages 285–295, 2001.
16. Badrul M. Sarwar, Joseph A. Konstan, Al Borchers, Jonathan L. Herlocker, Bradley N. Miller, and John Riedl. Using filtering agents to improve prediction quality in the GroupLens research collaborative filtering system. In *Proceedings of the ACM Conference on Computer Supported Cooperative Work*, pages 345–354, 1998.
17. U. Shardanand and P. Maes. Social information filtering: Algorithms for automating 'word of mouth'. In *Human Factors in Computing Systems ACM CHI*, pages 210–217, 1995.

Visualization in Digital Libraries

Enrico Bertini, Tiziana Catarci, Lucia Di Bello, and Stephen Kimani

Università degli Studi di Roma "La Sapienza"
Dipartimento di Informatica e Sistemistica
Via Salaria, 113 - 00198 Roma, Italy
{bertini, catarci, dibello, kimani}@dis.uniroma1.it

Abstract. In an age characterized by tremendous technological break-throughs, the world is witnessing overwhelming quantities and types of information. Digital Libraries (DLs) are a result of these breakthroughs, but they have not been spared by the challenges resulting from them. While DLs stakeholders are still struggling to come to terms with the massive quantities and complex types of information, the needs of the digital library as an information/knowledge environment is still evolving including new challenging needs. Information Visualization (Infovis) represents a viable solution to this. The human-vision channel has a high bandwidth and it can surveil a visual field in a parallel manner, processing the corresponding data to different levels of detail and recognition and understanding of overwhelming data can be done at an instant. It is an outstanding resource that can be exploited within a DLs in order to address issues arising from the conventional needs (such as the quantities and types of information) and the non-conventional needs. Here we analyze Infovis as a resource for DLs, relating visualization techniques to specific DLs needs, providing a classification of Infovis techniques and reporting about our analysis of DLs tasks and their correspondence with suitable visualizations.

1 Introduction

The revolutionary development of computing technologies, their techniques, and theories in late years, lead us to a new world where data is continuously produced and consumed at a rate never imagined before and where the access to it is made every day faster and easier. Thanks to the Internet and communication technologies, it is possible now for everyone to gain direct access to large information spaces and experience the unique opportunity to directly participate to the consumption and production of them. From this scenario, the disciplines object of our study, Information Visualization (Infovis henceforth) and Digital Libraries (DLs henceforth), were born, flourish and still evolve. Infovis with the main purpose of providing tools and techniques to analyze data, DLs with the main purpose of giving access to libraries' content and facilitating the search for specific library items.

Infovis techniques literally permit to obtain a view into these complex information spaces by mapping data features to visual features and visually presenting their content [9]. Interactively exploring abstract visualizations the user

M. Hemmje et al. (Eds.): E.J. Neuhold Festschrift, LNCS 3379, pp. 183–196, 2005.
© Springer-Verlag Berlin Heidelberg 2005

can explore, obtain overviews, search for trends, make comparisons, and present findings. DLs were originally born from the need of producing digital counterparts of physical libraries; with the driving idea of making everything in digital form [15] so giving wider and easier access to library materials and empowering people with powerful search facilities. For this reason, DLs have mainly been studied from the point of view of their provision through digital networks and the accuracy and efficiency of their searching tools. These two disciplines never touched each other before, but recently, there is a growing interest in the use of Infovis in the world of DLs. The reason for this is that both disciplines are assuming new roles and coping with new needs.

Infovis is expanding its vision, including the visual exploration of less structured and less well-defined data. The typical infovis scenario was that of an analyst trying to discover interesting trends in data coming from some sort of statistics. Now Infovis techniques are being more and more applied to new contexts where information is less structured (e.g. knowledge domains [11]), the tasks are less well defined, and individuals using it are more heterogeneous, comprising experts and non experts. Similarly, DLs are slowly transforming their role including new perspectives. For instance, there is a need for tools that permit to obtain overviews of digital library repositories. The typical paradigm of DLs has always been that of querying the repository with some sort of search tool, but now, given their heterogeneity and volume, it is necessary to provide techniques that permit to orient into large information spaces. Interestingly, the world of DLs is moving from a scenario in which people extract information, to one in which users are increasingly the producers of information. DLs are in fact becoming a collaboration space, where people not only obtain access to relevant information but also provides new information by adding commends, pursuing modifications, and creating new relations [3][7]. In this scenario, Infovis is confronted with an additional and challenging problem, that of visualizing and exploring human activities, relations between users and content, and relations between humans and humans.

Given these trends and these complex relations, we recognize there is a strong need for an analysis of the characteristics of these two fields. We believe that a systematization is necessary; a more formal analysis of Infovis' capabilities, DLs' needs and their relationship, can provide us new insights. Even if there already exist some attempt to systematize Infovis and DLs [16][12][8] we feel there is a need to put some order taking into account these two disciplines together. We classify existing techniques and synergies, to better understand what is their role in the whole spectrum of combinations, to find new aspects and unexpected roles. For this reason, this chapter provides a first part in which we present Infovis in its standard view, a second one mainly dealing with DLs, and a third one that puts them together.

Section 1 offers preliminary definitions and discusses why Infovis is becoming so largely used in a variety of different applications and fields. We expose what are the principal purposes of Infovis. Then, we provide a schematic classification of Infovis based on: data type, visualization technique, interaction and distortion technique. In Section 2, we pass considering possible future research developments of Infovis to DLs. We offer a view on how visual interfaces can offer significant improvements on current practices and technologies and point out the interesting challenges. In Section 3, we go deep into the matter of DLs. We give a brief description of DLs, followed by an extensive analysis of tasks. The analysis of tasks performed in DLs gives us the opportunity to embrace the whole spectrum of relevant activities, comprised those arising from the new role DLs are assuming. In Section 4, we pass considering the relationships between DLs tasks and techniques offered by Infovis. This permits to see the extent to which the needs posed by DLs are covered by Infovis and where future research should point to cover existing holes. Finally, in Section 5, we give indications for future research and final remarks.

2   Background Knowledge

2.1   Information Visualization

Introduction to Information Visualization. Infovis can be defined as the use of computer-supported, interactive, visual representations of abstract data to amplify cognition [9]. The ability of the human mind to rapidly perceive certain types of information from visual representations of data, makes Infovis a useful and often necessary tool. The visual perceptive system is particularly efficient in giving sense to complex graphical frameworks. In fact, it is characterized by a very high throughput and high degree of parallelism, since it partitions limited bandwidth between the conflicting needs for both high spatial resolution and wide aperture in sensing the visual environment. Visualizations can work indirectly reducing working memory requirements for a task by allowing the working memory to be external and visual. Infovis applications rely on basic features that the human perceptual system inherently assimilates very quickly: color, size, shape, proximity and motion. These features can be used to increase the data density of the information displayed. In this way, visualizations can reduce the search for data by grouping or visually relating information. While visualizations compact information into a small space, they can also allow hierarchical search by using overviews to locate areas for more detailed search. In fact, they also allow zooming in or popping up details on demand. Infovis, through aggregation and abstraction, enable users to immediately recognize gaps in the data, discover outliers or errors in the data, pinpoint minimum and maximum values, identify clusters, compare objects, visually draw some conclusions, discover trends and patterns. These patterns, in turn, suggest schemata at a higher level, which enable us to extract some knowledge that can be utilized to make new hypothesis, drive other ideas, propose solutions, and so on. Thus, visualizations are powerful tools that make some problems obvious, allowing fast perceptual inferences that are extremely easy for humans.

A Classification of Visualization Techniques. In the last decade, a large number of novel information visualization techniques have been developed, allowing visualizations of multidimensional data sets lacking of inherent two or three-dimensional semantics. These visualization techniques can be categorized according to three criteria: the underlying data types that the applications attempt to visualize, the specific type of visual technique applied, and the distortion and interaction technique used. Nevertheless, it is important to note that a specific system may also be designed to support different data types and it may use a combination of multiple visualization and interaction techniques. In the following, we present a visualization taxonomy based on: the underlying data types that the applications attempt to visualize, the specific type of visual technique applied, and the distortion and interaction technique used. In Infovis, the data usually consist of a large number of records, each consisting of a number of variables or dimensions. The number of attributes, also called dimensionality of the data sets, can differ from data sets to data sets. We can identify data sets according to both dimensionality and data format. Nevertheless, it is important to note that these two data characteristics can be assumed to be orthogonal i.e. any data may belong to both classes.

According to **dimensionality** we can identify the following types of data.

- *One-dimensional data*
- *Two-dimensional data*
- *Three-dimensional data*
- *Multi-dimensional data*

According to **data format** we can identify the following types of data.

- *Text* such as articles full text documents, web pages.
- *Algorithms and software*, such as debugging operations and visualizations support in software development by helping to understanding algorithms, e.g., by presenting the structure of thousands of source code lines as graphs.
- *Multimedia data*, such as audio, video or image.
- *Semi-structured data* such as hypertext or XML-based documents.
- *Records* such as data table as found in DBMS.

Along with these two data classifications, we can also identify:

- *Temporal data*, such as the age of a person or time series data.
- *Hierarchies and Graphs* such as data mainly exhibiting relationships among them. Trees and graphs are widely used to represent such relationships. Examples are the e-mail interrelationships among people, the file structure of the hard disk, or the hyperlinks in the World Wide Web. In particular, hierarchical data are usually represented by trees like Hyperbolic Tree [20], Cone Tree [26], Treemap [27].

The above types of data can be visualized in different ways using several kinds of **visualization techniques**. These visualization techniques can be classified as follows:

- *Standard 2D/3D displays*, such as scatter plots and bar charts.

- Geometrically transformed displays, such as landscapes and parallel coordinates [19].
- *Icon-based displays*, the idea is to map the attribute values of a multidimensional data item to the features of an icon. The icons can be arbitrarily defined, for example, stick figure icons, needle icons, color icons.
- *Stacked displays*, such as Tree-maps, Worlds-within-Worlds [14], Cone Trees and Dimensional Stacking [21].

The third criterion for classifying visualizations is the **interaction and distortion technique** used. These techniques may be classified as follows.

- *Interactive Projection*. The basic idea here is to change the projections in order to explore a multidimensional data set e.g. GrandTour system [5].
- *Interactive Filtering*. In exploring large data sets, it is important to focus on interesting subsets of data by a direct selection of the desired subset (browsing) or by a specification of properties of the desired subset, (dynamic query is an example of interaction technique that enables users to interactively filter data selecting ranges of values for some data attributes) (e.g., FilmFinder [4]).
- *Interactive Zooming*. In dealing with large amounts of data, it is important to present the data in a highly compressed form to provide an overview of the data, but, at the same time, allow a variable display of them on different resolutions. Zooming means that the data representation automatically changes to present more details on higher zoom levels (e.g., TableLens [25]).
- *Interactive Distortion*. Distortion is a visual transformation that modifies a Visual Structure to create focus+context views. Overview and details are combined into a single Visual Structure. The basic idea is to show portions of the data with a high level of detail while others are shown with a lower level of detail. Examples of distortion techniques can be found in Hyperbolic Tree and Perspective Wall [24].
- *Interactive Linking and Brushing*. Link-and-brush is a technique that permits to relate different representations of the same data in many different visual structures. The brushed points are highlighted in all visualizations, making it possible to detect dependencies and correlations (e.g., Polaris [29]).

Infovis is useful to the extent that it increases our ability to perform cognitive activities. It enables us to better understand complex systems, make better decisions, and discover information that might otherwise remain unknown. In the following section, we explain how Infovis can be exploited to better access, browse, and analyze DLs.

2.2   Digital Libraries

One particularly worthwhile definition of DLs is the one given by Borgman et al. in [6] which states: "Digital libraries are a set of electronic resources and associated technical capabilities for creating, searching and using information.

In this sense they are an extension and enhancement of information storage and retrieval systems that manipulate digital data in any medium (text, images, sounds; static or dynamic images) and exist in distributed networks. The content of DLs includes data, metadata that describe various aspects of the data (e.g., representation, creator, owner, reproduction rights), and metadata that consist of links or relationships to other data or metadata, whether internal or external to the digital library." According to the Digital Library Federation, "Digital libraries are organizations that provide the resources, including the specialized staff, to select, structure, offer intellectual access to, interpret, distribute, preserve the integrity of, and ensure the persistence over time of collections of digital works so that they are readily and economically available for use by a defined community or set of communities" [1]. Many others can be found but the main points are that: (1) DLs can comprise digital as well as non-digital entities, (2) the realm of libraries is constituted not only of library objects but also of associated processes, actors and communities, and (3) their content can be extremely heterogeneous.

It appears that the bottom line DLs issue in this matter is to provide a coherent view of the (possibly) large collection of the available materials [22]. With the foregoing statement in mind we may, to a large extent, regard DLs as an information/knowledge environment. In this environment, there are producers and consumers of information and knowledge; producers may also be consumers at the same time and vice versa. Ubiquitous computing is particularly important. For instance, DLs users may have a device and just plug it in to be connected not only to a network but also to an information/knowledge environment.

2.3   Information Visualization and Digital Libraries

DLs are content rich, multimedia, multilingual collections of documents that are distributed and accessed worldwide. We will take a work-oriented perspective on libraries, a perspective from which observations of people's actual work are used to critique and guide technology development. We refer to a simple framework which highlights three crucial aspects of libraries: the collections of documents [1] they house, their enabling technologies, and the work conducted in and by libraries. The work is the most fundamental element of all. Without understanding the forms of search toward which a library is oriented, we could not understand how its collections are selected and organized; and without understanding its internal services, we could not understanding how collections are maintained or how users' search is supported. In this perspective, work is placed on a par with documents and technology as a legitimate domain of investigation and source of innovation. By this work-oriented approach to DLs, we do not mean focus solely on people's work, but rather evaluate library collections and technology in relation to the work that is being done with them. In this context, we can list a range of issues related to DLs, such as to store, access and explore DLs, locate

---

[1] we use the term "document" in the broadest sense, including paper materials, electronic files, videotapes, and audiotapes

the required information and finally obtaining it, issues related to buying physical or electronic objects, copyright issues, and so on. Digital library interfaces are playing a crucial role in helping users to achieve an easy and effective access to the information that they need. Research in visual interfaces has a strong connection to the fast-moving field of Infovis and the design of visual interfaces can benefit from the advances of Infovis.

Good visualizations can help the design of visual interfaces in several ways, for example, by: reducing visual search time, providing a better understanding of a complex data set, revealing relationships otherwise not being noticed, enabling to see a data set from several perspectives simultaneously, conveying information effectively.

Advances in Infovis can be exploited to develop enhanced interfaces for improving retrieval, interaction, analysis, understanding and management of data stored in DLs. Visual interfaces to DLs apply powerful data analysis and Infovis techniques to generate visualizations which are intended to help users to organize, to electronically access and to manage large, complex information spaces and which can be seen as a value adding service to DLs. Visual interfaces represent one of the most exciting areas of research and development in DLs.

Both infovis research and research on visual interfaces to DLs is facilitated by several factors: (1) explosion of digitally available information, (2) decreasing cost of storage and computing power, (3) larger hard disk sizes which support faster information access, (4) accelerated graphics processors and high resolution color monitors.

We believe that visual interfaces to DLs can help to: providing rapid and efficient access to enormous amount of multimedia knowledge and information, providing new ways to analyze, manage, understand document collections, leverage information (annotation, footstep) from previous users, facilitate information sharing and collaborations.

Today, our primary means of accessing DLs are search engines that typically retrieve very large amounts of more or less relevant documents displayed in long scrollable lists. Search interfaces lack the ability to support information exploration to gain an overview of DLs, to locate resources, to monitor the evolution of their own and other knowledge domains, to track the influence of theories within and across domains. Thus, research on visual interfaces to DLs needs to focus on these aspects. In the following, we list the most common challenging issues for visual interfaces to DLs.

- To support visual representations of retrieval results in order to understand the interrelations of retrieved documents - Spatially mapping interrelations can be very effective and it is desirable [17]. Digital library search results are usually shown as a textual list. Viewing several thousand search results at once on a two-dimensional display is desirable. It is possible, for example, to organize search results retrieved from web search engines by topics and display them on a 2-dimensional map, each document is represented by an icon, its size represents the relevance of the document to the query, color-coded links suggest how the documents interrelate [7].

- To support visual representations for query refinement - Today, search engines lack of responsiveness, users are locked into a cycle of query refinement, in which query specification and result browsing are distinct activities. The users receive no feedback concerning the effect of query refinements until a new set of results for the refined query is returned. Users can waste time and effort in forming queries which return zero or near-zero matching documents or very large unmanageable numbers of matching documents. They receive no indication as to whether the query terms that they specify will identify documents of the appropriate nature. Visual interfaces that interactively enable refinement of visual query results are desirable [18].

- To gain an overview of the coverage of a digital library and to facilitate browsing - If users have to handle a large number of documents organized in a hierarchical database, it is possible, for example, to adopt two-dimensional displays that use categorical and hierarchical axes, allowing users to see the entire result set and browse it [28].

- To visualize user interaction data in relation to available documents, (online customer behavior data), in order to assess the effectiveness of the website design and improve DLs usage - Tools that use spatial metaphors to visualize the website structure, paths, flow through the site and common click streams are desirable [7].

- To create visualization of knowledge domains - A considerable body of recent research applies powerful mathematical techniques such as Factor Analysis, Multidimensional Scaling or Latent Semantic Analysis to extract the underlying semantic structure of documents, the special structure of a discipline, author co-citation pattern, changes in authors' influences in a particular field; cluster techniques and a modified Boltzman algorithm are used to spatially visualize co-citation patterns and semantic similarity networks of retrieved documents for interactive exploration. The algorithm works by computing attraction and repulsion forces among nodes based on the result of the data analysis. Nodes may represent articles or images which are attracted to other nodes to which they have a similarity link and repelled by nodes to which there is no link [11].

- To invent appropriate metaphor graphics for documents visualization. A metaphor graphics based interface further assists the user in intuitively understanding the library, providing an instant overview.

- To create appropriate software tools to manage different types of data, such as documents, image data and video - For example, creating tools that enable the user to explore the difference between various versions of the same full text document; tools that help the user navigating through relevant paragraphs within a full text document; tools to handle diverse and large scale multimedia and mixed-media data.

- To create cartographic interfaces to DLs, exploiting the role of cartographic principles in designing easy to understand and easy to use visual interfaces that implement map metaphors to visualize abstract information.

3   Digital Library Tasks

A digital library should enable the user to carry out various tasks. We have undertaken two main studies in the context of the DELOS Network of Excellence on Digital Libraries project [2] in order to understand the common DLs tasks: DLs case studies and questionnaire-based study. We were able to collect results from both DLs users and stakeholders. The results pertained to prevalent DLs tasks and their importance.

Content Management (or Integration of Knowledge), e.g., locating resources, creating cross-reference links among similar resources, storing metadata about resources (creator, content, technical requirements, etc).

Access to Knowledge (or locating information), e.g., search (keyword search, parametric search), navigation related functions (e.g., browsing predefined catalogues), index facilities.

Tool Creation and Management, e.g., bookmark facility , presentation of contents according to profile, profile definition (e.g., professional interests, personal interests, etc.).

Membership Management, e.g., unsubscribing and subscribing DLs users, maintaining a virtual help desk for end-users, updating end-users on new / refined services.

Some Services Interfaces for access to integrated knowledge, e.g., title, author(s)/editor(s), short description/ previews, related items.

Interfaces for sharing/integration of knowledge, e.g., e-mail, shared annotation facilities, message Boards, chat and video conferencing.

Other services to end-users, e.g., downloading/uploading facilities, printing/print preview facilities, glossaries.

4   Correspondence Between DLs Tasks and Visualizations

It would be beneficial to establish a correspondence between the realized set of DLs tasks and the various types of visualizations. In an attempt to come up with the correspondence, we have first grouped DLs tasks that are similar/related. For each such a group of similar DLs tasks, we propose visualizations that are appropriate for supporting the tasks.

Managing DLs resources (Locating resources, creating new resources, editing existing resources, deleting resources, organizing resources, archiving resources) - *Graphs* (such as trees and networks) can help representing relationships among different resources on the digital library. *Metaphors* can also be exploited in this case. It appears that they are appropriate for visualizing resources in the underlying domain. Many geographical DLs use the landscape metaphor to visualize resources (e.g., IDV [3]).

---

[2] http://www.delos.info

[3] http://my.unidata.ucar.edu/content/software/metapps/docs/userguide/
Introduction.html

Managing links to related/similar resources (Creating cross-reference links among similar resources, "See also" items) - *Graphs* would be a reasonable choice because crss-references (and "See also") tend to form graph structures. In [23], the authors describe a *metaphor-based* visualization tool for searching, browsing and accessing bibliographic materials using metaphors.

Storing metadata about resources (creator, content, technical requirements, etc.) - This task might benefit from *tree/hierarchical visualizations.*

Checking for inconsistencies in the metadata - A *multidimensional* visualization could be useful in detecting inconsistencies in metadata. One of the visualization tools that has been resourceful for such purposes is Spotfire DecisionSite [4]. Spotfire can be used to carry out a quality control analysis of metadata to ensure consistency of samples and microarrays.

Handling glossaries, index facilities, thesaurus, dictionaries, and classification schemes - *Trees and hierarchies* it may be a worthwhile choice to visualize this type of information. Considering thesauruses and dictionaries, we can use *graphs* or icons, thumbnail or miniature of the object representing the synonym or of the object represented by the term/word. An interesting example of such an application that uses such graphs is the Visual Thesaurus [5]. The application uses graphs, primarily tree structures, to represent relationships among/between words, e.g., to reflect the relationship among words synonyms. It is worth noting that a tree visualization might also help addressing navigation requirements.

Retrieving content/services usage statistics - A *multidimensional* visualization might be resourceful in this respect (such as the Spotfire DecisionSuite). However, it should also be pointed out that spatial metaphors could be used to visualize the website paths, flow through the site and common click streams [7].

Providing bookmark facility - Standard browsers such as Netscape and Internet Explorer provide bookmarks as a vertical list with the possibility to organize them in folders. In such browsers, it is difficult to manage and visualize bookmarks (for instance: bookmarks could be hidden in folders). In [2] the authors recommend for a global visualization of bookmarks visualizing a large number of bookmarks at the same time and providing time-based visualizations. A *tree visualization* might be desirable in this case. Bookmark features (e.g., time) could be encoded on nodes using visual attributes like color and size. As for visualizing a single bookmark, a typical choice would be to use icons to represent the bookmark or use a miniature of the document. The two visualizations (global view and individual view) could be integrated through a visualization interaction technique such as *Overview + Detail*

Supporting multilingual features - *Graphs* could be resourceful in this respect. An example of a multilingual support application is Meat (Multilingual Environment for Advanced Translations) [6]. In Meat, some intermediate results are presented as edges. The content of each edge can be seen below the visual-

---

[4] http://www.spotfire.com/products/decision.asp
[5] http://www.visualthesaurus.com
[6] http://crl.nmsu.edu/ ahmed/Meat/intro.html

ization. However, it should be pointed out that the tool and the visualization might require a lot of domain knowledge (e.g., in linguistics). *Providing history facility* Such a facility should make time information more apparent. Therefore, *temporal visualizations* could be help in that direction.

Supporting search mechanisms (e.g., keyword search, parametric search) - A lot of research has been done regarding this task and especially in the information retrieval community. It could be worthwhile to adopt some of the straightforward *1-dimensional* and yet profound visualization proposals; and that are relevant to DLs. They include: TileBars, AQUA, and Envision.

Providing navigation related functions (e.g., browsing predefined catalogues) - *Tree visualizations* could be a good choice for navigating materials in DLs.

Filtering search/browsing results (e.g., according to personal profile(s)) - *Multidimensional visualizations* are usually suitable for such a task. An example of an appropriate tool in this context is Tablelens. It should also be observed that web search results could be organized by topics and displayed on a *2-dimensional map*, in which each document is represented by an icon [7]. Document aspects (such as relevance of the document to the query, the document's interrelationship with other documents, etc) could be coded using visual attributes (such as color, size, etc).

Managing profiles (Presentation of contents according to profile, Profile definition, e.g., professional interests, Suggestions for content based on profile, Suggestions for discussion with other library members with similar interest profiles) - *Multidimensional visualizations* may be resourceful for the DLs task of visualizing profiles.

Monitoring usage and identifying common patterns of use - In the new or evolving perspective of DLs, we encounter information producers, information consumers (and collaborators). In fact, a DLs user can be an information producer or an information consumer at the same time or at different times. DLs users will produce/consume DLs material and move on to another, and may also interact/share with another DLs user(s). Such tasks therefore usually entail lots of interconnections. *Graphs* can be a worthwhile choice. Some of the efforts that have been carried out for the Web can be really resourceful in the arena of DLs as well.

5   Trends and Conclusions

DLs provide for collection development, organization, access, annotation and preservation, and deal both with information in digital form as well as digital management of information residing on physical media. It is important to place additional emphasis on the need to consider users and usage as part of any analytical framework used to study DLs; research on any visual interfaces to DLs should be based on a detailed analysis of users, their information needs, and their tasks.

Current digital library technology assumes that the user has a networked personal computer which is used to access server computers, to store content and to provide access to services. In practice, people increasingly use a variety of computing devices in their daily lives not all of which are continuously connected to a network. This growth of palm devices, hand-held computers, disconnected laptops, and embedded processors (e.g. "smart mobile telephones") offer exciting opportunities for the creation of *Personalized Information Spaces*: DLs with collections and services that correspond to targeted needs and situations. Mobile devices represent new opportunities for accessing DLs but also pose a number of challenges given the diversity of their hardware and software features. This diversity makes it difficult to access DLs using the existing user interfaces (suitable to conventional computers) and would make it necessary to redesign user interfaces for each kind of device [13], [10].

We believe that new software tools will enable individuals to exploit the mobility of these devices using them for storing, accessing, and updating information resources, even when network access is impractical or impossible. Developing and deploying these *Nomadic DLs* will require technology that is sensitive to two critical dimensions: device capabilities, (e.g., unique hardware characteristics, display capabilities, input mechanisms); device connectivity (e.g., connections' stability, coverage, and speed).

These new devices will offer the promise of anywhere, anytime access to vast online repositories. Along with all this, we should also consider that DLs users are changing their way of using DLs. The search and service work that users and librarians execute on DLs is highly collaborative and it needs new interfaces in order to integrate social structures with the organization of underlying DLs. Nevertheless, supporting collaborative work, that is, translating collaborative work into a visual form, is a challenging task [7]. Future research will have to address a set of issues, for example, how to represent participating parties through a visual interface, how to evaluate whether a particular visual interface is useful in a collaborative setting, how to allow users to store previously selected document sets in personal baskets or how to provide users with personal space to store new information. This will bring users and librarians towards a new digital library in which users will play more and more different roles at different times and places. In this context, consumers of information and knowledge may also be producers at the same time.

Personalization is another related and challenging issue to consider. Future visual interfaces should provide support tailoring screen and interaction to specific user needs, for instance, according to client's background and access history.

Finally, research on visual interfaces to DLs as a whole lacks of solid theoretical foundation. This is a crucial aspect since theoretical contributions can significantly drive new research in practice. Likewise, we need empirical studies to make clear which features prove successful across different techniques. A common test repository would also be necessary. It would allow to compare evaluative studies in terms of strengths and extent of applicability. All these efforts would permit designers to use common standards, to modularize visual interfaces, and to agree upon interface protocols.

6   Acknowledgements

This work is supported by the DELOS Network of Excellence on Digital Libraries. The network is funded by the EU's Sixth Framework Programme. More information can be found at http://www.delos.info

References

1. Digital library federation. a working definition of digital library.
2. David Abrams, Ron Baecker, and Mark Chignell. Information archiving with bookmarks: personal web space construction and organization. In *Proceedings of the SIGCHI conference on Human factors in computing systems*, pages 41–48. ACM Press/Addison-Wesley Publishing Co., 1998.
3. Mark S. Ackerman. Providing social interaction in the digital library. In *Proceedings of the First Annual Conference on the Theory and Practice of Digital Libraries*, 1994.
4. Christopher Ahlberg and Ben Shneiderman. Visual information seeking using the filmfinder. In *Conference companion on Human factors in computing systems*, pages 433–434. ACM Press, 1994.
5. Daniel Asimov. The grand tour: a tool for viewing multidimensional data. *SIAM J. Sci. Stat. Comput.*, 6(1):128–143, 1985.
6. Christine L. Borgman. What are digital libraries? competing visions. *Inf. Process. Manage.*, 35(3):227–243, 1999.
7. Katy Börner and Chaomei Chen. Visual interfaces to digital libraries: Motivation, utilization, and socio-technical challenges. In *Visual Interfaces to Digital Libraries [JCDL 2002 Workshop]*, pages 1–12. Springer-Verlag, 2002.
8. S. K. Card and J. Mackinlay. The structure of the information visualization design space. In *Proceedings of the 1997 IEEE Symposium on Information Visualization (InfoVis '97)*, page 92. IEEE Computer Society, 1997.
9. Stuart K. Card, Jock D. Mackinlay, and Ben Shneiderman. *Readings in information visualization: using vision to think*. Morgan Kaufmann Publishers Inc., 1999.
10. Nohema Castellanos and J. Alfredo Sánchez. Pops: mobile access to digital library resources. In *Proceedings of the third ACM/IEEE-CS joint conference on Digital libraries*, pages 184–185. IEEE Computer Society, 2003.
11. Chaomei Chen and Ray J. Paul. Visualizing a knowledge domain's intellectual structure. *Computer*, 34(3):65–71, 2001.
12. Ed H. Chi. A taxonomy of visualization techniques using the data state reference model. In *Proceedings of the IEEE Symposium on Information Vizualization 2000*, page 69. IEEE Computer Society, 2000.
13. Andy Dong and Alice Agogino. Designing an untethered educational digital library. In *Proceedings of the IEEE International Workshop on Wireless and Mobile Technologies in Education*, page 144, 2003.
14. S. K. Feiner and Clifford Beshers. Visualizing n-dimensional virtual worlds with n-vision. In *Proceedings of the 1990 symposium on Interactive 3D graphics*, pages 37–38. ACM Press, 1990.
15. Edward A. Fox, Robert M. Akscyn, Richard K. Furuta, and John J. Leggett. Digital libraries. *Commun. ACM*, 38(4):22–28, 1995.
16. Marcos Andrè Gonçalves, 0 Edward A. Fox, Layne T. Watson, and Neill A. Kipp. Streams, structures, spaces, scenarios, societies (5s): A formal model for digital libraries. *ACM Trans. Inf. Syst.*, 22(2):270–312, 2004.

17. Matthias Hemmje, Clemens Kunkel, and Alexander Willett. Lyberworld a visualization user interface supporting fulltext retrieval. In *Proceedings of the 17th annual international ACM SIGIR conference on Research and development in information retrieval*, pages 249–259. Springer-Verlag New York, Inc., 1994.

18. Steve Jones. Graphical query specification and dynamic result previews for a digital library. In *Proceedings of the 11th annual ACM symposium on User interface software and technology*, pages 143–151. ACM Press, 1998.

19. Matthias Kreuseler, Norma Lopez, and Heidrun Schumann. A scalable framework for information visualization. In *Proceedings of the IEEE Symposium on Information Visualization 2000*, page 27. IEEE Computer Society, 2000.

20. John Lamping, Ramana Rao, and Peter Pirolli. A focus+context technique based on hyperbolic geometry for visualizing large hierarchies. In *Proc. ACM Conf. Human Factors in Computing Systems, CHI*, pages 401–408. ACM, 1995.

21. Jeffrey LeBlanc, Matthew O. Ward, and Norman Wittels. Exploring n-dimensional databases. In *Proceedings of the 1st conference on Visualization '90*, pages 230–237. IEEE Computer Society Press, 1990.

22. Clifford Lynch and Hector Garcia-Molina. Interoperability, scaling, and the digital libraries research agenda. In *IITA Digital Libraries Workshop*, 1995.

23. Jock D. Mackinlay, Ramana Rao, and Stuart K. Card. An organic user interface for searching citation links. In *Proceedings of the SIGCHI conference on Human factors in computing systems*, pages 67–73. ACM Press/Addison-Wesley Publishing Co., 1995.

24. Jock D. Mackinlay, George G. Robertson, and Stuart K. Card. The perspective wall: detail and context smoothly integrated. In *Proceedings of the SIGCHI conference on Human factors in computing systems*, pages 173–176. ACM Press, 1991.

25. Ramana Rao and Stuart K. Card. The table lens: Merging graphical and symbolic representations in an interactive focus context visualization for tabular information. In *Proc. ACM Conf. Human Factors in Computing Systems, CHI*. ACM, 1994.

26. George Robertson, Jock D. Mackinlay, and Stuart K. Card. Cone trees: Animated 3d visualizations of hierarchical information. In *Proc. ACM Conf. Human Factors in Computing Systems, CHI*. ACM, 1991.

27. Ben Shneiderman. Tree visualization with tree-maps: 2-d space-filling approach. *ACM Trans. Graph.*, 11(1):92–99, 1992.

28. Ben Shneiderman, David Feldman, Anne Rose, and Xavier Ferré Grau. Visualizing digital library search results with categorical and hierarchical axes. In *Proceedings of the fifth ACM conference on Digital libraries*, pages 57–66. ACM Press, 2000.

29. Chris Stolte, Diane Tang, and Pat Hanrahan. Polaris: A system for query, analysis, and visualization of multidimensional relational databases. *IEEE Transactions on Visualization and Computer Graphics*, 8(1):52–65, 2002.

Modelling Interactive, Three-Dimensional Information Visualizations

Gerald Jaeschke[1], Piklu Gupta[2], and Matthias Hemmje[1]

[1] Fraunhofer IPSI, Dolivostr. 15, 64293 Darmstadt, Germany
{jaeschke, hemmje}@ipsi.fraunhofer.de
http://www.ipsi.fraunhofer.de

[2] Technische Universität Darmstadt, Hochschulstr. 1, 64289 Darmstadt, Germany
gupta@linglit.tu-darmstadt.de
http://www.linglit.tu-darmstadt.de

Abstract. Research on information visualization has so far established an outline of the information visualization process and shed light on a broad range of detail aspects involved. However, there is no model in place that describes the nature of information visualization in a coherent, detailed, and well-defined way. We believe that the lack of such a lingua franca hinders communication on and application of information visualization techniques. Our approach is to design a declarative language for describing and defining information visualization techniques. The information visualization modelling language (IVML) provides a means to formally express, note, preserve, and communicate structure, appearance, behaviour, and functionality of information visualization techniques and applications in a standardized way. The anticipated benefits comprise both application and theory.

1 Introduction

Research on information visualization has so far established an outline of the information visualization process and shed light on a broad range of detail aspects involved. However, there is no model in place that describes the nature of information visualization in a coherent, detailed, and well-defined way. We believe that the lack of such a lingua franca hinders communication on and application of information visualization techniques. This paper addresses this challenge.

Our approach is to design a declarative language for describing and defining information visualization techniques. The information visualization modelling language (IVML) provides a means to formally express, note, preserve, and communicate structure, appearance, behaviour, and functionality of information visualization techniques and their applications in a standardized way.

Such a language needs to rest on solid foundations. The information visualization modelling language puts into practice a formal model that reflects the concepts and relationships of information visualization as it is understood today. To the best of our knowledge, no such integrated model exists. On our way towards the information visualization modelling language, first we survey and discuss extant models of which each covers selected facets of (information) visualization (section 2). The survey fo-

M. Hemmje et al. (Eds.): E.J. Neuhold Festschrift, LNCS 3379, pp. 197–206, 2005.
© Springer-Verlag Berlin Heidelberg 2005

cuses on work that devised classification schemas. Our supposition that the presence of classifications indicate an elaborated level of formalization is the rationale behind this selection. Second, we provide an overview of the entire set of models under investigation and discuss the coverage of and the relationships between the models (section 3). Next, we present computational requirements as well as requirements imposed by the application the information visualization modelling language has to fulfil (section 4). We conclude by sketching an application scenario that illustrates the language's benefits (section 5). Throughout this paper, we will refer to the visualization reference model in order to organize our investigations.

2   Information Visualization Models

"Classification lies at the heart of every scientific field." (Lohse, Biolsi, Walker & Rueter, 1994) In striving for a better understanding of information visualization, a variety of classification schemes have been proposed over the past years. Depending on provenance and intention, they shed light on the information visualization process, its application, or its utility. Information visualization techniques, applications, systems, and frameworks can be classified according to the data types they can display, user tasks they support, characteristics of visual representations they deploy as well as cognitive aspects of their visual appearance.

Reference Model for Visualization. Card, Mackinlay & Shneiderman (1999) introduced a reference model for information visualization (Fig. 1), which provides a high-level view on the (information) visualization process.

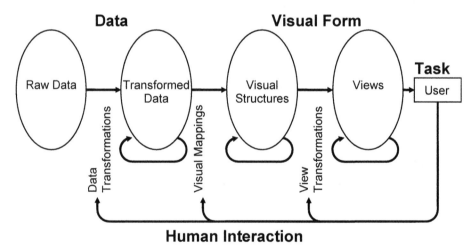

Fig. 1. Reference model for visualization

The model assumes a repository of raw data, which exist in a proprietary format, be it structured or unstructured. To get to a visualization of this data, data have to first undergo a set of transformations. Data transformations comprise filtering of raw data, computation of derived data as well as data normalization. These steps result in a set of transformed data in a unified structure. Visual transformations map the transformed data onto a corresponding visual structure. From this visual structure, a set of views can now be generated, which allow users to navigate through the display. User interactions can the transformation process at different stages. Users can adjust their view on the data, change the visual structure, or even affect the data transformation. The cyclic arrows in the diagram refer to the fact that the processes involved in the distinct steps are of an iterative nature and can occur repeatedly before the next step follows.

Data Type. Shneiderman (1996) suggested a taxonomy for information visualization designs built on data type and task, the type by task taxonomy (TTT). He distinguished seven data types: *1-dimensional, 2-dimensional, 3-dimensional, temporal, multi-dimensional, tree,* and *network*. High-level abstractions and specific datatypes are treated as subordinates of the types presented. A variety of consecutive taxonomies proposed extensions to the TTT, but were never as widely adopted as Shneiderman's work. In his summary, Keim (2002) discards few of the data types and introduces software and algorithms as new data types that could be visualized.

Visual Representations. Visual representations, in general, are structures for expressing knowledge. Long before computer technology emerged, visualizations were well-established and widely used. In their empirical study Lohse, Biolsi, Walker & Rueter (1994) investigate how people classify two-dimensional visual representations into meaningful categories. From this survey, a structural classification of visual representations became apparent: *graphs, tables, time charts, network charts, diagrams, maps, cartograms, icons,* and *photo-realistic pictures*.

Visualization Techniques. In the last decade, a large number of novel information visualization techniques have been developed. Good overviews of the approaches can be found in a number of recent books (Card, Mackinlay & Shneiderman, 1999) (Ware, 2000) (Spencer, 2000). Keim (2002) concentrates on the design of the visual environment and suggests a classification of visualization techniques that takes into consideration recent developments in information visualization: *standard 2D/3D displays, geometrically transformed displays, icon-based displays, dense pixel displays,* and *stacked displays*.

Tasks. Bundled with the type taxonomy, Shneiderman (1996) enumerated seven tasks users could perform on the data: *overview, zoom, filter, details on demand, relate, history,* and *extract*.

Interaction. The information visualization process of transforming data into visual representations is a one-way street unless the human perceiver is given the opportunity to intervene. Human interaction completes the loop between visual forms and control of the visualization process. It includes controlling the mappings performed in the visualization process (Card et al., 1999). Although interactive techniques and metaphors differ in design, Chuah & Roth (1996) have identified primitive interactive components visualization systems have in common. Composing these primitives can model the complex behaviour of visualization system user-interfaces at the semantic level of design. The functional classification distinguishes between three main types of basic visualization interactions: *graphical operations*, *set operations*, and *data operations*. Each main type ramifies to a hierarchy of more specific interaction types.

View Transformations. The visual mapping process results in graphical structures that represent information. In a final step, views render these graphical structures and make them accessible to the human perceiver, on computer screens, for example. View transformations specify graphical parameters that influence the view such as position, scaling, and clipping. Varying view transformations can reveal more information from one and the same graphical structure than static visualizations possibly could. Card, Mackinlay & Shneiderman (1999) distinguish three common view transformations: *location probes*, *viewpoint controls*, and *distortion*. Scales, as introduced by Theus (2003), encompass location probes and viewpoint controls. Leung & Apperley (1994) introduce transformation and magnification functions for various distortion-oriented presentation techniques.

Multiple View Coordination. Multiple view systems "use two or more distinct views to support the investigation of a single conceptual entity." (Wang Baldonado, Woodruff & Kuchinsky, 2000). To fully exploit the potential of multiple views, sophisticated coordination mechanisms between views are required: *navigation slaving*, *linking*, and *brushing*. Roberts (2000) identified three ways in which multiple views may be formed according to stages in the information visualization process comparable to the reference model (Fig. 1).

Cognition. By definition, the purpose of information visualization is to "communicate properties of information to a human". The research on information visualization must not stop at producing and designing visualization but must also consider how visualizations affect the human observer. Wiss & Carr (1998) propose a framework for classification of 3D information visualization designs based on three cognitive aspects: *attention*, *abstraction*, and *affordances*. A survey revealed that information visualization systems have come up with a variety of solutions in order to guide user attention, abstract from complex data and indicate available functionality and interaction modes.

Information Visualization Operating Steps. The data state reference model (Chi, 2000) describes visualization techniques with a focus on data and its transformations. The model breaks down the information visualization process into four data stages: value, analytical abstraction, visualization abstraction, and view. Three types of data transformation operators carry over into states: *data transformation*, *visualization transformation*, and *visual mapping transformation*. Based on the data state model, Chi decomposed the data processing pipelines of visualization techniques and identified operating steps they share.

3   Information Visualization Model Consolidation

With our approach, we do not intend to substitute information visualization models and classifications that have evolved so far. Instead, best-of-breed will be selected and combined into one consolidated formal model describing information visualization.

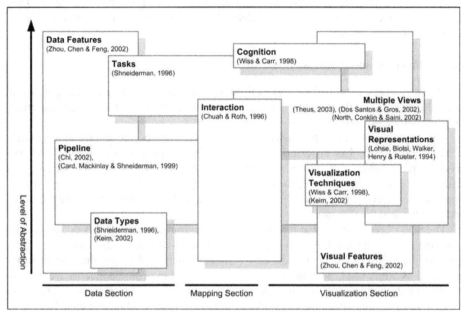

Fig. 2. Interrelationship of information visualization models in information visualization model space

3.1   Information Visualization Model Space

All the classification models presented describe selected subsets of the complex area of information visualization. Our attempt to arrive at a consolidated model for information visualization starts out with the analysis of what areas these discrete models cover and how they are mutually related (Fig. 2). To answer that question, we locate information-visualization models within *model space* for information visualization. There are two axes that span model space. The first dimension reflects the processing pipeline for (information) visualizations as introduced by the reference model for visualization (Fig. 1). Roughly speaking, three sections subdivide this pipeline. Beginning with the data section, data is transformed and mapped into graphical objects in the visualization section. Of course, models describing data properties, for example, are located to the left whereas multiple views and their coordination cover the area from the middle to the right. The second dimension expresses dependencies between models as well as the level of abstraction from the actual task of handling (computer) data. On the lowest level, models deal with data properties and visual attributes, whereas at the upper levels, models such as cognition abstract away from implementation details. Upper level models depend on their subordinates. The absence of visual objects and their properties would render talking about cognition futile.

Of course, as information visualization model space lacks metrics, positions and borderlines get blurred. So far, the diagram reflects our subjective assessment. Furthermore, drawing rectangles is a simplification. More often than not, single models do not handle all aspects at one constant level of abstraction and vice versa. This holds true especially for substantial models. Hence, the areas in the diagram depict an approximation of the real state of affairs.

3.2   Coverage and Ambiguity

The first overview reveals that there is little white space in the diagram. Judging from that, the extant models in total cover nearly all facets of information visualization as we know it today.

The frayed right side of the visualization section indicates that information visualization model space has no clearly marked border in this direction. Multiple views, visual representations, cognition, and interaction not only apply to information visualization exclusively. Partially, these models belong to visualization in general. From our point of view, visualization model space begins in the visualization section and extends beyond the diagram.

The next observation is that rectangles in the diagram overlap. If this occurs within one section, the models involved compete. Such conflict can be observed, for example, between data types, as introduced by Shneiderman's TTT, and the data features invented by Zhou et al. Sorting out the differences and matching concepts are the anticipated tedious tasks required in order to arrive at a joint model. The above presentation of information visualization models discusses corresponding models. Note that the collection of models portrays selected samples. Less important items have already been omitted.

Sections cannot always be clearly separated without ambiguity. Cross-section overlapping arises when one and the same phenomenon of information visualization is covered by various models starting out from different perspectives. For instance, interaction and the processing pipeline are closely interwoven. From the standpoint of the reference model, view transformations are modifications that are likely to be triggered by human interaction. Conversely, interaction claims that location probes and viewpoint controls are their terrain, and terms them interactive filtering, interactive zooming, interactive distortion, and interactive linking and brushing.

3.3   Quality and Level of Granularity

As the diagram suggests, the area of information visualization has been thoroughly researched and only few white spaces remain. Yet the stake the various models claim reflects neither the model quality nor its level of detail. There are always two sides to quality: correctness and completeness. Before they can be integrated into the coherent model, extant models need to be assessed with care. More easy to judge is the model's level of granularity. Classification systems vary in how detailed a way they have been conceived. Generally, coarse models leave space for alternatives and variations, whereas in depth models provide better guidance. To illustrate the difference, the interaction model with three hierarchy levels of classes is far more detailed than the data types according to the TTT. Then again, not all facets of information visualization share the same level of complexity. It is natural that different areas feature different numbers of classes.

4 Information Visualization Modelling Language

Current practice in information technology favours the use of formal languages as representation formalisms which abstract away from details of specific realisation. The information visualization modelling language enables the declarative description of an information visualization need or solution in preference to describing the steps required in order to realise the visualization process. It is a formal language; it has a set of strings which can be derived from a (formal) grammar consisting of a deductive system of axioms and inference rules (Partee, ter Meulen & Wall, 1990). We give the term information visualization modelling language *blueprint* to the formal description of an information visualization technique or application expressed by the language. A blueprint is composed of a number of sections. Blueprint sections are legal combinations of language elements derived from the grammar.

Conceiving the information visualization modelling language may follow two simple rules of thumb. First, concepts identified within the model constitute the vocabulary. Secondly, relationships between concepts determine the grammar. Presumably, however, relationships from the model will also contribute to the language vocabulary. The information visualization modelling language will constitute a specific encoding of the consolidated information visualization model. In order to be useful, its design has to meet requirements for both computation and application.

4.1   Computational Desiderata

The information visualization modelling language (IVML) carries knowledge about information visualization within its schema. Moreover, information visualizations denoted in the language are formal structures which represent knowledge about information visualization techniques, applications, and requirements, respectively. Hence, the information visualization modelling language can be considered a meaning representation language. Meaning representation languages need to meet a number of practical computational requirements (Jurafsky & Martin, 2000).

Verifiability is the most basic requirement for a meaning representation: "it must be possible to use the representation to determine the relationship between the meaning of a sentence and the world as we know it." In the case of the IVML, it can (say) describe information visualization techniques and data types these techniques are capable of displaying. These descriptions establish knowledge. Demands for visualization of data of a specific type can be considered a question expressed in IVML. If there is no visualization technique that can handle the requested data type, matching will fail. In general, sentences can have different meanings depending on the circumstances in which they are uttered. Since the IVML is intended to be the means we reason about and act upon, it is critical that blueprint sections expressed in the language (analogous to natural language sentences) have single unambiguous interpretations. The IVML is required to be an *unambiguous representation*. Conversely, distinct sentences in general may have the same meaning. Such a situation is highly problematic, since it hinders verification and adds complexity to reasoning. Therefore, the IVML should follow the doctrine of *canonical form*: Sentences that mean the same thing should have the same representation. More complex requests cannot be answered solely on the basis of verification and canonical form. Let's agree that whilst traditional diagrams in general are suitable for presentation purposes, they are not a good choice to pursue data exploration. Pie charts belong to this class of traditional visualization techniques. To meet the demand for visualization of data for presentation purposes using pie charts, *inference* is required. It must be possible to draw conclusions about propositions that are not explicitly represented, but are nevertheless logically derivable from the knowledge available. Finally, in order to be useful, the IVML must be *expressive* enough to treat a wide range of the subject matter of information visualization. But, since research in this area is ongoing, the IVML cannot be expected to be complete.

4.2   Applicational Desiderata

By analogy with design criteria that underlie related modelling languages (Web3D Consortium, 1997), the information visualization modelling language should meet a set of requirements in order to be useful in application.

Information visualization is a multifaceted subject matter. The formal description of information visualization techniques and applications using the IVML will be accordingly complex. *Composability* provides the ability to use and combine information visualization objects, like data sources, mapping formulas, or view definitions, within an IVML application and thus allows reusability. Depending on the application, the complete set of constructs is not always required. In a single-view application, for example, multiple-view coordination is pointless. The design of the IVML must permit the omission of constructs which are not essential for the given situation. The notion of language constructs which are independent by design is known as *orthogonality*. Since the IVML is anticipated not to cover all future inventions in the area of information visualization, the language has to be *extensible*, allowing the introduction of new concepts. Wherever concepts are missing in the language, *bypass*es help to fill the gaps with alternative solutions. Bypasses also stand in when IVML design does not meet particular requirements. In the case of parsers interpreting the IVML in order to render information visualizations, the bypass addresses purpose-built implementations. The IVML needs to be *authorable*: Computer programs must be capable of creating, editing, and maintaining IVML files, as well as automatic translation programs for converting related data into IVML. More generally, the language must be *capable of implementation* on a wide range of systems. Considering the implementation of software systems, language design must foster the development of scalable high-*performance* implementations. Finally, IVML must *scale* and enable arbitrarily large dynamic information visualization applications.

5   Application Scenario

Imagine a knowledge worker engaged in an information retrieval dialogue with a computer-based interactive information visualization system, seeking to meet an information need he cannot fully specify. Hence, it is impossible for him to formulate a question and have the system answer in a targeted way. Instead, the dialogue is of exploratory nature. During a series of iterative steps the user learns about the data source, locates relevant information, and refines his information need. This process is put into practice by human actions demanding the system to adapt in return. Beginning with an initial setup, interactions manipulate data transformations, visual mappings, and view transformations. Finally, if the dialogue succeeds, the user will not only have come to a relevant data set answering his information needs, but moreover end-up with an information visualization application tailored to the task performed.

Imagine the system was able to export its final state as a blueprint. The information visualization modelling language would then be deployed to formally *express* the information visualization technique that has evolved, allowing it to be *noted* down (electronically). Usually, only content retrieved is retained as a result of the dialogue, discarding the history and the supporting tool's setup. With the various blueprint sections, all these facets of the information retrieval dialogue can be *preserved* and reused in similar tasks or applied to diverse data sources. With the blueprint the information visualization technique can be communicated in its entirety to third parties.

6   Summary and Conclusion

This article outlines our approach towards the information visualization modelling language (IVML). To lay a sound foundation, we survey the state-of-the-art of information visualization, assess the coverage and relationships between extant models, and identify potential obstacles in the process of setting up an integrated formal model that reflects the concepts and relationships of information visualization as it is understood today. Finally, we present computational requirements as well as those imposed by the application the information visualization modelling language has to fulfil.

The survey focuses on work that devised classification schemas. To assess which facets of information visualization these discrete models cover and how they are mutually related, we established the notion of information visualization modelling space. The analysis suggests three findings. First, the extant models in total cover nearly all facets of information visualization as we know it today. Secondly, areas of information visualization model space are described by rival models, leading to ambiguity. Third, the models vary in the level of detail in which they have been worked out. The information visualization modelling language constitutes a specific encoding of the consolidated information visualization model. Its design has to meet requirements for both computation and application.

The modelling language should provide a means to formally express, note, preserve, and communicate structure, appearance, behaviour, and functionality of information visualization techniques and their applications. This claim will be further motivated in future work along with anticipated benefits in both application and theory.

References

Card, S., Mackinlay, J., Shneiderman, B.: Readings in Information Visualization. Morgan Kaufmann, San Francisco (1999) 1-34

Chi, E.H.: A Taxonomy of Visualization Techniques Using the Data State Reference Model. In: Proceedings of the IEEE Symposium on Information Visualization 2000. IEEE Scientific Press (2000) 69-76

Chuah, M.C., Roth, S.F.: On the Semantics of Interactive Visualizations. In: Proceedings of the IEEE Symposium on Information Visualization 1996 (InfoVis'96). IEEE (1996) 29-36

Dos Santos, C.R., Gros, P.: Multiple Views in 3D Metaphoric Information Visualization. In: Proceedings of the Sixth International Conference on Information Visualization 2002 (IV'02). IEEE (2002) 468-476

Fluit, C., Sabou, M., van Harmelen, F.: Ontology-based Information Visualization. In: Geroimenko, V., Chen, C. (Eds): Visualizing the Semantic Web. Springer, London (2003) 36-48

Jurafsky, D., Martin, J.: Speech and Language Processing. Prentice Hall, Upper Saddle River (2000)

Keim, D.A.: Information Visualization and Visual Data Mining. In: IEEE Transactions on Visualization and Computer Graphics, Vol. 8, No. 1. IEEE (2002) 1-8

Leung, Y, Apperley, M.: A Review and Taxonomy of Distortion-Oriented Presentation Techniques. In: ACM Transactions on Computer-Human Interaction, Vol. 1, No. 2. (1994) 126ff

Lohse, G.L., Biolsi, K., Walker, N., Rueter, H.H.: A Classification of Visual Representations. In: Communications of the ACM, Vol. 37, No. 12. ACM Press (1994) 36-49

North, C., Conklin, N., Saini, V.: Visualization Schemas for Flexible Information Visualization. In: Proceedings of the IEEE Symposium on Information Visualization 2002 (IV'02). IEEE (2002) 15-22

Partee, B., Ter Meulen, A., Wall, R.: Mathematical Methods in Linguistics. Kluwer Academic Publishers (1990)

Roberts, J.C.: Multiple-View and Multiform Visualization. In: Erbacher, R., Pang, A., Wittenbrink, C., Roberts, J. (eds.): Visual Data Exploration and Analysis VII, Proceedings of SPIE, Volume 3960. (2000) 176-185

Shneiderman, B., Card, S.: On-line Library of Information Visualization Environments (Olive). Online http://www.otal.umd.edu/Olive/ (1997)

Spence, B.: Information Visualization. Pearson Education Higher Education publishers, UK, (2000)

Shneiderman, B.: The Eyes Have It: A Task by Data Type Taxonomy for Information Visualizations. In: Proceedings of the IEEE Symposium on Visual Languages 1996 (VL '96). (1996) 336-343

Theus, M.: Navigating Data – Selections, Scales, Multiples. In: Stephanidis, C., Jacko, J. (Eds.): Human-Computer Interaction - Theory and Practice (Part II). Proceedings of HCI International 2003 (HCII 2003). Lawrence Erlbaum Associates (2003) 1323-1327

Wang Baldonado, M.Q., Woodruff, A., Kuchinsky, A.: Guidelines for Using Multiple Views in Information Visualization. In: Proceedings of the Working Conference on Advanced Visual Interfaces (AVI'00). ACM Press, New York (2000) 110-119

Ware, C.: Information Visualization: Perception for Design. Morgan Kaufman (2000)

Web3D Consortium: Information Technology - Computer Graphics and Image Processing - The Virtual Reality Modeling Language (VRML) - Part 1: Functional Specification and UTF-8 Encoding (VRML97), ISO/IEC 14772-1:1997 (1997)

Wiss, U., Carr, D.: A Cognitive Classification Framework for 3-Dimensional Information Visualization. Research report LTU-TR-1998/4-SE, Luleå University of Technology (1998)

Zhou, M.X., Chen, M., Feng, Y.: Building a Visual Database for Example-based Graphics Generation. Proceedings of the IEEE Symposium on Information Visualization 2002 (InfoVis'02). IEEE (2002) 23-30

A Knowledge Integration Framework
for Information Visualization

Jinwook Seo[1,2] and Ben Shneiderman[1,2,3]

[1]Department of Computer Science,
[2]Human-Computer Interaction Laboratory, Institute for Advanced Computer Studies, and
[3]Institute for Systems Research
University of Maryland, College Park, MD 20742
{seo, ben}@cs.umd.edu

Abstract. Users can better understand complex data sets by combining insights from multiple coordinated visual displays that include relevant domain knowledge. When dealing with multidimensional data and clustering results, the most familiar displays and comprehensible are 1- and 2-dimensional projections (histograms, and scatterplots). Other easily understood displays of domain knowledge are tabular and hierarchical information for the same or related data sets. The novel parallel coordinates view [6] powered by a direct-manipulation search, offers strong advantages, but requires some training for most users. We provide a review of related work in the area of information visualization, and introduce new tools and interaction examples on how to incorporate users' domain knowledge for understanding clustering results. Our examples present hierarchical clustering of gene expression data, coordinated with a parallel coordinates view and with the gene annotation and gene ontology.

1 Introduction

Modern information-abundant environments provide access to remarkable collections of richly structured databases, digital libraries, and information spaces. Text searching to locate specific pages and starting points for exploration is enormously successful, but this is only the first generation of knowledge discovery tools. Future interfaces that balance data mining algorithms with potent information visualizations will enable users to find meaningful clusters of relevant documents, relevant relationships among dimensions, unusual outliers, and surprising gaps [10].

Existing tools for cluster analysis are already used for multidimensional data in many research areas including financial, economical, sociological, and biological analyses. Finding natural subclasses in a document set not only reveals interesting patterns but also serves as a basis for further analyses. One of the troubles with cluster analysis is that evaluating how interesting a clustering result is to researchers is subjective, application-dependent, and even difficult to measure. This problem generally gets worse as dimensionality and the number of items grows. The remedy is to enable researchers to apply domain knowledge to facilitate insight about the significance of

M. Hemmje et al. (Eds.): E.J. Neuhold Festschrift, LNCS 3379, pp. 207–220, 2005.

the clustering result. Strategies that enable exploration of clusters will also support sense-making about outliers, gaps, and correlations.

A cluster is a group of data items that are similar to others within the same group and are different from items in other groups. Clustering enables researchers to see overall distribution patterns, and identify interesting unusual patterns, and spot potential outliers. Moreover, clusters can serve as effective inputs to other analysis method such as classification.

Researchers in various areas are still developing their own clustering algorithms even though there are already a large number of general-purpose clustering algorithms in existence. One reason is that it is difficult to understand a clustering algorithm well enough to apply it to their new data set. A more important reason is that it is difficult for researchers to validate or understand the clustering results in relation to their knowledge of the data set. Even the same clustering algorithm might generate a completely different clustering result when the distance/similarity measure changes. A clustering result could make sense to some researchers, but not to others because validity of a clustering result heavily depends on users' interest and is application-dependent. Therefore, researchers' domain knowledge plays a key role in understanding/evaluating the clustering result.

A large number of clustering algorithms have been developed, but only a small number of cluster visualization tools are available to facilitate researchers' understanding of the clustering results. Current visual cluster analysis tools can be improved by allowing researchers to incorporate their domain knowledge into visual displays that are well coordinated with the clustering result view.

This paper describes additions to our interactive visual cluster analysis tool, the Hierarchical Clustering Explorer (HCE) [9]. These additions include 1-D histograms and 2-D scatterplots that are accessed through coordinated views. These views are familiar projections that are more comprehensible than higher dimensional presentations. HCE also implements presentations of external domain knowledge. While HCE users appreciate our flexible histogram and scatterplot views, his paper concentrates on novel presentations for high-dimensional data and for domain knowledge:

- a parallel coordinates view enables researchers to search for profiles similar to a candidate pattern, which is specified by direct-manipulation
- a tabular or hierarchical view enables researchers to explore relationships that may be found in information that is external to the data set.

Visualization techniques can be used to support semi-automatic information extraction and semantic annotation for domain experts. For example, visual analysis by techniques such as dynamic queries has been successfully used in supporting researchers who are interested in analyses of multidimensional data [5][7]. Well-designed visual coordination with researchers' domain knowledge facilitates users' understanding of the analysis result.

This paper briefly explains the interactive exploration of clustering results using our current version, HCE 3.0. Section 3 describes the knowledge integration framework, including the design considerations for direct-manipulation search and dynamic queries. Section 4 presents a tabular view showing gene annotation and the gene ontology browser and section 5 covers some implementation issues.

2   Interactive Exploration of Clustering Results with HCE 3.0

Some clustering algorithms, such as k-means, require users to specify the number of clusters as an input, but it is hard to know the right number of natural clusters beforehand. Other clustering algorithms automatically determine the number of clusters, but users may not be convinced of the result since they had little or no control over the clustering process. To avoid this dilemma, researchers prefer the hierarchical clustering algorithm since it does not require users to enter a predetermined number of clusters and it also allows users to control the desired resolution of a clustering result.

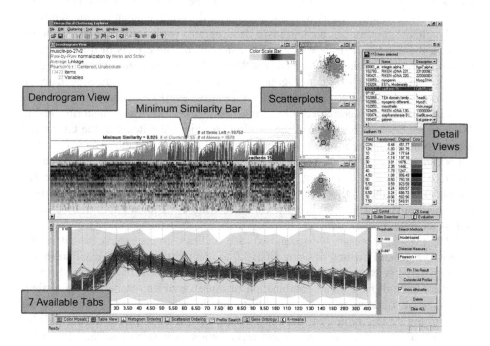

Fig. 1. Overall layout of HCE 3.0. Minimum similarity bar was pulled down to get 55 clusters in the Dendrogram View. A cluster of 113 genes (highlighted with orange markers below the cluster) is selected in the dendrogram view and they are highlighted in scatterplots, detail view, and parallel coordinates view tab window (see section 3). Users can select a tab among the seven tab windows at the bottom pane to investigate the data set coordinating with different views. Users can see the names of the selected genes and the actual expression values in the detail views.

HCE 3.0 is an interactive knowledge visualization tool for hierarchical clustering results with a rich set of user controls (dendrograms, color mosaic displays and etc.) (Fig. 1). A hierarchical clustering result is generally represented as a binary tree called dendrogram whose subtrees are clusters. HCE 3.0 users can see the overall clustering result in a single screen, and zoom in to see more detail. Considering that the lower a subtree is, the more similar the items in the subtree are, we implemented two dynamic controls, minimum similarity bar and detail cutoff bar, which are shown over the dendrogram display. Users can control the number of clusters by using the minimum similarity bar whose y-coordinate determines the minimum similarity threshold. As users pull down the minimum similarity bar, they get tighter clusters (lower subtrees) that satisfy the current minimum similarity threshold. Users can control the level of detail by using the detail cutoff bar. All the subtrees below the detail cutoff bar are rendered using the average intensity of items in the subtree so that we can see the overall patterns of clusters without distraction by too much detail.

Since we get a different clustering result as a different linkage method or similarity measure is used in hierarchical clustering, we need some mechanisms to evaluate clustering results. HCE 3.0 implements 3 different evaluation mechanisms. Firstly, HCE 3.0 users can compare two dendrograms (or hierarchical clustering results) in the dendrogram view to visually comprehend the effects of different clustering parameters. Two dendrograms are shown face to face, and when users double-click on a cluster of a dendrogram, they can see the lines connecting items in the cluster and the same items in the other dendrogram [9]. Secondly, HCE 3.0 users can compare a hierarchical clustering result and a k-means clustering result. When users click on a cluster in the dendrogram view, the items in the cluster are also highlighted in the k-means clustering result view (the last tab in Fig. 1) so that users can see if the two clustering results are consistent. Thirdly, HCE 3.0 enables users to evaluate a clustering result using an external evaluation measure (F-measure) when they know the correct clustering result in advance. Through these three mechanisms, HCE 3.0 helps users to determine the most appropriate clustering parameters for their data set.

HCE 3.0 was successfully used in two case studies with gene expression data. We proposed a general method of using HCE 3.0 to identify the optimal signal/noise balance in Affymetrix gene chip data analyses. HCE 3.0's interactive features help researchers to find the optimal combination of three variables (probe set signal algorithms, noise filtering methods, and clustering linkage methods) to maximize the effect of the desired biological variable on data interpretation [8]. HCE 3.0 was also used to analyze in vivo murine muscle regeneration expression profiling data using Affymetrix U74Av2 (12,488 probe sets) chips measured in 27 time points. HCE 3.0's visual analysis techniques and dynamic query controls played an important role in finding 12 novel downstream targets that are biologically relevant during myoblast differentiation [12]. In section 3 and 4, we will use this data set to demonstrate how HCE 3.0 combines users' domain knowledge with other views to facilitate insight about the clustering result and the data set.

Fig. 2 shows four tightly coupled components of HCE and linkages between them. Updates by each linkage in Fig. 2 are instantaneous (or, it takes less than 100ms) for most microarray data sets.

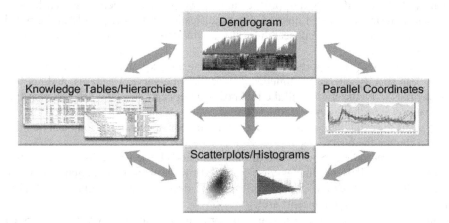

Fig. 2. Diagram of interactions between components of HCE 3.0. All interactions are bi-directional. This paper describes coordination between the dendrogram view, scatterplots/histograms views, parallel coordinates view, and knowledge tables/hierarchies views. Knowledge tables/hierarchies incorporate external domain knowledge while others show the internal data using different visual representations.

3   Combining Users' Domain Knowledge: Parallel Coordinates View

Many microarray experiments measure gene expression over time [2][12]. Researchers would like to group genes with similar expression profiles or find interesting time-varying patterns in the data set by performing cluster analysis. Another way to identify genes with profiles similar to known genes is to directly search for the genes by specifying the expected pattern of a known gene. When researchers have some domain knowledge such as the expected pattern of a previously characterized gene, researchers can try to find genes similar to the expected pattern. Since it is not easy to specify the expected pattern at a single try, they have to conduct a series of searches for the expression profiles similar to the expected pattern. Therefore, they need an interactive visual analysis tool that allows easy modification of the expected pattern and rapid update of the search result.

Clustering and direct profile search can complement each other. Since there is no perfect clustering algorithm right for all data sets and applications, direct profile search could be used to validate the clustering result by projecting the search result onto the clustering result view. Conversely, a clustering result could be used to validate the profile search by projecting the cluster result on the profile view. Therefore, coordination between a clustering result and a direct search result make the identification process more valid and effective.

'Profile Search' in the Spotfire DecisionSite (www.spotfire.com) calculates the similarity to a search pattern (so called 'master profile') for all genes in the data set and adds the result as a new column to the data set. The built-in profile editor makes it possible to edit the search pattern, but the editor view is separate from the profile chart view where all matching profiles are shown, so users need to switch between two views to try a series of queries. The modification of master profile in the profile editor view is interactive, but search results are not updated dynamically as the master profile changes.

TimeSearcher [5] supports interactive querying and exploration of time-series data. Users can specify interactive timeboxes over the time-varying patterns, and get back the profiles that pass though all the timeboxes. Users can drag and drop an item from the data set into the query window to create a query with a separate timebox for each time point over the item in the data set. Each timebox at each time point can be modified to change the query.

HCE 3.0 reproduces Spotfire's and TimeSearcher's basic functions with a novel interface, the parallel coordinates view powered by a direct-manipulation search, that allows for rapid creation and modification of desired profiles using novel visual metaphors. Key design concepts are:

– interactive specification of a search pattern on the information space : Users can submit their queries simply by mouse drags over the search space rather than using a separate query specification window.
– dynamic query control : Users get the query results instantaneously as they change the search pattern, similarity function, or similarity threshold.
– sequential query refinement : Users can keep the current query results as a new narrowed search space for subsequent queries.

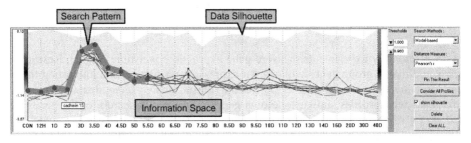

Fig. 3. Parallel coordinates view: Layout of the parallel coordinates view and an example of model-based query on the mouse muscle regeneration data. The data silhouette (the gray shadow) represents the coverage of all expression profiles (also known as 'data envelope' in Time-Searcher). The bold red line is a search pattern specified by users' mouse drags. Thin regular solid lines are the result of the current query that satisfies the given similarity threshold. The data set shown is a temporal gene expression profile on the mouse muscle regeneration [12].

The parallel coordinates view consists of three parts (Fig. 3): the information space where input profiles are drawn and queries are specified, the range slider to specify similarity thresholds, and a set of controls to specify query parameters. Users specify a search pattern by simple mouse drags. As they drag the mouse over the information space, the intersection points of mouse cursor and vertical time lines define control points. Existing control points, if any, at the intersecting vertical time lines are updated to reflect the dragging. A search pattern is a set of line segments connecting the contiguous control points specified. Users choose a search method and a similarity measure on the control panel. They can change the current search pattern by dragging a control point, by dragging a line segment vertically or horizontally, or by adding or removing control points. All modifications are done by mouse clicks or drags, and the results are updated instantaneously. This integration of the space where the data is shown and where the search pattern is composed reduces users' cognitive load by removing the overhead of context switching between two different spaces.

Incremental query processing enables rapid updates (within 100 ms) so that dynamic query control is possible for most microarray data sets. The easy and fast search for interesting patterns enables researchers to attempt multiple queries in a short period of time to get important insights into the underlying data set.

In the parallel coordinates view, users can submit a new query over the current query result. If users click "Pin This Result" button after submitting a query, the query result becomes a new narrowed search space (Fig. 3). We call this "pinning." Pinning enables sequential query refinement, which makes it easy to find target patterns without losing the focus of the current analysis process. If users click on a cluster in the dendrogram view, all items in the cluster are shown in the parallel coordinates view. By pinning this result, users can limit the search to the cluster to isolate more specific patterns in the cluster.

Genes included in the search result are highlighted in the dendrogram view. Conversely, if users click on a cluster in the dendrogram view, profiles of the genes in the cluster are shown in the parallel coordinates view so that users can see the patterns of genes in a different view other than color mosaic. Through the coordination between the parallel coordinates view and the dendrogram view, users can easily see the representative patterns of clusters and compare patterns between clusters. Since queries done in the parallel coordinates view identify genes with a similar profile, the search results should be consistent with clustering results if the same similarity function is used. In this regard, the parallel coordinates view helps researchers to validate the clustering results by applying their domain knowledge through direct-manipulation searches.

In the parallel coordinates view, users can run a text search (called search-by-name query) by typing in a text string to find items whose name or description contains the string. Moreover, two different types of direct-manipulation queries are possible in the parallel coordinates view: model-based queries and ceiling-and-floor queries.

Model-based queries: Users can specify a model pattern (or a search pattern) simply by mouse drags as shown in Fig. 3, and select a distance/similarity measure among 3 different ones and assign the similarity/distance threshold values. All profiles satisfying the similarity/distance threshold range will be rapidly shown in the information space. The three different measures are 'Pearson correlation coefficient', 'Euclidean distance', and 'absolute distance from each control point'. The first measure is useful when the up-down trends of profiles are more important than the magnitudes, while the second and the third measures are useful when the actual magnitudes are more important. When users know the name of a biologically relevant gene, they can perform a text-based search first by entering a name or a description of the gene (Fig. 4). Then they can choose one of the matching genes and make them a model pattern by right-clicking on the pattern and selecting "Make it a model pattern." They can adjust or delete some control points depending on their domain knowledge. Finally, they adjust the similarity thresholds to get the satisfying results and project them onto other views including the dendrogram view.

Ceiling-and-Floor queries: Ceilings and floors are novel visual metaphors to specify satisfactory value ranges using direct manipulation. A ceiling imposes upper bounds and a floor imposes lower bounds on the corresponding time points. Users can define ceilings and floors on the information space so that only the profiles between ceilings and floors are shown as a result (Fig. 4). Users can specify a ceiling by dragging with the left mouse button depressed and a floor by dragging with the right mouse button depressed. They can change ceilings and floors with mouse actions in the same way as they do for changing search patterns in model-based queries. This type of query is useful when users know the up-down patterns and the appropriate value ranges at the corresponding time points of the target profiles. Compared to model-based queries, ceiling-and-floor queries allow users to specify separate bounds for each control point.

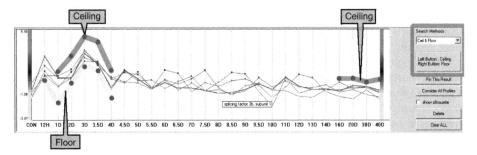

Fig. 4. An example of the Ceiling-and-Floor query. Bold line segments above the profiles define ceilings, and bold line segments below profiles define floors. Profiles below ceilings and above floors at the time points where ceilings or floors are defined are shown as a result. Users can move a line segment or a control point of ceilings or floors to modify current query. The highlighted region gives users informative visual feedbacks of the current query. The data set shown is a temporal gene expression profile on the mouse muscle regeneration [12].

Coordination example: Researchers performed a microarray experiment to generate a gene expression profile data that indicates relative levels of expression for each of these > 12000 genes in murine muscle samples [12]. They measured expression levels at 27 time points to find genes that are biologically relevant to the muscle regeneration process. They already have domain knowledge that MyoD is one of genes that are the most relevant to muscle regeneration. They run the hierarchical clustering with the data set, and identify a relevant cluster that peaks on day 3 (Fig. 5). In the parallel coordinates view, they search MyoD using search-by-name query, then make it a model pattern to perform a model-based query. They adjust the similarity thresholds to get the search result that mostly overlaps with the relevant 3 day cluster (Fig. 5). Finally, they confirm through other biological experiments that 2 genes (Cdh15 and Stam) in the overlapped result set are novel downstream targets of MyoD.

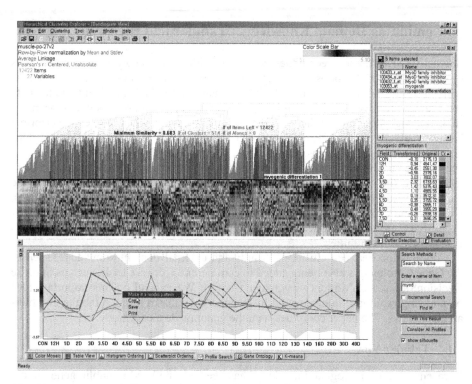

Fig. 5(a). Run a search-by-name query with 'MyoD' to find 5 genes whose name contains MyoD, and the 5 genes are projected onto the current clustering result visualization shown by triangles under the color mosaic. Select a gene (myogenic differentiation 1) and make it a model pattern for next query.

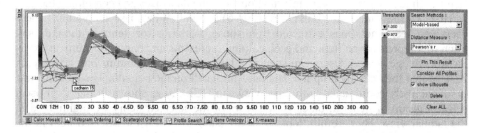

Fig. 5(b). Modify the model pattern to emphasize 3 day peak (notice the bold red line), and run a model base query to find a small set of candidate genes. The updated search result will be highlighted in the dendrogram view and the gene ontology browser (see section 4).

Fig. 5. An example of coordination with the parallel coordinates view

4   Combining Domain Knowledge: Tabular and Hierarchy Viewers

Interactive visualization techniques combined with cluster analysis help researchers discover meaningful groups in the data set. A direct-manipulation search coordinated with clustering result visualization facilitates insight into clustering result and the data set. Further improvement is possible if there is another well-understood and meaningful knowledge structure for the same data set. For example, when marketers perform a cluster analysis on the customer transaction data, they discover customer groups based on purchasing patterns. If they have another knowledge structure on the data such as the customer preferences or demographic information, they can acquire more insight into the clustering results by projecting the additional information onto the clustering result. In this market analysis example, if a geographic hierarchy of states, counties, and cities were available, it might be possible to discover that purchasers of expensive toys reside in large southern cities. They are likely to be older grandparents in retirement communities.

Coordination between clustering results and external domain knowledge, such as the Gene Ontology, is also being added to commercial software tools, such as Spotfire DecisionSite and CoMotion(www.mayaviz.com). We expand on this important idea by allowing rapid multiple selection in secondary databases through tabular and hierarchical views. The paper continues with the genomic data case study.

4.1   Tabular View

In recent decades, biological knowledge has been accumulated in public genomic databases (GenBank, LocusLink, FlyBase, MGI, and so on) and it will increase rapidly in the future [1]. These databases are useful sources of external domain knowledge with which biologists gain insights into their data sets and clustering results. Biologists frequently utilize those databases to obtain information about genomic instances that they are interested in. However, those databases are so diverse that researchers have difficulties in identifying relevant information from the databases and combining them.

HCE 3.0 implements a tabular view (Fig. 6) as a hub of database annotations where users can see annotations extracted from those databases for items in the data set. Each row represents an item and each column represents an annotation from an external knowledge source. Users can specify a URL for each column to link a web data base so that they can look up the data base for a cell on the column. The tabular view is interactively coordinated with other views in HCE 3.0 as shown in Fig. 2. If users select a group of items in other views, rows of the selected items are highlighted in the tabular view. By carefully looking at the annotations for the selected item in the table view and looking those up in the corresponding databases, users can gain more insight into the items by utilizing the domain knowledge from the databases. Conversely, if users select a bunch of rows in the tabular view, the selected items are also highlighted in other views. For example, after sorting by a column and selecting rows with the same value on the column, users can easily verify how closely those items are group together in the dendrogram view.

Researchers can do annotation either by using one or more of the public genomic databases or by using annotation files provided by gene chip makers. For example, Affymetrix provides annotation files for all their GeneChips, and users can easily import the annotation file and combine it with the data set.

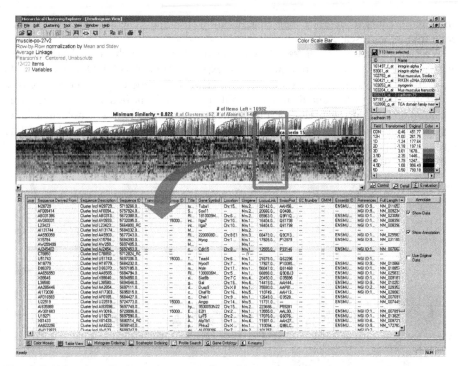

Fig. 6. Tabular view: Each row has annotations for a gene. Each column represents an annotation from an external database. All of 12422 genes are in the tabular view, and there are 28 annotation columns. When users select a cluster of 113 genes in the dendrogram view, the annotation information for those genes is highlighted in the tabular view. The Affymetrix U74Av2 chip annotation file downloaded from www.affymetrix.com was imported and combined with the data set. The data set shown is a temporal gene expression profile on the mouse muscle regeneration [12].

4.2   Hierarchy View: Gene Ontology Browser

One of the major reasons that biologists cannot efficiently utilize the abundant knowledge in public genomic databases is the lack of a shared controlled vocabulary. The Gene Ontology (GO) project [6] is a collaborative effort of biologists to build consistent descriptions of gene products in different databases. The GO collaborators have been developing three ontologies - structured, controlled vocabularies with which gene products are described in terms of their associated biological processes, molecular functions, and cellular components in a species-independent manner.

The good news is that Gene Ontology (GO) annotation is a widely accepted, well-understood and meaningful knowledge structure for gene expression data. GO annotations of genes in a cluster or a direct manipulation search result might reveal a clue about why the genes are grouped together. With the GO annotation, researchers can easily recognize the biological process, molecular function, and cellular component that genes in a cluster are associated with. Furthermore, it is possible to test a hypothesis that an unknown gene might have the same or similar biological role with the known genes in the same cluster. Interactive coordination with the GO annotation enables researchers to upgrade their insights by combining generally accepted knowledge from other researchers.

We can see many tools listed at www.geneontology.org such as MAPPFinder [3], and GoMiner[11] that integrate microarray experiment data with GO annotation. In those tools, users can input a criterion for a significant gene-expression change or a list of interesting genes, and then relevant GO terms are identified and shown in a tree structure or DAG display. HCE 3.0 integrates the three ontologies – molecular function, biological process, and cellular component into the process of understanding clusters and patterns in gene expression profile data. The ontologies are shown in a hierarchical structure as in Fig. 7.

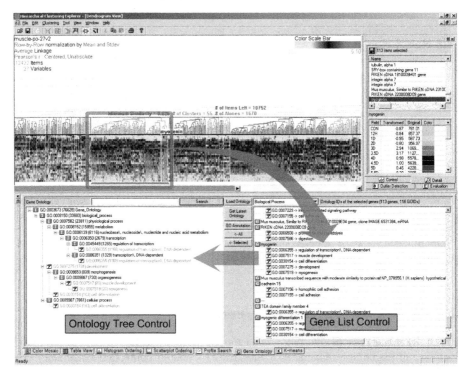

Fig. 7. HCE 3.0 with gene ontology browser on. Users can select a cluster in the dendrogram view (at the top left corner), which is highlighted with a rectangle. 113 genes in the selected cluster are shown in the gene list control at the bottom right corner. All paths to the selected GO terms (associated with myogenin) are shown with a flag-shape icon in the ontology tree control at the bottom left corner. 'I' represents 'IS-A' relationship and 'P' represents 'PART-OF' relationship. The data set shown is in vivo murine muscle regeneration expression profiling data using Affymetrix U74Av2 (12,488 probe sets) chips measured in 27 time points.

The gene ontology hierarchy is a directed acyclic graph (DAG), but we use a tree structure to show the hierarchy since the tree structure is easier for users to understand and easier for developers to implement than a DAG. Thus, a gene ontology term may appear several times in different branches, but the path from the root to a node is unique. Users can download the latest gene ontologies from the Gene Ontology Consortium's ftp server ('Get Latest Ontology' button), and browse the ontology hierarchy on its own ('Load Ontology' button). Coordination between the gene ontology browser and other views in HCE 3.0 is bi-directional.

5   Implementation

HCE 3.0 was implemented as a stand-alone application using Microsoft Visual C++ 6.0. The Microsoft Foundation Class (MFC) library was statically linked. HCE 3.0 runs on personal computers running Windows (at least Window 95) without special hardware or external library support. HCE 3.0 is freely available at http://www.cs.umd.edu/hcil/hce/ for academic or research purposes.

To achieve rapid response times, hash and map data structures were used because they enable constant time lookup of items, with only a modest storage overhead. Incremental data structures were used to support rapid query update in the parallel coordinate view by maintaining active index sets for intermediate query results.

Microarray experiment data set can be imported to HCE 3.0 from tab-delimited text or Excel spreadsheets. The latest gene ontology annotation data is automatically downloaded from the Gene Ontology Consortium's ftp server. The current annotation file with GO annotations for most Affymetrix chips is downloadable from www.affymetirx.com and can be automatically attached to the input data in HCE 3.0.

6   Conclusion

Cluster analysis has been the focus of numerous research projects conducted in various fields. It reveals the underlying structure of an input data set, interesting unusual patterns, and potential outliers. Understanding the clustering result has been a tedious process of checking items one by one. With HCE 3.0, we believe users can quickly apply their own or external domain knowledge to interpret a cluster by visual display in coordinated views. Users often begin with histograms and scatterplots, but these are only the first step.

This paper presented two coordinated views to incorporate users' domain knowledge with visual analysis of the data set and clustering results. First, when users know an approximate pattern of a candidate group of interest, they can use the parallel coordinates view to quickly compose the search pattern according to their domain knowledge and run a direct manipulation search. Second, when there is a well-understood and meaningful tabular or hierarchical information for their data set, they can utilize external knowledge from other researchers to make interpretations based on the clustering result. Well-designed interactive coordination among visual displays helps users to evaluate and understand the clustering results as well as the data set by visually facilitating human intuition.

This work is a part of our continuing effort to give users more controls over data analysis processes and to enable more interactions with analysis results through interactive visual techniques. These efforts are designed to help users perform exploratory data analysis, establish meaningful hypotheses, and verify results. In this paper, we show how those visualization methods can help molecular biologists analyze and understand multidimensional gene expression profile data. Empirical validation on standard tasks, more case studies with biological researchers, and feedback from users will help refine this and similar software tools.

Acknowledgements: We appreciate the support from and partnership with Eric Hoffman and his lab at the Children's National Medical Center, through NIH grant N01-NS-1-2339. We appreciate support from National Science Foundation Digital Government Initiative (EIA 0129978) "Towards a Statistical Knowledge Network."

References

1. Baxevanis, A.D.: The Molecular Biology Database Collection: 2003 update. Nucleic Acids Research, Vol. 31. (2003) 1-12
2. Butte, A.: The Use and Analysis of Microarray Data. Nature Reviews Drug Discovery, Vol. 1. No. 12. (2002) 951-960
3. Doniger, S., Salomonis, N., Dahlquist, K., Vranizan, K., Lawlor, S., Conklin, B.: MAPPFinder: Using Gene Ontology and GenMAPP to Create a Global Gene-expression Profile from Microarray Data. Genome Biology, (2003) 4:R7
4. Gene Ontology Consortium: Gene Ontology: tool for the unification of biology. Nature Genet, Vol. 25. (2000) 25-29
5. Hochheiser, H., Shneiderman, B.: Dynamic query tools for time series data sets: Timebox widgets for interactive exploration. Information Visualization, Vol. 3 (2004) 1-18
6. Inselberg, A., Avidan, T.: Classification and visualization for high-dimensional data. Proc. 6th ACM SIGKDD International Conference on Knowledge Discovery and Data Mining (2000) 370-374
7. Kandogan, E.: Visualizing multi-dimensional clusters, trends, and outliers using star coordinates. Proc. 7th ACM SIGKDD International Conference on Knowledge Discovery and Data Mining (2001) 107-116
8. Seo, J., Bakay, M., Zhao, P., Chen, Y., Clarkson, P., Shneiderman, B., Hoffman, E.P.: Interactive Color Mosaic and Dendrogram Displays for Signal/Noise Optimization in Microarray Data Analysis. Proc. IEEE International Conference on Multimedia and Expo (2003) III-461~III-464
9. Seo, J., Shneiderman, B.: Interactively exploring hierarchical clustering results. IEEE Computer, Vol. 35, No. 7. (2002) 80-86
10. Shneiderman, B., Inventing discovery tools: Combining Information Visualization with Data Mining, Proc. Discovery Science 4th International Conference 2001, Editors (Jantke, K. P. and Shinohara, A.), Springer-Verlag, Berlin Heidelberg New York (2002) 17-28. Also printed in Information Visualization, Vol. 1. (2002) 5-12
11. Zeeberg, B., Feng W., Wang, G., Wang, M., Fojo, A., Sunshine, M., Narasimhan, S., Kane, D., Reinhold, W., Lababidi, S., Bussey, K., Riss, J., Barrett, J., Weinstein, J.: GoMiner: A Resource for Biological Interpretation of Genomic and Proteomic Data: Genome Biology, Vol. 4(4):R2 (2003)
12. Zhao, P., Seo, J., Wang Z., Wang, Y., Shneiderman, B., Hoffman, E.P.: In Vivo Filtering of in Vitro MyoD Target Data: An Approach for Identification of Biologically Relevant Novel Downstream Targets of Transcription Factors. Comptes Rendus Biologies, Vol. 326, Issues 10-11. (2003) 1049-1065

Visualizing Association Rules in a Framework for Visual Data Mining

Paolo Buono and Maria Francesca Costabile

Dipartimento di Informatica, Università degli Studi di Bari, Italy
{buono,costabile}@di.uniba.it

Abstract. The abundance of data available nowadays fosters the need of developing tools and methodologies to help users in extracting significant information. Visual data mining is going in this direction, exploiting data mining algorithms and methodologies together with information visualization techniques. The demand for visual and interactive analysis tools is particularly pressing in the Association Rules context where often the user has to analyze hundreds of rules in order to grasp valuable knowledge. In this paper, we present a visual strategy that exploits a graph-based technique and parallel coordinates to visualize the results of association rule mining algorithms. This helps data miners to get an overview of the rule set they are interacting with and enables them to deeper investigate inside a specific set of rules. The tools developed are embedded in a framework for Visual Data Mining that is briefly described.

1 Introduction

The evolving demands of the market and the increasing competition force companies to support their business plans with tools that help managers to make decisions in a rapid and more effective way. Presenting data in a convincing and understandable way requires a lot of work when data changes dynamically.

Business Intelligence refers to concepts and methodologies of different disciplines whose aim is to provide decision support by transforming the information usually stored in huge distributed databases into knowledge useful to optimize the company processes as well as the customer relationships. Business Intelligence includes data mining techniques that should allow users to get insights from the data by extracting patterns or models or relationships among the data that can be easily interpreted and understood.

Visual Data Mining (VDM) is an emerging area in explorative data analysis and mining. VDM refers to methods for supporting exploration of large data sets by allowing users to directly interact with visual representations of data and dynamically modify parameters to see how they affect the visualized data. Graphically presenting data enables users to discover specific patterns, as well as new and useful properties in the data, their correlations, and also detect possible deviations from the expected values.

M. Hemmje et al. (Eds.): E.J. Neuhold Festschrift, LNCS 3379, pp. 221–231, 2005.

The enormous amount of data accessible by the current technology provides additional information that can be integrated into people knowledge. Using good visualizations to present the information hidden in various company repositories can improve the decision process. Advances in information visualization offer promising techniques for presenting knowledge structures [5] and for permitting explorative analysis of the data [7,12].

VDM combines both classical data mining and visual representation techniques. We strongly believe that this "approach could lead to discovery tools that enable effective data navigation and interpretation, preserves user control, and provides the possibility to discover anything interesting or unusual without the need to know in advance what kind of phenomena should be observed"[6].

This paper illustrates a framework for VDM that we have developed as a result of the work within the European funded project FairsNet (IST-2001-34290). The aim is to provide various visualization techniques to assist the users in their decision making processes. Even if FairsNet focused on a specific application domain, namely trade fair management, the framework is quite general and applicable to different domains. Several data visualizations are generated to browse among the data and to present the retrieved information in appropriate ways for each user category. The demand for visual and interactive analysis tools is particularly pressing in the association rules context where often the user needs to analyze hundreds of rules in order to grasp valuable knowledge. In this paper we focus on the techniques for association rules visualization that are embedded in the proposed framework.

This paper has the following organization: after a brief description of the framework for VDM, we present our approach to explore association rules in Section 3. Section 4 describes other tools for visualizing association rules and Section 5 concludes the paper.

2   The Framework for VDM

The objective of FairsNet is to offer on-line innovative services to support the business processes of real trade fairs as well as to provide information services to main actors in the fair business, namely fair organizers, exhibitors, professional visitors. By organizers we mean all the people involved in the organization of the trade fair, more specifically the organizer is the person, or the group of people, that should take decisions about organizing and running the fair. The exhibitor is the client of the fair who has products or services to exhibit during the fair. Professional visitors are people or companies that visit the fair for business reasons.

The framework for VDM we have developed within FairsNet is called DAE (Data Analysis Engine). DAE is primarily related to decision support tasks, it aims at managing and improving interactive relationships among the trade fair users; detect profiles of exhibitors and visitors; find possible relationships between some behavioral profiles and commercial performance; segment exhibitors and visitors along different dimensions; find possible relationships among data in the trade fair database. DAE address the needs of specific types of users, primarily fair organizers and exhibitors, by allowing them to easily retrieve information with the use of appropriate visualization techniques, in accordance with the results on VDM [15].

The DAE architecture is shown in Fig. 1. It is a module directly accessible by the users. In the FairsNet context DAE is connected to the FairsNet database. As we said, the framework is general and DAE can be used in other contexts by connecting it to the proper databases.

The application server is composed by a local database and the DaeMine module. This is the data mining component which implements descriptive data mining algorithms to find interesting patterns inside data. We included algorithms for association rules generation and algorithms for clustering. Clustering aims at identifying a finite set of categories or clusters to describe the data. Data of interest are divided into groups using some criteria such as similarity. Association rules is another well known data mining technique that will be briefly described later in the paper.

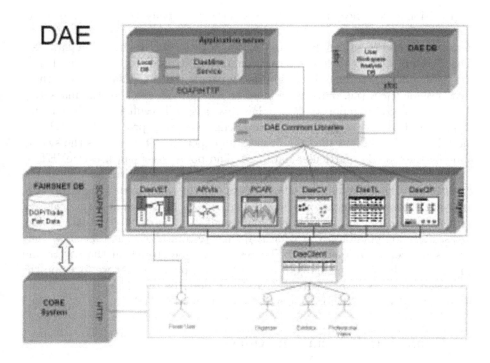

Fig. 1. DAE architecture

DaeDB stores the results of data mining algorithms as well as the results of queries on the application domain databases (e.g. FairsNet DB in our example). DAE Common Libraries includes all libraries that permit communication among the DAE components. DAE may include several visual modules that are accessible by users to allow them to analyze the stored data. They constitute the UI (User Interface) layer in the architecture in Fig. 1. Currently, there are the following visual modules:

- DaeVET enables the user to select relevant data and to create analysis;
- ARVis visualizes association rules using graphs and allows the user to interact with them. ARVis presents the overview of the dataset, then permits the user to zoom, filter and get the details on demand.
- PCAR uses Parallel Coordinates to visualize association rules in a way that is complementary to ARVis;
- DaeCV allows the user to analyze the result of the clustering algorithms used in DaeMine;
- DaeTL allows the user to analyze the data by using a technique based on Table Lenses [14];
- DaeQP allows the user to analyze the data by using a technique based on Query Preview [16].

Decision makers need to analyze data in their company's database in order to make the right decisions. Following the knowledge discovery process [8], the first action to do before any analysis can be done is data selection from the database. This is often a long and difficult task, and often, it needs to be iterated before the right selection is done, because usually people that need data are not those that provide them (i.e. database administrators provide data for the marketing division to produce reports). Improving this task will result in a reduced time to acquire data and to perform the knowledge discovery process. DaeVET is a module used by the so-called power user, an expert user that knows the system and the data of the particular database. The power user can use DaeVET to explore the database and select relevant tables and attributes as well as the types of users that will use the selected data and the tools needed to perform the analysis. Interaction techniques like dragging, selection, zooming and panning help the power user in this task. For some analysis, in particular for data mining tasks, it is not possible to provide real-time results to the user because they need some computational time. The results will be stored on the server and will be available for the eligible users. In the rest of this paper we focus on the visualization of Association Rules (ARs) and describe the visual techniques we have embedded in DAE for supporting users to analyze ARs.

3   Exploring Association Rules

The demand for visual and interactive analysis tools is particularly pressing in the Association Rules context where often the user has to analyze hundreds of rules in order to grasp valuable knowledge. The proposed VDM framework includes a visual strategy to face this problem, that exploits a graph-based technique and parallel coordinates to visualize the results of the association rules mining algorithms used by DAE. Combining the two approaches provides both an overview of the ARs structure and the possibility to deeper investigate inside a specific set of rules selected by the user. Association rules can be defined as follows: let $I = i_1, i_2, \ldots, i_n$ be a set of items called literals (in the market basket analysis the items could be the products sold in a supermarket). The database consists of a set of transactions $\mathrm{T} = T_i, A_p, \ldots, A_q$, where $A_i \in I$ for $i = p, \ldots, q$ and T_i is the identifier of the transaction. Each transaction $T_i \in \mathrm{T}$ is a set of items, such that $T \subset \mathrm{T}$. An association rule is a condition of the form $X \rightarrow Y(s, c)$, where $X \subseteq I$ and $Y \subseteq I$, $X \cap Y = \emptyset$, s and c are called respectively support and confidence. The support s of the rule R is $s = n_R/n$, where n_R is the number of transaction in T holding $X \cup Y$ and n is the total number of transaction. The support represents the proportion of transactions containing both the antecedent and the consequent. The confidence c of a rule R is $c = n_R/n_X$ where n_X is the number of transactions with X in the left side of the implication. The confidence is a measure of the conditional probability of the consequent, given the antecedent. The confidence expresses the strength of the logical implication described by the rule.

The main goal of researchers working in this area is to mine association rules, i. e., to produce as many significant rules as possible, discarding those with low meaning. The task of discarding rules is called pruning. Typically rules are pruned if they don't reach minimum thresholds for support and confidence threshold. Some authors introduced other parameters to improve the pruning phase and keep interesting patterns, see for example the Difference of Confidence in [11] and the Item Utility in [3].

In order to improve data mining task, it is useful to produce good visualization tools that allow to perform explorative analysis of ARs. The graph-based technique to visualize ARs we use in DAE was first proposed in [4]. Providing interaction features, the user may find interesting information exploring association rules. This graph visualization is very useful to see the overall distribution of the rules, it is possible to immediately recognize relationships among different rules and between the antecedent and the consequent of the rules. The adopted technique maps the ARs into a graph representing each single side of the rules as a node, the edge of the graph represents the logical implication of a rule. Fig. 2 depicts an example of output of a data mining step in the geographic domain. The rules have the same antecedent: "$A \rightarrow B$" and "$A \rightarrow C$" (in Fig. 2 A is the string "$ed\_on\_M63(A)$", B is the string "$close\_to(A, B)$", and C is the string "$relate\_meet(A, B)$"). The nodes may be visualized as colored rectangles (left frame) or as colored circles (middle frame). In the graph, red is used to represent antecedents and green to represent consequents, in case a node is antecedent for a rule and consequent for another rule it appears half red and half green. The rectangles are useful when there are few rules to visualize, since they provide the text of the rule. The user may expand to a rectangle as many rules as needed. The default visualization of rules is the one shown in the middle frame of Fig. 2, i.e. colored circles are used to reduce screen cluttering. Details are provided when the user goes with the cursor over an edge or on a node, as it is visible

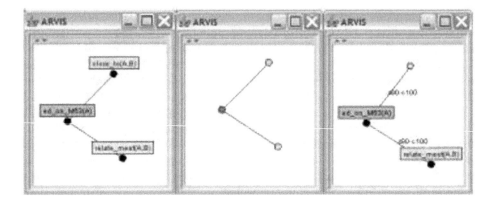

Fig. 2. Two association rules represented in a graph

in the right frame of Fig. 2. The confidence of a rule is coded by the length of the edge, the bigger is the confidence, the longer is the edge. The support is coded by color saturation of the edge: light blue means low support values, dark blue means high support values, black means 100% support. This graph representation easily reveals association rules that share the antecedent or the consequent. As we will see in Section 4, such information is not always available in other visualizations. To overcome occlusion and scalability, various interaction mechanisms are provided, that allow the user to move nodes with dragging operations.

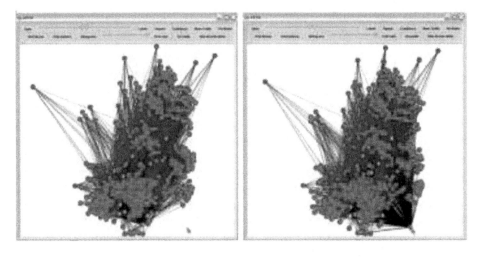

Fig. 3. 9785 association rules shown in one screen

In Fig. 3 two different visualizations of the same rule set consisting of 9785 ARs are shown. To produce the visualization in the right frame of Fig. 3, the user has moved a node at the bottom center of the screen, so that the relationships with other nodes are now better visible. We generate dynamic visualizations with the use of animation to overcome the occlusion problem. The graph moves according to the force-directed technique [17], showing the user a more clear view of a sub-graph. In the example of Fig. 3, the user may easily see that there is a node (shown half red and half green at the bottom of the right frame of Fig. 3) that has almost all the links with the black color. The black color on the links means that the group of rules has 100% confidence. The user can understand that he is interacting with rules with a strong significance, so it could be interesting to better explore them.

When the user discovers potential interesting patterns he may want to further investigate on that group of rules using another visualization. In our approach we integrated the graph-based technique with the parallel coordinates technique [2]. The user can select a group of rules of interest and send them to the parallel coordinates visualization tool to explore them in more details.

The approach of parallel coordinates to visualize ARs has been illustrated in [3]. A measure to indicate the utility of an item in a rule is called Item Utility (IU). The IU indicates how good is an item into a rule, for instance, if there is a rule of the form: $x, y \Rightarrow z$ with confidence CR it is possible to get the value of the confidence of the rule removing the item y $CR(y)$. The formula to compute IUy leads to three different cases: $IUy < 0$ means that y is dangerous for the rule, $IUy > 0$ means that y is useful for the rule, and $IUy = 0$ means that y is neutral. In order to generate the visual representation, the axes representing the parallel coordinates are normalized to $[-1; 1]$ (IU range, see Fig. 4). Each item is an axis and each rule is a line, the line crosses each axis according to the value of the IU for that item. This technique allows users to perform useful operations, such as identifying interesting rules according to some parameters specified by the user, pruning uninteresting rules according to some criteria (i.e. those whose items have a IU below a specific threshold).

Both tools are integrated in the VDM framework since they permit to perform complementary tasks. If graph visualization is very useful to describe the overview of the rules and the relationships among the items, parallel coordinates work better if used as a visual pruning tool. Due to these different goals, the two visualizations can be profitably used together by exploiting their synergic power. First the user may visualize the overview of all the rules produced by a classical data mining algorithm using the graph-based technique. Once the user selects a subset of rules, he passes them to the parallel coordinates tool for a deeper analysis that will allow him to filter some uninteresting rules. The reduced set of rules can then be returned to the graph-based tool for further analysis.

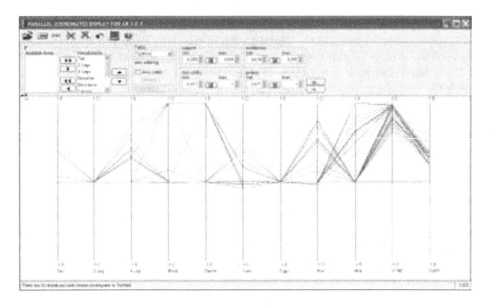

Fig. 4. Association rules visualization using parallel coordinates

4   Tools for Visualizing Association Rules

Despite the big amount of algorithms and methods for the production and management of ARs, there are not so many tools that provide good visualizations of the discovered rules. We present some tools according to the main visualization techniques they use. We divide the techniques in two categories: those visualizing ARs using 2D, which are described first, and those using 3D, described later.

Tabular visualization. The most immediate way to visualize ARs is using a table in which each row is a rule and columns represent the item set. The last two columns typically store the values of support and confidence of the rules. The advantage of this approach is that it is easy to order rules according to an attribute, e.g. by confidence. The main disadvantage is that the user may analyze few rules at once and it is very hard to look at the overview of the rule set or at relationships among them. Even if there are few rules to analyze but for each of them there are many items, it is hard to look at them.

Twokey plot. Unwin et al. use a scatter plot in which they represent the rules as colored circles [18]. The combination of support and confidence of the rule determines the position of the rules in the scatter plot. The Y axis represents the confidence values and the X axis the support values. The color indicates the cardinality of the rules (how many items has the rule). This technique is effective to represent the relationship among support, confidence and cardinality. It is also possible to see relationships between ancestor and descendants of the rules (a rule is child of another if the child has one more item). Even though the user can get some information about the rules, it is difficult to analyze the rules in detail, the items of the rules are not easily visible so this technique need to be associated to other techniques to better explore ARs.

Double-Decker plot. This approach uses mosaic plots to visualize all possible combinations of items in the antecedent that implies a consequent composed of a single item. The visualization is composed of several bins. The support of an association rule is represented by the area of highlighting in the corresponding bin. The confidence of the rule can be deduced from the proportion of the highlighted area in a bin and the total area of the bin [11]. This is an interesting technique but does not scale very well.

Circular graph. This technique adopts a circular graph layout where items involved in rules are mapped around the circle [13]. Associations are plotted as lines connecting these points, where a gradient in the line color, from blue(dark) to yellow(light), indicates the direction of the association from the antecedent to the consequent. A specific color shows bi-directional links. This technique has been successfully used to highlight relationships among items and it is able to display high information volumes. Unfortunately it is difficult to represent support and confidence, therefore another technique should be combined with this to be able to perform a more complete analysis.

Directed graph. This is a reticular representation of the ARs. The graph technique may visualize ARs in different ways, representing relationships among items (nodes of the graph) or relationships among rules. A tool that uses this technique is DBMiner [9], that represents two kinds of relationship among nodes: *inter-attribute* association and *intra-attribute* association. The former is an association among different attributes (or items); whereas the latter is an association within one or a set of attributes. The problem with this technique is that the graph may become cluttered. In ARVis, which uses a similar technique, this problem has been addressed by allowing the user to directly manipulate the graph to get different views and to filter the rules.

2D matrix. The leading idea of a 2D matrix is to represent an AR with the antecedent and the consequent on the x-axis and y-axis respectively. Confidence and support where originally coded only with color. Different colors represented different confidence value ranges. Color hue indicated the support. This use of color is not efficient. To overcome this problem, DBMiner introduces a third dimension in which the height of bars represents the confidence and the color represents the support [9]. The best use of this technique is for one-to-one ARs, because the user may be confused about which item is in the antecedent and which one in the consequent.

Matrix visualization. The application developed by Wong et al visualizes relationships using a 3D matrix in which the rows represent the items and the columns represent the rules [19]. The third dimension is exploited to visualize the values of support and confidence of each rule. The cell (i, j) shows a small cube colored with blue if the item i is in the antecedent of the rule j and colored with red if the item i is in the consequent of the rule j. This tool gives an overview of all the rule set. The user can rotate the matrix, zoom and pan, avoiding typical 3D problems such as occlusion. Unfortunately, this technique does not scale well and it is difficult to see relationships among rules and between antecedents and consequents.

3D graph visualization. In the Ming C. et al. approach [10], a 3D graph is used. Items are represented as spheres linked by edges. Items that are strongly correlated are grouped in elliptical clusters. The support is represented by edge length and the confidence by color. This technique is similar to the one we developed in a 3D version of ARVis. We found that the third dimension does not improve the rule analysis, it gives only a fascinating display.

Virtual arenas. This is an alternative visualization that exploits the metaphor of virtual arenas [1]. The ARs are represented as spheres positioned on the steps of an arena. The radius of the spheres is proportional to the support. The spheres are set on a cone whose height represents the confidence. This tool allows the users to select a rule (sphere) and to analyze in more details the rules related to the items of the selected rule. This new approach is attractive but does not appear suitable for many rules.

5   Conclusions

The big amount of available data makes its analysis a complex task. We have presented a framework for VDM that may help people to analyze the data present in company databases using various tools. The integration of several tools over the same data allows to the user to manage multiple views for discovering novel and unexpected insights.

The framework is open to the integration of more data mining and visualization tools to increase the range of possibilities for looking at the data and analyzing them, hence to better support the decision makers in their activities.

6   Acknowledgments

The support of EC through grant FAIRSNET IST-2001-34290 is acknowledged.

References

1. J. Blanchard, F. Guillet, and H. Briand. Exploratory visualization for association rule rummaging. In *Proceedings fourth International Workshop on Multimedia Data Mining MDM/KDD2003*, pages 107–114, 2003.
2. D. Bruzzese and P. Buono. Combining visual techniques for association rules exploration. In M. F. Costabile, editor, *Proceedings Working Conference on Advanced Visual Interfaces AVI 2004*, pages 381–384. ACM Press, 2004.
3. D. Bruzzese and C. Davino. Visualizing association rules. In S. J. Simeoff, M. Noirhomme, and M. Boehlen, editors, *Visual Data Mining: Theory and Applications*, Lecture Notes in Artificial Intelligence. Springer-Verlag, to appear.
4. P. Buono. Analysing association rules with an interactive graph-based technique. In C. Stephanidis, editor, *Proceedings HCI International, Special Session on Visual Data Mining*, volume 4, pages 675–679. Lawrence Erlbaum, 2003.

5. C. Chen. *Information Visualisation and Virtual Environments*. Springer-Verlag, London, 1999.
6. M. F. Costabile and D. Malerba. Special issue on visual data mining, editor's foreword. *Journal of Visual Languages & Computing*, 14(6):499–501, December 2003.
7. G. S. Davidson, B. Hendrickson, D. K. Johnson, C. E. Meyers, and B. N. Wylie. Knowledge mining with VxInsight: Discovery through interaction. *Journal on Intelligent Information Systems*, 11(3):259–285, March 1998.
8. U. Fayyad, G. Piatetsky-Shapiro, and P. Smyth. From data mining to knowledge discovery in databases. *AI Magazine*, 17(3):37–54, 1996.
9. J. Han, Y. Fu, W. Wang, J. Chiang, W. Gong, K. Koperski, D. Li, Y. Lu, A. Rajan, N. Stefanovic, B. Xia, and O. R. Zaiane. DBMiner: A system for mining knowledge in large relational databases. In *Proceedings International Conference on Data Mining and Knowledge Discovery (KDD'96)*, pages 250–255, Portland, Oregon, 1996.
10. M. C. Hao, U. Dayal, M. Hsu, T. Sprenger, and M. H. Gross. Visualization of directed associations in E-Commerce transaction data. In *Proceedings VisSym'01*, pages 185–192, 2001.
11. H. Hofmann, A. P. J. M. Siebes, and A. F. X. Wilhelm. Visualizing association rules with interactive mosaic plots. In *Proceedings sixth ACM SIGKDD international conference on Knowledge discovery and data mining*, pages 227–235. ACM Press, 2000.
12. D. Keim and M. Ankerst. Visual data mining and exploration of large databases, a Tutorial. In *ECML/PKDD 2001*, 3-7 September 2001. Freiburg, Germany.
13. C. P. Rainsford and J. F. Roddick. Visualisation of temporal interval association rules. In *Proceedings 2nd International Conference on Intelligent Data Engineering and Automated Learning, (IDEAL 2000)*, pages 91–96. Springer-Verlag, 2000.
14. R. Rao and S. K. Card. The table lens: Merging graphical and symbolic representations in an interactive focus context visualization for tabular information. In *Proceedings ACM Conf. Human Factors in Computing Systems, CHI 94, Boston*, pages 318–322. ACM Press, 1994.
15. B. Shneiderman. Inventing discovery tools: combining information visualization with data mining. *Information Visualization*, 1(1):5–12, 2002.
16. B. Shneiderman, C. Plaisant, K. Doan, and T. Bruns. Interface and Data Architecture for Query Preview in Networked Information Systems. *ACM Transaction on Information System*, 17:320–341, 1999.
17. I. G. Tollis, G. D. Battista, P. Eades, and R. Tamassia. *Graph Drawing: Algorithms for Drawing Graphs*. Prentice Hall, 1998.
18. A. Unwin, H. Hofmann, and K. Bernt. The twokey plot for multiple association rules control. AT&T Florham Park.
19. P. C. Wong, P. Whitney, and J. Thomas. Visualizing association rules for text mining. In G. Wills and D. Keim, editors, *Proceedings IEEE Symposium on Information Visualization*, pages 120–123. IEEE Computer Society, 1999.

From Human-*Computer* Interaction to Human-*Artefact* Interaction: Interaction Design for Smart Environments

Norbert A. Streitz

Fraunhofer IPSI, Darmstadt, Germany

Abstract. The introduction of computer technology caused a shift away from real objects as sources of information towards desktop computers as *the* interfaces to information now (re)presented in a digital format. In this paper, I will argue for returning to the real world as the starting point for designing information and communication environments. Our approach is to design environments that exploit the affordances of real world objects and at the same time use the potential of computer-based support. Thus, we move from human-*computer* interaction to human-*artefact* interaction. Combining the best of both worlds requires an integration of real and virtual worlds resulting in hybrid worlds. The approach will be demonstrated by sample prototypes we have built as, e.g., the Roomware® components and smart artefacts that were developed in the project "Ambient Agoras: Dynamic Information Clouds in a Hybrid World" which was part of the EU-funded proactive initiative "The Disappearing Computer"(DC).

Introduction

The spread of information technology has caused a significant shift: away from real objects in the physical environment as the sources of information towards monitors of desktop computers as the interfaces to information and thus an increasing emphasis on virtual environments. In this paper, I argue for returning to the real world as the starting point for designing future information and collaboration environments. The goal is to design environments that exploit the affordances provided by real objects but at the same time make use of the potential of computer-based support available via the virtual world. This combination of the best of both worlds requires an integration of real and virtual worlds resulting in hybrid worlds. Thus, we move from human-computer interaction to human-artefact interaction.

Cooperative Buildings

The overall context of this approach is our notion of so called Cooperative Buildings that we introduced some time ago (Streitz et al., 1998). We used the term "building" (and not "spaces") in order to emphasize that the starting point of the design should be the real, architectural environment. By calling it a "cooperative" building, we wanted to indicate that the building serves the purpose of cooperation and communication. At

M. Hemmje et al. (Eds.): E.J. Neuhold Festschrift, LNCS 3379, pp. 232–240, 2005.

the same time, it is also "cooperative" towards its users, inhabitants, and visitors by employing active, attentive and adaptive components. This is to say that the building does not only provide facilities but it can also (re)act "on its own" after having identified certain conditions. It is part of our vision that it will adapt to changing situations and provide context-aware information and services.

Roomware®

The major constituents of cooperative buildings are provided by what we called Roomware components (Streitz et al., 1998, 1999, 2001) [www.roomware.de]. We define Roomware® as the result of integrating information and communication technology in room elements such as doors, walls, and furniture. This is part of our approach that the "world around us" is the interface to information and for the cooperation of people. In this approach, the computer as a device disappears and is almost "invisible" (see also "The Disappearing Computer" in the next section) but its functionality is ubiquitously available via new forms of interacting with information as it is also envisioned in ubiquitous computing (Weiser, 1991). Thus, the roomware approach moves beyond the limits of standard desktop environments on several dimensions and extends usage into the architectural environment as well as outside of buildings into public spaces, etc.

Fig. 1. Examples of Roomware components:
DynaWall, InteracTable, CommChair, ConnecTables

Our design of the roomware components and the associated software exploits the affordances provided by real objects. Thus, we build on general knowledge and specific experiences people have when interacting with everyday artefacts as, e.g., a table, a wall or a pin board. This motivated also our gesture-based approach of interaction that is realized via the BEACH software (Tandler, 2003, Prante et al. 2004). It allows to throw, to shuffle and to rotate digital information objects, e.g., on the DynaWall and the InteracTable similar to real objects in the real world. Examples of the second generation of roomware components (Streitz et al., 2001) are the following (see also figure 1):

The *DynaWall* is a large interactive, electronic wall, representing a touch-sensitive vertical information display and interaction device that is 4.50 m wide and 1.10 m high. Two or more persons can either work individually in parallel or they share the entire display space. The size of the DynaWall provides challenges as well as opportunities for new forms of human-computer interaction that are provided by our BEACH software

The *InteracTable* is an interactive table for informal group discussion and planned cooperation. It is 90 cm high with a display size of 63 cm x 110 cm. The horizontal workspace is realized with a touch-sensitive plasma-display integrated into the tabletop. People can use pens and fingers for gesture-based interaction with information objects. Using BEACH, they can create and annotate information objects that can also be shuffled and rotated to accommodate different view orientations around the table.

The *CommChair* combines the mobility and comfort of armchairs with the functionality of a pen-based computer. It has an independent power supply and is connected to all other roomware components via a wireless network. The BEACH software provides a private workspace for personal notes and a public workspace that allows moving them to other roomware components, for example to the DynaWall. Using the CommChair, one can interact remotely with all objects displayed on the DynaWall.

The *ConnecTable* is a modular version of the CommChair and can be used in different positions: either sitting in front of it on a regular chair or using it in a stand-up position as a high desk. Its particular name – ConnecTable – results from the functionality that its workspace area can be easily extended by "connecting" several ConnecTables (Tandler et al., 2001). The coupling of the individual displays resulting in a common shared workspace is achieved by simply moving the ConnecTables together in physical space which is detected by sensors. No additional login or typing of IP addresses is needed.

The *Passage* mechanism (Konomi et al., 1999) provides an intuitive way for the physical transportation of virtual information structures using arbitrary physical objects, so called "Passengers". The assignment is done via a simple gesture moving the information object to (and for retrieval from) the "virtual" part of the so called "Bridge" that is activated by placing the Passenger object on the physical part of the Bridge. No electronic tagging is needed. Passengers can be viewed as "physical bookmarks" into the virtual world.

We also developed the dedicated software infrastructure BEACH (Tandler, 2003) and applications on top of it as, for example, PalmBeach, MagNets, BeachMap (Prante et al, 2004) and the Passage mechanism (Konomi et al., 1999) in order to exploit the full potential of roomware. Furthermore, we used non-speech audio in order to provide sound augmentation for the different types of interaction and collaboration , especially on the DynaWall (Müller-Tomfelde et al., 2003).

The Disappearing Computer

"The Disappearing Computer" (DC) [www.disappearing-computer.net] is an EU-funded proactive research initiative of the Future and Emerging Technologies (FET) section of the Information Society Technologies (IST) research program. The goal of the DC-initiative is to explore how everyday life can be supported and enhanced through the use of collections of interacting smart artefacts. Together, these artefacts will form new people-friendly environments in which the "computer-as-we-know-it" has no role. There are three main objectives:
1. Developing new tools and methods for the embedding of computation in everyday objects so as to create artefacts.
2. Research on how new functionality and new use can emerge from collections of interacting artefacts.
3. Ensuring that people's experience of these environments is both coherent and engaging in space and time.

These objectives are addressed via a cluster of 17 related projects under the umbrella theme of the DC-initiative. The cluster is complemented by a variety of support activities provided by the DC-Network and coordinated by the DC Steering Group, an elected representation of all projects. For more details please visit the website www.disappearing-computer.net

Ambient Agoras

"Ambient Agoras: Dynamic Information Clouds in a Hybrid World" is a project of the "Disappearing Computer" initiative [www.ambient-agoras.org]. It started in January 2001 and lasted until December 2003. The interdisciplinary approach of the project required a range of expertise provided by the different consortium partners.

Fraunhofer IPSI in Darmstadt (Germany) was the scientific and technical as well as the administrative project coordinator. The contributions were provided by its AMBIENTE research division. For the development of some of the artefacts, AMBIENTE cooperated closely with product designers and architects. *EDF (Electricité de France)*, the French electrical power utility, was the user organization in the consortium. As part of its R&D division, the Laboratory of Design for Cognition (LDC) in Paris provided the test bed for the evaluation studies and contributed to the observation and participatory design methods. *Wilkhahn,* a German manufacturer of office furniture, contributed to the design and development of some artefacts. They had previously gained experience in designing the second generation of roomware® developed in cooperation with Fraunhofer IPSI's AMBIENTE in the previous 'Future Office Dynamics' consortium.

Objectives

The project investigated how to turn everyday places into social marketplaces (= 'agoras' in Greek) of ideas and information where people can meet and interact. Therefore, the objective of Ambient Agoras was to address the office environment as an integrated organization located in a physical environment and having particular information needs both at the collective level of the organization, and at the personal level of the worker. The overall goal was to augment the architectural envelope in order to create a social architectural space (Streitz et al., 2003) to support collaboration, informal communication, and social awareness. Ambient Agoras aimed at providing situated services, place-relevant information, and feeling of the place ('genius loci') to users, enabling them to communicate for help, guidance, work, or fun in order to improve collaboration and the quality of life in future office environments.

While the initial objective was targeted at office environments it became obvious during the project that a number of results can be transferred to similar support situations in other domains, for example, public spaces and extended home environments.

Approach

The project promoted an approach of designing individual as well as team interaction in physical environments using augmented physical artefacts. It applied a scenario-based approach, starting out with a large number of "bits-of-life", aggregated them to scenarios and presented them, e.g., via video mock-ups, to focus groups for user-feedback. This served, in combination with extensive conceptual work as the basis for the development of artefacts and software prototypes and their evaluation. Design, development, and evaluation followed an iterative approach. Ambient Agoras coupled several interaction design objectives (disappearance and ubiquity of computing devices) with sensing technologies (active and passive RFID, WaveLAN-based triangulation), smart artefacts (walls, tables, mobile devices), ambient displays, and investigated the functionality of two or more artefacts working together. It addressed the following three major issues, investigated their interaction and combination, and presented results for arriving at solutions for these issues. The issues are:

1) supporting informal communication and atmosphere in organizations,
2) the role and potential of ambient displays in future work environments, and
3) the combination of more or less static artefacts integrated in the architectural environment with mobile devices carried by people.

Results

This project provided substantial contributions to the emerging domain of ubiquitous computing, smart artefacts, and ambient intelligence. It built upon our previous work on interweaving information technology with architectural spaces (roomware). Within the project, we developed a conceptual framework that analyzed the architectural constraints for the design of future work environments. During the three years of the project, seven functional prototypes of smart artefacts were developed and tested in combination with four major software prototypes in several evaluation cycles.

The Hello.Wall (see figure 2) is a prominent example of the artefacts that were developed. It is an XL-size compound artefact with sensing technology. It does not have a standard type of display but a so called "ambient display" communicating information via a range of dynamic light patterns. The current realization uses 124 light emitting cells organized in an array structure with 8 rows. It provided awareness

Fig. 2. The Hello.Wall – an ambient display communicating awareness information between different locations via a range of dynamic light patterns

and notifications to people passing by or watching it via different light patterns. Different patterns correspond to different types of information, in our scenarios, e.g., information about "presence" and "mood" at different locations of a distributed project organisation. In order to monitor and identify people passing-by, a state-of-the-art sensing infrastructure was set up at Fraunhofer IPSI. People can access details of the information that is communicated via the Hello.Wall by using a mobile device that is called ViewPort (see figure 3 and 4). The ViewPort is a wavelan-equipped PDA-like computer for creating and presenting personal as well as background information.

Fig. 3. Observing light patterns on the Hello.Wall and using the ViewPort to access additional information

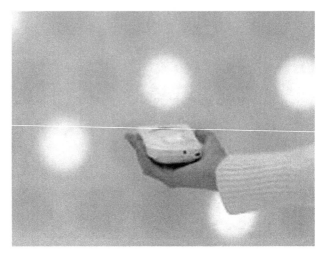

Fig. 4. The ViewPort in front of the Hello.Wall

We call this interaction between the artefacts: 'the Hello.Wall is "borrowing" the display of another artefact for displaying the information'. The sensor infrastructure allowed to define three different zones of interaction around the Hello.Wall and thus implements a "distance-dependent semantics", i.e., the distance of an individual from the wall defines the interactions offered and the kind of information shown on the Hello.Wall and the ViewPort.

An important aspect in sensor-based environments is "privacy". Therefore, we developed a checklist on privacy issues in ubiquitous computing environments and guidelines for the development of privacy enhancing technology. As a dedicated example of privacy enhancing technology, we developed the Personal Aura in order to give users control over RFID-based identification in smart environments (Röcker et el.., 2004)

Another direction in the project was the development of augmented table-top surfaces. The ConsulTable presents a stand-up interactive table supporting face-to-face discussions. It was turned into a product and is now marketed by our industrial partner Wilkhahn. The Inter.Sur.Face is an interactive high-resolution surface to be mounted on a table or at a wall. It can display large overviews and works towards smooth transitions from individual to small group work use. Finally, the ConverTable is a folding table with integrated display and a multi-touch frame which supports flexible usage in a creative team work space. To ensure that the artefacts smoothly work together and facilitate user identification, most of them are provided with integrated sensor technology.

All our systems support work-related processes in office buildings while at the same time fostering informal communication and awareness. The InfoRiver system (shown on the wall-sized InforMall display) implements the information river metaphor and supports the flow of information through an office building or an organization, e.g., company-related news and announcements or messages. SIAM is a lightweight task-management system with synchronous groupware functionalities implemented based on Microsoft's .NET. Aimed at nomadic work groups, it supports group communication and provides awareness. The Hello.Wall software infrastructure enables the synchronous communication of distributed Hello.Walls and ViewPorts. The ContextDrive (Prante, et al. 2004) supports personal information management. Our prototypes are multi-user and multi-device systems enabling coherent and engaging interaction experiences with sensor-enhanced smart artefacts.

In order to evaluate the approach, a living-lab evaluation was run with distributed Hello.Walls connecting two remote sites, i.e., lounge spaces at EDF-LDC in Paris and Fraunhofer IPSI in Darmstadt. The Hello.Wall served as an awareness and notification tool about the availability of people for chance encounters and as a starting point for initiating video-based communication between the two remote sites.

Acknowledgements

The work reported was supported in various ways by the "Future Office Dynamics (FOD)" industrial R&D Consortium and the European Commission (contract IST–2000-25134) as part of the "Disappearing Computer" initiative. Thanks are due to Jörg Geißler, Torsten Holmer, Carsten Magerkurth, Christian Müller-Tomfelde, Daniela Plewe, Thorsten Prante, Carsten Röcker, Peter Tandler, Daniel van Alphen, our cooperation partners in the different projects, e.g., Wilkhahn, wiege, Quickborner Team, EDF, DALT, and to further members and students of the research division AMBIENTE [www.ipsi.fraunhofer.de/ambiente] for their contributions in realizing the different components and environments.

References

Konomi, S., Müller-Tomfelde, C., Streitz, N. (1999). Passage: Physical Transportation of Digital Information in Cooperative Buildings. In: N. Streitz, J. Siegel, V. Hartkopf, S. Konomi (Eds.), *Cooperative Buildings - Integrating Information, Organizations, and Architecture. Proceedings of Second International Workshop (CoBuild'99).* Springer LNCS 1670. pp. 45-54.

Müller-Tomfelde, C., Streitz, N., Steinmetz, R. (2003). Sounds@Work - Auditory Displays for Interaction in Cooperative and Hybrid Environments. In: C. Stephanidis, J. Jacko (Eds.): *Human-Computer Interaction: Theory and Practice (Part II).* Lawrence Erlbaum Publishers. Mahwah. pp. 751-755.

Prante, T., Petrovic, K., Stenzel, R. (2004). Kontextbasiertes Individuelles Informations-management für das Ubiquitous Computing. In: *Proceedings of Mensch & Computer 2004 (M&C '04),* Oldenbourg Verlag, München, pp. 291-300.

Prante, T., Streitz, N., Tandler, P. (2004). Roomware: Computers Disappear and Interaction Evolves. *IEEE Computer,* December 2004, pp. 47 – 54.

Röcker, C., Prante, T., Streitz, N., van Alphen, D. (2004). Using Ambient Displays and Smart Artefacts to Support Community Interaction in Distributed Teams. Proceedings of OZCHI-2004 Conference (22.-24. November 2004, University of Wollongong, Australia.)

Streitz, N. Geißler, J., Holmer, T. (1998). Roomware for Cooperative Buildings: Integrated Design of Architectural Spaces and Information Spaces. In: N. Streitz, S. Konomi, H. Burkhardt, H. (Eds.), *Cooperative Buildings - Integrating Information, Organization, and Architecture. Proceedings of the First International Workshop (CoBuild '98).* Springer LNCS Vol. 1370. pp. 4-21.

Streitz, N., Geißler, J., Holmer, T., Konomi, S., Müller-Tomfelde, C., Reischl, W. Rexroth, P., Seitz, P., Steinmetz, R. (1999). i-LAND: an Interactive Landscape for Creativity and Innovation. In: *Proceedings of ACM Conference CHI'99* (Pittsburgh, USA). pp. 120-127.

Streitz, N., Tandler, P., Müller-Tomfelde, C., Konomi, S. (2001). Roomware: Towards the Next Generation of Human-Computer Interaction based on an Integrated Design of Real and Virtual Worlds. In: J. Carroll (Ed.), *Human-Computer Interaction in the New Millennium.* Addison-Wesley. pp. 553-578.

Streitz, N., Röcker, C., Prante, Th., Stenzel, R., van Alphen, D. (2003). Situated Interaction with Ambient Information: Facilitating Awareness and Communication in Ubiquitous Work Environments. In: D. Harris, V. Duffy, M. Smith, C. Stephanidis (Eds.): *Human-Centred Computing: Cognitive, Social, and Ergonomic Aspects.* New Jersey, Lawrence Erlbaum Publishers. Mahwah. pp. 133-137.

Streitz, N., Prante, T., Röcker, C., van Alphen, D., Magerkurth, D., Stenzel, R., Plewe, D. (2003). Ambient Displays and Mobile Devices for the Creation of Social Architectural Spaces: Supporting informal communication and social awareness in organizations. In: K. O'Hara, M. Perry, E. Churchill, D. Russell (Eds.): *Public and Situated Displays: Social and Interactional Aspects of Shared Display Technologies.* Kluwer Publishers. pp. 387-409

Tandler, P., Prante, T., Müller-Tomfelde, C., Streitz, N., Steinmetz, R. (2001). ConnecTables: Dynamic Coupling of Displays for the Flexible Creation of Shared Workspaces. In: Proceedings of the 14. Annual ACM Symposium on User Interface Software and Technology (UIST'01), ACM Press (CHI Letters 3 (2)). pp. 11-20.

Tandler, P. (2003). The BEACH application model and software framework for synchronous collaboration in ubiquitous computing environments. In: *The Journal of Systems & Software*, Vol 69/3 pp 267-296, 2003. Special issue on Ubiquitous Computing edited by J.J. Barton, R. Cerqueira and M. Fontoura.

Weiser, M., (1991). The Computer for the Twenty-First Century. *Scientific American*, pp. 94-10, September 1991.

Cooperation in Ubiquitous Computing:
An Extended View on Sharing

Peter Tandler and Laura Dietz

Fraunhofer Integrated Publication and Information Systems Institute (IPSI),
Dolivostr. 15, 64293 Darmstadt, Germany
{Peter.Tandler, Laura.Dietz}@ipsi.fraunhofer.de

Abstract. Many ubiquitous computing scenarios deal with cooperative work situations. To successfully support these situations, computer-supported co-operative work (CSCW) concepts and technologies face new challenges. One of the most fundamental concepts for cooperation is sharing. By analyzing applications of sharing in the context of ubiquitous computing it can be shown that ubiquitous computing enables an extended view on sharing. In this paper, we show that this extended view seamlessly integrates the view of "traditional" CSCW and additionally incorporates ubiquitous, heterogeneous, and mobile devices used in a common context.

1   Introduction

Ubiquitous computing environments offer a wide range of devices in many different shapes and sizes [21]. Today, the desktop computer is present in every office and many homes. Portable information appliances, such as personal digital assistants (PDAs), are increasing in popularity. In the future, collaboration between users and environments with multiple interconnected devices will determine work and everyday activities to a large degree. Then, heterogeneous devices will complement each other to provide a consistent usage experience. User interfaces and interaction techniques will take advantage of the different properties of the devices. The devices will be closely connected and integrated with the environment and context in which people use them.

Research on computer-supported co-operative work (CSCW) has developed suc-cessful concepts and technology to support collaborating people sharing information to fulfill a common task. This includes mechanisms for distributing and updating data, activity awareness, and building a mental context. However, traditionally CSCW assumes that the devices different users have at hand are rather homogeneous, with similar interaction capabilities, such as a display, mouse, and keyboard.

In ubiquitous computing (UbiComp), this homogeneity cannot be assumed. People bring a variety of devices into meetings that carry information people might want to share. In many cases, people want to benefit from sharing and editing information synchronously using different devices such as laptops, handhelds, and large interac-tive walls (figure 1). Then, it is no longer possible to use the same representation and interaction techniques for all devices used. If the users' context is considered, sharing can be adapted to the current situation. For instance, if a group stands in front of a

M. Hemmje et al. (Eds.): E.J. Neuhold Festschrift, LNCS 3379, pp. 241–250, 2005.

large public display they can use their handhelds to access functionality for working with the shared information. If the group is physically distributed and no large display is available, their personal devices have to show the shared information as well.

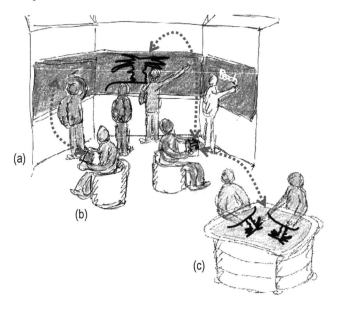

Fig. 1. In ubiquitous computing environments, heterogeneous devices are used to support synchronous collaboration. (a) An interactive wall with a large visual interaction area. (b) Interactive chairs, or handhelds with small displays. (c) A horizontal tabletop surface for multiple users

Especially in co-located settings, users expect to be able to use some devices, such as public displays or interactive tables, concurrently, which leads to issues for sharing the *devices* themselves. As an opposite of this, a user may want to use multiple devices for his or her task. All of these devices store some of the user's information, but are rarely aware that there are other devices around that are owned by the same user who would enjoy if they share their information and complement each other to help the user fulfilling his or her tasks. These are examples, where CSCW sharing technology serves as a good basis, but needs to be extended for UbiComp applications.

1.1   Aspects of Sharing

Sharing (in general) is a generic concept to enable collaboration (e.g. file sharing, application sharing, information sharing etc.). It can be seen both conceptually at the user level and technically at the software level. At the *user level*, sharing describes a technique how users can access the same information, which could be manifested as a document that is shown on a large common display. Concepts are defined, how users interact with shared information. Also, users can share the same device, which needs concepts that describe which actions are concurrently possible and which have to be coordinated. At the *software level*, sharing expresses the ability to access and manipulate the same entity, for instance digital documents. At this level, it is investigated how sharing can be implemented and how technical challenges such as concurrent and conflicting actions can be solved. The same sharing concept can be implemented by the software using different approaches.

This section discusses different aspects related to sharing: synchronous work, sharing and distribution, and sharing and coupling.

Synchronous and Asynchronous Sharing. Sharing can support different working modes [5]. When people work simultaneously with the same information, it is often desirable that the information is *synchronously* shared. This means that multiple users can modify the same document while conflicts are detected at a fine granularity. When information is *asynchronously* shared, different users work on different versions of the same document, which requires merging changes into a single document.

Difference between Sharing and Distribution. Sharing, as it is used in this paper, refers to a general concept. *Distribution*, in contrast, is a technology that can be used for implementing the technical part of sharing. As explained in [9], distribution alone does not lead to cooperative software. The system also has to transmit the mental concept of what is shared, what will happen to the user's actions, social, and physical context.

In this paper it is argued that when designing software systems supporting cooperation, developers should think of information as shared among users and devices, and not simply as distributed among computers.

Sharing and Degree of Coupling. In contrast to sharing, *coupling* describes the level of collaboration ranging from informing, coordinating, collaborating to cooperating, according to the degree of communication [1]. One extreme is *individual work*, i.e. people work on their own without exchanging any information with others. Working *loosely coupled*, people may share some documents and artifacts and are to some degree aware of the others' actions. In *tightly-coupled work*, people work very closely together, use the same documents, work on the same task, and share the same view.

Now, depending on the degree of coupling, various aspects of the software have to be shared. As a general rule, the tighter the collaboration, the more sharing is needed. However, the degree of coupling also leads to what to share, which is discussed in section 2.

1.2   Sample Usage Scenario

In order to illustrate different aspects of cooperation in ubiquitous computing, this section presents a team meeting in an UbiComp environment as a sample usage scenario.

Shortly before the meeting all participants enter the room. As soon as each one arrives, the meeting room detects the user's presence and devices brought into the room. Devices and users are automatically logged into the shared virtual workspace for the current meeting. The workspace provides documents and tools that have been used in the previous project's meeting; some documents were updated during the week. By default, participants view public documents on the large-scale display composed from three independent hardware segments (fig. 1a). Private documents are shown on one of their personal devices (fig. 1b). During the meeting they open a communication channel to a specialist working somewhere in the same building, to get her opinion. Although she is currently not in her office, she receives the message on her mobile phone. She uses a nearby desktop computer to log into the virtual meeting workspace. Then, she can navigate together with the other participants through the documents.

Suddenly, a discussion arises between some participants and the specialist. While the others are arguing, three participants withdraw to the back of the meeting room and work out a solution using one of the electronic meeting tables with touch sensitive surface on which they scribble simultaneously (fig. 1c). Meanwhile, the specialist decides to join the others in the meeting room. She found a spreadsheet document with important information for the ongoing discussion stored on her PDA. In order to make it accessible within the meeting, she adds the document to the shared workspace and opens it on the public display to discuss it with the whole team. One of the participants opens a personal view of the common spreadsheet on his laptop in order to perform some advanced calculations. Since his device has only limited memory and computational power, the device shows the user interface only, while the calculations are performed on a server associated with the meeting room.

In the following text, we examine the different aspects of sharing that are mentioned in the scenario. We present a design model that provides a basis to analyze the different aspects of our broader view on sharing.

2   Extending the View on Sharing

Many aspects of UbiComp applications are perceived by users as shared and thus have to match their intuition. In order to be able to get a deeper understanding of the new aspects of sharing that become relevant in ubiquitous computing, this section analyzes the extended view on sharing in detail, based on a conceptual software design model of UbiComp and CSCW applications, which is introduced first. This model is used to discuss various aspects of sharing: first for "traditional" CSCW applications, then the extensions introduced by ubiquitous computing.

2.1   A Conceptual Software Design Model

This section briefly describes the conceptual software design model, which is used in this paper to analyze aspects of sharing. This model is discussed in detail in [20]. It defines three design dimensions: separation of concerns, coupling and sharing, and level of abstraction (figure 2). In the following, we focus on the *separation of concerns* dimension, as it is used to analyze the *coupling and sharing* dimension of applications. The *level of abstraction* dimension is not further discussed in this paper.

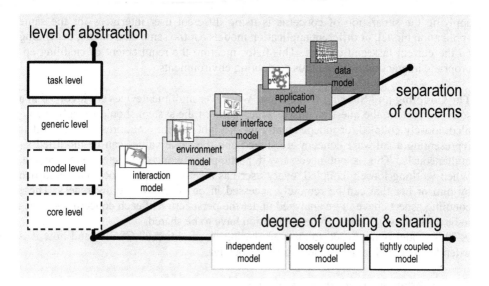

Fig. 2. Notation for the three design dimensions of the conceptual software design model

The Separation of Concerns Dimension. Separation of concerns is a common software technique to enable independent modifications and extensibility of software components. The conceptual design model suggests separating five basic concerns (i.e. aspects of the software); each concern is represented by its own model when designing software. The *data model* specifies the artifacts users create and interact with. This can be text-documents, spreadsheets, drawings, as well as a group folder or the items of a shared desktop. To work on data, an *application model* describes the necessary functionality to access and manipulate artifacts. On a conceptual level, these two models are independent of the currently used device. Instead, available devices and other relevant parts of the context and environment are described by the *environment model*. The environment model provides information about the presence of users and their tasks [9], and their devices as well as devices that are permanently installed in their near surrounding. Software being aware of its context can act depending on the state of the environment [4; 15]. The *user-interface model* deals with everything that is needed to describe the user interface of an application. Typical examples are arrangements of widgets such as windows, menus, scrollbars, and toolbars. The user interface model, however, does *not* describe how these concepts are presented to the user or how the user can control the widgets. These issues are modeled separately by the *interaction model*.

This separation of concerns enables, for instance, the selection of an appropriate user interface and interaction forms for the different devices found in ubiquitous computing, based on the information provided by the environment model. The *same user interface model* can be used with *different interaction models* representing different (device-dependent) interaction forms and modalities. For instance, a form can be visually presented by a projection while keyboard or voice recognition can be used to enter text into this form and eye tracking or hand gestures can control the input focus. This way, multiple interaction modalities can be combined. Other examples of applying the separation of concerns is using different user interfaces for the same application model, or different application models for the same data model, depending on the current task and context. This helps meeting the requirement of enabling appropriate interaction in ubiquitous computing environments.

The Coupling and Sharing Dimension. Whenever multiple devices are involved in a software system, the question arises, which parts of the system should be tightly coupled, loosely coupled, or independently used. Tight coupling requires that all models representing a software concern are shared and the same values can be modified simultaneously. This is not necessary if participants work completely independent. When working loosely coupled, every user has a set of shared values only modified by him or her that can be remotely accessed in order to provide awareness. These coupling aspects have to be analyzed under the perspective of each concern and it has to be decided which parts of the application have to be shared.

This model is now used to analyze sharing in "traditional" CSCW, and how it is extended by the ubiquitous computing perspective.

2.2   Sharing in "Traditional" CSCW

The traditional focus of CSCW is on sharing the data, application, and user interface models. One can build upon the *shared data model* for cooperative data editing.

The *shared application model* provides the basis to give activity awareness and to control the degree of coupling [16].

Similarly, a *shared user interface model* can be used to implement a tightly-coupled user interface that enforces the same scroll bar position for all users, but also to provide awareness information about other users' individual scroll bar positions [8]. Again, in the first case, a single shared value is used for all users' scroll bar positions, in the second, each user has a separate value that is shared in order to provide awareness [16].

A *shared interaction model* in traditional CSCW is often referred to as application sharing, such as Microsoft Netmeeting. This means that all participants have exactly the same view, while (in the case of Netmeeting) only one can control the application.

Finally, most groupware systems have only a limited view on their *environment* e.g. a list of participants or the network address of their computers.

2.3   Sharing in the Context of UbiComp

In addition to what has been described so far, ubiquitous computing brings in new aspects of sharing. In fact, there are new ways of sharing the user interface and interaction models, and it becomes especially relevant to share the model of the environment.

Shared User Interface. As mentioned in the usage scenario, it is often desirable to distribute the user interface among several devices, which is called *cross-device* or *multi-machine user interface* [11]. There are many examples in literature where a PDA-like device is used concurrently with a digital whiteboard, a table, or PC [6; 7; 11; 12; 14]. A large display is used for presentation to the group, while a personal device can be used to provide additional personal information or to control the shared material simultaneously (see figure 1a–b).

Another application of a shared user interface model is devices that are (statically or dynamically) composed from multiple computers. The ConnecTables [19] are small mobile interactive tables that dynamically form a homogeneous tabletop surface that shows a shared user interface when placed next to each other.

In general, if the user interface model is shared, interaction devices that are present in the environment can be dynamically employed to extend the interaction capabilities of a mobile device [13].

Shared Interaction Devices. Another often described UbiComp scenario is *disaggregated computing* [17]: interaction devices are no longer connected to a single computer, but can be flexibly combined to route input and output data among available devices. For instance, a keyboard can be used to input text in the personal laptop, a nearby PDA, or a large display mounted at a wall. In figure 1, the user sitting in the chair on the right (figure 1b) could enter information at the interactive wall (figure 1a) or at the interactive table (figure 1c). In these cases, the interaction model is shared.

The purpose of a shared *user interface model* is to enable accessing the same user interface from different interaction devices. In contrast, a shared *interaction model* allows routing the input events from an interaction device to an arbitrary computer, and routing the generated presentation from a computer to an arbitrary output device. Here, from a user perspective the interaction *devices* are shared. Examples are Mouse Anywhere from the Microsoft EasyLiving project [3] and PointRight in iROS [10].

Another form of shared interaction is Single Display Groupware (SDG) [18]. Here, the same output device is shared among cooperating users. One of the first SDG applications was MMM (Multi-Device, Multi-User, Multi-Editor) [2], which allowed the use of up to three mice concurrently to edit rectangles and text. While these kinds of systems use mice or pens connected to a PC, the Pebbles project explored how PDAs can be used to provide concurrent input to a shared PC [11]. They have in common that a *single output* device (here: a display) is shared by users having *multiple input* devices.

Shared Environment. The devices within a ubiquitous computing environment are not treated in isolation; instead, they are often perceived within the context of their environment.

For ubiquitous computing to be successful, all users and devices that are at the same place for a common purpose must be perceived as *sharing* the same environment, and not as an arbitrary collection that is not aware of its context. To meet the user's intuitive view on the devices (and applications) within an environment as a consistent whole, software *developers* must create applications that also share a common "understanding" of the environment. For instance, when the software realizes that a public display is available in a meeting room, it can be used as default for opening shared documents, as described in the usage scenario; a personal device would be the default for private information.

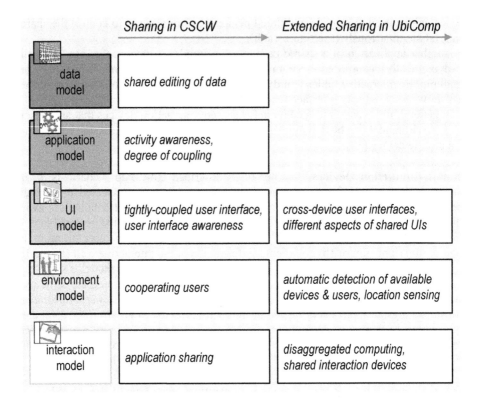

Fig. 3. Ubiquitous computing extends the CSCW view on sharing

The analysis presented in this section shows that for ubiquitous computing the concept of *sharing*—as known from CSCW—has to be extended to function as a guiding principle for application design. Figure 3 summarizes the aspects of sharing in CSCW and ubiquitous computing discussed here.

3   Conclusions and Future Work

When designing a system that supports cooperation in ubiquitous computing, it is especially important to emphasize on the concept of sharing instead of distribution. We extended the traditional CSCW view on sharing with special regard to shared user interfaces, shared interaction devices, and shared environments. We introduced five basic models for data, application, user interface, interaction and environment that utilize each other but take care about different concerns of the software. For software design, each of these concerns has to be examined for issues on coupling, and it has to be decided which devices it has to support.

The extended view on sharing has implications for the design of software, both on the user and on the technical level. Sticking tightly to the five concerns on both levels will result in a straightforward mapping of concepts at the user level to the software design.

At the user level, sharing is a natural way to represent the users' perception of the concerns. When designing user experiences, software systems have to consider the users' shared view. This also implies that imposing unintuitive and (from a users' point of view) unnecessary tasks on him will lead to low acceptance rates. Collaborating users have a natural common understanding of their task and its relevant context. Especially co-located people normally have a quite similar idea about their environment and the relationship of objects such as devices and documents within. Participants are used to employ multiple devices to complete their task. They automatically choose the device that seems most appropriate. If the application shares the view on the environment, the software can often guess the device that can best support the current task.

Using sharing in the context of ubiquitous computing introduces new requirements for sharing toolkits. Besides allowing one participant to use many devices, the system must also support multiple people sharing the same device, as explored in single display groupware, as well as transitions in between. The same concepts of sharing will have to be implemented on various devices. An optimal division between generic functionality and device-dependent implementations is still an open research question. A further issue is how to augment well known concurrency control mechanisms with different format conversions. Additionally, building a sufficient environment model is essential for nearly all concerns, especially when trying to provide appropriate support for the available devices.

References

1. Bair, J. H. Supporting cooperative work with computers: Addressing meeting mania. In *Proceedings of the 34th IEEE Computer Society International Conference–CompCon Spring*, pp. 208–217, San Francisco, Feb. 27–Mar. 3 1989.
2. Bier, E. A. and Freeman, S. MMM: A User Interface Architecture for Shared Editors on a Single Screen. In *Proceedings of ACM SIGGRAPH Symposium on User Interface Software and Technology (UIST'91)*, pp. 79–86. ACM Press, New York, NY, 1991.
3. Brummit, B., Meyers, B., Krumm, J., Kern, A., and Shafer, S. Easyliving: Technologies for Intelligent Environments. In *Proceedings of the 2nd International Symposium on Handheld and Ubiquitous Computing (HUC'00)*, vol. 1927, no. 1927 in Lecture Notes in Computer Science, pp. 12–29, Bristol, UK, Sep. 25–27 2000. Springer, Heidelberg, New York.
4. Dey, A. K. Providing Architectural Support for Building Context-Aware Applications. Ph.D. thesis, Georgia Institute of Technology, Nov. 2000.
5. Ellis, C. A., Gibbs, S. J., and Rein, G. Groupware: some issues and experiences. *Communications of the ACM*, 34(1):39–58, 1991. http://doi.acm.org/10.1145/99977.99987.
6. Fox, A., Johanson, B., Hanrahan, P., and Winograd, T. Integrating Information Appliances into an Interactive Workspace. *IEEE CG&A*, 20(3):54–65, May/June 2000. http://graphics.stanford.edu/projects/iwork/papers/ieee-pda00/.
7. Greenberg, S., Boyle, M., and LaBerge, J. PDAs and Shared Public Devices: Making Personal Information Public, and Public Information Personal. *Personal Technologies*, 3(1):54–64, March 1999.
8. Gutwin, C., Roseman, M., and Greenberg, S. A Usability Study of Awareness Widgets in a Shared Workspace Groupware System. In *Proceedings of the ACM 1996 Conference on Computer Supported Cooperative Work (CSCW'96)*, pp. 258–267, Boston, Mass., USA, November 16–20 1996. ACM Press, New York, NY.

9. Gutwin, C. and Greenberg, S. Design for Individuals, Design for Groups: Tradeoffs between power and workspace awareness. In *Proceedings of the ACM 1998 conference on Computer supported cooperative work*, pp. 207–216, Seattle, Washington, United States, 1998. ACM Press. http://doi.acm.org/10.1145/289444.289495.

10. Johanson, B., Hutchins, G., Winograd, T., and Stone, M. PointRight: Experience with Flexible Input Redirection in Interactive Workspaces. In *Proceedings of the 15th annual ACM symposium on User interface software and technology (UIST'02)*, vol. 4, no. 2 in CHI Letters, pp. 227–234, Paris, France, Oct 27–30 2002. ACM Press, New York, NY. http://graphics.stanford.edu/papers/pointright-uist2002/.

11. Myers, B. A. Using Handhelds and PCs Together. *Communications of the ACM*, 44(11):34–41, Nov. 2001.

12. Myers, B. A., Malkin, R., Bett, M., Waibel, A., Bostwick, B., Miller, R. C., Yang, J., Denecke, M., Seemann, E., Zhu, J., Peck, C. H., Kong, D., Nichols, J., and Scherlis, B. Flexi-modal and Multi-Machine User Interfaces. In *IEEE Fourth International Conference on Multimodal Interfaces*, pp. 343–348, Pittsburgh, PA, October 14–16 2002. IEEE CS Press. http://www.cs.cmu.edu/~cpof/papers/cpoficmi02.pdf.

13. Pierce, J. S. and Mahaney, H. Opportunistic Annexing for Handheld Devices: Opportunities and Challenges. Paper presented at the Human Computer Interaction Consortium 2004 Winter Workshop (HCIC'04), Feb. 4–8 2004. http://www.cc.gatech.edu/projects/PIE/pubs/.

14. Rekimoto, J. A Multiple Device Approach for Supporting Whiteboard-based Interactions. In *Proceedings of the ACM Conference on Human Factors in Computing Systems (CHI'98)*, pp. 344–351. ACM Press, New York, NY, 1998.

15. Schmidt, A., Beigl, M., and Gellersen, H. There is more to Context than Location. *Computer & Graphics*, 23(6):893–902, Dec. 1999. http://www.elsevier.com.

16. Schuckmann, C., Schümmer, J., and Seitz, P. Modeling Collaboration using Shared Objects. In *Proceedings of International ACM SIGGROUP Conference on Supporting Group Work (GROUP'99)*, pp. 189–198, Phoenix, Arizona, USA, November 14–17 1999. ACM Press, New York, NY. http://www.opencoast.org.

17. Shafer, S. A. N. Ubiquitous Computing and the EasyLiving Project. 40th Anniversary Symposium, Osaka Electro-Communications University, Nov. 2001. http://www.research.microsoft.com/easyliving/.

18. Stewart, J., Bederson, B. B., and Druin, A. Single Display Groupware: A Model for Co-present Collaboration. In *Proceeding of the CHI 99 conference on Human factors in computing systems (CHI'99)*, pp. 286–293. ACM Press, New York, NY, 1999. http://www.cs.umd.edu/hcil.

19. Tandler, P., Prante, T., Müller-Tomfelde, C., Streitz, N., and Steinmetz, R. ConnecTables: Dynamic Coupling of Displays for the Flexible Creation of Shared Workspaces. In *Proceedings of 14th Annual ACM Symposium on User Interface and Software Technology (UIST'01)*, vol. 3, no. 2 in CHI Letters, pp. 11–20, Orlando, Florida, USA, Nov. 11–14 2001. ACM Press, New York, NY. http://ipsi.fraunhofer.de/ambiente/publications/.

20. Tandler, P. The BEACH Application Model and Software Framework for Synchronous Collaboration in Ubiquitous Computing Environments. *Journal of Systems & Software (JSS) Special issue on Ubiquitous Computing*, 69(3):267–296, Jan 2004. http://ipsi.fraunhofer.de/ambiente/publications/, http://authors.elsevier.com/sd/article/S0164121203000554.

21. Weiser, M. Some Computer Science Issues in Ubiquitous Computing. *Communications of the ACM*, 36(7):75–84, 1993.

A Metaphor and User Interface for Managing Access Permissions in Shared Workspace Systems

Till Schümmer, Jörg M. Haake, and Anja Haake

FernUniversität in Hagen, Computer Science VI
Informatikzentrum, Universitätsstr. 1
D-58084 Hagen, Germany
joerg.haake@fernuni-hagen.de

Abstract. This paper presents an intuitive metaphor and user interface for managing access permissions of a shared workspace. It is based on a combination of the room and key metaphor, which represent shared workspaces and the users' access permissions. Keys and rooms can be used for different modes of group formation. We report on experiences with the metaphors in the context of the collaborative learning environment CURE.

Keywords: Shared workspaces, virtual environments, CSCW, access control, group formation

1 Introduction

Collaboration among distributed team members is often supported by shared workspaces. Within the shared workspace, users interact with each other and with shared artifacts. Current shared workspace systems such as BSCW [251] allow users to create a shared workspace and to invite other users into the workspace, thereby creating distributed teams anchored in the workspace. This works well in situations that do not require dynamic adaptation. But in other situations such as project work in collaborative learning, students are required to form, structure, and adapt their own teams and workspaces. Emerging forms of group formation in particular pose the problem of adapting access permissions to shared spaces with changing membership. Already in 1991, Ellis, Gibbs and Rein [4] argued for groupware: "Since access information changes frequently, there must be lightweight access control mechanisms that allow end-users to easily specify changes".

In shared workspace systems, such as BSCW [1], access control is managed by granting file or workspace permissions to individual users or groups of users. Internally, these systems use access control lists or role-based access control lists, which are presented directly in the user interface. According to our experience from using BSCW for supporting group work in distributed project settings at the FernUniversität in Hagen, this approach suffers from two limitations: Firstly, lay users find the functionality too difficult to understand and therefore reject to use it – which implies that teachers have to perform the role of workspace administrators. Secondly, all assign-

M. Hemmje et al. (Eds.): E.J. Neuhold Festschrift, LNCS 3379, pp. 251–260, 2005.
© Springer-Verlag Berlin Heidelberg 2005

ments of access permissions require explicit transfer of access permissions from the workspace owner to individual users. This paradigm is often inappropriate, e.g. when students are supposed to assign themselves to team workspaces. Here, the workspace owner should be able to specify a number of open slots with special access permissions for users of the workspace. Users taking an empty slot should get the appropriate access permissions.

Much research has focused on making access control more understandable and usable for end users. A good overview on existing approaches for access control in collaborative environments has been provided by Bullock and Benford [2]. Haake et al. [6] review the state of the art in group formation and access control in shared workspace systems concluding that in today's shared workspace systems access rights management by end-users is insufficiently supported, either due to too complex role-models, access control parameters and user interfaces that end-users cannot easily understand, or due to insufficient functionality.

We propose to combine the room and the key metaphor to manage access permissions. Rooms represent shared workspaces. Only users having a key for a room may enter it. Rooms and keys, human artifacts known from real world situations, are represented at the user interface. The human computer interaction required to manage access permissions in shared workspace systems thus consists of manipulating rooms and keys, i.e. virtual representations of artifacts rather than abstract concepts such as roles [1], boundaries [2], or access matrixes [12].

By assigning room keys to users, the functionality of traditional shared workspace systems can be achieved. But also new ways of group formation in a shared workspace system become possible: by putting keys on the door of a room, users can take a room key from it. If no keys are available, users may contact the room owner and ask for one.

We implemented the proposed metaphors in CURE [3], a web-based system supporting distributed collaborative learning and working. The system is currently being used by students and teachers in three departments of the university. Our experiences show that distributed groups of students are able to create new rooms and to define and tailor the access permissions of their shared workspaces using keys. While other papers on CURE [5, 6] reported about tailoring of room structures and content, this paper focuses on managing access permissions. The remainder of this paper is organized as follows: The next section presents the combined room and key metaphor and the corresponding user interface. We then report about our usage experiences followed by a comparison to related work. Finally, we summarize our contribution.

2   Managing Access Permissions in CURE

In this section, we present a combination of two metaphors and a corresponding user interface that support end-users in managing access permissions for their shared workspaces. We begin with the room metaphor and then extend it with the virtual key metaphor. Then, we discuss the user interface and show how end-users are supposed to use it by manipulating the shared artifacts rooms and keys.

2.1   Rooms as Metaphoric Places for Interaction

Room metaphors [5, 11] have been widely used to structure collaboration. The room metaphor uses the room as the representation of a virtual place for collaboration. Rooms can contain documents and participants. Users, who are in the same room at the same time, can communicate by means of a communication channel that is automatically established between all users in the room. They can also perceive all documents that are in the room. Changes of these documents are visible to all members in the room.

Users can enter a room, whereby they can now access the room's communication channel and may participate in collaborative activities. Users can also add documents or artifacts to rooms. This means that, e.g., if they add a new document, this is from then on accessible by all other users in the room. When users leave the room, the content stays there to allow users to come back later and continue their work on the room's documents.

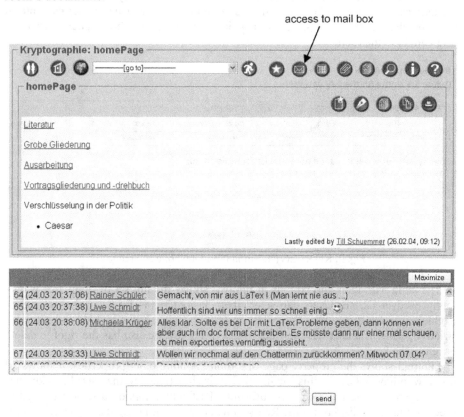

Fig. 1. A room in CURE

Figure 1 shows a typical room in CURE. It contains documents (in the example, a user reads the document "homePage" in the room "Kryptographie") that can be edited by those users, who have sufficient edit rights. It provides two room-based communication channels: a mail box and a chat. Users can use the room-based e-mail to send a mail to the room. Users of the room (with communication rights) will receive this message.

By providing a plenary room, sharing and communication in a whole class or organization can be supported. By creating new rooms for sub groups and connecting those to the classes' or organization's room, work and collaboration can be flexibly structured. However, in order to support evolving structures of group work, access permissions for rooms must be managed by the users themselves.

2.2   The Metaphor of Virtual Keys

We apply the metaphor of virtual keys to the metaphor of rooms in order to provide access control to rooms. Each room is equipped with a lock, and users need a key matching this lock in order to get access to this room. Furthermore, the key represents not only the permission to enter a room but also specifies what the key holder can do in the room. We identified three different classes of rights: key-rights defining what the user can do with the key, room-rights defining whether or not a user can enter a room or change the room structure, and interaction-rights, which specify what the user can do in the room.

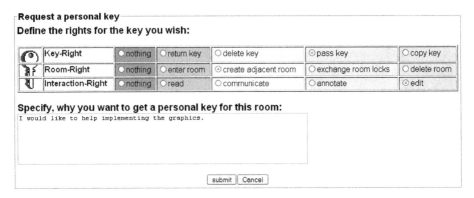

Fig. 2. Key-rights (shown in the context of a key request)

The table with the radio buttons in figure 2 shows the full set of rights that is currently used in CURE. Users can select their desired rights for each class of rights. Rights are ordered in a way that a less restrictive right always includes all more restrictive rights. If a user has the right to pass on a key, he also has the right to delete or return the key.

Figure 3 shows the property page of a room. Among other properties, it shows all users, who have a key for this room. The key is shown next to the user. Each key has three segments, one for each class of rights. Different colors on a scale from red to green are used to display rights. Red segments represent no rights, while green segments represent the full right. The user "Lukosch" has for instance a key with a yellow part for the key-rights (delete the key), an orange part for the room rights (enter the room) and a green part for the interaction rights (edit pages).

To support public areas, which can be entered by all users, so-called public rooms are equipped with a default-key specifying the default-rights for all users.

Fig. 3. Properties of a room in CURE

2.3 Managing Access Permissions Using Virtual Keys

In a shared workspace system using rooms and keys, users enter the system via a public entry hall (indicated by the first entry in the room directory shown in figure 4). From there, they can either navigate to accessible rooms (i.e., other public rooms or rooms for which they hold a key) or create a new room. If a new room is created, the user automatically becomes the room owner and the holder of the master key (cf. the green key behind the room "Entwicklungsraum" in fig. 4). This key permits every possible operation on its room. The room owner can then create copies of the master key with potentially restricted access permissions and make them available to other users.

Two distribution schemes are supported: Firstly, the room owner may explicitly assign keys to registered users. Secondly, the owner may put keys on the door of the room. In addition, users may actively ask room owners for a key to gain access to a room. These different uses of replicable keys allow different modes of group formation, e.g. by invitation, by free enrollment (placing the keys on the room's door), or by confirmed enrollment (to request a key from the owner by using a door knocker, symbolized by a yellow ring in figure 4).

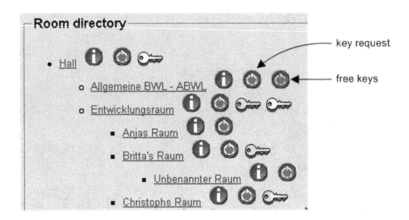

Fig. 4. A user's overview of existing rooms

For groups with invitations, the creator of the room can determine the group's members. In this case, she invites other users by creating copies of the replicable key and passing one to each user, who should be in the group.

In case of a group with free enrollment, the creator of the room creates a set of copies of her key (which are usually copy protected) and puts them on the room's door (outside the restricted area). These free keys are visualized as green door knockers in fig. 4 (e.g. behind the room "Allgemeine BWL – ABWL"). If a user wants to join the group, he clicks on the green door knocker, grabs a key from the door, and enters the room. The creator of the room can control the group's size by putting only a limited number of keys on the door. One example for this use of keys could be a virtual seminar: The teacher creates a public lobby for the seminar and a participant's room with as many keys, as the seminar should have participants. Students enroll in a seminar by taking one of these keys. To ensure that enrollment takes place in a given time frame, the teacher will remove the keys from the door when enrollment ends.

In case, where the enrollment in the group has to be confirmed by the room owner, a user can join the group by knocking on the room (clicking on a yellow door knocker in figure 4 – e.g. behind the room "Anjas Raum"). The user can then specify the desired rights as shown in fig. 2 and explain why he should be part of the group. By submitting the form, the room owner will be notified by e-mail and can create an appropriate personal key for the user.

Sometimes, a user may want to leave a group. In case of groups with free enrollments, he can do so by putting his key back on the door. This clears his place in the group for another user. In other groups, he can return the key to the room owner (or delete it, if he has sufficient key-rights).

3   Experiences

We used the system in three different courses in the winter term 2003/04: a virtual seminar in psychology, a one term project-based course in computer science and tutor-guided learning groups in mathematics. For these courses, the teachers provided an initial learning environment (a set of rooms) and managed the formation of the groups.

In addition to these settings, all students of the university could use the system in the context of other courses. Examples of groups that formed on their own are study groups for business administration or discussion groups for university politics. These groups did not receive any administrative help from the system administrators.

In this paper, we report about a study of the system's use during the first 120 days. All user actions were logged in a log file. The interpretation of the log files are backed by the results of questionnaires answered by 28 computer science students and interviewing the teachers of the virtual seminar in psychology.

We counted a total of 290 users. Since the basic system architecture is a web application, we can restore the full interaction from the log files, which means that the files contain information for each web request (each click) of the users. Our main objective was that lay users can control and tailor access permissions to their shared workspaces. We will therefore report on an analysis of the log files regarding activities that were concerned with room and key management. We will compare the amount of activities done by employees of our university (who were trained to use the system) with those performed by lay users (mainly students) regarding the use of CURE.

Before groups can form in CURE, they have to create a room. At the end of the 120 days, the system had 91 rooms. These rooms have been in use for an average period of 48 days. In total, the users created 257 rooms. The difference between created and deleted rooms indicates that the rooms were used for short term collaboration (and were removed after the group finished their work). 27 rooms were created by lay people. 19 of them are still in use, the other eight rooms were removed by the lay people again. We conclude that teachers and students were able to create rooms and adopt the room structure to their evolving needs.

Users generated 1127 keys. 590 of these were free keys that were attached to the room. This method of key distribution was popular for situations, where access should not be limited, but the place owner wanted to stay aware of the group that could access the place. Free keys were taken by the users 381 times. 105 keys were returned after interacting in the room. Thus, we can conclude that users changed their group membership over time.

The other way of distributing keys was to send them directly to the users. This was done 537 times. Although this number is close to the number of free keys, one has to distinguish two different cases: keys assigned to users without their requests, and keys requested by users. The first case reflects a situation, where the creator of a room knows the group of people, who should collaborate in the room. 429 keys were distributed in this way. The second case reflects a situation, where a user wants to join an existing group. 150 requests for keys were sent by users, most of them (136) by lay people. 108 requests were answered positively. 88 key requests had to be answered by lay people. The average time from a key request to the first use of a key by the requesting user was 12 hours. Most requests were answered below the average time (median time 8.25 minutes). The above numbers indicate that the users were able to fulfil the task of room administration. They decided which rights they granted to other users and created new keys for them. Most administrative tasks were completed in a short time. From the log, we can also see that users used their keys to work in the desired rooms.

Finally, we could observe that additional keys were often created several days after the room creation and that keys were created while group work had already started. This highlights the need for key distribution at run time.

4   Comparison with Related Work

While other access control models for shared workspace systems are based on rather abstract concepts such as roles (e.g. in BSCW [1]), boundaries (e.g. SPACE [2]), or access matrixes (e.g. [11]), our approach for managing access permissions in shared workspace systems is based on human artifact interaction: The shared workspace represented as a room is equipped with a lock and users need a key matching this lock in order to get access to this room. Thus, using the room and virtual key metaphors, users can manage access control to their workspaces easily and in a more flexible manner.

Equipping an object with a lock and providing accessing subjects (i.e. users) with keys is close to the proposal of [15]. While [15] uses a single-key-lock approach for implementation, we use keys and locks as metaphoric complements of a room-based groupware system. Consequently, in our model a room has a single lock, but a user may possess more than one key for that lock.

Looking at the classic access matrix of Lampson [10], which has been extended by Shen & Dewan [12] for groupware, protected objects are rooms, subsuming the protection of all documents contained in the room, and access requesting subjects are individual users. The matrix' cells are filled up with keys, specifying the access control a single user has on a certain room.

Virtual keys correspond to capabilities and key-rights to capability-rights in HYDRA [16]. HYDRA has no notion of object ownership. Instead, they allow capabilities for protected objects to be passed to others, by associating a capability not only with the rights to the referenced object but also with a special copy right to the capability itself. Similarly, keys may be passed to other subjects and are not only associated with the rights to the referenced object but also with a special copy right to the key itself (cf. Key-Right "copy key" in Figure 2).

To keep the model simple and understandable for non-expert computer users, we do not provide inheritance among rights nor negative rights [12]. We found conflict resolution [12] being too difficult to understand for non-expert users, and role models [1] too difficult to use. Simply, the set of rights a given user possesses on all the objects in a room is determined by the union of all keys the user is holding for that particular room.

Our model supports several means for group formation including invitation, free enrollment, and confirmed enrollment. In particular, the ability to request a key for a room via the yellow door knocker is provided for every room. This is a solution for uno-tempore access control [13], i.e. specification of access rights at the moment of the access. Using the yellow door knocker for a key request results in access control resolution via *negotiation* [14]: Initially a semi-structured message (i.e. structured specification of requested room rights and unstructured request justification, cf. Figure 2) is sent to the room owner. Using the communication channels provided by the workspace system, key distribution may be further discussed among the users.

5   Conclusions

In this paper, we combined the room and the key metaphor to enable end users to manage access permissions in shared workspace systems. We have shown how keys can be used to grant and transfer access rights. Furthermore, we also discussed the role of keys in the context of group formation. The metaphors have been implemented in the collaborative learning environment CURE. Logs from 120 days of system usage were analysed to see how the metaphors are used.

In summary, our observations indicate success of the combination of the key- and room-metaphor to manage access permissions in shared workspaces. This approach supports structuring collaboration in terms of (1) usage of the system by lay users, (2) change of room and group membership over time, and (3) creation of new rooms and teams over time (i.e. flexible group formation).

In CURE, teachers and students managed their collaboration spaces and created new room structures for changing group constellations, enabling them to interact flexibly with each other and with shared artefacts. Collaboration proceeds through communication and cooperation among humans, which is mediated by shared artefacts (rooms with communication channels, documents, and keys). Group formation and access management is supported through interaction with the key and room artefacts.

Acknowledgements

We thank Britta Landgraf and Mohamed Bourimi, who participated in the design and implementation of CURE.

References

1. Appelt, W., Mambrey, P.: "Experiences with the BSCW Shared Workspace System as the Backbone of a Virtual Learning Environment for Students", Proc. of ED-MEDIA99, bscw.gmd.de/Papers/EDMEDIA99/, 1999.
2. Bullock, A., Benford, S.: "An access control framework for multi-user collaborative environments", Proc. Of GROUP'99, Phoenix Arizona, 1999, pp. 140-149.
3. CURE, http://cure.pi6.fernuni-hagen.de, accessed 2003.
4. Ellis, C.A., Gibbs, S.J., and Rein, G.L.: Groupware: Some issues and experiences, CACM, 34, 1, pp.38-58, Jan. 1991
5. Greenberg, S., Roseman, M.: "Using a Room Metaphor to Ease Transitions in Groupware", in Ackermann, M., Pipek, V., Wulf, V. (Eds.): "Beyond Knowledge Management: Sharing Expertise", MIT Press: Cambridge, MA, 2002.

6. Haake, J.M., Haake, A., Schümmer, T., Bourimi, M., Landgraf, B.: End-User Controlled Group Formation and Access Rights Management in a Shared Workspace System. Proc. of ACM CSCW'04, Chicago, November 7-9, 2004. ACM Press. in press.

7. Haake, J. M., Schümmer, T., Haake, A., Bourimi, M., Landgraf, B.: "Two-level tailoring support for CSCL Groupware: Design, Implementation, and Use." Proceedings of the 9th International Workshop (CRIWG2003), LNCS 2440, Springer: Heidelberg, 2003, pp. 74-82.

8. Haake, J.M., Schümmer, T., Haake, A., Bourimi, M., Landgraf, B.: "Supporting flexible collaborative distance learning in the CURE platform." Proc. of HICSS-37, January 5-8, 2004. IEEE Press.

9. Hess, E.: "Yib's Guide to Mooing: Getting the Most from Virtual Communities on the Internet", Trafford Publishing, http://yibco.com/ygm/ygm/, 2003.

10. Lampson, B.: Protection, in: ACM Operation Systems Review, Vol. 8, 1974, pp. 18 – 24.

11. Schümmer, T.: "Room" Pattern, CSCW2002 workshop on Socio-Technical Pattern Languages, http://www.groupware-patterns.org/room, 2002.

12. Shen, H. and Dewan, P.: Access Control for Collaborative Environments, In *Proc. of the ACM CSCW 92*, ACM Press, New York, 1992, pp. 51 – 58.

13. Stevens, G. and Wulf, V.: A New Dimension in Access Control: Studying Maintenance Engineering across Organizational Boundaries, In *Proc. of the ACM CSCW 02*, New Orleans, 2002, pp. 196 – 205.

14. Stiemerling, O. and Wulf, V.: Beyond 'Yes or No' – Extending Access Control in Groupware with Awareness and Negotiation; In *Group Decision and Negotiation*; Vol. 9, 2000, pp. 221-235.

15. Wu, M. and Hwang,T., Access Control with Single-Key-Lock, in IEEE Transactions on Software Engineering, Vol. SE-10, No. 2, March 1984, pp. 185-191.

16. Wulf, W., Cohen, E., Corwin, W., Jones, A., Levin, R., Pierson, C. and Pollack, F.: HYDRA: The Kernel of a Multiprocessor Operating System. CACM, 17(6), June 1974.

Ambient Intelligence:
Towards Smart Appliance Ensembles*

José L. Encarnação and Thomas Kirste

Fraunhofer Institute for Computer Graphics, Fraunhoferstraße 5, 64283 Darmstadt, Germany
jle@igd.fraunhofer.de, tkirste@igd.fraunhofer.de

Abstract. The vision of Ambient Intelligence is based on the ubiquity of information technology, the presence of computation, communication, and sensorial capabilities in an unlimited abundance of everyday appliances and environments. Today's experimental smart environments are carefully designed by hand, but future ambient intelligent infrastructures must be able to configure themselves from the available components in order to be effective in the real world.

We argue that enabling an ensemble of devices to spontaneously act and cooperate coherently requires software technologies that support self-organization. We discuss the central issues pertaining to the self-organization of interactive appliance ensembles and outline potential solution paradigms: Goal-based interaction and distributed event processing pipelines.

1 Introduction

The vision of Ambient Intelligence (AmI) [1,3,11] is based on the ubiquity of information technology, the presence of computation, communication, and sensorial capabilities in an unlimited abundance of everyday appliances and environments.

"Ambient Intelligence", a term coined by the European Commission's Information Technologies Advisory Group (ISTAG) and Philips, is the vision of a world, in which we are surrounded by smart, intuitively operated devices that help us to organize, structure, and master our everyday life. The notion "Ambient Intelligence" specifically characterizes a new paradigm for the interaction between a person and his everyday environment: Ambient Intelligence enables this environment to become aware of the human that interacts with it, his goals and needs. So it is possible to assist the human proactively in performing his activities and reaching his goals.—If my car stereo tunes in to exactly the station I just listened to at the breakfast table, then this is a simple example for such an aware, pro-active environment; just as the mobile phone that automatically redirects calls to my voice mail in case I am in a meeting, or the bathroom mirror that reminds me of taking my medications.

Hitherto, it is the user's responsibility to manage his personal environment, to operate and control the various appliances and devices available for his support. But, the more technology is available and the more options there are, the greater is the challenge to master your everyday environment, the challenge not to get lost in an abundance of

---

* This work has been partially supported by the German Federal Ministry of Education and Research under the grant signature BMB-F No. FKZ 01 ISC 27A.

M. Hemmje et al. (Eds.): E.J. Neuhold Festschrift, LNCS 3379, pp. 261–270, 2005.

Fig. 1. Environments we'd like to be smart: Conference rooms (left) and living rooms (right)

possibilities. Failing to address this challenge adequately simply results in technology becoming inoperable, effectively useless. Through Ambient Intelligence, the environment gains the capability to take over this mechanic and monotonous control task from the user and manage appliance activities on his behalf. By this, the environment's full assistive potential can be mobilized for the user, tailored to his individual goals and needs.

Technical foundation of Ambient Intelligence is *Ubiquitous* resp. *Pervasive Computing*: the diffusion of information technology into all appliances and objects of the everyday life, based on miniaturized and low cost hardware. In the near future, a multitude of such "information appliances" and "smart artifacts" will populate everyone's personal environment. In order to make the vision of Ambient Intelligence come true, a coherent teamwork between the environment's appliances has to be established that enables a co-operative, proactive support of the user. Wireless ad-hoc networking and embedded sensors provide the basis for coherent and coordinated action of an appliance ensemble with respect to the current situation. By enabling multi-modal interaction— such as speech and gestures—an intuitive interaction becomes possible. On top of this, strategies, models, and technologies for the self-organization of appliance ensembles are required that allow an adaptation to the user's needs and desires.

Clearly, Ambient Intelligence covers more aspects then just supporting the interaction of a human being with its environment. In general, any "active" entity engaging in situated behavior can benefit from a responsive environment, which provides smart assistance for this behavior – this holds for human beings, for livestock, for robots, as well as for smart goods (in logistics and smart factory applications). However, within the scope of this paper, we will concentrate on a specific sub-area of Ambient Intelligence: the software infrastructure needed for supporting user interaction with smart environments.

2   A Scenario ...

A rather popular scenario illustrating this application area is the *smart conference room* (or *smart living room*, for consumer-oriented projects, see Figure 1) that automatically

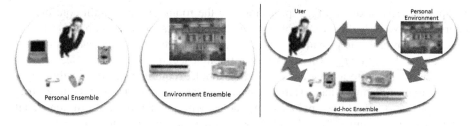

Fig. 2. Appliance Ensembles: physical constituents (left), and compound ad-hoc ensemble (right)

adapts to the activities of its current occupants (cf. e.g. [2,5,9,12]). Such a room might, for instance, automatically switch the projector to the current lecturer's presentation as she approaches the speaker's desk[1], and subdue the room lights—turning them up again for the discussion. Of course, we expect the environment to automatically fetch the presentation from the lecturer's notebook.

Such a scenario doesn't sound too difficult, it can readily be constructed from common hardware available today, and, using pressure sensors and RFID tagging, doesn't even require expensive cameras and difficult image analysis to detect who is currently at the speaker's desk. Setting up the application software for this scenario that drives the environment's devices in response to sensor signals doesn't present a major hurdle either. So it seems as if Ambient Intelligence is rather well understood, as far as information technology is concerned. Details like image and speech recognition, as well as natural dialogues, of course need further research, but building smart environments from components is *technologically* straightforward, once we understand what kind of proactivity users will expect and accept.

3   ... and Its Implications

But only as long as the device ensembles that make up the environment are anticipated by the developers. Today's smart environments in the various research labs are usually built from devices and components whose functionality is known to the developer. So, all possible interactions between devices can be considered in advance and suitable adaptation strategies for coping with changing ensembles can be defined. When looking at the underlying software infrastructure, we see that the interaction between the different devices, the "intelligence", has carefully handcrafted by the software engineers, which have built this scenario. This means: significant (i.e. unforeseen) changes of the ensemble require a manual modification of the smart environment's control application.

This is obviously out of the question for real world applications, where people continuously buy new devices for embellishing their home. And it is a severe cost factor for institutional operators of professional media infrastructures such as conference rooms and smart offices. Things can be even more challenging: imagine a typical ad hoc meeting, where some people meet at a perfectly average room. All attendants bring notebook

---

[1] For the smart living room this reads: "switch the TV set to the user's favorite show, as he takes seat on the sofa."

computers, at least one brings a projector, and the room has some light controls. Of course, all devices will be accessible by wireless networks. So it would be possible for this chance ensemble to provide the same assistance as the deliberate smart conference room above. Enabling *this* kind of Ambient Intelligence, the ability of devices to configure themselves into a coherently acting ensemble, requires more than setting up a control application in advance. Here, we need software infrastructures that allow a true self-organization of ad-hoc appliance ensembles, with the ability to afford non-trivial changes to the ensemble. (See also [13] for a similar viewpoint on this topic.)

Besides providing the middleware facilities for service discovery and communication, such a software infrastructure also has to identify the set of fundamental interfaces that characterize the standard event processing topology to be followed in all possible ensembles. This *standard topology* is the foundation for an appliance to be able to smoothly integrate itself into different ensembles: In a conference room, the user's notebook may automatically connect to a projector and deliver the user's presentation, while it will hook up to the hi-fi system and deliver an MP3 playlist when arriving back home.

When looking at the challenges of self-organization indicated above, we can distinguish two different aspects here:

Architectonic Integration – refers to the integration of the device into the communication patterns of the ensemble. For instance, the attachment of an input device to the ensemble's interaction event bus.

Operational Integration – describes the aspect of making new functionality provided by the device (or emerging from the extended ensemble) available to the user. For instance, if you connect a CD player to an ensemble containing a CD recorder, the capability of "copying" will now emerge in this ensemble.

Clearly, both aspects eventually have to be accounted for by an "Ambient Intelligence Software Architecture". In this paper, we will concentrate on the aspect of architectonic integration.

4   Appliances and Event Processing Pipelines

When developing at a middleware concept, it is important to look at the communication patterns of the objects that are to be supported by this middleware. For smart environments, we need to look at *physical devices*, which have at least *one* connection to the physical environment they are placed in: they observe user input, or they are able to change the environment (e.g. by increasing the light level, by rendering a medium, etc.), or both. When looking at the event processing in such devices, we may observe a specific *event processing pipeline*, as outlined in Figure 3: Devices have a User Interface component that translates physical user interactions to events, the Control Application is responsible for determining the appropriate action to be performed in response to this event, and finally the Actuators are physically executing these actions. It seems reasonable to assume that *all* devices employ a similar event processing pipeline (even if certain stages are implemented trivially, being just a wire connecting the switch to the light bulb).

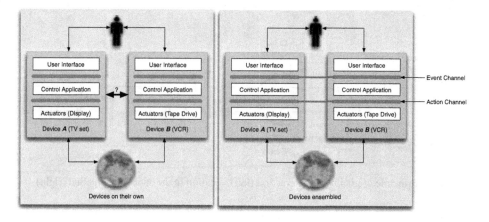

Fig. 3. Devices and Data Flows

It would then be interesting to extend the *interfaces* between the individual process-ing stages across multiple devices, as outlined in the right side of Figure 3. This would allow a dialogue component of one device to see the input events of other devices, or it would enable a particularly clever control application to drive the actuators provided by other devices. By turning the private interfaces between the processing stages in a device into public *channels*, we observe that the event processing pipeline is imple-mented cooperatively by the device ensemble on a per-stage level. Each pipeline stage is realized through the cooperation of the respective local functionalities contributed by the members of the current ensemble.

So, our proposal for solving the challenge of architectonic integration is to provide a middleware concept that provides the essential communication patterns of such data-flow based multi-component architectures. Note that the *channels* outlined in Figure 3 are not the complete story. Much more elaborate data processing pipelines can easily be developed (such as outlined in [7]). Therefore, the point of such a middleware concept is not to fix a *specific* data flow topology, but rather to allow *arbitrary* such topologies to be created ad hoc from the components provided by the devices in an ensemble.

In the next section, we will look one additional channel of particular importance for interaction with ad-hoc ensembles: the *goal* channel.

5   Goal-Based Interaction

When interacting with appliances in everyday settings, we are used to think of interaction in terms of the individual "functions" these devices provide: functions such as "on", "off", "play", "record", etc.. When interacting with devices, we select, parameterize, and then execute functions these devices provide. When these functions are executed, they cause an effect: a broadcast is recorded on videotape, the light is turned brighter, and so on.

Of course, different devices have different functions, similar functions in different devices behave differently, and staying on top of all features is not altogether easy. So,

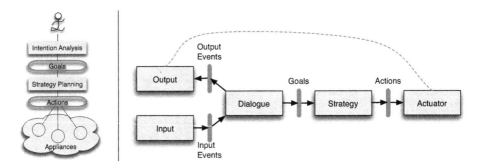

Fig. 4. Principle of goal based interaction (left); location in the appliance pipeline (right)

interaction with devices is usually not intuitive and straightforward—as anybody trying to coax an unfamiliar projector into adjusting his contrast or programming a new VCR will probably acknowledge. Such activities can get very much in the way and interfere massively with user's foreground task, such as giving a lecture or enjoying a show on TV.

The proliferation of computational capabilities and the advent of ad-hoc ensembles will not make things easier. On the contrary: interesting devices in an ad-hoc ensemble may be completely invisible to a user, such as a rear-projection facility in an unfamiliar conference venue. Now: how is a user expected to interact with components and devices he is not even *aware* of (even *if* he knew, how to operate them . . .)?

But then, a user is not really interested in the *function* he needs to execute on a device – it is rather the function's *effect* which is important.

This observation immediately leads to the basic idea of goal-based interaction. Rather than requiring the user to invent a sequence of actions that will produce a desired effect ("goal") based on the given devices and their capabilities, we should allow the user to specify just the goal ("I want to see 'Chinatown' now!") and have the *ensemble* fill in the sequence of actions leading to this goal (Find the media source containing media event "Chinatown". Turn on the TV set. Turn on the media player—*e. g.*, a VCR. Position the media source to the start of the media event. Make sure the air condition is set to a comfortable temperature. Find out the ambient noise level and set the volume to a suitable level. Set ambient light to a suitable brightness. Set the TV input channel to VCR. Start the rendering of the media event.).

Once we abstract from the individual devices and their functions, we arrive at a system-oriented view, where the user perceives the *complete* ad-hoc ensemble as a single system of interoperating components that helps him in reaching his specific goals. Once we abstract from (device) actions and have the system communicate with the user in terms of (user) goals, we also have effectively changed the domain of discourse from the system's view of the world to the user's view of the world.

Goal-based interaction requires two functionalities: *Intention Analysis*, translating user interactions and context information into concrete *goals*, and *Strategy Planning*, which maps goals to (sequences of) device operations (see Figure 4, left). With respect to the information processing inside appliances as outlined in Section 4, these two functionalities can be interpreted as components of the Control Application, resulting in the extended processing pipeline (shown in Figure 4, right).

Note that goal based interaction is able to account for the operational integration, called for in Section 3: Operational integration can now be realized based on an explicit modeling of the semantics of device operations as "precondition/effect" rules, which are defined over a suitable environment ontology. These rules then can be used by a planning system for deriving strategies for reaching user goals, which consider the capabilities of all currently available devices (see [7] for details).

We will now briefly look at the core concepts of a middleware for supporting the dynamic instantiation of the distributed event processing pipeline that coordinates the operation of an appliance ensemble.

6   Towards a Middleware for Self-Organizing Ensembles

From an engineering point of view, it is not sufficient just to enumerate the desired features of a software system – one would also like to know if it is possible to construct a effective *solution* to this feature set, lest we should follow a pipe dream. And we are well aware of the fact that the set of features we have called for in the previous sections is a rather tall order.

Therefore, we have begun investigating potential solutions for software infrastructures supporting self-organizing ensembles. In this section, we outline the basic properties of the SODAPOP infrastructure, a prototype middleware for ambient intelligence environments based on appliance ensembles. SODAPOP[2] development is currently pursued within the scope of the DYNAMITE project—the interested reader is referred to [4,8] for a more detailed account.

The SODAPOP model introduces two fundamental organization levels:

- Coarse-grained self-organization based on a data-flow partitioning, as outlined in Section 4.
- Fine-grained self-organization of functionally *similar* components based on a kind of "Pattern Matching" approach.

Consequently, a SODAPOP system consists of two types of elements:

Channels, which read a single message at time *point* and map them to multiple messages which are delivered to components (conceptually, *without delay*). Channels have no externally accessible memory, may be distributed, and they have to accept *every* message.

Channels provide for *spatial distribution* of a single message to multiple transducers. The specific properties of channels enable an efficient distributed implementation.

Transducers, which read one or more messages during a time *interval* and map them to one (or more) output messages. Transducers are *not* distributed, they may have a memory and they do not have to accept every message.

---

[2] The acronym SODAPOP stands for: **S**elf-**O**rganizing **D**ata-flow **A**rchitectures su**P**porting **O**ntology-based problem decom**P**osition).

SODAPOP provides the capability to create channels—message busses—on demand. On a given SODAPOP channel, messages are delivered between communication partners based on a refined publish / subscribe concept. Every channel may be equipped with an individual strategy for resolving conflicts that may arise between subscribers competing for the same message (the same request).

Once a transducer requests a channel for communication, a check is performed to see whether this channel already exists in the ensemble. If this is the case, the transducer is attached to this channel. Otherwise, a new channel is created. Through this mechanism of dynamically creating and binding to channels, event processing pipelines emerge automatically, as soon as suitable transducers meet.

When subscribing to a channel, a transducer declares the set of messages it is able to process, how well it is suited for processing a certain message, whether it allows other transducers to handle the same message concurrently, and if it is able to cooperate with transducers in processing the message. These aspects are described by the subscribing transducer's *utility*, which encodes the subscribers' handling capabilities for the specific message.

When a channel processes a message, it evaluates the subscribing transducers' handling capabilities and then decides, which transducer(s) will effectively receive the message. Also, the channel may decide to *decompose* the message into multiple (presumably simpler) messages, which can be handled better by the subscribing transducers. (Obviously, the transducers then solve the original message in cooperation.)

How a channel determines the effective message decomposition and how it chooses the set of receiving transducers is defined by the channel's *decomposition strategy*. Both the transducers' utility and the channel's strategy are eventually based on the channel's ontology—the semantics of the messages that are communicated across the channel. A discussion of specific channel strategies for SODAPOP is out of the scope of this paper. It may suffice that promising candidate strategies for the most critical channels—the competition of Dialogue Components for Input Events, the competition of Strategists for goals on the Goal Channel, and the cooperative processing of complex output requests—have been developed and are under investigation (see [6,8] for further detail on SODAPOP).

7   Ensemble Organization by SODAPOP

To summarize, self-organization is achieved by two means in SODAPOP:

1. Identifying the set of channels that completely cover the essential message processing behavior for any appliance in the prospective application domain.
2. Developing suitable channel strategies that effectively provide a distributed coordination mechanism tailored to the functionality, which is anticipated for the listening components.

Then, based on the standard channel set outlined in Figure 4, any device is able to integrate itself autonomously into an ensemble, and any set of devices can spontaneously form an ensemble.

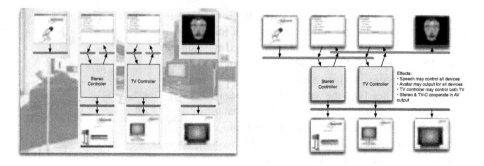

Fig. 5. A simple Smart Living Room Ensemble. Before assembly (left), and after topology formation (right)

Currently, SODAPOP is available as experimental software from the DYNAMITE web site [4]. Formation of an ensemble based on experimental SODAPOP is outlined in Figure 5. On the left, the individual appliances are shown (the green boxes symbolize their hardware packages), where this example contains a stereo and a TV set (both with standard WIMP-type user interfaces), a solitary speech input, a solitary display, and a solitary avatar (possibly on a mobile display). For all devices, their internal transducers and channel segments are shown. On the right, the resulting "ensembled" appliance set is shown, after the matching channel segments have linked up by virtue of SODAPOP. Note how the vertical overall structure at left has been replaced by a horizontal overall structure. Note also, that now stereo and TV both afford speech control, output may be done anthropomorphic through the avatar by all components, and the audio for a movie will be automatically rendered by the stereo system (winning competition with the TV-set's audio system by offering a higher quality).

8 Conclusion

Ambient Intelligence promises to enable ubiquitous computing technology to provide a new level of assistance and support to the user in his daily activities. An ever growing proportion of the physical infrastructure of our everyday life will consist of smart appliances. In our opinion, an effective realization of Ambient Intelligence therefore inherently requires to address the challenge of self-organization for ad-hoc ensembles of smart appliances.

We argue that a possible solution should be based on the fundamental concepts of *goal based interaction* and *self-assembling distributed interaction pipelines*. In guise of the SODAPOP middleware, we have given evidence that such an approach indeed is viable.

We do not expect the solution proposal we have outlined above to be the only possibility. However, we hope that we have convinced the reader that there is *at least one* possible and sufficiently concrete approach towards solving the substantial challenges of dynamic ensembles, which are raised by the proliferation of ubiquitous computing technology.

As stated in the introduction, Ambient Intelligence is in the focus of important European research initiatives such as the Ambient Agoras project coordinated at Fraunhofer IPSI (headed by Prof. Neuhold). As can bee seen from our discussion, software infrastructures for Ambient Intelligence need to cope with complex systems, being able to readjust themselves dynamically to changing circumstances. European research has a strong and successful background in designing and implementing complex systems—Europe therefore is well positioned to response to the challenge of Ambient Intelligence.

So we are looking forward to exciting new research and results in this important area of future ICT infrastructures.

Fig. 7. Ambient displays and beyond: Fraunhofer IPSI Hello.Wall, part of *Ambient Agoras* development [10]

References

1. Aarts E. Ambient Intelligence: A Multimedia Perspective. *IEEE Multimedia*, 11(1):12–19, JanÐMar 2004.
2. Brummitt B, Meyers B, Krumm J, Kern A, Shafer S. Easy Living: Technologies for Intelligent Environments. *Proc. Handheld and Ubiquitous Computing*. Springer, 2000.
3. Ducatel K, Bogdanowicz M, Scapolo F, Leijten J, Burgelman J-C. Scenarios for Ambient Intelligence 2010, ISTAG Report, European Commission, Institute for Prospective Technological Studies. Seville, 2001.
   ftp://ftp.cordis.lu/pub/ist/docs/istagscenarios2010.pdf
4. DynAMITE -Ð Dynamic Adaptive Multimodal IT-Ensembles (Project Web Site)
   http://www.dynamite-project.org
5. Franklin D, Hammond K. The intelligent classroom: providing competent assistance. *Proc. fifth Int'l Conf. on Autonomous Agents*. ACM Press, 2001.
6. Heider T, Kirste T. Architectural considerations for interoperable multi-modal assistant systems. In Forbig P (Ed.) *Proc. Interactive Systems, Design, Specification, and Verification (DSV-IS 2002)*. Springer, 2002.
7. Heider T, Kirste, T. Supporting goal-based interaction with dynamic intelligent environments. *Proc. 15th European Conf. on Artificial Intelligence (ECAI'2002)*, Lyon, France, 2002.
8. Hellenschmidt M, Kirste T. Software Solutions for Self-Organizing Multimedia-Appliances. *Computers & Graphics, Special Issue on Pervasive Computing and Ambient Intelligence* 28(5), 2004.
9. MIT Project Oxygen, Pervasive, Human-centered Computing. (Project Web Site)
   http://oxygen.lcs.mit.edu/
10. Prante Th, Ršcker C, Streitz N A, Stenzel R, Magerkurth C, van Alphen D, Plewe D A. Hello.Wall – Beyond Ambient Displays. *Video Track and Adjunct Proc. fifth Int'l Conf. on Ubiquitous Computing (UBICOMP'03)*, Seattle, USA. 2003.
11. Shadbolt N. Ambient Intelligence. *IEEE Intelligent Systems*, 18(4):2Ð3. Jul/Aug 2003.
12. Stanford Interactive Workspaces—iWork. (Project Web Site)
    http://iwork.stanford.edu/
13. Servat D, Drogoul A. Combining amorphous computing and reactive agent-based systems: a Paradigm for Pervasive Intelligence? *Proc. first Int'l Joint Conf. on Autonomous Agents and Multiagent Systems*. ACM Press, 2002.

Enterprise Information Integration – A Semantic Approach

Thomas Kamps, Richard Stenzel, Libo Chen, and Lothar Rostek

Fraunhofer IPSI, Dolivostr. 15, 64293 Darmstadt, Germany
{kamps, stenzel, chen, rostek}@ipsi.fhg.de
http://www.ipsi.fhg.de/orion

Abstract. Nowadays, we witness the advent of a new era in information technology as an enabler for an often proclaimed "knowledged society". Many aca-
demicians – computer scientists, computational linguists and others – but also
researchers in corporate settings investigate the use of "knowledge" as a means
for intelligent information access in enterprises. Ontologies are commonly considered a formal means for modelling and instantiating conceptual structures
upon which implicit knowledge can be inferred. In an industrial context, however, domain-specific conceptual information is only one corporate information
resource. Relevant business information comprises facts on goods, projects, experts, customers, competitors and many other information bits as they are stored
in enterprise information systems. A great wish of many executives is, however,
to gain an integrated view on these assets and their relationships, thus deriving
new insights relevant for their business. To achieve this goal, ontologies can
help with respect to semantic data integration. A problem is, however, that the
construction and maintenance of ontologies is expensive. Another problem is
that the business data are usually stored redundantly in different heterogeneous
data repositories and the connectivity – a prerequisite for intelligence – is not
explicit. The approach discussed in the remainder will show how a mix of information extraction and classification methods can be used to automatically
set-up and update a network of business objects serving as a corporate memory
index. The latter represents a rich semantic access structure for filtering and in-
dividualizing the retrieval of relevant business information.

1   Introduction

Managers take the decisions for the introduction of corporate IT-systems usually in a
pragmatic way, i.e. local business processes need to be supported and thus software
systems will be installed in a rather independent way. As a consequence, the operational systems are in many cases neither synchronized on the data level nor on the
application level. These circumstances have severe implications on the accessibility of
the stored data. To explain this, consider the following example. A company maintains an expert-database containing data relating the experts to their expertise and to
the organizational unit they belong to. The same company maintains projects in a
project database relating the projects to their project managers and to the thematic
information describing what the projects are about (see figure 1). To achieve the "single point of view" on the data, questions of the following kind need to be answered:

M. Hemmje et al. (Eds.): E.J. Neuhold Festschrift, LNCS 3379, pp. 271–279, 2005.

what are the information objects shared by the given databases and how can their connectivity be established and exploited for search without significant effort by the information seeker?

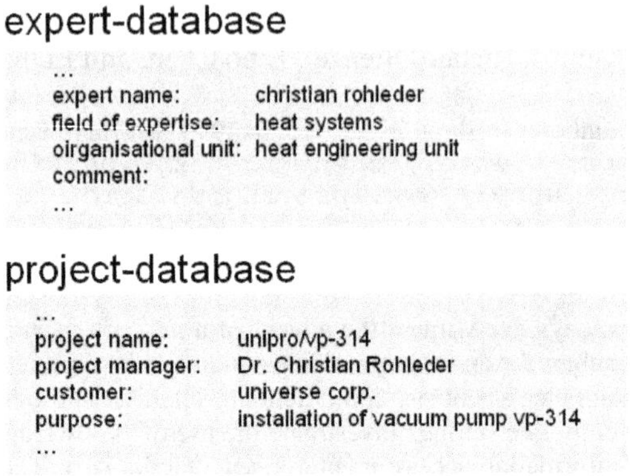

expert-database

...
expert name:	christian rohleder
field of expertise:	heat systems
oirganisational unit:	heat engineering unit
comment:	

...

project-database

...
project name:	unipro/vp-314
project manager:	Dr. Christian Rohleder
customer:	universe corp.
purpose:	installation of vacuum pump vp-314

...

Fig. 1. Simple unification of database fields

With the exception of some minor inconsistencies concerning the spelling of the names the example shows a rather simplistic integration problem where the data analyst only needs to find out that the two fields "expert name" and "project manager" contain the same person. For an information seeker the situation is not trivial since he needs to log in two databases, retrieve information from the two different sources and merge them without machine support. A straight forward technical approach could be to offer appropriate views on the two databases by merging selected fields and their values. In this way we could ask for experts in heat engineering who have installed the vp-314 vacuum pump and get the result "Christian Rohleder". Such an approach becomes quiet awkward if the database structure is more complex, or worse, if many complex databases are involved.

Besides connectivity aspects such as those discussed before there is another important issue relating to the circumstance that much valuable corporate information is not stored by means of discretely structured database formats but by means of unstructured text. What is the connection between these texts and the structured information above? To give an answer let us extend the scenario above by introducing sample corporate documents (see figure 2) storing domain-specific information. These could be glossaries defining corporate terminology, technical documentations on products and technologies but also commercial texts describing the company's expertise.

Analyzing these examples we find definitions of manufacturing devices such as "vacuum pump", "extraction well" etc. It is intuitive that "diaphragm vacuum pumps" are a specific form of vacuum pumps and that vacuum pumps are used as part of an "extraction well" to extract any kind of fluids. We can also read that the more specific "liquid ring vacuum pump" is part of the expertise of "Universe Corporation". The latter relates domain-specific information to the business expertise of the company. Taking into account the facts given in the expert and project database, respectively, an information seeker might conjecture that "Christian Rohleder" could be a candidate expert for liquid ring vacuum pumps, too. To gain such insights would require to

> **vacuum pump** - A pumping apparatus which exhausts gas or air from an enclosed space to achieve a desired degree of vacuum.
>
> **Diaphragm vacuum pumps** are becoming increasingly popular for small to medium size applications as an alternative to...
>
> **Extraction well:** a well employed to extract fluids (either water, gas, free product, or a combination of these) from the subsurface. Extraction is usually accomplished by either a pump located within the well or suction created by a vacuum pump at the ground surface.
>
> **_Universe Corporation, the Experts for Liquid Ring Vacuum Pumps_**
>
> _Finder Vacuum Pumps_
> Finder Pumps offer single stage and two stage liquid ring vacuum pumps, also available in monobloc execution.

Fig. 2. Sample thematic text documents

major analyses by the information seeker. He had to connect the bits of the data puzzle by himself requiring – similar as above – research through the available information resources not knowing where to begin. Machine support would be helpful. However, commercially available search engines allow only for limited access. They rely mostly on pure syntactic indexing principles that are not able to relate terminology of different languages automatically (not even synonyms of the same language). Thus, we need a more advanced technology that overcomes these limitations.

We summarize that we need a central repository storing both terminology and facts relating to the corporate assets. We have argued in the introduction that this is a promising approach towards establishing data connectedness as a prerequisite for the creation of synergies in information access. A major problem we encounter here is that most of the terminology and facts need to be extracted from the given corporate resources and if needed from external sources. Existing ontology engineering systems (see [3]) support a manual feed for knowledge acquisition or automatic feed if the ontology is already stored in an explicit format (RDF, RDF-Schema, DAML-OIL, OWL, Topic Map). However, if the terminology and the facts are only implicit they need to be carved out of the unstructured material. Then the "discretized" data structures have to be transformed in one of the machine readable formats mentioned before. Only in this way a machine can make use of reasoning processes allowing for intelligent proposals to the user. Because of the size of the corporate data repositories the extraction process needs to be widely automatic. On top of that the extracted data of different repositories should be integrated automatically and back-linked to serve as a centralized semantic index structure. Since corporate knowledge is undergoing continuous changes it needs to be assured that the underlying knowledge model, both for the terminology and for the facts, is extensible. This is one of the reasons why the results of the extraction process should be stored using an ontology engineering system. Another one is that we can exploit the reasoning capabilities of such a system, too. The most important one is, however, that the heterogeneous structure of the index represents a corporate ontology extended by the business facts. So the use of an ontology system to store the index structure suggests itself.

2   The Approach

As outlined above, the goal of the information extraction process is to establish a semantic index structure by which the user is able to flexibly access the corporate resources. This should be possible depending on individualized access rights. An elegant way to implement such a feature is by exploiting the structure of a business ontology connecting, e.g., persons and projects as well as persons and their roles in the company (department head, accountant, etc.). A role-based accessing mechanism is thus easily realized. Because of the connectivity it can even be used to establish basic workflow patterns such as a substitution rule replacing, e.g., the access rights of the project manager with those of his subordinate for the time of his vacation. The basic integration paradigm is illustrated in figure 3.

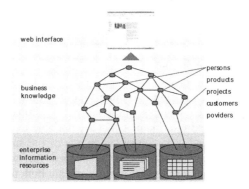

Fig. 3. Basic paradigm for semantic enterprise integration

2.1   The Structure's Structure

The network itself comprises two levels: the "concepts" and the "individuals". Concepts are abstract things that can be instantiated or refined (e.g., company, biology, microbiology, etc.) whereas individuals are concrete things that only exist once in the world (Germany, Thomas Kamps, Coca Cola etc.). We may thus distinguish between

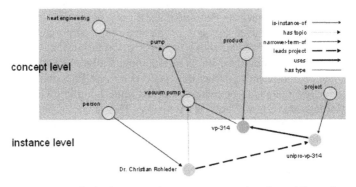

Fig. 4. Part of a business ontology part representing data of figure 1

concept-concept relations (terminology), individual-individual relations (facts) and concept-individual relations (instantiations). Because individuals are instantiations of concepts the separation of concepts on the upper level and the individuals on the lower is quite intuitive. The connectivity thus reflects the possible semantic interpretations of real-world things by means of thematic structure. In other words, thematic structure helps expanding a topic under which certain facts are located and relate them to others.

2.2   The Business Data Integration Design

The construction of the semantic index structure will be described in this section. As already mentioned above, the rationale behind our approach is to automatically create a semantic indexing structure and store it using a fact-extended business ontology.

Before we can create this structure we need to develop an (extended) ontology schema in the first step. It reflects the design of the models of its principal components such as the *organization structure*, the *project structure*, the *thematic space(s)*, the *business processes* and the *business objects* as well as *relations* connecting the components. On the research side great effort has been spent to come up with business ontology models (see [10]). And it will be interesting to observe if there will be standardized reference models in the future to be used in practical business applications. Today this is not the case. In fact, researchers have found (see [9]) that for the construction of ontologies it is most relevant to start from the user-requirements. What is the application the user needs? This question directly leads to the identification of the most relevant business objects. Is it a marketing application? Then it is most likely that we have to deal with customers and competitors. Is it a skill-management application? In this case we probably deal with persons, their skills, projects in which these skills were applied. Another question relates to the character of the application. Is it a semantic search scenario? Then the search technology should lead the searcher to relevant hits even when the input keywords and the text vocabulary do not match. Is it a fact-retrieval scenario in which high precision plays an important role? Then this scenario will induce higher requirements on the ontology model and on the inferencing technology.

The Construction of the Business Ontology

In the case of "pure semantic integration and search" which is the most likely case concerning business integration scenarios we propose the following approach for the integration of corporate data resources ranging from strongly structured (structured databases) to completely unstructured (plain text).

In the *first step*, the database structures of the strongly structured corporate repositories are analyzed with respect to their applicability as the basic building blocks for the initial business ontology model. The first instantiation of the model is then achieved by transforming the values of the database fields into the respective business object instances representing them. The *second step* is achieved by adapting the model with respect to the thematic structure found in the weakly structured contents of the corporate assets (glossaries, encyclopedias) and in the (possibly external) reference works to be used. To this purpose, we need to answer a number of questions. What kind of thematic relations need to be modeled? Are hierarchy relations such as "broader concept of-" or "part of- " relations needed. Is it necessary to define them on a more detailed level distinguishing more specific cases? The important question is then: How can we derive these structures automatically from the weakly structured or other contents? What are the structures we can expect from the given information extraction technologies? Once it is clear what the concepts, individuals and relations are, the business ontology model can be extended in the *third step*. In the *fourth step* the extraction technologies are applied and the results of these processes are imported into the business ontology in the same way as described before. During this process it is most likely that the business ontology undergoes several passes of extension and refinement. Since it is clear from the extraction processes what information is extracted from what documents we can exploit this knowledge for the indexing of the contents. The construction is schematically presented in figure 5.

2.3   Automatic Extraction Technologies to Build Up the Index Structures

The automatic construction of the business ontology requires two major steps: The first is concerned with *terminology extraction*. Here, the relevant vocabulary needs to be identified out of a set of company-specific corpora, and most likely, also from external content resources such as reference works, glossaries etc. The second step is concerned with *fact extraction*. For fact extraction we will enhance the results of state of the art extraction technologies [6] employing pattern-oriented parsing and by making use of controlled vocabularies such as lists of names, roles, products etc. as they can pragmatically be computed from company resources. We will not elaborate on the detection of facts in this paper, however.

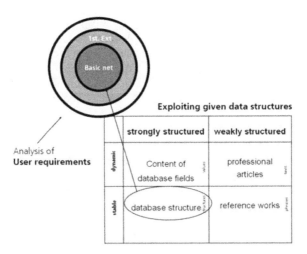

Fig. 5. Iterative modeling and instantiation of the business ontology with extracted content. The fat circles represent the model extensions starting with the inner circle. The fill between the circles represents the amount of instantiation of the business ontology

Terminology Extraction
Terminology extraction may happen by identifying vocabulary – phrases consisting of one or more words of text. Finding relations between such chunks leads in the sim-

plest case to statements such as those we have encountered in the ontology examples above (e.g., a vacuum pump is a pump). The way in which we can identify these statements depends on the applied technology. An interesting statistics-based approach is that of [1], a further development of the approach proposed by [8]. The idea is here to first extract the vocabulary from multiple relevant information sources (both internal and external sources) and then apply the layer-seeds method developed by [2] to automatically construct "thematically-more-specific" hierarchies and association relations. This approach allows the enhancement of existing thesaurus or categorization material. It can also be combined with the symbolic approach of [7] that may refine the results of the layer-seeds method by distinguishing "thematically-more-specific" tuples into true "broader-concept-of" tuples and "differentiation" tuples.

The terminology extraction approaches discussed so far produce hierarchical and non-hierarchical binary relations. This is so because the extracted vocabulary essentially consists of one-word or two-word chunks. An interesting approach for the detection of more-word chunks based on noun-phrase analysis was proposed by [7]. In the remainder of this section we will show how noun-phrases (more-word chunks with the noun as the kernel) can be used to index unstructured material in a more accurate way. Consider the example phrase "Universe Corporation, the Experts for Fluid-Ring Vacuum Pumps" in figure 2. Its semantic structure may be captured as displayed in figure 6. The complete phrase is represented on the bottom-level relating the individual "Universe Corporation" to the sub-phrase fluid-ring vacuum pump. This is in fact more than a noun-phrase, it is a full sentence, a malapropism for "Universe corporation is the expert for fluid-ring vacuum pumps". However, for the human observer it is obvious that "Universe Corporation" is a corporation related to the noun phrase "fluid ring vacuum pump" by the relation "is expert of". The noun-phrase can be decomposed into the narrower-term-of hierarchy "fluid-ring vacuum pump", "vacuum pump", "pump". The node "vacuum" differentiates the type of the pump and this works analogously for the term "fluid-ring". As the results of noun-phrase analysis are of the same form as those detected with the extraction methods discussed above it extends in a natural way the semantic structures by introducing "higher-order" searchable concepts – the noun phrases.

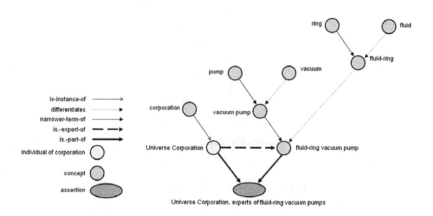

Fig. 6. Semantic structure of an example noun-phrase

2.4   Classification Methods

Semantic structures as a means for intelligent navigation on the abstract business ontology level may be complemented by a navigation structure that is based on classification methods allowing for navigation on the document level. If a user sends a query and reads some documents from the search results, we know more about the user than his pure query. Each document itself can be seen as a heavily extended query. Using this extended query, it is possible to present for each document (or even the user's complete history) a list of documents, containing "similar" information (e.g. backgrounder about the same topic). A simple and powerful method to find similar documents to a given one is the use of a weighted vector space model. This is in principle an extended full text search where the query string contains all words of the given document. All documents which have some words in common with the query string are retrieved and ranked. The measured similarity (a number) of two documents is the sum of all word co-occurrences in the two documents. Because not all words (or word bi-grams and tri-grams) are semantically equal important (e.g. "and" is less important than "fluid-ring vacuum pump") each word gets a weight. Surprisingly, the simple vector space model works very well. On the other hand, it does not detect real semantic connections. For the purpose of solving the latter, the vector space model can be combined with methods trying to extract semantic information about the document corpus. The methods Latent Semantic Indexing (LSI) (see [4]) and Probabilistic Latent Semantic Indexing (pLSI) extend the vector space model (VSM) (see [5]).

2.5   The Semantic Integration Architecture

The overall software architecture covering the technologies discussed above is presented in figure 7 below. Here it can be seen that the results of all the different analyses are uniformly stored by means of a business ontology instance. Even the document-document relations can be stored there because they are represented as all other individuals as instances of the concept "document".

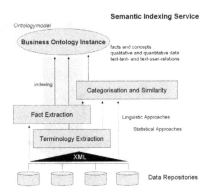

Fig. 7. Semantic Indexing Architecture

3   Summary and Conclusions

We have introduced a highly automated approach for business data integration based on information extraction as well as on classification methods. The approach aims at integration of a variety of state-of-the-art methods and elaborates on the promising technology noun phrase analysis. Interesting research problems relate to the exploitation of the internal structure of noun-phrases for the construction of semantic index structures and to the interplay of statistical and symbolic extraction methods.

4   References

[1] L. Chen, M. L'Abbate, U. Thiel, E. Neuhold: "Increasing the Customer's Choice: Query Expansion based on the Layer-Seeds Method and its Application in E-Commerce", In Soe-Tsyr Yuan and Jiming Liu (eds), proceedings of the IEEE international conference on e-Technology, e-Commerce and e-Service (EEE-04), 28 - 31 March 2004, Taipei, Taiwan, IEEE computer society press, Los Alamitos, California, 2004, pp. 317-324.

[2] L. Chen, U. Thiel: "Language Modeling for Effective Construction of Domain Specific Thesauri", In Proceedings of the 9th International Conference on Applications of Natural Language to Information Systems (NLDB04), Manchester, United Kingdom, 2004, Lecture Notes in Computer Science, Springer Verlag, Berlin, pp.242-253.

[3] O. Corcho, M. Fernández-López, A. Gómez Pérez: "Ontoweb, Technical Roadmap v1.0", Universidad Politécnica de Madrid, http://ontoweb.aifb.uni-karlsruhe.de/About/Deliverables.

[4] S.T. Dumais: "Latent semantic indexing (LSI)": Trec-3 report. In Proceedings of the Text Retrieval Conference (TREC-3), D. Harman, Ed., pp. 219, 1995.

[5] T. Hofmann: "Probabilistic latent semantic indexing". In Proceedings of the 22nd International Conference on Research and Development in Information Retrieval, pp. 50-57, 1999.

[6] C. Manning, H. Schütze: "Foundations of Statistical Natural Language Processing", MIT Press. Cambridge, MA: May 1999.

[7] L. Rostek, D. Fischer: "Konzepte für ein thesaurusbasiertes Information Retrieval am Arbeitsplatz", In Sprachverarbeitung in Information und Dokumentation, GLDV/GI Tagung, März 1985, Hannover, Hrsg. J.Krause, B.Endres-Niggemeyer, Informatik Fachberichte, Springer Verlag Heidelberg.

[8] M. Sanderson & B. Croft, "Deriving concept hierarchies from text", In proceedings of the 22nd ACM Conference of the Special Interest Group in Information Retrieval, pp. 206-213, 1999.

[9] M. Uschold, R. Jasper: "A Framework for Understanding and Classifying Ontology Applications", In KAW99 Twelfth Workshop on Knowledge Acquisition, Modeling and Management, Banff, Alberta, Canada, 1999.

[10] M. Uschold, M. King, S. Moralee, Yannis Zorgios: "The Enterprise Ontology The Knowledge Engineering Review", Vol. 13, Special Issue on Putting Ontologies to Use (eds. Mike Uschold and Austin Tate), 1998

Ontology-Based Project Management for Acceleration of Innovation Projects

Hans-Jörg Bullinger[1], Joachim Warschat[2],
Oliver Schumacher[2], Alexander Slama[2], and Peter Ohlhausen[2]

[1] Fraunhofer-Gesellschaft zur Förderung der angewandten Forschung e.V.,
Postfach 120420, D-80031 München
`hans-joerg.bullinger@zv.fraunhofer.de`
[2] Fraunhofer Institut für Arbeitswirtschaft und Organisation,
Nobelstraße 12, D-70569 Stuttgart
`{joachim.warschat; oliver.schumacher;`
`alexander.slama; peter.ohlhausen}@iao.fraunhofer.de`

Abstract. Shortening time-to-market for new product innovations is now and in future one of the critical success factors for market competitiveness and ability. The ability to faster and better arrive at innovative products is based on the knowledge, what constellations are excessively time-consuming and how this time barrier can be broken down in order to achieve acceleration. The ability to develop new things fast and effectively and to introduce them on the market does nowadays substantially depend on the increasingly complex knowledge and creative performance of all employees during the entire innovation project. At the moment we do, however, lack a computer-supported solution, aiming to provide the employee working on the innovation process with an appropriate support for an effective acceleration of innovations. A system for the acceleration of innovation, on the on hand, has to be backed up with a model allowing to represent innovation projects - and the occurring time-consuming constellations with all their complex interrelations and their semantics - in an information system. On the other hand, the system must be equipped with all knowledge concerning undesired time consumers and the respective avoidance strategies, the so-called innovation-acceleration knowledge. Ontology-based models and methods enable computer-supported representation of innovation projects, computer aided identification of time-consuming constellations and serve to infer and provide innovation-acceleration knowledge to ensure faster and better innovations.

1   Current Situation

Innovations are the central instrument of control for nations as well as companies, enabling them to get ahead of the international competition - and to stay on top. As innovations create a new lead, fresh employment and new growth, this is just what we need to be able to further afford our wealth. Nations as well as companies, however, find themselves confronted with a growing obligation for innovation. Figure 1 compares the nation-wide R&D expenses of the leading economic countries. The graph shows that, compared to our most important competitors, we commit only very few resources to our power-for-the-future in Germany.

M. Hemmje et al. (Eds.): E.J. Neuhold Festschrift, LNCS 3379, pp. 280–288, 2005.

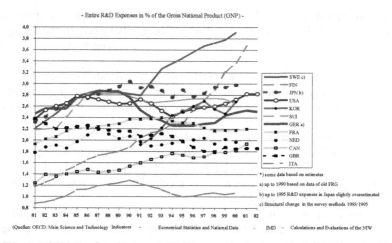

Fig. 1. R&D intensity of selected OECD countries in the period of 1981 to 2002*

Especially in a changing world, and particularly in Germany, it is necessary to retain and strengthen the position in the world market through the development of new products and services as well as through the acquisition of new customer groups. In reality this means that companies nowadays have to face growing global competitive pressure, an increasing complexity and variety of technically excellent and individual products or services. Due to increased customer orientation this also involves a trend from serial products to mass-customized and service-intensive product packages. In spite of time and cost pressure, companies are still forced to exploit extensively the growth potentials of their value-added chain. At the same time, they are confronted with ever more complex framework conditions, e. g. extensive legislations.

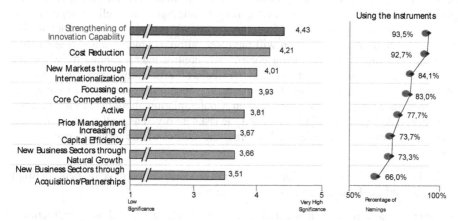

Fig. 2. Innovation capability – most important instrument of control for an increase in profitability and growth [3]

However, the innovation-compass [1] as well as our own analyses show that over the last 10 years (1991 18,4 % and 2000 13,9 %) the world-market share of research and development intensive goods dropped significantly. More and more companies reduce their R&D budget or completely step out of this field. But according to the innovation-compass, research and development intensive goods belong to the fast growing sectors. This results in a definite need for action to keep up with our international competitors.

In particular within a knowledge-based society, accelerated cycles of change in technology, economy and society and the dynamics of international partners and competition represent a challenge but also a fresh chance for a "management of innovation".

In order to enable companies to take a leading position within the international competitive field, innovation processes need to be accelerated and a networked and agile economic organisation has to be built up. In this context, the acceleration of innovation processes also serves as a safety mechanism in the innovation rivalry for top and state-of-the-art technologies.

Innovations are those new ideas or inventions that manage to successfully mass-implement themselves as better solutions within the working, living or learning environment of people. Innovations may be technological innovations which permit the creation and implementation of new products or services. But innovations can also be structural or process innovations which form working, living or learning environments that foster creativity, ability for change or productivity. In these environments, inventions can turn into innovations. And last but not least, innovations can take place in politics and society.

2   Accelerating Innovation as Ultima Ratio

Innovation is a colourful expression and a complex process with many varieties, especially where technological innovations are concerned with supplying the market with new, attractive products and services. Besides the time criterion, another essential phenomenon consists of the fact that mainly technological as well as structural and process innovations during the 21st century have their origin at inter-disciplinary borders. Better and faster innovation will therefore enforce companies and organisations to be able to cope with increasing complexity, control interdisciplinarity while supporting creativity and productivity and, particularly, efficiently foster the integration of knowledge between specialist sectors and/or functional sectors. To succeed, we need to broaden our concept of innovation. Contemplating about innovation means to be concerned with new technologies and the risks involved as well as to establish the necessary creative force. We need a three-fold notion of the term innovation. This involves:

- Technological innovations, i.e. investments in research and development aiming to design and implement new products and services

- Structural and process innovations, i.e. the development and implementation of concepts for variable working, learning and living environments that enhance creativity

- And last but not least, innovations in society and politics serving to design fit-for-the-future location factors and to mobilise individual and cooperative creative power

Several surveys of academic circles and consultants show that there is a definite need for action within companies.[2] Figure 3 clearly shows that in order to secure the competitive lead, the economy has to focus more and more on the time factor.

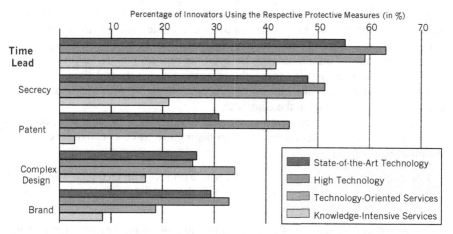

Fig. 3. Accelerated innovation processes as protective measure [4]

The Fraunhofer Institute has dedicated itself to this issue and initiated a project concentrating on the areas of technical innovations and the respective structural and process innovations. As companies and organisations are faced with shorter product life cycles and increasing international competition, it is not only the innovation force to stay competitive in today's complex markets, but also the time period at which new products and services are brought to the market. Hence in this project, the time factor of innovation activities has been moved into focus. This means, solutions are worked out which support companies and organisations in accelerating their innovation processes without loosing sight of the entire context of excellent innovation management.

On developing fit-for-the-future solutions, scientists of various disciplines work in close cooperation. Experts for innovation management and performance rating as well as specialists of ontology development are creating a framework model for innovation excellence and are working out ontology-based, technological solutions for mastering complexity and supporting interdisciplinary knowledge-integration during innovation processes. Specialists from six Fraunhofer Institutes provide empirical data and experience gained in innovation projects within the pilot areas adaptronics, optoelectronics, polytronics and services, and are accompanying the development and testing of the solutions.

3   Ontology-Based Project Management for Acceleration of Innovation Projects

The ability to faster and better arrive at innovative products is based on the knowledge, what constellations are excessively time-consuming and how this time barrier can be broken down in order to achieve acceleration.

Excessive time consumers are impediments hindering the (full) exploitation of the current and future innovation potential. They can be traced back to specific constellations within the innovation process. One excessive time consumer detected during a project in the medical technology sector was, e. g.: "disregarded government guidelines for technical equipment". The constellation was based on the following: some prototype equipment had been installed in an eye-clinic, and was to be tested on patients. It was, however, overlooked that equipment not bearing the CE-logo must not be used. This caused an unnecessary delay of the process run. To represent such constellations, it is necessary to make the respective elements and their interrelations accessible, in order to make innovation processes, together with their excessive time consumers, representable on the computer.

The thus achieved "innovation-acceleration knowledge" permits to speed up the innovation process. In this context we can distinguish three effective levels of time-optimisation:

- **Paradigm/Strategy Level** looks at the whole project with its typical characteristics and strategic scheduling - comparable with the creation of a complete DNS - and its overall functional alignment

- **Process-Component Level** looks at single phases of the project - comparable to the creation of a DNS-section - and the functional alignment of this sector

- **Methods Level looks** at the single activities of a project phase - comparable to the atoms of a DNS, which are providing the DNS section with its functionalities

The ability to develop new things fast and effectively and to introduce them on the market does substantially depend on the knowledge and creative performance of all employees during the entire innovation process. At the moment we do, however, lack a computer-supported solutions, aiming to provide the employee working on the innovation process with an appropriate support for an effective acceleration of innovations. A system for the acceleration of innovation, on the on hand, has to be backed up with a model allowing to reproduce innovation projects – and the occurring time-consuming constellations with all their complex interrelations and their semantics – in the computer. On the other hand, the system must be equipped with all knowledge concerning undesired time consumers and the respective avoidance strategies, the so-called innovation-acceleration knowledge. Ontology-based models and methods enable computer-supported representation of innovation projects, computer aided identification of time-consuming constellations and serve to infer and provide innovation-acceleration knowledge to ensure faster and better innovations.

Ontologies represent the knowledge structure of a relevant part of the real world reproduced on the computer. Just the conveyance of a simple occurrence of the real world essentially requires the comprehensive use of typical terms and depiction of meanings and interrelations in order to achieve understanding. To keep control of the complexity it is however important only to consider the absolutely essential phenomena of the real world. The phenomenon to be represented in this context is the innovation process along with its excessive time consumers and possible avoidance-strategies on all three levels.

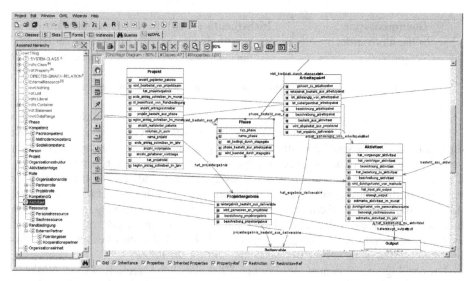

Fig. 4. Section of the innovation-process ontology (OWL standard) developed in Protégé-2000

An analysis of excessive time consumers in context with innovative products, and the competence of numerous experts of the Fraunhofer Gesellschaft regarding single sectors of the knowledge structure, enables the construction of an ontology, which allows a representation of innovative processes with their potential excessively-time-consuming constellations. The following essential elements of the innovation-process ontology were derived (see figure 4):

- Project, Project Objective, Change of Objective, Project Results, Project Team, Phase, Work Package, Deliverable, Activity, Sequence of Activities, Output, Method, List of Parameters and Stage-Gate

- Organisational Structure, Project-, Matrix-, Divisional-Organisation and Functional Organisation, Unit of Organisation

- Role, Organisational Role, Project Role, Partner Role, Project Management, Work Package

- Resource, Material Resource, Human Resource, Person

- Competence and Requirements

- Allocation Period, Allocation of Role as well as Competence, Organisational Unit, Organisational Role and Human Resources

Ontologies provide on the one hand the basis to describe complex interrelations and to turn process information into knowledge and on the other hand a rule-based determination of excessive time consumers. Ontologies serve to make innovation processes representable, analysable and interpretable on the computer and according to Gruninger and Lee [5] there are three different fields of applications in which ontologies can be used profitably: (computer-based) communication between humans, computer-based reasoning and structuring and re-use of knowledge.

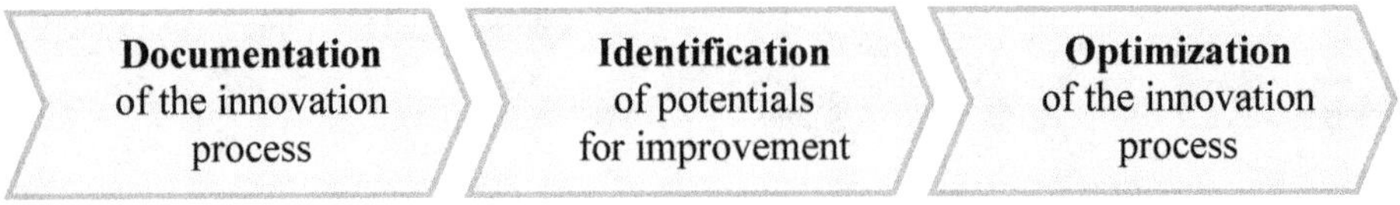

Documentation of the innovation process	Identification of potentials for improvement	Optimization of the innovation process

Fig. 5. Phases of the computer-supported acceleration of innovation

The knowledge for acceleration of innovation - backed up by ontologies - allows the identification of potentials for improvement. The system provides the diagnosis based on which the user is supplied with suitable suggestions on how to optimise the innovation process (see figure 5). The creative treatment of knowledge however still remains a privilege of the human being. This system aims to support the employees working on the innovation process with knowledge about the acceleration of innovations and thus to enable them to accelerate processes more effectively. Knowledge on how new things are developed in a better and faster way, can be effectively supported by ontology-based innovation management. This knowledge thus becomes an essential feature influencing competitiveness that is fit for the future.

The ontology-development tool Protégé-2000 allows the creation of input masks in order to support an efficient knowledge acquisition for relevant innovation process information, within we will identify unwanted time consuming constellation, besides the development of ontology itself. Thus it is possible to set up different instances for continuously testing an ontology for innovation processes and therefore to improve the quality of a process model and its resulting ontology. E. g. for an unwanted time consuming constellation: it is necessary in order to perform the activity "creation of a physical prototype" (a typical process step in mechanical engineering) to have a certain experience with the use of a stereo lithography machine. Furthermore it is essential to describe the different competencies of employees as it is already done in different skill management databases. If there is a discrepancy found between requirements and abilities, there is a strong indicator that there could be a project constellation which results in time loss. This approach is very useful during the development of ontology for innovation projects to validate practically the fundamental but theoretical ideas in terms of necessity and completeness.

For ontology-based innovation management ontology should not only support knowledge acquisition but also the chance of analysing and reasoning of knowledge. Rule-based languages, e. g. F-Logic, which are already implemented in software systems like OntoEdit, see figure 6, or FLORA as plug-in for Protégé-2000, facilitate the definition of if-then-constraints and the use of inference mechanisms that involve the identification of time-consuming constellations like "discrepancy between requirements and abilities".

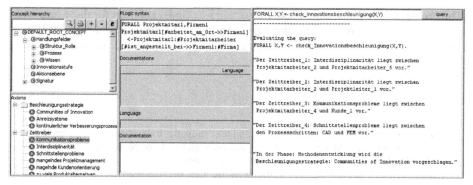

Fig. 6. Ontology-based identification of potentials for improvement by use of F-Logic in On-toEdit

The use of specialised software agents has the potential to provide even more sophisticated solution strategies than discovering disadvantageous constellations and to provide check lists. Based on a project structure it is possible for a software agent to analyse this structure regarding different target functions like use of resources, time or costs and to provide alternatives to overcome weaknesses. The application of software agents for re-structuring development projects has already been investigated in the collaborative research project "Entwicklung und Erprobung innovativer Produkte" founded by German DFG [6], [7].

A further approach to shorten development time is to provide support to project managers by selecting useful methods or procedures to perform the activities during design and development. By describing the typical methods of an application domain as well as the associated requirements appropriately a software agent can be used to recommend use of methods or materials. The criteria for the selection on the one hand is typically a result of the product or technology which is to be developed like chemical or mechanical requirements or on the other hand or they are determined by the personnel involved in the development project. In the field of rapid prototyping different selection procedures based on the requirements of physical prototypes have been described in the EU-project BE-S2-5661 [8].

4   Outlook

From this spot-light like the consideration of the complex matter innovation and the challenges companies have to face, we would like to draw up some problems which, in our opinion, science and economy will have to deal with soon:

- What devices do we require o allow companies to more systematically and efficiently evaluate their innovation capability?

- Is the acceleration of innovation compatible with the necessity to reduce costs in the companies?

- How can the most important tasks of knowledge-integration be realised more effectively than before?

The project of the Fraunhofer Gesellschaft aims to find a solution for these and other problem fields. We assume that the project results and empirical findings will lead to further needs for research and development focussing on the acceleration of innovation processes.

References

1. VDI-Nachrichten (2001): Innovations-Kompass: radikale Innovationen erfolgreich managen; Handlungsempfehlungen auf Basis einer empirischen Untersuchung, Düsseldorf: VDI-Verlag, 2001 (Sonderpublikation der VDI-Nachrichten)
2. Wildemann, H. (2003): Schneller zum neuen Produkt, In: Harvard Business Manager März 2003, S. 33 – 39
3. Little, A. D. (2004), Innovation Excellence Studie 2004
4. BMBF (2002), Zur technologischen Leistungsfähigkeit Deutschlands, 2002
5. Gruninger, M.; Lee, J. (2002): Ontology Applications and Design. Communications of the ACM. February 2002, Vol. 45, No. 2, pp 39-41.
6. Wörner, K. (1998): System zur dezentralen Planung von Entwicklungsprojekten im Rapid Product Development. Berlin, Heidelberg: Springer, 1999, Stuttgart. Universität Stuttgart, PhD-Thesis.
7. Leyh, J.; Diederich, M. K. (2001): Distributed Planning in the Rapid Product Development using adaptable process modules. In: Proceedings for the Conference on Product Development, 1st Automotive and Transportation Technology Congress and Exhibition (1st ATTCE). Barcelona, October, 1st-3rd 2001, Barcelona.
8. Schumacher, O.; Langbeck, B. and Laios, L. (2000): Development of a Software Tool Supporting the Selection of RP Processes and Materials. In: Proceedings of ISATA 2000, Dublin, Ireland.

Understanding and Tailoring Your Scientific Information Environment:
A Context-Oriented View on E-Science Support

Claudia Niederée, Avaré Stewart, Claudio Muscogiuri, Matthias Hemmje, and
Thomas Risse

Fraunhofer IPSI
Integrated Publication and Information Systems Institute
Dolivostrasse 15, 64293 Darmstadt, Germany
{niederee,stewart,muscogiuri,hemmje,risse}@ipsi.fhg.de

Abstract. R&D efforts in the area of e-Science aim at building an infrastructure
that supports researchers' work processes in a flexible way relying on Grid-based,
on-demand resource assignment. We believe, that within the developing e-Science
environments an improved awareness of researchers for their scientific context as
well as a more flexible support for the interaction of the researcher with this context
is desirable. This paper discusses approaches for context exploitation in support
of an increased awareness for the scientific context as well as approaches for more
active context construction by the researcher for specific research projects.

1 Introduction

Accelerated innovation cycles and the general trend toward globalization, on the one
hand, and tighter research budgets, on the other hand, impose new challenges for the
work of today's researcher. In addition, the digital age facilitates information access
but also dramatically increases the amount of information that has to be processed and
assessed in order to keep track of the newest research developments.

Current work in e-Science aims at building an infrastructure that supports researchers'
work processes, more flexibly contributing to the aforementioned challenges. Based on
a Grid infrastructure, resources are assigned on demand enabling to fulfill high demands
with respect to resources like storage space and computational power. Recent developments in this area focus on higher level resources, i.e. Grid services, aiming for more
integrated and targeted information provision and support of scientific processes.

A systematic consideration of context within the developing e-Science environments
contributes to this goal. This includes an improved awareness for the context, in which
the research takes place, and a more flexible support for the interaction of the researcher
with this context:

- *Awareness for Scientific Context:* Creating an improved awareness of the researcher
  for the community and domain as well of the researcher's role within this network
  facilitates more targeted interactions with scientific resources (documents, other
  researchers, events, etc.);

M. Hemmje et al. (Eds.): E.J. Neuhold Festschrift, LNCS 3379, pp. 289–298, 2005.

– *Construction of Scientific Context:* Enabling researchers and research teams to build up a working context by tailoring information environments and processes to their needs, eases collaboration and the focus on the "real" research work.

This paper discusses these issues in more detail and considers different approaches and methods for supporting improved awareness as well as the construction of tailored working contexts. Section 2 gives an overview of the role of context for in e-Science and library services and discusses relevant context types. Section 3 and section 4 consider the aspects of Awareness for Scientific Context and Construction of Scientific Context, respectively, and present concrete approaches and projects in these areas. Related work is not discussed separately, but together with the different approaches for considering context in e-Science. The paper concludes with issues for future work.

2   Context in E-Science and Information Mediation

Before discussing context-enabled services in support of e-Science in section 3, we will give an overview of current e-Science efforts, requirements for information and knowledge environments for e-Science and the relevant types of context in this section.

2.1   e-Science: Next Generation Support for the Researcher

R&D activities in e-Science aim at improving the support for researchers by enhanced services and on-demand resource assignment. Current e-Science projects mainly focus on the primary requirements of application domains which produce very high volumes of data and/or have extreme requirements with respect to computing power, i.e. the traditional Grid application domains (e.g. particle physics, astronomy, earth science, biotechnology and medical applications. The projects deal, for example, with the Grid-based processing of very large data sets (e.g. GridPP) and with the management and access support for the large sets of data produced e.g in earth observation. The projects in the area of e-Science are supported by the construction of national Grid-based infrastructures (e.g. UK e-Science, D-Grid) and by European efforts in this area (e.g. EGEE).

More recent e-Science projects go beyond the on-demand assignment of the traditional Grid resources computing power and storage space. Web or Grid services are considered as Grid resources on a higher level of abstraction. The semantic description of raw data, information objects and services, the on-demand instantiation and combination of services, and the flexible integration of raw and experimental data with scientific information objects contribute to the construction of tailored and demand-oriented information and knowledge environments.

2.2   Information and Knowledge Environments for e-Science

In building information and knowledge environments in support of e-Science, two central processes have to be considered: the scientific innovation process itself and the orthogonal lifecycle of scientific information and knowledge that contains the process of creating and publishing new scientific information artifacts (see figure 1). Important

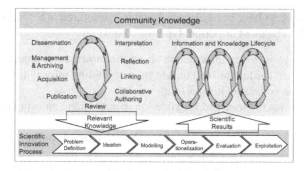

Fig. 1. The Scientific Innovation Process and the Information and Knowledge Lifecycle

aspects of the interaction between the two processes is the bidirectional flow of information between the community knowledge and the innovation process: In the one direction, relevant parts of the community knowledge flow into the innovation process, which is fostered by an adequate dissemination and mediation of the available information within a domain. In the other direction, the timely and quality controlled flow of information about new scientific results into the community knowledge is fostered by an adequate support of the content creation and publication process.

In summary, the researcher has to be supported in information use (by adequate mediation) as well as in information creation. Both activities take place in a specific scientific context, which can be taken into account in various ways by e-Science services, in order to better support the researcher in his working processes.

2.3   A Taxonomy of Context Types

"The context of something consists of the ideas, situations, events, or information that relate to it and make it possible to understand it fully"[1]. If context is represented explicitly (e.g. in knowledge representation [2]), it can be used for reasoning and decision making and enables interpretation in spite of diverging contexts. For an effective use of context, it is important that the "right" aspects of context are modeled and used.

Fig. 2. A Taxonomy of Context Types

In e-Science environments different types of contexts are relevant. Starting from the information and knowledge lifecycle different types of context relevant for the information mediation process have been identified and are structured in a context taxonomy in [3] (see figure 2). The most important types of context are:

information context includes information about the information object that is directly related to the individual artifact and to its surrounding information structures like an information collection it is part of;

user context captures the user and his situation in accessing and using information objects;

community context considers the information object as part of community processes like scientific discourse, censorship, content commentary. These process may stimulates other work in the domain or new ways of interpreting the information object.

Information about these context types can be modeled, collected and used to provide services that take this context into account. However, for information creation, which is another important activity in an e-Science environment, a further type of context becomes relevant: the working context that is created, shared and modified by a team of researches in creating new information artifacts. Such working context consists of the relevant information and its form as needed for the scientific task.

3   Fostering Context Awareness and Context Exploitation

e-Science is characterized by distributed, global collaborations between researchers supported by a Grid-based infrastructure. e-Science supports building virtual organizations (research teams and communities) and enables flexible and coordinated resource sharing [4]. In order to foster context awareness in e-Science, an individual must be considered in a community context and services have to be provided which exploit this context. We discuss several approaches to community context models and context aware services which exploit this context to support the e-Science researcher.

3.1   Modeling Community Context

Following theories such as Communities of Practice [5] and Social Network Analysis [6] the influence of communities plays a central role in collaboration processes. The decisions and resource needs of a human is defined and affected by their role within one or more communities. In e-Science, considering the community context can facilitate the discovery of a researcher's position with respect to the interrelationships among the set of interacting and collaborating units. Moreover, these relationships can be exploited to support the dissemination of information, the brokering of the vast amounts of e-Science resources or to stimulate the creation of new scientific information artifacts.

An example of a community model is the RDF-based FOAF vocabulary that provides a collection of basic terms for describing people and the links they have to other entities in a domain such as documents, events or other people[7]. Importantly, the FOAF vocabulary provides for a extensible framework: FOAF-based descriptions can be mixed with models described in other RDF vocabularies. In e-Science, FOAF can provide the basis for extensible descriptions of e-Science communities and support the researcher in exploring their role in the scientific community.

Another example of a community model applicable in e-Science is the Relationship-based approach. This approach defines a person's context within a community using ontology-based domain models. The ontologies are used to represent the salient relationships and entities in a given domain as well as to model the user in this domain [8,9,10]. One benefit of using domain ontologies is that they support the design of sharable, agreed-upon models for e-Science stakeholders. A promising Relationship-based approach developed by our group is the Personal Web Context (PWC)[10]. The goal of this approach is to analyze known relationships in order to infer and explicate implicit relationships between resources. The core of this approach is a match-making process that supports discovering sequences of relationships from which a single relation can be compositionally inferred to support inferencing processes for extending and exploiting the user's context. The PWC can support these types of activities with the so-called Semantic Resource Network which is an information infrastructure, which can be layered on top of an e-Science information space (as done in the VIKEF Integrated EU project, http://www.vikef.net). More specifically, based on a relevant application domain ontology, the Semantic Resource Network contains instances of ontology-defined entities in a given e-Science community collection. Such an information infrastructure takes into account the model of users as well as the community, in which they are embedded, and can be viewed a promising model toward fostering context awareness in e-Science.

3.2 Community Aware Services

The second aspect for fostering context awareness is the provision of services which take, for example, the previously mentioned context models into account. One particular type of service that is identified in e-Science is the need for visualization services to support the individual e-Science user by showing him part of his context. Other types of services include support for online-collaboration and community building, personalization as well as community landscape analysis, that is, understanding the greater structure of some domain. The example services described below can be considered as a starting point for defining e-Science services which exploit community context.

A number of recent studies in information visualization focus on identifying statistical properties and topographical structures in networked as well as ontology based systems [11,12,13,10]. They attempt to reveal implicit information about the data relationships embedded in them, exposed through the visualization of some underlying physical graph structure. The tools focus on analyzing a variety of properties, for example: co-relationships (co-author, co-participation), citations, small-world property, network transitivity, determinancy and prominence as well community structure, in which network nodes are joined together in tightly knit groups, between which there are only looser connections. FOAFnaut [14], for example, is an application built with the SVG open standard for visually mapping distributed communities. In e-Science, FOAFnaut can be extended to also visualize e-Science based RDF vocabularies describing not only people, but also scientific information objects and services.

Additionally, recent trends in the visualization of bibliographic metadata are growing in importance [15]. So far, comprehensive meta-indices, in combination with helpful graphical user interface are missing in most areas of science [16]. In e-Science this is relevant for two reasons: Such metadata (and semantic descriptions) will be available for a wider range of resources including primary (experimental) data and service descriptions in addition to the more traditional scientific documents. The descriptions can be exploited to support visualization and navigation of e-Science resources and services. Second, compared to the dynamic nature and rapid growth of bibliographical metadata collections of e-Science resources will grow faster by orders of magnitude. Adequate tools to support the user in targeting their interaction with large volume collections and supporting scientific processes are this even more important in this area.

Considering the models and tools discuss in this section, e-Science can come one step closer to fostering context awareness and providing more flexible support for improving the interaction of the researcher with this context.

4   Constructing Your Own Context

Researchers can also take a more active role with respect to context by tailoring their own working context within an e-Science environment. The idea is to construct a project-oriented working context or working environment for a team of researchers that, in the ideal case, contains all and only the information the team of researchers needs for their current project and also in a form that serves their current purpose best. This section discusses projects and preliminary work in active working context construction, which requires an adequate infrastructure that enables the following functionalities:

- the construction and management of reference libraries or virtual libraries as a project-oriented view on the information and metadata collections as well as selected library services of an underlying digital library infrastructure;
- the definition and execution of processes composed from services that process and transform information resources as required for the respective project;

4.1   Personal Reference Libraries and Virtual Digital Libraries

Digital libraries are tailored to the information interests of an entire community [17]. For a concrete scientific project (e.g. authoring a publication, creating a report or organizing a community event), temporal information collections tailored to a specific purpose and group are required. The setup and management of such temporal project-oriented views (possibly based on the content of different information collections) are considered in work on personal (reference) libraries (PRLs). In addition to more traditional digital library functionality, the following main challenges have to be considered:

- adequate languages and tools that support the definition and configuration of a PRL (included services, information and metadata collections, etc.);
- services for the management of the PRLs following an adequate lifecycle model;
- clear and customizable strategies for deciding which type of content to copy into the PRL and for controlling access and visibility;
- strategies for storing and managing content objects that are created within the working context like e.g. annotations

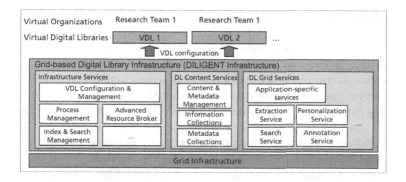

Fig. 3. DILIGENT Virtual Digital Library Infrastructure

A possible PRL lifecycle model consists of an initialization and a termination phase and repeated development and consolidation phases [18]. The consolidation phase is dedicated to incrementally integrating further information into the PRL and to propagating results from the project into the underlying digital library. Both information flows raise issues of adequate synchronization and integration as well as of quality assurance. Alternatively to just archiving a PRL, it should be possible in the termination phase to make insights captured in the PRL visible to a broader community in a controlled way. Special services are required for these purpose like services for managing the controlled coexistence of different PRLs or for merging PRLs (see e.g. [19]).

DILIGENT (http://diligentproject.org), a current European Integrated Project, addresses several of the aforementioned challenges and implements such project-oriented libraries -Virtual Digital Libraries (VDLs)- on the basis of a Grid infrastructure. The infrastructure is used to enable temporary and on-demand provision of storage space for content and metadata collections in setting up VDLs. This also includes storage space and computing power for extracting and storing project-specific (semantic) metadata. Furthermore, the infrastructure enables on-demand instantiation of library services.

Figure 3 shows an architecture overview of the DILIGENT infrastructure. Based on the Grid infrastructure it contains three types of services. The *Infrastructure Services* are a group of services that are specific for operating the infrastructure. This group contains the services for the configuration and management of VDLs. The *DL Grid Services* are a set of specific library services. On one hand, existing DL services are wrapped as Grid Services or adapted to the new Grid-based environments. On the other hand, new services are implemented that specifically take into account the operation environment, e.g. services for distributed search. Besides generic services like annotation and search services, this group also contains application specific services. Finally, the *DL Content Services* include services for content and metadata management as well as existing information and metadata collections wrapped as Grid services. This DILIGENT infrastructure is used to create VDLs in support of virtual organizations.

4.2   Tayloring Your Work Processes

In the DILIGENT project the tailoring of the VDLs is not restricted to content and meta-data collections, but also includes the definition of customized information processing workflows based on available services. In the earth science application domain this may, for example, be a process that extracts oil spill pattern from satellite images and prepares the resulting annotated images for integration in a VDL for a workshop on sea pollution. Such processes have to be composed from available services in a dynamic way. This requires both task-oriented support for the selection of adequate services for the process tasks and enactment of the process based on the selected services.

While the second activity is strongly supported by the Web service paradigm, and current efforts in Web services composition or orchestration, the first activity requires proper service mediation process, which is discussed in more detail in this section.

The mediation paradigm is based on models of the available resources and their capabilities, resource needs, and the matchmaking logic to match needs and available resources [20]. As a basis for the mediation of services all involved parties, service providers, mediators and requestors, have to agree to a common description vocabulary formalized either in one of the agent capabilities description languages (ACDL) defined for service mediation platforms (e.g. [21,22,23]) or by exploiting the recent standardized service description frameworks WSRF [24] or OWL-S [25].

Matching of resource requests is a process at three levels [26,23]: 1) Syntactic matching, 2) Semantic matching, on the basis of data types and constraints for the accessible content, as specified in the advertisement and 3) Pragmatic matching, considering properties in additional dimensions like performances and security. At this three levels, services advertisement, request and matching are based on formal descriptions of the following dimensions [26,21]: Types (in service signature), Input/Output (service signature), Pre/Post conditions (constraints on input and output), concepts and text used in descriptions. Different matchmaking algorithms can be used to compute best matches from the values specified for the properties in the different dimensions, in requests and service advertisement (see e.g. [26,21,23,27]).

We are currently developing a resource mediation approach that heavily relies on the exploitation of taxonomies combining the reasoning support enabled by taxonomies with ease of resource description as it is required in Grid-based environments where new services regularly come up and have to be described in a efficient way.

Taxonomies are in our approach used for task modelling, representing task properties that are relevant for assigning adequate services to a process. The task model consist of a taxonomy of tasks/subtasks. For each task, the researcher can specify a task profile including I/O requirements, Pre/Post conditions, and capabilities required from a service to perform the task. These capabilities might again be described by a special taxonomy. In the ideal case the capabilities are described on the basis of the same taxonomy as the tasks or the taxonomies are related by some ontology.

Besides using taxonomies for resource description, the exploitation of taxonomies is pushed one step further (see also [28]). Service are described by properties along the syntactical, semantic, and pragmatic dimensions. Instead of developing matchmaking methods for each individual property, the properties themselves as well as the matchmaking methods are classified by a taxonomy of principle matchmaking situations. These situations depend upon the type and other characteristics of the respective property as well as upon the role of the property for the matchmaking. Properties that are classified in the same way can be handled by analogous matchmaking methods. By following this approach, the set of properties considered for mediation can be easily adapted and extended by assigning adequate matchmaking situations to new properties.

5 Conclusions and Future Work

In this paper we discussed approaches to provide improved and better tailored e-Science services by taking a closer look to the context, in which research takes place in. Two types of scientific context "use" have been considered: 1) increasing context awareness both by making context visible to the researcher and by exploiting collected context information in context-aware services like e.g. personalization services and 2) supporting the construction of tailored working contexts for groups of researchers.

For both types of scientific context use, various approaches exist. However, there are still considerable R&D activities in different areas required for a more in depth exploitation of context information, for creating improved awareness for the relevant parts of a researcher's context as well as for powerful and user friendly support of working context construction. This includes, beneath others, specification languages for the definition of VDLs and working contexts, together with the associated tools and services, extended context models together with methods for collecting and exploiting the associated context information, advanced methods for flexible context visualization, and further methods and tools for service description and mediation.

Acknowledgements This study has been partly funded by the European Commission through grant to the project VIKEF under the number IST-507173, and to the project DILIGENT under the number IST-004260.

References

1. Akman, V., Surav, M.: Steps toward formalizing context. AI Magazine **17** (1996) 55–72
2. D.B., L.: Cyc: Large-scale investment in knowledge infrastructure. Communications of the ACM **38** (1995) 33–38
3. Neuhold, E., Niederée, C., Stewart, A., Frommholz, I., Mehta, B.: The role of context for information mediation in digital libraries. In: To appear in: 7th International Conference on Asian Digital Libraries. Lecture Notes in Computer Science, Springer-Verlag (2004)
4. eScience Councils UK: escience. http://www.rcuk.ac.uk/escience/ (2004)
5. O'Hara, K., Alani, H., Shadbolt: Identifying communities of practice: Analysing ontologies as networks to support community recognition. In: In Proceedings IFIP World Computer Congress. Information Systems: The E-Business Challenge. (2002)
6. Wasserman, S., Galaskiewicz, J., eds.: Advances in Social Network Analysis. Sage, Thousand Oaks, California (1994)
7. Brickley, D., Miller, L.: Foaf vocabulary specification namespace document 13 march 2003. http://xmlns.com/foaf/0.1/ (2003)
8. Liana Razmerita, Albert A. Angehrn, A.M.: Ontology-based user modeling for knowledge management systems. User Modeling (2003) 213–217

9. Middleton, S.E., Shadbolt, N.R., De Roure, D.C.: Ontological user profiling in recommender systems. ACM Trans. Inf. Syst. **22** (2004) 54–88

10. Stewart, A., Niederée, C., Mehta, B., Hemmje, M., Neuhold, E.:   Extending your neighborhood-relationship-based recommendations using your personal web context. In: Proceedings of the Sevetn International Conference on Asisan Digital Libraries. Lecture Notes in Comuter Science, Springer-Verlag (2004)

11. Mutton, P., Golbeck, J.: Visualization of semantic metadata and ontologies. In: IEEE In Seventh International Conference on Information Visualization (IV03. (2003) 300–305

12. Freeman, L.C.: Visualizing social networks. Journal of Social Structure: Visualizing Social Networks **1** (2003)

13. Newman, M.E.J.:   Who is the best connected scientist? a study of scientific coau-thorship networks.   Working Papers 00-12-064, Santa Fe Institute (2000) available at http://ideas.repec.org/p/wop/safiwp/00-12-064.html.

14. Turner, E.: Mapping distributed communities using svg.
http://liz.xtdnet.nl/MappingDistributedCommunities.html (2003)

15. Deussen, O.and Hansen, C., Keim, D., Saupe, D., eds.: VisSym 2004, Symposium on Visu-alization, Konstanz, Germany, May 19-21, 2004. In Deussen, O.and Hansen, C., Keim, D., Saupe, D., eds.: VisSym, Eurographics Association (2004)

16. Klink, L., Ley, M., Rabbidge, E., Reuther, P., Weber, W., Weber, A.: Browsing and visualizing digital bibliographic data. In: VisSym, Eurographics Association (2004)

17. Neuhold, E.J., Niederée, C., Stewart, A.: Personalization in digital libraries: An extended view. In: Proceedings of ICADL 2003. (2003) 1–16

18. Niederée, C.: Personalization, Cooperation and Evolution in Digital Libraries (in German). PhD thesis, University Hamburg-Harburg, Germany (2003)

19. Matthes, F., Niederée, C., Steffens, U.: C-merge: A tool for policy-based merging of resource classifications. In Constantopoulos, P., Solvberg, I.T., eds.: Research and Advanced Tech-nology for Digital Libraries, Proceedings of the Fifth European Conference, ECDL 2001, Darmstadt, Germany, Springer-Verlag (2001)

20. Wiederhold, G.: Mediators in the architecture of future information systems. In Huhns, M.N., Singh, M.P., eds.: Readings in Agents. Morgan Kaufmann, San Francisco, CA, USA (1997) 185–196

21. Sycara, K., Wido, S., Klusch, M., Lu, J.: Larks: Dynamic matchmaking among heterogeneous software agents in cyberspace (2002)

22. Rogers, T.J., Ross, R., Subrahmanian, V.S.: Impact: A system for building agent applications. J. Intell. Inf. Syst. **14** (June) 95–113

23. Nodine, M.H., Fowler, J., Ksiezyk, T., Perry, B., Taylor, M., Unruh, A.: Active information gathering in infosleuth. Int. Journal of Cooperative Information Systems **9** (2000) 3–28

24. Czajkowski, K., Ferguson, D.F., Foster, I., Frey, J., Graham, S., Sedukhin, Snelling, D., Tuecke, S., Vambenepe, W.: The ws-resource framework. (2004)

25. Coalition, T.O.S.: Owl-s semantic markup for web services.
available at http://www.daml.org/services/owl-s/1.0/owl-s.pdf (2003)

26. Klusch, M., Sycara, K.: Brokering and matchmaking for coordination of agent societies: a survey. In: Coordination of Internet agents: models, technologies, and applications. Springer-Verlag (2001) 197–224

27. Paolucci, M., Kawamura, T., Payne, T., Sycara, K.: Semantic matching of web services capabilities. In Horrocks, I., Hendler, J.A., eds.: The Semantic Web - ISWC 2002, First International Semantic Web Conference, Springer-Verlag (2002)

28. Muscogiuri, C., Paukert, M., Niederée, C., Hemmje, M.:   Dimensions of innovation: Knowledge-based resource mediation for innovation process engineering. In: Proceedings of the 5th European Conference on Knowledge Management (ECKM2004). (2004)

TV Scout: Lowering the Entry Barrier
to Personalized TV Program Recommendation[*]

Patrick Baudisch[1] and Lars Brueckner[2]

[1] Inf. Sciences and Technologies Lab.
Xerox Palo Alto Research Center
Palo Alto, CA 94304, U.S.A.
patrick.baudisch@acm.org

[2] IT Transfer Office (ITO)
Darmstadt University of Technology
64283 Darmstadt, Germany
brueckner@ito.tu-darmstadt.de

Abstract. In this paper, we present *TV Scout,* a recommendation system providing users with personalized TV schedules. The TV Scout architecture addresses the "cold-start" problem of information filtering systems, i.e. that filtering systems have to gather information about the user's interests before they can compute personalized recommendations. Traditionally, gathering this information involves upfront user effort, resulting in a substantial entry barrier. TV Scout is designed to avoid this problem by presenting itself to new users not as a filtering system, but as a retrieval system where all user effort leads to an immediate result. While users are dealing with this retrieval functionality, the system continuously and unobtrusively gathers information about the user's interests from implicit feedback and gradually evolves into a filtering system. An analysis of log file data gathered with over 10,000 registered online users shows that over 85% of all first-time users logged in again, suggesting that the described architecture is successful in lowering the entry barrier.

1 Introduction

Information filtering systems [7] suffer from a bootstrapping problem. Before they can give personalized recommendations to a user, they have to find out what the user's interests are. Only then can filtering systems build user profiles and compute personalized recommendations. The problems resulting from this undesirable order of required user effort and delayed benefit is a well-known phenomenon in collaborative filtering, the so-called *cold start* problem [17]. Users are reluctant to invest effort, especially if they don't know whether the offered service will be worth the effort. This approach bears the risk that users will avoid the gamble and stick with a system offering more immediate benefit, such as a retrieval-oriented system. Users making this decision, however, will never come to discover the long-term benefits the filtering system would have offered. For additional studies on incentive structures and the results of the lack of incentives see [11].

---

[*] The work presented in this paper was carried out during the authors' affiliation at GMD-IPSI

M. Hemmje et al. (Eds.): E.J. Neuhold Festschrift, LNCS 3379, pp. 299–309, 2005.
© Springer-Verlag Berlin Heidelberg 2005

In this paper, we describe an architecture designed to address this incentive problem and we will demonstrate this architecture at the example of our TV program recommendation system TV Scout. We will begin by briefly introducing the field of TV recommendation. We will then discuss TV Scout and its user interface and discuss the underlying filtering architecture. Finally, we will report results of an analysis of TV Scout online usage data, discuss our findings, and present conclusions and future work.

2   Recommending TV Programs

In 1992, Belkin and Croft wrote "In particular, applications such as the recreational use of television programming pose special problems and opportunities for research in filtering" [7, p.37]. Several current trends make TV an interesting application area for information filtering. TV viewers are facing an information overload situation [10]. A number of technical improvements, such as cable, satellite, and digital TV technology have resulted in an increasing number of available TV channels. Today, hundreds of channels broadcast thousands of programs every day. Since the amount of content that is of interest for a given viewer has not increased proportionally, and especially since the time users have for watching TV has not increased, *planning* ones TV consumption has become a challenge. The amount of TV programs will soon exceed the limits of what can reasonably be printed and inspected by the viewer. Also channel surfing is no longer fast enough to allow getting an overview of all channels [11]. Attempting to meet the changing requirements, web-based TV program guides (e.g. TV Guide, http://www.tvguide.com), set-top boxes with electronic program guides (EPGs, [20]), and digital VCRs (e.g. *Tivo* http://www.tivo.com) have emerged in the past few years.

There have been several research projects around TV recommendation in the past [11, 9], but most of them focused on set-top boxes and on the technical possibilities for monitoring user behavior rather then on web-based systems and usability. Current research in personalized TV evolves still around personalized EPGs [1], but also around new concepts, such as multi-agent recommender systems [14]. A more thorough overview of current research in the field of personalized TV recommendation can be found in [18].

3   TV Scout

TV Scout [3, 4] is a web-based TV recommendation system. Its goal is to support users in planning their personal TV consumption.

In order to understand the design requirements for such a system, we began our research with an informal survey among students [3]. The survey indicated that expectations about the functionality of an ideal TV recommendation system were dominated by experiences with printed TV program guides. While our goal was to eventually provide users with a personalized TV program at a single mouse click, our survey indicated that only a minority of the users we had interviewed would be willing to invest the required effort. We concluded that in order to attract users, a successful TV recommendation system would first have to emulate the expected print-like functionality, as well as the straightforward usage of printed guides: pick up the TV guide, find today's listing, pick a program, and watch TV. The challenge was to provide a seamless transition from this scenario to the filtering functionality we had in mind. To prevent the filtering functionality from conflicting with the user expectations and system learnability, we decided to create a system that would progressively disclose its filtering features to users.

3.1 Implementation

The TV Scout project was conducted in cooperation with the TV program guide publisher TV TODAY. While this resulted in TV Scout getting implemented as a web-based system, we see no architectural problems in porting the resulting architecture to a set-top box. To allow maintaining personal user profile data, first-time users have to create an account, which they access using a self-selected login name and password. The web-based TV Scout front end is implemented in HTML, Java, and JavaScript.

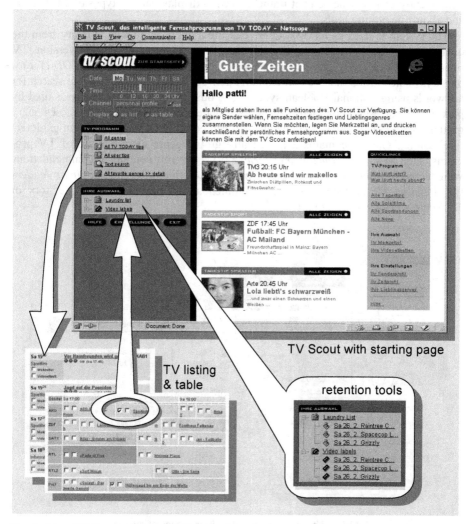

Fig. 1. How TV Scout presents itself to first-time users (screenshots partially translated from German)

3.2   Retrieving Program Descriptions

To users entering TV Scout for the first time, the system presents itself as a retrieval system. Its functionality at this stage restricts itself to the functionality of a printed TV program guide, with a graphical user interface. Users specify a query (or simply hit a button for the default "what's on now"), sort through the resulting list and select programs to watch. Users can also print the list of selected programs for later use.

Fig. 1 shows how users accomplish this using the TV Scout user interface. The interface consists of the menu frame on the left and the content frame on the right. The menu frame provides users with access to all retrieval and filtering functions and is permanently visible. The content frame is used to display various types of TV listings and all profile editing tools.

The system is used as follows. Users execute a query by picking a query from the query menu. Fig. 2 shows several close-ups of this menu. In its current version, TV Scout offers four query groups: *text search*, *genres*, *user tips*, and *TV TODAY tips*, plus a *favorites* group that we will explain later. Text search allows users to search for keywords using optional Boolean syntax. The other three submenus are executed by picking the corresponding menu entry. To provide more precise queries, theses query groups contain hierarchies of submenus that can be browsed in a file system explorer-like fashion. *Genres* contains a historically grown genre classification of TV programs, such as *sports*, *comedy*, and *series* [14]. *User tips* contains recommendations volunteered by users who serve as self-proclaimed editors, so-called *opinion leaders* [4]. Finally, *TV TODAY tips*, are recommendations provided by the editors of TV Scout's printed counter part.

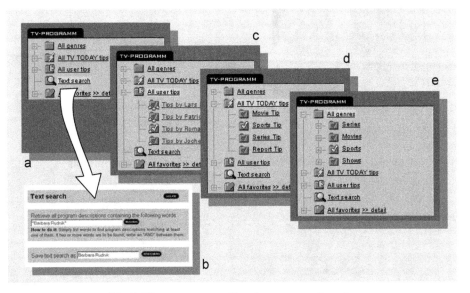

Fig. 2. The query menu offers four groups of queries

By default, all queries are restricted to the programs starting within the current hour, but TV Scout provides customized controls that allow specifying arbitrary time and date intervals using mouse drag interactions (Fig. 4a). Channels can be selected from two predefined sets or can be selected in detail using a paintable interface (Fig. 4b) [6].

When a query is executed, the resulting set of TV program descriptions (Fig. 1 bottom left) is displayed in the content area. Descriptions consist of the program title, a rating describing how well the program matches the query, an extract of the program description, and links to a more detailed description. Users can choose between the display styles *ranked list* and *table*.

Two toggle switches per program description allow users to retain programs they plan to watch in the so-called *retention tool* (Fig. 1 bottom left, circled). The retention tool *laundry list* can be used to print a list of programs; *video labels* are designed to retain and print programs to be videotaped. The retention menu allows users to display the content of their retention tools for reviewing or printing. The printed list can be used to remind users of the programs that they plan to watch.

3.3   Filtering Functionality: Creating "Bookmarks"

Using the functionality described so far, the effort for repeated usage is the same each time the service is used. The next step therefore is for the system to reduce the effort required of the user when querying, since the primary purpose of information filtering systems is to be "time-saving devices" [2].

When a user enters a query that is broader than necessary, the user is forced to sort through an unnecessarily long listing when trying to find desired programs. When the system detects that the user has used such a sub-optimal query repeatedly while another query with better precision exists, it makes a suggestion. Fig. 3 shows an example. Let's assume that the user has repeatedly used the query "movies" to exclusively find and retain comedies and horror movies. By computing the overlap between the retained programs and all available queries [3], the system detects that the retained programs can also be covered by the more specific queries "horror movies" and "comedies". A dialog box opens and suggests using these queries instead. The user can execute the suggested queries like any other query, i.e. by clicking their names.

The more important function of the dialog box, with respect to our filtering concept, is that it also suggests retaining these queries as *bookmarks*. Users can do this by clicking the toggle switch that accompanies each query (a folder symbol with a check mark, see Fig. 3a). Retained queries pop up in the user's *favorites* (Fig. 3b). The *favorites* folder is collocated with the other query groups and can be executed the same way. Retained queries are listed in a flat hierarchy, thereby providing the users with convenient access to queries that would otherwise be hidden in multiple different submenus. This functionality corresponds to the bookmark folder in a web browser. Unlike web bookmarks these bookmarks are stored on the TV Scout server, allowing TV Scout to use them as input for additional computation.

Retention check boxes accompany all queries in the system (see Fig. 3b), so users can bookmark queries anytime, independent of suggestions. The primary purpose of query suggestions is to inform users about the bookmaking concept and to encourage its usage.

Note the special importance of the retention tools. Although the declared purpose of the retention tools is to allow users to memorize programs and print schedules, their primary purpose from the system's point of view is to serve as an information source about the user's interests. The content of the retention tools is considered an implicit positive rating for the retained programs, making the retention tools serve as a source of implicit retention feedback [16]. Although implicit feedback is commonly agreed to be a less reliable source of rating information than explicit feedback, it has the benefit of being unobtrusive, which we considered essential for this type of filtering system. See [3, 4] for how TV Scout uses the same implicit input for various types of filtering functionality based on collaborative filtering.

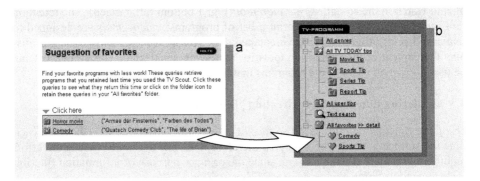

Fig. 3. By clicking a checkmark-shaped button, queries can be retained in *All favorites*.

3.4   Filtering Functionality: One-Click Personalized TV Schedules

To provide a container for bookmarked queries is not the only purpose of the *favorites* folder. The real value of this folder lies in the fact that users can execute it as a whole by clicking the top menu entry labeled *all favorites*. This executes all retained queries at once. The result listings of the individual queries, however, are not appended to each other—they are merged into a single relevance-ordered result list. This is the most powerful function of the TV Scout system—it fulfills the initial goal of generating personalized TV schedule with a single mouse click.

How are the individual query results merged in order to obtain a useful result? When the query profile *all favorites* is executed, a script running inside the TV Scout server executes all contained queries. This is done by delegating each query to the corresponding subsystem; text search, for example, is executed by FreeWAIS, while genre queries are executed by a relational database. As a result, the subsystems deliver sets of pairs (program, rating). The task of the query profile script is to merge all these results into a single ranked list. This requires transforming the individual ratings such that they include the user's perceived importance of the interest represented by the query. In order to express this perceived importance, the query profile stores a linear function (i.e. a factor and an offset) for each retained query. The resulting ratings are computed by transforming the ratings returned by the subsystem using this function. If a TV program is returned by multiple queries its ratings are summed up. Finally, programs are sorted by their result rating and returned to the user.

The critical factor is the parameters of the linear transformation. The system acquires these parameters through initialization, learning, and manual updating. When queries are bookmarked, their functions are initialized using Zipf's law [19, p. 60]. This means that more specific queries are given positive offsets, propagating the results of these queries towards the top ranks of the resulting listings, thus preventing them from being buried inside the large result sets of less specific queries.

After initialization, the parameters of the rating transformations can be improved by two means. First, TV Scout continuously optimizes the query profile based on the same implicit retention feedback that was already used for suggesting queries. See [3] for a description of the algorithm. Second, interested users are allowed to manually inspect and update their profile. Clicking the ">>details" link in the *all favorites* menu invokes a profile editor. The simplest version of this editor provides users with a single pull-down menu per query (Fig. 4c), allowing users to assign a symbolic rating to each query, such as "*Action movies* are [very important] to me" [3, 5].

Through the use of relevance feedback the query profile improves continuously, so that the quality of the rankings obtained by clicking *all favorites* increases over time.

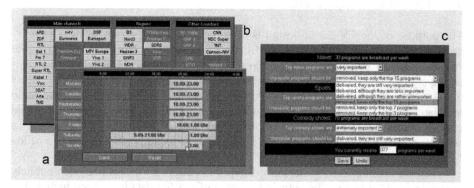

Fig. 4. The TV Scout profile editing tools (a) viewing time profile editor, (b) channel profile editor, and (c) query profile editor.

3.5   Summary

Fig. 5 summarizes how the usage of TV Scout by a given user can evolve over time. Each transition to a more personalized phase can be suggested by the system (T1-T3) or initiated by the user (U1-U3). However, users are not forced through these phases and may equally well settle with the functionality of one of the earlier phases.

1. **Query phase (S1):** Users can pick predefined queries (T1) or can formulate queries, such as text searches, manually (U1).
2. **Bookmark/reuse phase (S2):** If the system detects reoccurring or sub-optimal queries it proposes better-suited queries and suggests retaining them as *favorites* (U2). Independent of suggestion, users can bookmark queries anytime (T2).

   Profile creation (T*): The user's query profile is created automatically when the first query is bookmarked.

3. **Profile phase (S3):** Initially, the query profile provides users with a convenient way of executing all their bookmarks with a single click. Continuous supply of relevance feedback(T3) or manual profile manipulation(U3) improves the profile.

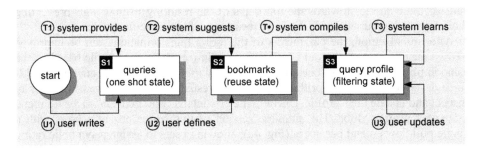

Fig. 5. Evolving usage of a proposed filtering architecture

4   TV Scout Usage Data

The purpose of the TV Scout design is to reduce the entry barrier for new users by using a progressive disclosure of the filtering functionality. How can we verify the success of our interaction design? A controlled experimental comparison with a competing system would be problematic because of the vast amount of interface variables that would be difficult to control. In addition, modeling a realistic web-usage scenario in a lab setting is challenging. Alternatively, a naturalistic study of web use would provide more realistic data, but we would be unable to measure factors such as subjective satisfaction. Ultimately, we decided to conduct an informal analysis of log file data from actual web usage.

When we conducted our data analysis April 20, 2000, TV Scout had been publicly available for 18 months. The entire 18 months of log file data have been included in this study. All usage data was extracted from the web server log files and the system's database. With respect to the filtering functionality, this data was slightly biased, in that the suggestion feature became available later. Because of this, we expected that the usage of bookmarking would be underrepresented.

The main purpose of the analysis was to verify whether our filtering system design fulfilled the primary goal, namely to provide a low entry barrier. If our design was appropriate, then TV Scout would meet the expectations of first-time users and would not overwhelm them. Repeated usage would indicate that users had taken the entry hurdle; one-shot users would suggest the opposite.

We were also interested in learning more about the users' demand for the offered filtering functionality. How many users would adopt bookmarking functionality; how many would make use of their personal query profiles? Based on our informal survey, we expected the majority to be satisfied with the initial retrieval functionality, but we had no clear expectations about the percentages. Finally, we were interested in seeing how useful users would find the query profile. Once they had created one, would they continue to use it or would they abandon it rapidly?

4.1   Results

At the day we examined the log data, TV Scout had 10,676 registered users. In total, users had executed 48,956 queries. 53% of all queries (25,736 queries) were specific queries different from the default query.

Repeated log-ins: We found that 9,190 of the 10,676 registered users had logged in repeatedly, i.e. twice or more. This corresponds to a percentage or 86% repeated users. The most active user with 580 logins had logged in almost daily.

Bookmarks: 1770 users had bookmarked one or more queries. Together, these users had bookmarked 4383 queries, mostly genres. The most frequently executed queries were the genres movies (736 times) and information (364 times), and TV TO-DAY Movie tips (369 times). Over 300 text searches were bookmarked.

Query profiles: Out of the 1770 users who had bookmarked at least one query, 270 users (about 15%) executed their query profile at least once to obtain personalized listings. These users executed their query profiles a total of 5851 times, which corresponds to an average of 21 times per user. These users manually fine-tune their profiles a total of 1213 times, with an average of 4.5 times per user. These results indicate that query profiles were highly appreciated by those who used them.

5   Conclusions

We interpret the measured percentage of repeated users as a confirmation of our design. 86% of all first time users logged in repeatedly; we consider this to be a very high percentage for a web-based system. This indicates that presenting first-time users with a retrieval setting is a successful approach to keeping the entry barrier for first-time users low.

Only 17% of users made use of the bookmark feature; out of these, only 15% made used of the query profile. These numbers seem low even taking into account that the suggestion feature was not available most of the logged time. Does this result indicate that the filtering functionality is inappropriate or difficult to learn? Why did the majority of the users not reach the "goal" of the system?

This is not how we interpret these results. In an earlier TV usage survey [3] we found TV users to plan their TV consumption for very different timeframes. Most of these users only planned a TV schedule for the following day or they did not plan at all. Many users only used a guide to determine what was currently on TV. Only 12% of the users planned a TV schedule for the entire week. Considering that the filtering functionality of TV Scout addresses the relatively small subgroup of users who plan their TV consumption, the observed results seem appropriate. The majority of users who only used the retrieval functionality may have found the retrieval functionality of TV Scout to be the appropriate support for *their* information seeking strategy. An online survey as well as an experimental study should help to verify this interpretation.

6   Acknowledgements

We would like to thank Dieter Böcker, Joe Konstan, Marcus Frühwein, Michael Brückner, Gerrit Voss, Andreas Brügelmann, Claudia Perlich, Tom Stölting, and Diane Kelly.

References

1. L. Ardissono, F. Portis, P. Torasso. F. Bellifemine, A. Chiarotto and A. Difino Architecture of a system for the generation of personalized Electronic Program Guides. In *Proceedings of the UM 2001 workshop "Personalization in Future TV"*, July 13 to July 17, 2001, Sonthofen, Germany.

2. P.E. Baclace. Information intake filtering. In *Proceedings of Bellcore Workshop on High-Performance Information Filtering*, Morristown, NJ, November 1991.

3. P. Baudisch. Dynamic Information Filtering. Ph.D. Thesis. GMD Research Series 2001, No. 16. GMD Forschungszentrum Informationstechnik GmbH, Sankt Augustin. ISSN 1435-2699, ISBN 3-88457-399-3. Also at http://www.patrickbaudisch.com/publications

4. P. Baudisch. Recommending TV Programs on the Web: how far can we get at zero user effort? In Recommender Systems, Papers from the 1998 Workshop, Technical Report WS-98-08, pages 16-18, Madison, WI. Menlo Park, CA: AAAI Press, 1998.

5. P. Baudisch. The Profile Editor: designing a direct manipulative tool for assembling profiles. In *Proceedings of Fifth DELOS Workshop on Filtering and Collaborative Filtering*, pages 11-17, Budapest, November 1997. ERCIM Report ERCIM-98-W001.

6. P. Baudisch. Using a painting metaphor to rate large numbers of objects. In Ergonomics and User Interfaces, Proceeding of the HCI '99 Conference, pages 266-270, Munich, Germany, August 1999. Mahwah: NJ: Erlbaum, 1999.

7. N.J. Belkin and W.B. Croft. Information filtering and information retrieval: two sides of the same coin? CACM, 35(12):29-37, Dec. 1992.

8. A. Borchers, J. Herlocker, J. Konstan, and J. Riedl. Ganging up on information overload. Computer, 31(4):106-108, April 1998.

9. D. Das and H. ter Horst. Recommender systems for TV. In Recommender Systems, Papers from the 1998 Workshop, Technical Report WS-98-08, pages 35-36, Madison, WI. Menlo Park, CA: AAAI Press, 1998.

10. P. Denning. Electronic junk. CACM, 23(3):163-165, March 1982.

11. M. Ehrmantraut, T. Härder, H. Wittig, and R. Steinmetz. The Personal Electronic Program Guide—towards the pre-selection of individual TV Programs. In Proc. of CIKM'96, pages 243-250, Rockville, MD, 1996.

12. L. Gravano and H. García-Molina. Merging ranks from heterogeneous Internet sources. In Proceedings of the 23rd VLDB Conference, pages 196-205, Athens, Greece, 1997.

13. J. Grudin. Social evaluation of the user interface: who does the work and who gets the BENEFIT? In *Proc. of INTERACT'87*: pages 805-811, 1987.

14. M. Kuhn. The New European Digital Video Broadcast (DVB) Standard. ftp://ftp.informatik.uni-erlangen.de/local/cip/mskuhn/tv-crypt/dvb.txt.

15. K. Kurapati, S. Gutta, D. Schaffer, J. Martino and J. Zimmerman. A multi-agent TV recommender. In *Proceedings of the UM 2001 workshop "Personalization in Future TV"*, July 13 to July 17, 2001.

16. D.M. Nichols. Implicit ratings and filtering. In *Proceedings of Fifth DELOS Workshop on Filtering and Collaborative Filtering*, pages 31-36, Budapest, November 1997. ERCIM Report ERCIM-98-W001. Le Chesnay Cedex, France, European Research Consortium for Informatics and Mathematics, 1998.

17. P. Resnick and H. Varian (Eds.). Special issue on Recommender Systems. Communications of the ACM, 40(3):56-89, March 1997.

18. Proceedings of the UM 2001 workshop "Personalization in Future TV", July 13 to July 17, 2001, Sonthofen, Germany. Online at http://www.di.unito.it/~liliana/UM01/TV.html

19. G. Salton and M.J. McGill. *Introduction to Modern Information Retrieval*. New York: McGraw-Hill, 1983.

20. H. Wittig and C. Griwodz. Intelligent media agents in interactive television systems. In *Proc. of the International Conference on Multimedia Computing and Systems '95*, pages 182-189, Boston, May 1995. Los Alamitos, CA: IEEE Computer Science Press, 1995.

Intelligent Home-Enjoying Computing Anywhere

Junzhong Gu

Lab. of Multimedia Information Technology (MMIT)
East China Normal University (ECNU), 200062 Shanghai, China
jzgu@ica.stc.sh.cn

Abstract. The computing mode is changing. Computer is disappearing, Information Appliances, especially Internet Appliances, are increasingly used for computing. Most devices that usually appear at home are involving computing now. The questions are, how to integrate them to a distributed computing environment, for example, how to integrate entertainment facilities, communication facilities, as well as traditional computing devices (PC, Laptop, printer, scanner,) in a system? How to guarantee their effective and conditional access to Internet? How to provide effective information service to such home facilities? Taking iHome (intelligent Home) as example, which is a project launched in Shanghai, supported by the company SVA[1] and ECNU, as well as IBM, this paper intends to answer these questions. The architecture of Intelligent Home, the software architecture for device UPnP, as well as the distributed information service structure are presented.

1   Introduction

Virtual information and knowledge environments are not only located in working space, but have also extended to home. This kind of home will be named as intelligent home here.

Actually, computing mode is changing. Distributed computing, pervasive computing are more and more popular. Computing devices are changing. Computer is disappearing. Information Appliances, especially Internet Appliances, are increasingly used for computing. Nowadays, Internet, mobile and broadcast islands exist at home. Technology about how to integrate the islands through a seamless, interoperable network will provide a unique opportunity for manufacturers and consumers alike. A digital home contains one or more intelligent platforms, such as an advanced set-top box (STB) or a PC. These intelligent platforms will manage and distribute rich digital content to devices such as TVs and wireless monitors from devices like digital cameras, camcorders and multimedia mobile phones.

To solve the problems, such as internetworking, UPnP of software, global service and conditional access, some organizations appear. And some efforts have already been made, for example, IBM's pervasive computing, efforts of **DLNA**[2], **IGRS**[3] (In-

---

[1] http://www.sva.com.cn
[2] http://www.dlna.org
[3] http://www.igrs.org.cn

M. Hemmje et al. (Eds.): E.J. Neuhold Festschrift, LNCS 3379, pp. 310–319, 2005.

telligent Grouping and Resource Sharing) and **ITopHome**[4] in China, etc. A short blink of them is as follows.

DLNA

DLNA (Digital Living Network Alliance,), former DHWG[5], is organized in industry and focused on delivering an interoperability framework of design guidelines based on open industry standards to complete the cross-industry digital convergence.

IGRS

IGRS (Intelligent Grouping and Resource Sharing) appeared in China in 2003. Some Companies and research institutions jointly set up IGRS, to realize the intelligent interconnection among information devices, consumer electronics and communications devices, and to sharpen the industry competitive edge and further drive the healthy development of the industry.

ITopHome

ITopHome alliance was set up in China in 2004 to unify standards and platform of home networking systems. Initial members include top CE/PC vendors in China and telecom companies, VLSI vendors, and so on.

There are also other related organizations, such as OSGi (Open Service Gateway initiative) Alliance[6], IHA (Internet Home Alliance)[7], UPnP Forum[8] and so on.

This paper, taking iHome as an example, discusses the information and knowledge environment at home-intelligent home. In Section 2, a network reference model of intelligent home is presented. Section 3 is about the new application scenarios at intelligent home and the corresponding requirements to system and software are derived. The system architecture of intelligent home is presented in Section 4. Software structure and related topics are in Section 5.

2   Home Networking

For computing anytime, anywhere and with any device, especially at home (or car), interconnecting of home devices and connecting them to service providers is the first thing. It is named as **Home Networking** here.

Nowadays ISDN, DSL, Cable Modem, as well as FTTP+LAN are widely used to get access to Internet from home. For more computers (desktop PC, Laptop, and so on) at home to get access to Internet, a simple solution is that they directly connect with Internet via any available communication media (e.g. Telephone line, Cable, etc.) separately. A shortage is that it will expend too much communication resources. And in most cases it's also impossible. Another approach is to set up a gateway as a public channel for varied devices to get access to Internet. This is a view of PC Internet world, as shown in Fig. 1.

---

[4] http://www.itophome.org.cn
[5] Digital Home Working Group (http://www.dhwg.org)
[6] http://www.osgi.org
[7] http://www.internethomealliance.com/
[8] http://www.upnp.org

Actually, at least three worlds appear at home, as in Fig. 1. PC Internet world is about Internet-connected computer-based devices. Mobile world involves Laptop, Phone, etc. The CE Broadcast world converges entertainment devices, sensors, energy meters, and so on. Human being can at home enjoy entertainment, have access to broadband portal, and control the light via Internet. It means, not only PCs but also other devices should be interconnected, and have access to Internet.

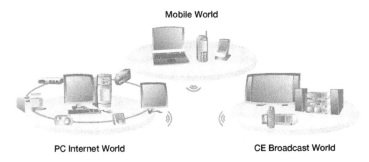

Fig. 1. Different Worlds around Human Being (Source: [1])

But, three worlds are islands at home up to now. How to connect these devices in an integrated network? How to connect them to Internet?

If each device is assigned to a connecting media, path, etc., it will be very complex, unmanageable and also impossible. Therefore another case is to set up a gateway as a public channel to connect Internet and connect the islands at home.

Unfortunately, devices at home are in a large quantity, varied and quite different (in size, power, function, communication possibility, etc). To integrate such varied devices to an interconnected network is a hard task. In addition, building a comprehensive gateway to directly serve too many varied and quite different devices is also difficult.

In this way, designing a universal gateway is one of the keys. That is, a gateway to provide varied connections to many devices in different communication media (Ethernet, IR, WLAN, Bluetooth, Power line, Phone line, IEEEE 1394, USB, etc.) but to serve them is not easy. Therefore in our practice, we decide to design it in a multilayer architecture. That is, it's a hierarchy with a main gateway as root, and subgateways, and next level sub-gateways follow the root.

A reference model of home networking can be illustrated as in Fig. 2.

As shown in Fig. 2, a main gateway is the unique channel at home to connect Internet, and it connects to some sub-gateways in order to integrate islands at home. Different devices connect with sub-gateways or sometimes directly with the main gateway. A sub-gateway can connect and service to next level sub-gateways. Digital devices at home interconnect via sub-gateway(s) and main gateway. And they get access to Internet via a unique channel-main gateway. Remote users (even thousands miles away from the home) can visit/control/operate devices at home via Internet through the main gateway. This is a multi-layer structure.

Fig. 3 is a sample of iHome[9]. As shown in Fig. 3, the residential service gateway is the main gateway as in the referential model. The controller, CE network modular and networked wall switch play the role of sub-gateways.

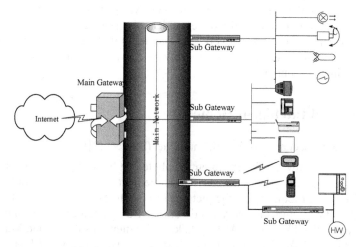

Fig. 2. Reference Model of Home Networking

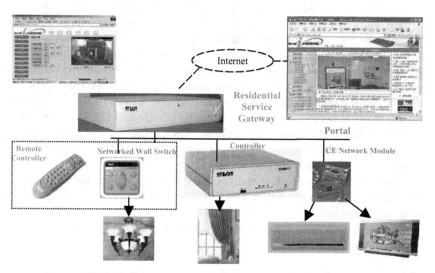

Fig. 3. iHome

A digital home consists of a network of CE (Consumer Electronics), mobile and PC devices that cooperate transparently, delivering simple, seamless interoperability that enhances and enriches user experiences. This is the communications and control backbone for the home network and is based on IP networking and UPnP technology.

---

[9] http://www.ihome.sh

A residential service gateway plays the role of main gateway here. It is named as **residential service gateway**, because it doesn't only play the role of communication channel, but also as service broker. A home security system consists of IR sensors, alarms, intruder detector/tracing systems, etc. connecting to a sub-gateway which interconnects with the residential service gateway. And some devices, e.g. home video systems, can connect directly to the residential service gateway.

Thus inter-communication, network architecture, software UPnP, conditional access, information service platform and software architecture are main topics in an intelligent home environment.

3   Home and Intelligent Home

Let's review some scenarios of intelligent home. (Source: [2])

- Mary wants to show her friend Karen the photos on her computer when she comes to visit. Mary picks up the infrared (IR) remote control that works with her plasma TV in the living room, selects the pictures she is interested in from a list displayed on the TV (the pictures actually reside on her PC in another room), and displays the photos on the TV screen. As they talk, Karen mentions travel, and Mary recalls that her husband, Jim, recently returned from a business trip to China where he bought a brand new camera phone and has saved most of the pictures he took on his laptop computer. Karen mentions she'd like to see Jim's China pictures, as well as some more of Mary's. Mary picks up the remote again and selects "pictures" as before. A listing of all the photos on their digital home network shows up on the screen, including both the den PC and Jim's laptop in the kitchen. (Source: [2])
- While Mary and Karen are chatting downstairs, Jim comes into his bedroom and turns on the bedside TV and the digital media adapter (DMA). He selects "Home Servers" on the menu using the IR remote for the TV. A listing appears on the screen, showing his PC, his wife's PC and the living room DVR (digital video recorder) are listed. He selects "Living Room DVR" from the list, picks a title "The Tonight Show, NBC" from the program list and pushes "play", stretching out on the bed to enjoy the monologue. (Source: [2])
- A wireless PDA is used to find and select content on a server, then to select a specific digital television for output, and finally to initiate streaming of the content to the digital television.
- A wireless PDA is used to download images or audio files from a PC so they can be taken out of the home.

...

Fig. 3 is a scenario of iHome. As shown in the figure, light, curtain, TV set, air conditioner and other CE devices are interconnected and able to get access to Internet. A residential gateway is at the central position as the broker to connect home devices to service providers. A controller is as a sub-gateway connecting some controllable curtains. Users can draw the curtain via WWW remotely. A networked wall switch here plays also a role of sub-gateway which connects/controls lights. CE network module is designed as PCI board to control air conditioners and TV set via PLC (Power Ling Communication).

It can be concluded, that an intelligent home system should meet the following requirements:

- Transparent connectivity between devices inside the digital home;
- Unified framework for device discovery, configuration and control;
- Interoperable media formats and streaming protocols;
- Interoperable media management and control framework;
- Compatible quality of service mechanisms;
- Compatible authentication and authorization mechanisms for users and devices

...

Nowadays, different service providers, for example, mobile telecom operators, online music service provider, etc., set up gateway in their systems separately. SMS (Short Message Service) providers have SMS gateway for SMS customers. Mobile phone service providers set up their WAP gateway for WAP users. Each of such gateways has its customer authentication and authorization mechanism, fee accounting mechanism, and others. In this way, if a user requires a service, he should apply for the service to different services providers. Therefore he will have different user names, use different passwords, and get various bills. Accompanied with home digitalization and more intelligent, gateways are moved closer to home. Various service gateways on the services provider side is moving near the customer and at last converges to a comprehensive residential service gateway. This is our vision in iHome. It's an evolution of computing mode.

4   System Architecture of Intelligent Home

Actually a digital home involves service provider, service and home devices.

In the applications, Service Provider, Service and Home Devices form a chain. Service providers, such as Telecom, Cable (TV), Utility and Portals, as sources, provide service via different communication media (e.g. fibre, coax, power line, and DSL/coax). The corresponding services are, for example, Telephony/Internet Access, Entertainment/Internet Access, Energy Management and Information/Commerce. Different home devices, such as telephone, PC, Television, utility meter, appliances are as user terminals to get services. An intelligent home is not only a digitalized home, but also an intelligent environment. For example, sensing intelligence at home enhances quality of life by monitoring activity. Communication Intelligence improves well-being by stimulating interaction. In such a situation, the system architecture should not be limited at home. We should consider the whole chain of service providers-service-home device.

Fig. 4 is the illustration of the corresponding system architecture. As shown in the figure, Home Network integrates devices at home. A service gateway is the main gateway as the portal for the device to get access to Internet. Via the service gateway people can enjoy rich services, such as broadband portal, intelligent kitchen, entertainment, security, HVAC (Heating Ventilation and Air-Conditioning), home monitoring, and so on.

A number of authentication and authorization mechanisms are being considered by device manufacturers and application developers to provide appropriate security for access and control. It is imperative to settle on a compatible authentication and

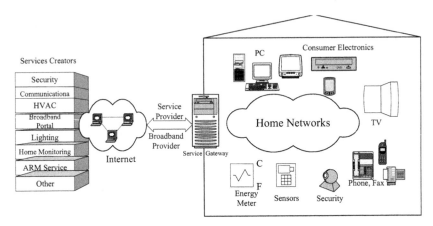

Fig. 4. System Architecture of Intelligent Home

authorization mechanism to enable devices to request and/or grant access to other devices and services at home. The residential service gateway plays such a role.

Now we discuss some important aspects in the system architecture.

Software Architecture

The software architecture should focus on devices transparent connectivity, unified devices discovery/configuration/control, interoperable media management and control, compatible authentication and authorization mechanisms, and other features as described in Section 3.

The software architecture of intelligent home in iHome is as in Fig. 5, similar to the proposal by OSGi.

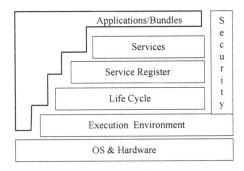

Fig. 5. Software architecture

Digital devices at home are built with different hardware and embedded with different operating systems. Therefore the execution environment should be designed to unify such heterogeneous systems. Java environment is a nice choice for it.

Here the execution environment is a Java virtual machine (JVM). Because each service has a life cycle, a life cycle management module is built on the execution environment. Service register is in charge of service registering. Then the services and applications are above it. As shown in the figure, security mechanism should accompany with all levels on the execution environment. In the architecture, "Bundles" play an important role. Actually, bundles are applications packaged in a standard Java ARchive (JAR) file.

Access to the bundle installation function is via an API that is available to every bundle.

UPnP

UPnP and interoperation between different devices is important for transparent connectivity between devices.

The UPnP™ Forum is an industry initiative designed to enable simple and robust connectivity among stand-alone devices and PCs from many different vendors. It defines different interconnecting standards. For example, **'FanSpeed:1'** provides programmatic control and status information for air fans used in Heating Ventilation and Air-Conditioning (HVAC) applications. **'AVTransport:1'** service type enables control over the transport of audio and video streams. This service type defines a 'common' model for A/V transport control suitable for a generic user interface. It can be used to control a wide variety of disc, tape and solid-state based media devices such as CD players, VCRs and MP3 players. A minimal implementation of this service can be used to control tuners.

In China, IGRS also defines an UPnP software architecture as shown at the left in Fig.6. The right of Fig. 6 is the UPnP™ Forum's architecture. Fig. 6 is the comparison of both architectures. In our practice, an IGRS compatible architecture is used.

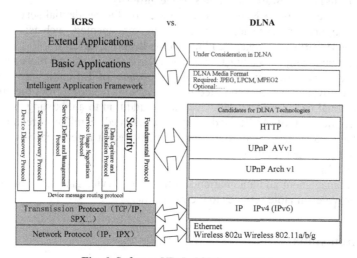

Fig. 6. Software UPnP: IGRS vs. DLNA

Gateway

Obviously, the main gateway (i.e. residential service gateway) plays an important role in an intelligent home.

In IBM pervasive computing vision, the home service gateway (HSG) is an intelligent "Home Network Hub". [4] It is a service platform designed to bridge external data networks to internal home networks and to enable customers to receive a whole new class of home services. The HSG can be defined as a device that combines a thin server architecture with traditional router/hub functions acting as the intersection between wide area networks (WANs) and local area networks (LANs). [4] A residential gateway is always online and could detect a new media server. The concept is similar to OSGi.

Some features of the gateway are stressed as follows:

- **Security**

Security lapses can affect data stored on private computing devices such as PCs or personal digital assistants (PDAs) as well as data sent over the Internet [4]. Gateway's functions should include an integrated firewall to isolate the home network from the Internet, except for a restricted set of authorized connections (e.g. VPNs), to protect information sent over the Internet by using encryption.

In the service gateway, the security mechanism consists of firewall, authentication, VPN, and encryption at least. In the devices, three functions (authentication, VPN, and encryption) are embedded.

- **Software Platform**

In our practice, service gateway software is based on LINUX operating system. As shown in Fig. 6, a Java Virtual Machine is built over the OS; then is a service framework facilitating service execution (life cycle management, registry, etc.) together with a collection of core services. Actually iHome project is running in the joint Lab. of SVA and IBM in China. Therefore more IBM's pervasive computing concepts are used in it.

- **Value added application based on service gateway**

Besides intelligent "Home Network Hub", based on the residential service gateway, some other applications expected long ago can be implemented, such as:

- **Remote Monitoring** (Meter Reading, Home Security, Safety)

AMR (automatic meter reading) and home security are more and more important to people. AMR has not been broadly deployed because of difficulties proving that the cost of deployment can be supported by cost savings resulting from the elimination of the manual meter reading. However, as an addition to an existing home service gateway, the cost of AMR is dramatically reduced. Similarly, remote security monitoring and home safety alerts can be deployed at a reduced cost by using a common service gateway.

- **Energy Management**

Energy management and automation solutions via service gateway will allow utilities to provide valuable services to their customers.

5   Conclusions

The iHome is a project launched a few years ago at the joint Lab. of SVA and IBM in China, and cooperated with MMIT, ECNU.

In the project, we try to define the home network model, build a sample network and make it really work. Communication media used in our systems are Ethernet, WLAN, paging, GSM, Power line communication (PLC), Bluetooth, USB, IEEE 1394 and so on. In AMR and home security PLC is widely used by us.

In the designing and implementation of the residential service gateway we adopt the OSGi concept. Conditional access and remotely operating devices at home via

Internet, such as control the operation of microwave oven, light and curtain, are supported by the residential service gateway. Alarm by intruder detecting can efficiently inform hosts via paging and SMS immediately.

But it's only at a beginning stage, vast realm is waiting for us to explore.

Intelligent home, such as iHome, actually means the evolution of computing mode. It's a new distributed computing mode. 24 years ago I studied distributed database systems POREL under the guidance of Prof. Dr. Erich Neuhold. Distributed database technology is rapidly changing. Data grid, Information grid and P2P computing are coming to us. Similarly, intelligent home involves a new pattern of distributed data management and distributed computing. Computing units are small, smart, intelligent, flexible, networked and varied. They come to and quit the distributed computing environment at any time, reinlessly. And Internet is too flexible. Service provider and services provided by them are varied and different. Data/information involved in an intelligent home are located anywhere, in heterogeneous systems/environment. So it's better to focus on the main gateway. In our practice, the residential service gateway is designed as the key, so that different service providers, different services and different digital home devices can work harmoniously together.

I would like to express my thanks to Prof. Dr. Erich Neuhold. His research achievements in heterogeneous multimedia database systems, in Peer-to-Peer- and GRID-based information environments, and in web-based distributed information technologies are very helpful to our work.

References

1. DLNA: Overview and Vision White Paper (2004)
2. DLNA: Use Case Scenarios White Paper (2004)
3. OSGi Alliance: About the OSGi Service Platform, Technical Whitepaper, Revision 3.012. July (2004)
4. IBM Pervasive Computing Division: Service Gateway-Strategy, White Paper, Networked Home Platform, Version 1.5 (1999)
5. Guo-hua Jiang, Junzhong Gu: Research on Application Model and Key Technology of Pervasive Computing. J. of East China Normal University, No. 2. (2004) (in Chinese)
6. Michael Jeronimo: It Just Works: UPnP in the Digital Home. The Journal of Spontaneous Networking, October 5, 2004, http://www.artima.com/spontaneous/upnp_digihome.html
7. Declan McCullagh: Digital home entertainment hits the road, http://news.com.com/2102-1041_3-5417159.html?tag=st.util.print (2004)
8. Syed Sibte Raza ABIDI: TIDE: An Intelligent Home-Based Healthcare Information & Diagnostic Environment, In: P. Kokol, et al (eds.): Medical Informatics in Europe (MIE '99), IOS Press, Amsterdam (1999)720-725

Author Index

Aberer, Karl   138

Baker, Thomas   61
Basilico, Justin   173
Baudisch, Patrick   299
Bertini, Enrico   183
Bock, Axel   69
Böhm, Klemens   31
Brocks, Holger   117
Brueckner, Lars   299
Buchmann, Erik   31
Bullinger, Hans-Jörg   280
Buono, Paolo   221

Catarci, Tiziana   183
Chen, Libo   271
Costabile, Maria Francesca   221

Darlagiannis, Vasilios   69
Degemmis, Marco   162
Di Bello, Lucia   183
Dietz, Laura   241
Dirsch-Weigand, Andrea   117
Dittmann, Jana   79

Encarnação, José L.   261
Everts, André   117

Fox, Edward A.   96
Frommholz, Ingo   117
Furuta, Richard   128

Gonçalves, Marcos André   96
Gu, Junzhong   310
Gupta, Piklu   197

Haake, Anja   251
Haake, Jörg M.   251
Hartmann, Jens   41
Heckmann, Oliver   69
Hemmje, Matthias   51, 197, 289
Hofmann, Thomas   173

Jaeschke, Gerald   197

Kamps, Thomas   271
Kimani, Stephen   183

Kirste, Thomas   261

Liebau, Nicolas   69
Lops, Pasquale   162

Mauthe, Andreas   69
Meissner, Andreas   87
Motz, Regina   21
Muscogiuri, Claudio   289

Niederée, Claudia   289

Ohlhausen, Peter   280

Peters, Carol   152

Qiu, Zhanzi   51

Risse, Thomas   1, 289
Rostek, Lothar   271

Schmidt-Thieme, Lars   41
Schmiede, Rudi   107
Schönfeld, Wolfgang   87
Schumacher, Oliver   280
Schümmer, Till   251
Semeraro, Giovanni   162
Seo, Jinwook   207
Shen, Rao   96
Shneiderman, Ben   207
Slama, Alexander   280
Stein, Adelheit   117
Steinebach, Martin   79
Steinmetz, Ralf   69
Stenzel, Richard   271
Stewart, Avaré   289
Stojanovic, Nenad   41
Streitz, Norbert A.   232
Studer, Rudi   41

Tandler, Peter   241
Thiel, Ulrich   117

Warschat, Joachim   280
Wombacher, Andreas   11
Wu, Jie   138

Lecture Notes in Computer Science

For information about Vols. 1–3289

please contact your bookseller or Springer

Vol. 3412: X. Franch, D. Port (Eds.), COTS-Based Software Systems. XVI, 312 pages. 2005.

Vol. 3403: B. Ganter, R. Godin (Eds.), Formal Concept Analysis. XI, 419 pages. 2005. (Subseries LNAI).

Vol. 3398: D.-K. Baik (Ed.), Systems Modeling and Simulation: Theory and Applications. XIV, 733 pages. 2005. (Subseries LNAI).

Vol. 3397: T.G. Kim (Ed.), Artificial Intelligence and Simulation. XV, 711 pages. 2005. (Subseries LNAI).

Vol. 3391: C. Kim (Ed.), Information Networking. XVII, 936 pages. 2005.

Vol. 3388: J. Lagergren (Ed.), Comparative Genomics. VIII, 133 pages. 2005. (Subseries LNBI).

Vol. 3387: J. Cardoso, A. Sheth (Eds.), Semantic Web Services and Web Process Composition. VIII, 148 pages. 2005.

Vol. 3386: S. Vaudenay (Ed.), Public Key Cryptography - PKC 2005. IX, 436 pages. 2005.

Vol. 3385: R. Cousot (Ed.), Verification, Model Checking, and Abstract Interpretation. XII, 483 pages. 2005.

Vol. 3382: J. Odell, P. Giorgini, J.P. Müller (Eds.), Agent-Oriented Software Engineering V. X, 239 pages. 2004.

Vol. 3381: P. Vojtáš, M. Bieliková, B. Charron-Bost, O. Sýkora (Eds.), SOFSEM 2005: Theory and Practice of Computer Science. XV, 448 pages. 2005.

Vol. 3379: M. Hemmje, C. Niederee, T. Risse (Eds.), From Integrated Publication and Information Systems to Information and Knowledge Environments. XXIV, 321 pages. 2005.

Vol. 3376: A. Menezes (Ed.), Topics in Cryptology – CT-RSA 2005. X, 385 pages. 2004.

Vol. 3375: M.A. Marsan, G. Bianchi, M. Listanti, M. Meo (Eds.), Quality of Service in Multiservice IP Networks. XIII, 656 pages. 2005.

Vol. 3368: L. Paletta, J.K. Tsotsos, E. Rome, G. Humphreys (Eds.), Attention and Performance in Computational Vision. VIII, 231 pages. 2005.

Vol. 3366: I. Rahwan, P. Moraitis, C. Reed (Eds.), Argumentation in Multi-Agent Systems. XII, 263 pages. 2005. (Subseries LNAI).

Vol. 3363: T. Eiter, L. Libkin (Eds.), Database Theory - ICDT 2005. XI, 413 pages. 2004.

Vol. 3362: G. Barthe, L. Burdy, M. Huisman, J.-L. Lanet, T. Muntean (Eds.), Construction and Analysis of Safe, Secure, and Interoperable Smart Devices. IX, 257 pages. 2005.

Vol. 3361: S. Bengio, H. Bourlard (Eds.), Machine Learning for Multimodal Interaction. XII, 362 pages. 2005.

Vol. 3360: S. Spaccapietra, E. Bertino, S. Jajodia, R. King, D. McLeod, M.E. Orlowska, L. Strous (Eds.), Journal on Data Semantics II. XI, 223 pages. 2004.

Vol. 3359: G. Grieser, Y. Tanaka (Eds.), Intuitive Human Interfaces for Organizing and Accessing Intellectual Assets. XIV, 257 pages. 2005. (Subseries LNAI).

Vol. 3358: J. Cao, L.T. Yang, M. Guo, F. Lau (Eds.), Parallel and Distributed Processing and Applications. XXIV, 1058 pages. 2004.

Vol. 3357: H. Handschuh, M.A. Hasan (Eds.), Selected Areas in Cryptography. XI, 354 pages. 2004.

Vol. 3356: G. Das, V.P. Gulati (Eds.), Intelligent Information Technology. XII, 428 pages. 2004.

Vol. 3355: R. Murray-Smith, R. Shorten (Eds.), Switching and Learning in Feedback Systems. X, 343 pages. 2005.

Vol. 3353: J. Hromkovič, M. Nagl, B. Westfechtel (Eds.), Graph-Theoretic Concepts in Computer Science. XI, 404 pages. 2004.

Vol. 3352: C. Blundo, S. Cimato (Eds.), Security in Communication Networks. XI, 381 pages. 2004.

Vol. 3350: M. Hermenegildo, D. Cabeza (Eds.), Practical Aspects of Declarative Languages. VIII, 269 pages. 2005.

Vol. 3349: B.M. Chapman (Ed.), Shared Memory Parallel Programming with Open MP. X, 149 pages. 2005.

Vol. 3348: A. Canteaut, K. Viswanathan (Eds.), Progress in Cryptology - INDOCRYPT 2004. XIV, 431 pages. 2004.

Vol. 3347: R.K. Ghosh, H. Mohanty (Eds.), Distributed Computing and Internet Technology. XX, 472 pages. 2004.

Vol. 3346: R.H. Bordini, M. Dastani, J. Dix, A.E.F. Seghrouchni (Eds.), Programming Multi-Agent Systems. XIV, 249 pages. 2005. (Subseries LNAI).

Vol. 3345: Y. Cai (Ed.), Ambient Intelligence for Scientific Discovery. XII, 311 pages. 2005. (Subseries LNAI).

Vol. 3344: J. Malenfant, B.M. Østvold (Eds.), Object-Oriented Technology. ECOOP 2004 Workshop Reader. VIII, 215 pages. 2004.

Vol. 3342: E. Şahin, W.M. Spears (Eds.), Swarm Robotics. IX, 175 pages. 2004.

Vol. 3341: R. Fleischer, G. Trippen (Eds.), Algorithms and Computation. XVII, 935 pages. 2004.

Vol. 3340: C.S. Calude, E. Calude, M.J. Dinneen (Eds.), Developments in Language Theory. XI, 431 pages. 2004.

Vol. 3339: G.I. Webb, X. Yu (Eds.), AI 2004: Advances in Artificial Intelligence. XXII, 1272 pages. 2004. (Subseries LNAI).

Vol. 3338: S.Z. Li, J. Lai, T. Tan, G. Feng, Y. Wang (Eds.), Advances in Biometric Person Authentication. XVIII, 699 pages. 2004.

Vol. 3337: J.M. Barreiro, F. Martin-Sanchez, V. Maojo, F. Sanz (Eds.), Biological and Medical Data Analysis. XI, 508 pages. 2004.

Vol. 3336: D. Karagiannis, U. Reimer (Eds.), Practical Aspects of Knowledge Management. X, 523 pages. 2004. (Subseries LNAI).

Vol. 3335: M. Malek, M. Reitenspieß, J. Kaiser (Eds.), Service Availability. X, 213 pages. 2005.

Vol. 3334: Z. Chen, H. Chen, Q. Miao, Y. Fu, E. Fox, E.-p. Lim (Eds.), Digital Libraries: International Collaboration and Cross-Fertilization. XX, 690 pages. 2004.

Vol. 3333: K. Aizawa, Y. Nakamura, S. Satoh (Eds.), Advances in Multimedia Information Processing - PCM 2004, Part III. XXXV, 785 pages. 2004.

Vol. 3332: K. Aizawa, Y. Nakamura, S. Satoh (Eds.), Advances in Multimedia Information Processing - PCM 2004, Part II. XXXVI, 1051 pages. 2004.

Vol. 3331: K. Aizawa, Y. Nakamura, S. Satoh (Eds.), Advances in Multimedia Information Processing - PCM 2004, Part I. XXXVI, 667 pages. 2004.

Vol. 3330: J. Akiyama, E.T. Baskoro, M. Kano (Eds.), Combinatorial Geometry and Graph Theory. VIII, 227 pages. 2005.

Vol. 3329: P.J. Lee (Ed.), Advances in Cryptology - ASIACRYPT 2004. XVI, 546 pages. 2004.

Vol. 3328: K. Lodaya, M. Mahajan (Eds.), FSTTCS 2004: Foundations of Software Technology and Theoretical Computer Science. XVI, 532 pages. 2004.

Vol. 3327: Y. Shi, W. Xu, Z. Chen (Eds.), Data Mining and Knowledge Management. XIII, 263 pages. 2004. (Subseries LNAI).

Vol. 3326: A. Sen, N. Das, S.K. Das, B.P. Sinha (Eds.), Distributed Computing - IWDC 2004. XIX, 546 pages. 2004.

Vol. 3323: G. Antoniou, H. Boley (Eds.), Rules and Rule Markup Languages for the Semantic Web. X, 215 pages. 2004.

Vol. 3322: R. Klette, J. Žunić (Eds.), Combinatorial Image Analysis. XII, 760 pages. 2004.

Vol. 3321: M.J. Maher (Ed.), Advances in Computer Science - ASIAN 2004. XII, 510 pages. 2004.

Vol. 3320: K.-M. Liew, H. Shen, S. See, W. Cai (Eds.), Parallel and Distributed Computing: Applications and Technologies. XXIV, 891 pages. 2004.

Vol. 3319: D. Amyot, A.W. Williams (Eds.), Telecommunications and beyond: Modeling and Analysis of Reactive, Distributed, and Real-Time Systems. XII, 301 pages. 2005.

Vol. 3318: E. Eskin, C. Workman (Eds.), Regulatory Genomics. VIII, 115 pages. 2005. (Subseries LNBI).

Vol. 3317: M. Domaratzki, A. Okhotin, K. Salomaa, S. Yu (Eds.), Implementation and Application of Automata. XII, 336 pages. 2005.

Vol. 3316: N.R. Pal, N.K. Kasabov, R.K. Mudi, S. Pal, S.K. Parui (Eds.), Neural Information Processing. XXX, 1368 pages. 2004.

Vol. 3315: C. Lemaître, C.A. Reyes, J.A. González (Eds.), Advances in Artificial Intelligence - IBERAMIA 2004. XX, 987 pages. 2004. (Subseries LNAI).

Vol. 3314: J. Zhang, J.-H. He, Y. Fu (Eds.), Computational and Information Science. XXIV, 1259 pages. 2004.

Vol. 3313: C. Castelluccia, H. Hartenstein, C. Paar, D. Westhoff (Eds.), Security in Ad-hoc and Sensor Networks. VIII, 231 pages. 2004.

Vol. 3312: A.J. Hu, A.K. Martin (Eds.), Formal Methods in Computer-Aided Design. XI, 445 pages. 2004.

Vol. 3311: V. Roca, F. Rousseau (Eds.), Interactive Multimedia and Next Generation Networks. XIII, 287 pages. 2004.

Vol. 3310: U.K. Wiil (Ed.), Computer Music Modeling and Retrieval. XI, 371 pages. 2005.

Vol. 3309: C.-H. Chi, K.-Y. Lam (Eds.), Content Computing. XII, 510 pages. 2004.

Vol. 3308: J. Davies, W. Schulte, M. Barnett (Eds.), Formal Methods and Software Engineering. XIII, 500 pages. 2004.

Vol. 3307: C. Bussler, S.-k. Hong, W. Jun, R. Kaschek, D.. Kinshuk, S. Krishnaswamy, S.W. Loke, D. Oberle, D. Richards, A. Sharma, Y. Sure, B. Thalheim (Eds.), Web Information Systems - WISE 2004 Workshops. XV, 277 pages. 2004.

Vol. 3306: X. Zhou, S. Su, M.P. Papazoglou, M.E. Orlowska, K.G. Jeffery (Eds.), Web Information Systems - WISE 2004. XVII, 745 pages. 2004.

Vol. 3305: P.M.A. Sloot, B. Chopard, A.G. Hoekstra (Eds.), Cellular Automata. XV, 883 pages. 2004.

Vol. 3303: J.A. López, E. Benfenati, W. Dubitzky (Eds.), Knowledge Exploration in Life Science Informatics. X, 249 pages. 2004. (Subseries LNAI).

Vol. 3302: W.-N. Chin (Ed.), Programming Languages and Systems. XIII, 453 pages. 2004.

Vol. 3300: L. Bertossi, A. Hunter, T. Schaub (Eds.), Inconsistency Tolerance. VII, 295 pages. 2005.

Vol. 3299: F. Wang (Ed.), Automated Technology for Verification and Analysis. XII, 506 pages. 2004.

Vol. 3298: S.A. McIlraith, D. Plexousakis, F. van Harmelen (Eds.), The Semantic Web - ISWC 2004. XXI, 841 pages. 2004.

Vol. 3296: L. Bougé, V.K. Prasanna (Eds.), High Performance Computing - HiPC 2004. XXV, 530 pages. 2004.

Vol. 3295: P. Markopoulos, B. Eggen, E. Aarts, J.L. Crowley (Eds.), Ambient Intelligence. XIII, 388 pages. 2004.

Vol. 3294: C.N. Dean, R.T. Boute (Eds.), Teaching Formal Methods. X, 249 pages. 2004.

Vol. 3293: C.-H. Chi, M. van Steen, C. Wills (Eds.), Web Content Caching and Distribution. IX, 283 pages. 2004.

Vol. 3292: R. Meersman, Z. Tari, A. Corsaro (Eds.), On the Move to Meaningful Internet Systems 2004: OTM 2004 Workshops. XXIII, 885 pages. 2004.

Vol. 3291: R. Meersman, Z. Tari (Eds.), On the Move to Meaningful Internet Systems 2004: CoopIS, DOA, and ODBASE, Part II. XXV, 824 pages. 2004.

Vol. 3290: R. Meersman, Z. Tari (Eds.), On the Move to Meaningful Internet Systems 2004: CoopIS, DOA, and ODBASE, Part I. XXV, 823 pages. 2004.